Walter Schatzberg

Scientific Themes
in the Popular Literature
and the Poetry of the
German Enlightenment,
1720 - 1760

German Studies in America

Edited by Heinrich Meyer

No. 12

Walter Schatzberg

Scientific Themes
in the Popular Literature
and the Poetry of the
German Enlightenment,
1720 - 1760

Herbert Lang
1973

Walter Schatzberg

Scientific Themes
in the Popular Literature
and the Poetry of the
German Enlightenment,
1720–1760

Herbert Lang
1973

ISBN 3 261 00317 0

Printed by Lang Druck Ltd., Liebefeld/Berne (Switzerland)

TABLE OF CONTENTS

ACKNOWLEDGEMENTS

This book is based on my Ph.D. dissertation which was submitted to The Johns Hopkins University in May, 1966. It is with pleasure that I acknowledge the encouragement and guidance of Professor Harold Jantz. I am most indebted to him for the use of his private collection of books. There, amidst the sources, I began my research and made my first discoveries. I also want to express my gratitude to Joan C. Neikirk who proofread the manuscript and prepared the Index of Names. I received a generous grant from the Clark University Research Fund towards the completion and publication of this book.

Walter Schatzberg
Clark University
Worcester, Massachusetts

INTRODUCTION

The impact that science has had on civilization has been a subject of increasing interest in recent years. Through its technological applications, science has revolutionized many aspects of society in the nineteenth and twentieth centuries. Yet in the seventeenth and eighteenth centuries, prior to the triumph of technology, the new sciences were already challenging many traditional notions about nature, about the cosmos, about man.

Our awareness that the sciences and the humanities have gone separate ways in the twentieth century has aroused curiosity about the reception of the sciences by men of letters in that earlier age when these sciences were achieving their first successes. Historians of science have continued to pay much attention to this early period in the development of modern science. Through numerous publications, the story of the significant discoveries made in astronomy, physics, and natural history in the seventeenth and eighteenth centuries have become readily accessible to the non-specialist. Thus, historians of literature have dared to venture out of their literary domains and have become curious about the scientific interests of men of letters in an age when the sciences still had humanistic roots.

The natural sciences introduced a new point of view and a new method. The scientist was not to rely on tradition and authority but on direct encounter with natural phenomena. He was to experiment, to use his senses and to reason about his perceptions in a consistent, logical manner as is done in mathematics. The discipline of the experiment and the discipline of mathematics characterized the new approach at its best.

However, this strict discipline did not yield immediate answers to many questions. Imagination and speculation were frequently introduced to suggest explanations that could not possibly be verified. This, too, is a part of the science of the time; it is certainly a part of the science that had an impact on culture. These speculations that were associated with science as it was then understood will be included in this study of scientific themes.

Historians of science at times consider only those discoveries and speculations that directly contributed to the progress of science. In cultural and literary history such a limitation is not valid. A historical point of view demands that we try to ascertain what was considered significant at the time and not simply what in retrospect has turned out to be so. To cultivate such a historical point of view, I have not examined the proceedings of scientific academies or the scientific treatises of individual scientists, many of whom, especially in Germany, wrote in Latin. Instead, I turned to the popular literature, written in German and intended to have a circulation beyond the circle of scientists. I consider as popular scientific literature works written in German which conveyed, in part or wholly, scientific subject matter and which were intended for the educated

layman. Thus, I shall include scientific compendiums, written solely for the
purpose of teaching science to the layman, as well as periodicals which contain
scientific material as one of several subjects. It was popular literature of this
sort that diffused the sciences to a reading public that was essentially
humanistically oriented. Any study which seeks to trace the assimilation of
scientific subject matter by men of letters must consider this popular literature.
It transmitted the work of the specialist and, frequently, added reflections that
transcended the limits and purpose of scientific method.

Numerous studies have already been made concerning the diffusion of the
sciences, the reception of the new sciences by men of letters and the presence of
scientific themes in poetry. This is especially true in English literary history, and
to a lesser extent in French and German literary history. Bibliographical sources
that are particularly helpful for an orientation on publications in this area are
the annual critical bibliography of *Isis*[1] and the annual bibliography issued by
General Topics VII (Literature and Science), a discussion group of the Modern
Language Association of America.[2] A few selections from these bibliographies
will give the reader some idea of the kind of studies that have been undertaken
in this field of research.

During the last forty years historians of English literature have produced a
considerable quantity of books, dissertations and articles on many aspects of the
relations of science and English literature. The outstanding example is Marjorie
H. Nicolson's *Science and Imagination* (Cornell University Press, 1956), a
collection of essays the author had published between 1935 and 1940. Her
studies of scientific themes in English poetry are accompanied by an
examination of the sources, the popular literature, from which the poets drew
much of the scientific knowledge that stirred their imagination. The impact of
the telescope and the microscope on the English imagination is so well
documented in these essays, that one can only wonder why scholars did not
recognize it earlier. Of her later works, *Newton Demands the Muse* (Princeton
University Press, 1946) examines the place of Newton's *Opticks* in English
poetry of the eighteenth century and *Mountain Gloom and Mountain Glory*
(Cornell University Press, 1959) studies the controversy over Thomas Burnet's

---

[1] *Isis.* An international review devoted to the history of science and its cultural
influences. It was founded in 1912 by George Sarton and is currently published by the
Johns Hopkins Press.

[2] General Topics VII (Literature and Science) was organized at the MLA convention
held in New Orleans in 1939. Since then, mimeographic lists of relevant studies have been
published annually; in 1940 and 1941 the lists were carried to about 1930. In 1949 Fred
A. Dudley edited *The Relations of Literature and Science. A Selected Bibliography,
1930—1949* (Pullman, Washington, 1949), and in 1968 the same editor extended his
compilation to include the lists up to 1967. *The Relations of Literature and Science. A
Selected Bibliography, 1930—1967* is obtainable from University Microfilms, Ann Arbor,
Michigan.

mountain theory in English poetry and prose. Well known are also her book on imaginary space voyages, *Voyages to the Moon* (New York, 1948) and her studies about the effect of science on seventeenth century English poetry, *The Breaking of the Circle* (Northwestern University Press, 1950).

Arthur O. Lovejoy's *The Great Chain of Being* (Harvard University Press, 1936) has been a stimulus for many studies of science in literature. Of great significance to the present work were those chapters of the book that trace the development of certain ideas, derived from astronomy and the life sciences and cherished by poets and philosophers in the seventeenth and eighteenth centuries. Another study in the history of ideas that has illuminated important aspects of intellectual history in the seventeenth and eighteenth centuries is Grant McColley's "The Seventeenth-Century Doctrine of a Plurality of Worlds" (*Annals of Science*, 1936, 385–430). Here he traces the history of this idea which so fascinated poets and scientists with the advent of the new astronomy.

English scientific and popular scientific literature is discussed in Richard Foster Jones' *Ancients and Moderns* (St. Louis, 1936). He examines the rise of the scientific movement in seventeenth-century England and shows that in England the famous controversy between the upholders of antiquity and those of modernity involved science as much as literature. Francis Rarick Johnson's *Astronomical Thought in Renaissance England* (Baltimore, 1937) is a study of English scientific writings from 1500 to 1645. By developing the background of the new astronomy it has been invaluable to students of the relations of science and literature. For popular speculations on the subject of cosmogony in the seventeenth and eighteenth centuries, Katherine Brownell Collier's *Cosmogonies of our Fathers* (Diss., Columbia University Press, 1934) is the best survey. The work, which treats mostly English and French authors, is a valuable background study of themes that so frequently appear in the poetry and prose of the time.

There have, of course, been a large number of dissertations, articles and books on science in English literature that benefitted from the highly original scholarship of the 1930's described above. Only a few can be mentioned here. Douglas Bush in his *Science and English Poetry* (New York, 1950) traces the repercussions of scientific thought, especially scientific materialism, on the great body of English poetry from 1590 to 1950. A.J. Meadows in *The High Firmament* (Leicester University Press, 1969) focuses on a single science, astronomy. He presents a history of astronomy of the last 500 years from the point of view of the layman's understanding. We learn about some of the popular debates over science and thus acquire background information to help in understanding literary references to astronomy.

The book that comes closest to the present study on science in the literature of the German Enlightenment is William Powell Jones' *The Rhetoric of Science* (University of California Press, 1966). The actual subject matter of the book is best summarized by the sub-title, "A Study of Scientific Ideas and Imagery in

Eighteenth-Century English Poetry". What our two works demonstrate is the extraordinary continuity and pervasiveness of this phase of the eighteenth-century European Enlightenment.

As evidence that research in the relations of science and English literature of the Enlightenment is not yet exhausted, I can cite George S. Rousseau's article "Science and the Discovery of the Imagination in Enlightened England" (*Eighteenth-Century Studies*, 1969, 108–35). He presents the original thesis that scientists and philosophers of the time discovered the imagination as a material substance and that this new belief in the physical existence of the imagination contributed to the transition from mimetic art to symbolic art in the eighteenth century.

Essential to studies of the impact of science on French literature is Daniel Mornet's *Les sciences de la nature en France au dix-huitième siècle* (Paris, 1911). Since Mornet is interested in the social implications of science, the subject of the diffusion of science through popular works is treated here at greater length than is usual in histories of science.

An interesting investigation of science in the periodical literature in France is Minnie M. Miller's "Science and Philosophy as Precursors of the English Influence in France" (PMLA, 1930, 856–896). The author maintains that an examination of French periodicals published during the seventy years preceding Voltaire's *Lettres philosophiques* in 1734 shows that the influence of English science and philosophy was at its height prior to the publication of Voltaire's *Lettres*.

A valuable background study on the diffusion of science in France is Leonard M. Marsak's dissertation, *Bernard de Fontenelle: The Idea of Science in the French Enlightenment* (Cornell University Press, 1957).[3] Marsak discusses Fontenelle as a philosopher and spokesman for science in eighteenth-century France and as a social scientist who tried to explain the meaning that science had for man and society.

A highly informative contribution to our understanding of science in the French Enlightenment is Colm Kieran's *Science and the Enlightenment in eighteenth-century France* (Genève, 1968). Kieran calls attention to the debate on science which continued in France throughout the eighteenth century. It was a debate between those who wanted to mechanize the world picture and the foes of the mechanists, the organicists, who sought a scientific rationale for their theories in the life sciences.

One of the earliest studies of the impact of science on French poetry is Casimir Alexandre Fusil's *La poésie scientifique de 1750 à nos jours* (Paris, 1918). He discusses popular scientific literature, didactic scientific poetry and

---

[3] The dissertation was the basis of a publication which appeared in the *Transactions of the American Philosophical Society*, N.S. Vol. 49, Part 7 (Philadelphia, 1959).

scientific themes in poetry, letters and essays. The influence of science on poetry in an earlier period is covered by Albert-Marie Schmidt's *La poésie scientifique en France au seizième siècle* (Paris, 1939), in which he reconstructs the history of French Renaissance learned poetry.

Specific scientific themes in French literature are treated in Donald Lawrence King's *L'influence des sciences physiologiques sur la littérature française de 1670 à 1870* (Paris, 1929) which deals primarily with the influence of medicine on literature.

The question concerning the nature of the animal soul has been the subject of several publications. One of the earliest was George Boas' *The Happy Beast in French Thought of the Seventeenth Century* (John Hopkins Press, 1933). It was followed by the Johns Hopkins dissertation of Hester Hastings, *Man and Beast in French Thought of the Eighteenth Century* (1936). A few years later came Leonora C. Rosenfield's *From Beast-Machine to Man-Machine* (New York, 1941), which examined the theories about the animal soul from Descartes to La Mettrie. The subject received another elaborate treatment in Hélène Naïs' *Les animaux dans la poésie de la Renaissance: science, symbolique, poésie* (Paris, 1961). These works, covering the period from the sixteenth to the eighteenth centuries, examine the scientific literature on the subject of the animal soul, the popular literature through which the new theories were diffused and the treatment of these theories in poetry and belles lettres.

Astronomy in French poetry has been the subject of several articles. The earliest was Jean Plattard's "Le système de Copernic dans la littérature française au seizième siècle" (*Revue du seizième siècle,* 1913, 220—237). The author discusses the slow acceptance of the Copernican system in France in the sixteenth century. His examination of the poetry of that century, including poems that deal specifically with astronomy, revealed that Copernicus had almost no influence on the imagination in France.

Beverly S. Ridgely in his article "Dalibray, Le Pailleur and the 'New Astronomy' in French seventeenth-century poetry" (JHI, 1956, 3—27) confirms the tardy impact of the new astronomy on French poetry. The uniqueness of Dalibray's forty sonnets, written between 1640 and 1646, on the subject of the earth's movement, illustrate that point. The same author treats another astronomy theme in a later article, "The cosmic voyage in French sixteenth century learned poetry" (*Studies in the Renaissance,* 1963, 136—162). He maintains that the cosmic voyage was a device used in the learned poetry to capture the interest of the reader and facilitate his instruction in the wonders of the cosmos. This theme was developed in the years 1555—1585, when there was a great vogue in France of scientific and philosophic verse.

The Newtonian system of the world was a theme of interest to the French poets of the eighteenth century. Ruth T. Murdoch, in her article "Newton and the French Muse" (JHI, 1958, 323—334), shows that by the middle of the eighteenth century, Newtonian thinking had become quite influential; the influence of the *Opticks,* however, was more widespread than that of the *Principia.* It is also pertinent to mention here the article by James R. Naiden, "Newton demands the Latin Muse" (*Symposium,* 1952, 111—122), in which he considers the didactic verse in Latin of three Italian Jesuits: Carolus Nocet, Roger John Boscovich and Benedict Stay. In the years 1729 to 1760 these three wrote 32,000 lines of "Newtonian poetry".

Turning now to the German scene, there are several publications that have made important contributions to our understanding of the popular literature in eighteenth-century Germany, especially the kind that aided the rapid diffusion of the new sciences. These books have escaped the attention of most literary historians which is unfortunate, because there we find a phase of the social history of the German Enlightenment not entirely unrelated to its literary history.

Historians of science have generally ignored the popular appeal that science enjoyed in Germany during the Enlightenment, with more attention being paid to this phenomenon in England and France. There are some exceptions, however. Friedrich Klemm in his article, "Die Physik im Zeitalter der Aufklärung" is aware of the dissemination of science in Germany by the middle of the eighteenth century and calls attention to the popular fascination with Newtonian thought that existed in Germany as well as in England and France.[4] In an earlier article, "Martin Frobenius Ledermüller: Aus der Zeit der Salon-Mikroskopie des Rokoko", the same author gives an account of the progress of microscopy in Germany and a view of the popular delight with the world revealed by the microscope.[5] Hans Schimank's lecture before the Joachim Jungius-Gesellschaft in 1967, "Stand und Entwicklung der Naturwissenschaften im Zeitalter der Aufklärung", is by far the best introduction to the history of science in the German Enlightenment.[6] This is especially due to the fact that Schimank does not simply tell the history of scientific discoveries, but delves into the scientific and popular scientific literature that was actually read by the enlightened public of the time.

The diffusion of the new astronomy in Germany receives its best treatment in *Entstehung und Ausbreitung der Copernicanischen Lehre* (Erlangen, 1943) by Ernst Zinner, a historian of astronomy. It is apparent that for the German scene, this work is more useful than the well-known book by Dorothy Stimson, *The Gradual Acceptance of the Copernican Theory* (New York, 1917). In pursuing

4 *Die BASF (Zeitschrift der Badischen Anilin- und Soda-Fabrik),* Jg. 8 (1958), Heft 3, pp. 99—108.
5 *Optische Rundschau,* Sonderdruck aus Nr. 45 bis 48, Jahrg. 1927 (Schweidnitz, 1928).
6 An expanded version of the lecture appeared in *Lessing und die Zeit der Aufklärung* (Göttingen, 1968), pp. 30—76.

his thesis, Zinner examines a vast literature on astronomy from the sixteenth to the eighteenth centuries, including popular works in German, as well as Latin treatises.

Indispensable to the study of science's impact on culture in Germany is *Geschichte der Beziehungen zwischen Theologie und Naturwissenschaft*[7] by Otto Zöckler, a Lutheran church historian. Once again, for the German scene this relatively unknown work is much more valuable than Andrew D. White's widely read *A History of the Warfare of Science with Theology* (New York, 1896). Zöckler devotes a large section of his second volume to popular science literature — insofar as it pertains to theology — in Germany from the last decade of the seventeenth to the middle decades of the eighteenth century. We have here an excellent bibliography of those numerous physicotheological works by scientists and clergymen who tried to demonstrate harmony between science and faith. An even more exhaustive study of this physicotheological literature is provided by Wolfgang Philipp in *Das Werden der Aufklärung in theologiege-schichtlicher Sicht* (Göttingen, 1957). Although Philipp's claims for the theological significance of this movement are controversial, his book proves beyond a doubt that there was a vast popular literature with a physico-theological orientation that contributed to the diffusion and acceptance of the new science.

For the periodical literature in the eighteenth century in Germany, the most useful work is Joachim Kirchner's *Die Grundlagen des deutschen Zeitschriften-wesens* (Two volumes, Leipzig, 1928, 1931). The second volume is a bibliography of German periodicals from their beginnings in the seventeenth century to 1790. The author identifies the scientific periodicals and distinguishes between those that are purely scientific and those that are of a more popular nature. David A. Kronick's *A History of Scientific and Technical Periodicals* (New York, 1962) focuses on scientific periodicals in Europe in approximately the same period. His statistical surveys reveal the unusual quantity of scientific periodicals in Germany as compared to other European nations. Whatever judgment one may pass on the quality of many of these periodicals, it is undeniable that they were a significant factor in the diffusion of science in Germany. Another valuable study of periodical literature in the eighteenth century is Wolfgang Martens' *Die Botschaft der Tugend* (Stuttgart, 1968), which is an extensive and thorough account of the German moral weeklies in the eighteenth century. It is a thematic study and one of the themes the author encountered was the popular interest in science.

Reference works for English and French popular science literature in German

---

[7] (Gütersloh, 1877–1879). Two volumes: Volume I, *Von den Anfängen der Christ-lichen Kirche bis Newton und Leibniz;* Volume II, *Von Newton und Leibniz bis zur Gegenwart.*

translations are Lawrence M. and Mary Bell Price's *The Publication of English Humaniora in Germany in the Eighteenth Century* (University of California Press, 1955) and Hans Fromm's *Bibliographie deutscher Übersetzungen aus dem Französischen 1700–1948*, 6 volumes (Baden-Baden, 1950–1953). I have been able to make occasional additions in the identity of a translator or the date of an early edition.

As regards science in German literature of the seventeenth and eighteenth centuries, there have been only a few publications. Gertrud Bieder in her *Natur und Landschaft in der deutschen Barocklyrik* (Zürich, 1927) contends that contemporary scientific developments did not influence the world view of the German lyricists from 1635 to 1674. Christof Junker comes to the same conclusion in his *Das Weltraumbild in der deutschen Lyrik von Opitz bis Klopstock* (Berlin, 1932). He demonstrates that the new astronomy and its new conception of space were not accepted by lyricists until the third decade of the eighteenth century. In Karl Richter's "Die kopernikanische Wende in der Lyrik von Brockes bis Klopstock" (*Schiller-Jahrbuch*, 1968, 132–169), we find beautiful speculations about the influence of science on the creation of a new lyric poetry. Unfortunately, his speculations are based on only a few examples from Brockes, Haller and Klopstock, and thus he neither proves his thesis nor presents adequate material. These three authors confine themselves to lyric poetry and do not deal with the problem of the diffusion of the sciences through popular literature.

A more thorough work is Frederick H. Wagman's *Magic and Natural Science in German Baroque Literature* (Columbia University Press, 1942) which studies the influence of the natural sciences on prose forms in the last four decades of the seventeenth century. The author found side by side vestiges of the medieval-theological or the primitive-occult views of nature and a more modern belief in the autonomy of nature, as well as the trend toward sceptical questioning of authority and insistence on empirical observation. Wagman's judgments about the attitudes toward nature in the prose works examined by him seem to be well founded. Occasionally, however, he makes generalizations about the seventeenth century such as, "In Germany there seems to have been but little popular interest in the progress of experimental science . . ." (116). Although he considers some of the popular science literature of the time, the material he presents is not sufficient to warrant such conclusions. The diffusion of the sciences in Germany in the seventeenth century requires much more systematic study than has yet been provided.

Of great value to the subject of science and literature in the German Enlightenment is Lois Armour Westen's "Melitto-Logia" the Mythology of the Bee in Eighteenth-Century German Literature (Diss., University of Illinois, 1952). Although the author confined herself to a single natural history theme, the bee, she uncovered valuable material in her examination of the background.

Her study of apiculture in the eighteenth century led her to the popular science literature of the time and especially to physicotheological treatises.

As far as the later period is concerned, that is, the age of Goethe, the significant publication on science in literature is Alexander Gode-von Aesch's *Natural Science in German Romanticism* (Columbia University Press, 1941). He touches on the earlier period, up to 1770, only peripherally, except for his careful treatment of the scientific and philosophic themes in Wieland's long didactic poem of 1750, "Die Natur der Dinge" (39—52). Gode-von Aesch's book, however, is oriented more toward an analysis of dominant ideas in the philosophic literature of German Romanticism. It is not a systematic examination of science in the "belle lettres" of the time.

It is well known that the age of Goethe had numerous literary figures with wide interests including the sciences. In addition to the many publications about Goethe's scientific interests, there have been such studies of Lichtenberg, Schiller, Matthisson and Novalis. However, the subject of science in the literature of the age of Goethe has not yet been treated systematically. Before this can be done, the earlier period must be studied, and it is hoped that the present undertaking will serve such a purpose.

The topic of this study is scientific themes in the poetry and popular literature of the German Enlightenment in the years 1720 to 1760. It is in this period that the diffusion of the sciences in Germany gathered momentum and that the educated layman became enlightened about the new sciences. I have studied the popular literature through which this diffusion took place, and the poetry in which the scientific interests of men of letters are reflected.

By popular literature in the sciences I mean works written in German and intended entirely or in part for the educated layman. Thus, for example, the publication of the German scientific society, Collegium Naturae Curiosorum, or the learned journal, *Acta Eruditorum,* are not popular science literature, for they were written in Latin and directed primarily toward scientists and scholars.

The first part of this study considers the main foreign and native sources for the dissemination of science. German translations of works by foreign authors are examined; these were books that aroused interest in the sciences and conveyed a variety of scientific themes. Compendiums of science by German scientists or men trained in the sciences are taken up; these books were specifically designed to teach science to the layman. Then comes the physicotheological literature, works that intended to demonstrate the harmony between faith and science and, in so doing, taught much scientific material. Significant samples from the vast periodical literature in this period are cited to show how they contributed to the popularization of science. Finally, popular scientific works on astronomy and natural history by German scientists and amateurs of science are examined.

Thus, in the first part the contents of a diverse popular science literature are discussed. These are the books that brought science to the men of letters. Here are the sources for the scientific themes that are reflected in the poetry. In the second part, the poets of the period are taken up individually, in chronological order, and the scientific themes in their poetry are identified. The works of more than fifty poets are involved in this section. Some poets are treated at length, others more briefly, depending on the quantity and variety of scientific material that appears in their poetry. In the third part the dominant themes are selected and traced through the authors discussed in the second part. Thus, in the second part the profile of each poet in regard to the scientific themes in his poetry is described, whereas in the third part the various scientific themes in the poetry of the period under study are taken individually and traced through the poetry examined in the second part.

Part I:
THE POPULAR LITERATURE

In this first part I am concerned with the scientific material that is found in the popular literature. It will introduce the science of the eighteenth century in the way men of letters at the time were introduced to it. This will be a much more fruitful approach than simply summarizing the development of the new sciences. That can be found in any history of science. What can not be found in a history of science or, for that matter, in any history at all, is a discussion of the content of the popular literature of the time.

The term popular literature is used to mean approximately what Price means by "humaniora" in his *The Publication of English Humaniora in Germany in the Eighteenth Century* (University of California Press, 1955). He includes works belonging to the humanistic disciplines other than "belles lettres" and technical or professional publications. Thus, "humaniora" is a very inclusive term, encompassing that vast literature that presented learning to those who were pursuing it for the sake of amusement and enlightenment, rather than for professional purposes. Johann Christoph Gottsched, very much alert to the cultural needs and trends of his time, devoted two of his periodicals to "humaniora", namely *Neuer Büchersaal der schönen Wissenschaften und der freyen Künste* (1745–1750) and *Das Neueste aus der anmuthigen Gelehrsamkeit* (1751–1762). By "freye Künste" and "anmuthige Gelehrsamkeit" he meant liberal learning, that is, a learning which is not confined to any one discipline and which offers its material for the amusement, enlightenment and edification of the layman, the non-specialist. As shall be seen when these two periodicals are discussed, science was very much a part of Gottsched's conception of liberal learning. In the present study of the popular literature, the focus, of course, will be primarily on those works that contributed in some measure to the diffusion of the sciences.

Thus, popular literature, in this sense of "humaniora" or liberal learning, includes many books that were well known and considered significant in their own time, but which have fallen into oblivion. However justifiable oblivion may be for some of these books, they must be examined for an understanding of the widespread acceptance of science in the German Enlightenment. The reflection of science in the poetry of the time is part of that acceptance.

The discussion of the popular literature is divided into five sections. First come the German translations of "humaniora", containing scientific subject matter by English, French and Dutch writers. Studies of German translations in the eighteenth century have confined themselves to "belles lettres". Yet, translations of the sort considered here are a part of the cultural history of the German Enlightenment. The second section takes up some of the popular compendiums of science of the time. These compendiums are characteristic of the attempts to enlighten the public about science. The third section examines physicotheological works, which are usually dismissed as examples of the naive optimism of the time. They belong to a type of popular literature that contributed much to the diffusion of science and, thus, has a place in any history of the German Enlightenment. The fourth section turns to periodicals. Histories of literature usually refer only to a few literary periodicals, about which there are also specialized studies available. But a discussion of the content of periodicals that belong to "humaniora" is rare. Here, again, there is a species of writing that characterizes the German Enlightenment and should be rescued from limbo for that reason. Finally, popular scientific works by German scientists and amateurs of science are considered. The role of the amateur scientist in eighteenth-century Germany has never been studied. This subject is touched on here because it is an example of the popular interest in the sciences. In this last section there is also a brief consideration of science in the encyclopedias and histories of learning of the time, a subject which deserves more attention than it has received. Thus, in this first part a neglected literature is rescued to tell one aspect of the story of science in the German Enlightenment.

A. THE TRANSLATIONS

German translations of popular scientific works by English, French and Dutch authors significantly aided the dissemination of scientific themes in Germany. I shall consider translations of works by the Englishmen, Thomas Burnet, John Ray, John Woodward, William Whiston, William Derham, John Wilkins; the Frenchmen, Bernard de Fontenelle, Antoine Pluche, George Louis Leclerc, Comte de Buffon, François de la Mothe Fénelon; the Dutch, Christian Huygens, Bernhard Nieuwentyt, Pieter van Musschenbroek and Jan Swammerdam. It will also be appropriate in this section to refer to translations of two long didactic scientific poems by the Frenchmen, Charles Claude Genest and Melchior de Polignac. These works are cosmogonies, popular astronomies, physicotheologies, natural histories, compendiums of science and didactic scientific verse.[1]

These certainly were not the only scientific books translated into German.[2] They are, however, the ones most often referred to by German poets and popular writers and are frequently reviewed in the journals of the time. As shall be seen, the subject matter of these popular works in translation appears repeatedly in the poetry and popular literature.

I do not maintain that these works would have remained unread and unknown in Germany had they not been translated. Most of these works were available in Latin and French. Most were reviewed in the Latin *Acta Eruditorum,* and all were reviewed in the German learned journals. However, the translations and numerous editions of some of them indicate the popularity of the books and the extent to which their material was being carried to the German reading public.

Thomas Burnet (1635–1715)

Thomas Burnet originally wrote his *Sacred Theory of the Earth* in Latin, with the English translation following soon afterwards.[3] A good account of Thomas

---

[1] First or early editions of the German translations of works by Ray, Whiston, Derham, Wilkins, Fontenelle, Pluche, Buffon, Genest, Nieuwentyt, Musschenbroek and Swammerdam were available for this study. For Burnet, Woodward and Huygens early English editions were used and for Fénelon a French edition.

[2] The only reference works for translations of this type of literature are: *The Publication of English Humaniora in Germany in the Eighteenth Century* by Mary Bell Price and Lawrence M. Price (University of California Press, 1955) and Hans Fromm's *Bibliographie deutscher Übersetzungen aus dem Französischen 1700–1948,* 6 volumes (Baden-Baden, 1950–1953).

[3] *Theoria Sacra Telluris . . .* Books I and II (London, 1681). In 1689 Burnet published a new Latin edition which included two more books. The first edition of the complete English translation was London, 1684–1689.

Burnet's unusual theories and the controversies they engendered in England can be found in Katherine Brownell Collier's *Cosmogonies of our Fathers* (Columbia University Press, 1934) and in Marjorie Nicolson's *Mountain Gloom and Mountain Glory* (Cornell University Press, 1959).

In Elisabeth Haller's dissertation on Burnet's style,[4] we find the full title of the German translation of the *Sacred theory*: "Theoria Sacra Telluris, d.i. *Heiliger Entwurff oder Biblische Betrachtung des Erdreichs, begreiffend, neben dem Ursprung, die allgemeine Enderung welche unser Erd-Kreiss einseits allschon ausgestanden, und anderseits noch auszustehen hat;* (Anfangs von Herrn Thomas Burnet in Latein zu London herausgegeben. Anjetzo aber ins Hochteutsche übersetzt, und dem curiosen Leser zu Dienste mit einem doppelten Register, mehreren Figuren und diensamen Anmerckungen erläutert. Durch M. Johann Jakob Zimmermann, Hamburg, 1698)". According to Price[5] there was an earlier translation with the following title: *Heiliger Entwurf oder biblische Betrachtung des Erdreichs . . .* (Frankfurt und Leipzig, 1693) and another edition of the Zimmermann translation, (Hamburg, 1703).

The story of the reception of Burnet's unusual theories in Germany has not yet been told. At this point, however, I shall state only that the theories were well known and often cited in German and poetry and prose.

Thomas Burnet was one of many authors who attempted to harmonize the new sciences with the Bible. He assumes that the Biblical account of the creation applies only to this planet. Then, using Cartesian principles, he tries to explain, according to natural laws, the creation (Book I), the primeval world and Noah's flood (Book II), the final conflagration (Book III) and the millenium and the fate of the planet after the Last Judgment (Book IV). In Germany, his account of the flood and the origin of mountains received most attention.

The original chaos consisted of particles of different density which in the course of time settled to the center of the chaos in accordance with their specific gravity. Thus, at the center there was a solid core surrounded by a sphere of liquid particles, beyond which existed an even larger sphere of gaseous particles. The oily portions of the liquid floated to the surface and there became mixed with the particles of solid matter that descended from the air, thereby forming the crust of the earth. Originally, therefore, the surface of the earth was entirely smooth and unbroken by mountains and seas. The earth at the time did not have an oblique axis and so had continuous spring. The heat of the sun eventually dried the earth's crust and 1656 years after the creation, the crust collapsed causing the Biblical deluge and leaving the earth marred with mountains. This briefly is the content of the first two books.

---

[4] *Die Barocken Stilmerkmale in der englischen, lateinischen und deutschen Fassung von Dr. Thomas Burnet's "Theory of the Earth"* (Bern, 1940).

[5] Mary Bell Price and Lawrence M. Price, *The Publication of English Humaniora in Germany in the Eighteenth Century* (University of California Press, 1955).

John Ray (1628–1705)

John Ray's reflections on cosmogony appeared in his *Three Physico-Theological Discourses* (London, 1693), first translated into German in 1698 under the title, *Sonderbares Klee-Blättlein, der Welt Anfang, Veränderung und Untergang* (Hamburg, 1698). In 1732 there was another translation, *Drey Physico-Theologische Betrachtungen von der Welt Anfang, Veränderung und Untergang* (Leipzig, 1732) by Theodor Arnold.[6]

As can be gathered from the title, Ray's cosmogony is about the creation of the world, the transformations caused on earth by the Biblical deluge and the anticipated final conflagration. Like all writers of cosmogonies in the seventeenth century, he seeks to find a theory that is in accord with both Biblical statements and scientific principles.

He claims that the earth was created out of an original chaos and that water and earth were separated from one another according to gravity, so that the land, being heavier, was submerged by the water. Dry land appeared as a result of eruptions precipitated by subterranean fires. He considered fossils real organic remains and evidence that the deluge was universal. He suggests that the flood was caused either by a shift in the earth's center of gravity or by an enormous pressure on the earth's oceans, thereby forcing the water down into the abyss and up through the earth's surface. As possible causes of the final conflagration, he suggests the eruption of the central fires or the gradual drying up of the earth, thereby predisposing it for a conflagration.

The Wisdom of God Manifested in the Works of the Creation (London, 1691) was another of Ray's works which was translated into German. It appeared under the title, *Spiegel der Weissheit und Allmacht Gottes* ... (Goslar, 1712), translated by Caspar Calvöer. It was one of several English physicotheologies around 1700 that used the new scientific knowledge of nature to praise God in his works and demonstrate his qualities out of his creation. It is a compendium of science including astronomy, physics, natural history and anatomy.

John Woodward (1665–1728)

John Woodward's *Essay toward a Natural History of the Earth* (London, 1695) was translated into Latin (Zürich, 1705) by Johann Jacob Scheuchzer, into French (Paris, 1735) and into German under the title *Physikalische Erdbeschreibung oder Versuch einer natürlichen Historie des Erdbodens* (Erfurt, 1744), a second edition appearing in 1746.

6 This translation was available to me.

Woodward's point of departure for his speculations about the origin and formation of the earth was fossils, of which he possessed a large collection. He was one of the first to maintain that the fossils of shells and other marine bodies are the remains of living animals that once lived in the sea. To explain the existence of fossils in all parts of the world, he had recourse to the Biblical deluge which he claimed to have been universal. Furthermore, since fossils are found not only on the surface but in various strata of the earth, he maintained that they sank to different depths according to their respective gravities mingling with terrestrial matter of the same specific gravity; thus, we find the heavier shells in stone and the lighter in chalk. In Woodward's cosmogony, gravity was also the means of creation, in that particles settled out of the primordial chaos according to their specific gravity.

Woodward's *An Attempt towards a Natural History of the Fossils of England* (London, 1728–1729) was also translated into German under the title, *Abhandlung über Fossilien* (Erfurt, 1746). The title page of the English original gives a good statement of the contents of this catalog: "A description and historical account of each [fossil]; with observations and experiments, made in order to discover, as well the origin and nature of them, as their medicinal, mechanical and other uses". He does this for some 1574 specimens which he divides into thirty-six species. The popular interest in fossils was already considerable in Germany, so that this translation was undoubtedly received with interest.

William Whiston (1667–1752)

William Whiston's *A New Theory of the Earth* (London, 1696) aroused controversy and discussion during the first half of the eighteenth century in Germany both before and after the German translation was published in 1713.[7] Undoubtedly this translation, which was well known, contributed to the general familiarity with Whiston's interesting cosmogony.

Whiston's theory concerning the creation of the earth was an attempt to explain the Genesis account of the creation by the application of Newtonian principles, and as such is one of the earliest accounts in the German language of Newton's *Principia*. In 1753 Lessing reviewed this translation which had appeared under a new title: *Willhelm Whistons . . . gründlicher Beweis, dass die in der Offenbahrung befindliche Geschichte von der Schöpfung der Welt und die allda geschehene Verkündigung von dem Untergange der Welt mit der gesunden Vernunft keinesweges streite* (Wittenberg, 1753). In his review which appeared

---

[7] *Neue Betrachtung der Erde* (Frankfurt, 1713), translated into German by Michael Swen.

in the *Berlinische privilegirte Staats- und gelehrte Zeitung,* October 30, 1753, Lessing makes the following comment about the work:

> ... Die neure Weltweisheit des Newtons, besonders die neuen Entdeckungen dieses unsterblichen Messkünstlers in dem physischen Theile der Astronomie, schlossen dem Verfasser einen neuen Weg auf, den Spöttereyen der Ungläubigen über einige der wichtigsten Puncte der Schrift, über die Schöpfung, über die Sündfluth und über den bevorstehenden Untergang der Welt, mit ungewohnten Waffen entgegenzugehen. Und hieraus entstand dieses Werk, welches auch noch alsdann, wann man der Weltweisheit längst wieder eine neue Form wird gegeben haben, ein Monument der menschlichen Scharffsinnigkeit sein wird.[8]

The text, divided into postulates, lemmata, hypotheses, phenomena and solutions, in that order, indicates that the author wished to provide his theory with mathematical rigor. The eighty-six lemmata of book I, with their corollaries and scholiums, include some of the main features of the Newtonian celestial mechanics, the laws of motion, the law of gravity as it applies to tides, planets, comets. The Newtonian system is, then, presupposed in Whiston's development of his theory.

In the second book the hypotheses begin to present aspects of Whiston's own ingenious speculations about the creation. The first hypothesis tells us that the chaos of which the Bible speaks was the atmosphere of a comet and that the earth originally was a comet. In fact, in the lengthy preface and throughout the text, he maintains emphatically that the Biblical story of creation applies only to our planet earth. Further hypotheses are that the earth acquired a perfectly circular annual motion about the sun at the beginning of the Mosaic creation, but did not get its diurnal rotation until after the Fall of Adam, and that a comet intersected the plane of the ecliptic in its descent toward its perihelion and thereby caused the deluge.

In book III he presents a multitude of phenomena which describe his conception, in detail, of the circumstances on this planet during the Mosaic creation, the circumstances of the primitive earth prior to the deluge, the effects of the deluge on the earth and, finally, the anticipated circumstances on the earth during the conflagration, the ensuing millenium and the Last Judgment. Book IV presents solutions, that is, attempts to explain the phenomena of book III according to the principles laid down in the lemmata and hypotheses.

What stirred the interest and imagination of German poets and writers most about Whiston's speculations was the role played by comets. The earth itself originally was a comet in Whiston's system and after the Last Judgment is to

---

[8] *Sämtliche Schriften,* hrsg. von Karl Lachmann (Stuttgart, 1886–1924), Band V, p. 207.

resume that role. A comet gave the earth its diurnal motion after the Fall and the comet that caused the Flood changed the earth's circular orbit into an elliptical one. This latter comet caused the cataclysmic inundation in three ways. When the earth passed through the atmosphere and tail of the comet, its gravitational pull attracted some of the vapors which rose again into the atmosphere and then returned in torrential rains. Secondly, the comet's gravitational force caused enormous tides in the waters of the earth's interior. The resulting pressure caused cracks and fissures in the crust of the earth permitting this reservoir of interior waters to escape and flood the entire globe. Finally, the earth entered the comet's tail a second time in its ascent from the perihelion. This time, however, the earth passed only through the tail of the comet and not through its atmosphere as well and thus, the rains were not as heavy but lasted longer than the first time. This last rain explains the Biblical account that the waters continued to mount after the forty days rain and, at the same time, it is in agreement with his computations of the comet's orbit.

Whiston explains the final conflagration also as caused by a comet coming very near to the earth. Such a proximity could force the earth out of its orbit and draw it so close to the sun that it would burn up. However, he considers another possibility, for the final conflagration in his view is not the complete destruction of the planet but a transformation of the planet into a new condition appropriate for the saints and martyrs who would dwell there for a millenium. Thus, he considers more likely that the comet would merely drain away the cold surface waters and heat the air so that the interior heat of the earth would no longer be offset and, consequently, devastate the surface. At the conclusion of the millenium, a comet would collide with the earth and, thereby, force it out of its planetary orbit into a cometary one.

William Derham (1657—1735)

From the cosmogonies we shall turn to William Derham's two physico-theologies, *Physico-Theology* and *Astro-Theology*, whose influence in Germany was impressive. In 1711 and 1712 William Derham, a member of the Royal Society and later a canon of Windsor, gave sixteen sermons as the Boyle lectures to prove the existence and attributes of God from His works. These sermons were published in book form in 1713 under the title of *Physico-Theology*,[9] which became the name of this type of literature. The work was so popular in England, that between 1713 and 1754 there were twelve editions. The work was

---

9 *Physico-Theology; or a demonstration of the Being and Attributes of God from His works of creation* (London, 1713). Other editions: 1714 (3), 1720 (4), 1723 (6), 1727 (7), 1732 (8), 1737 (9), 1742 (10), 1749 (11), 1754 (12).

almost as popular in Germany where the translation, based on the seventh English edition, had six editions between 1730 and 1764.[10] More than half of the text consists of footnotes by the author in further explanation of the scientific material presented in the lectures. Religious considerations are scattered throughout the text with the eleventh and final part entirely devoted to pious reflections.

The *Physico-Theology* is a compendium of science dealing with natural phenomena pertaining to our planet. The first three parts cover physical phenomena above, beneath and on the surface of the earth. The remaining seven parts discuss the inhabitants of the earth with a thoroughness that is unusual for compendiums of science of the time. The senses, organs and various functions of animals and man are considered in detail. The plant world is also taken up but to a much lesser extent. The work is indeed a storehouse of an enormous quantity of facts and figures. The title of the book, thus, is somewhat misleading, since three fourths of the book treats anatomy and physiology of animals and man, and only a relatively few pages in this lengthy text have a religious subject matter. Finally, as far as the diffusion of science in Germany is concerned, from the foregoing we can conclude that this translation played a not insignificant role in the popularization of science in Germany.

Derham's *Astro-Theology*,[11] the companion volume to his *Physico-Theology*, was almost as popular in Germany as in England. Between 1714 and 1750 there were nine English editions of the work and between 1728 and 1765 there were six editions in Germany of the German translation by Johann Albert Fabricius.[12]

Fabricius dedicated his translation to his patron, Barthold Heinrich Brockes, who, we are informed, repeatedly encouraged him with the translation. As a further service, Fabricius added to his translation a bibliography of ancient, medieval and modern writers who like Derham ventured to lead men to God through the contemplation of nature. In the second edition of 1732, this bibliography contains some three hundred titles (pp. XIII–LXXX). Most of these works are in Latin, about twenty in German, as many in English, and a few each in French, Dutch and Italian. Of the modern works in Latin, that is, those published in the sixteenth, seventeenth and early eighteenth centuries, many were published in Germany, thus demonstrating that this tradition was very well known in that country.

10 *Physicotheologie, oder Natur-Leitung zu Gott* (Hamburg, 1732), translated by Johann Albert Fabricius. The first translation of 1730 was made by Christian Ludewig Wiener. Other editions of the Fabricius translation were: 1736, 1741, 1750 and 1764.
11 *Astro-Theology; or a demonstration of the Being and Attributes of God from a survey of the Heavens* (London, 1714). Other editions: 1715 (2), 1719 (3), 1721 (4), 1726 (5), 1741 (8), 1750 (9).
12 *Astrotheologie, oder Himmlisches Vergnügen in Gott, bey aufmercksamen Anschauen des Himmels, und genauer Betrachtung der Himmlischen Cörper . . .* (Hamburg, 1732). Other editions of the translation were: 1728, 1739, 1745, 1750, 1765.

Since this work is undoubtedly one of the sources of many astronomy themes that we have found in the poetry of our period, a brief examination of the text is in order. In his preface to the fifth edition, the one that Fabricius translated, Derham speaks of three systems of the world, the Ptolemaic, the Copernican and what he calls the new system. The first one is treated very briefly; the Copernican is shown to be the most acceptable one and completely in harmony with Scripture. By the new system he means the expanded conception of the universe in which there is no sphere of fixed stars as was still the case in the Copernican system, but where the stars are scattered throughout an unlimited space, where each star is a sun about which revolve inhabited planets. He is very emphatic about the last point, for it answers for him the question why God created all these solar and planetary systems.

The text itself presents a thorough account of the astronomy of the day. Sizes, distances, orbits and movements of heavenly bodies are presented in detail. As sources for his facts and figures, he sometimes cites his own observations but more often the work of contemporary astronomers like Hooke, Halley, Flamsteed, Cassini, Picard and de La Hire. The sixth book is of special interest, for here Derham presents the Newtonian theory of gravity and, due to the popularity of this work in Germany, it must be considered as a source for the spread of Newtonian thinking. The last section of the book is entirely concerned with pious and religious reflections which also occur occasionally throughout the text. However, the astronomy is for the most part kept separate and distinct from the pious considerations. Therefore, though the material is presented within a religious framework, it is a serious popular text on astronomy.

John Wilkins (1614—1672)

Finally, the last of the English popular scientific books we shall consider is John Wilkins' *Vertheidigter Copernicus*[13] which is the title of the German translation of the first two books of his *Mathematical and Philosophical Works*.[14] The defense of the Copernican theory is actually the topic of the second book only, "Dass die Erde ein Planet seye", whereas the first book, "Dass der Mond eine Welt oder Erde seye" presents the many arguments so popular for the next hundred years, to prove that the moon is an inhabited

[13] Johannis Wilkins, *Vertheidigter Copernicus* (Leipzig, 1713), translated by Johann Gabriel Doppelmayr.
[14] *The Mathematical and Philosophical Works ... Containing, I. The Discovery of a New World: Or a Discourse tending to prove, that 'tis probable there may be another Habitable World in the Moon. II. That 'tis probable our Earth is One of the Planets. ...* (London, 1707, 1708). These first two volumes were published anonymously as early as 1638 under the title: *The Discovery of a World in the Moon.*

world like the earth. As the translator points out, Wilkins is not the only author to treat this subject, but he does it so thoroughly and beautifully that the work deserves to be translated. Similarly, since the work contains many of the arguments repeated so often between 1650 and 1750 in favor of the moon's inhabitation and the Copernican theory, the German translation of this work deserves to be considered in the present study.

In the early chapters of the first book, he proves that the notion of a plurality of worlds is not contrary to any principle of faith and reason and that contrary to tradition, all heavenly bodies are composed of the same materials and subject to decay and corruption. As proof that changes do occur in the heavens, he cites the phenomena of sun spots and the existence of comets. He then turns to the moon and accumulates arguments which contend that circumstances exist on the moon that make life there probable. The moon is a dense, opaque body that does not have its own light, as can be observed during eclipses. The dark and light areas observed on the moon by the naked eye represent water, due to light rays being observed and reflected. Furthermore, relying on Galileo's telescopic observations, he cites the presence of high mountains and deep valleys in the moon. He also maintains that the moon has an atmosphere, a subject that was debated throughout the following century. Among his arguments that were frequently repeated are first, the part of the moon that is illuminated makes a larger circle than the dark part and second, during a solar eclipse we see the moon in its natural size, that is, smaller than when it is illuminated. Both these observations, he maintains, are best explained by assuming that the moon is surrounded by a thick atmosphere that reflects and refracts the rays of the sun.

He vigorously defends the belief that the moon is inhabited, by resorting to the authority of both ancients and moderns and by arguments from nature. Of ancient supporters of the notion that the moon is a world like ours, he names Anaxagoras, Democritus, Heraclides, Xenophon, Pythagoras, Lucian; the moderns he names are Cusanus, Bruno, Nicolaus Hill, Michael Maestlin, Kepler and Galileo. He grants that nothing can be known with certainty about the moon's inhabitants but it is absurd to suppose that God would have created so many spacious, appropriate and comfortable homes if not to provide them with inhabitants. He frequently returns to the problem of the physical possibility of inhabitation. For example, as regards the possibility of all too great heat on the moon, he says that the long cold nights would offset the heat of the days, and thunderstorms during the day would regularly obscure the sun and provide cooling periods. He also suggests that the living creatures there might be of such a nature as we cannot conceive on the basis of our limited experience. Since there is such a great gap or difference between men and angels, it may be that the moon and the other planets are inhabited by intermediary creatures. These are some of the arguments that had become standard by the early eighteenth century.

In his concluding chapter he makes some ingenious suggestions about the possibility of space travel. He considers the main objection to space travel, namely weight, surmountable, because he does not believe that weight is an absolute quality of a body. Since the earth functions as a magnet, its attractive force would diminish with distance. Once a body has risen twenty miles above the earth, it would be practically weightless, he maintains. With similar arguments he presents a likely story for the possibility of space travel and shows a lively scientific imagination.[15]

The second book translated by Doppelmayr is a defense of the Copernican theory. Much of his effort is devoted to showing that Scripture is not against the heliocentric hypothesis and that Scripture nowhere supports the immovability of the earth nor its central position. He uses the often repeated argument that the Bible speaks of natural phenomena according to the understanding of man and not as they really are. He warns against the superstition that all science and knowledge can be found in the Bible. In the concluding chapters he presents a variety of arguments in support of the Copernican theory and challenges objections to it. He maintains the heliocentric hypothesis is simpler than the cumbersome Ptolemaic and awkward Tychonian system, that it explains the planetary orbits better and that the sun at the center can more easily transmit light and heat to the planets. He especially defends the diurnal motion of the earth against popular arguments based on the evidence of the senses and common sense.

It is difficult to say how much of an influence this book had in Germany. His arguments in favor of the inhabitation of the planets and in defense of the Copernican theory had become common property by the early decades of the eighteenth century. It seems, however, that the German reading public was more familiar with the popular astronomies of Fontenelle and Huygens.

Bernard LeBovier de Fontenelle (1657–1757)

The first French popular scientific work we shall consider is *Entretiens sur la pluralité des mondes* (Paris, 1686) by Fontenelle, which was probably the most beloved work on popular astronomy in Europe in the eighteenth century. The catalogs of the British Museum and Bibliothèque Nationale list some twelve editions of the book in its original French, as well as twelve editions of English translations. Neither catalog lists a German translation. There are several references to an early German translation (Leipzig, 1698), which according to three sources was made by the German scientist and mathematician, Ehrenfried

---

[15] See Marjorie Nicolson's *Voyages to the Moon* (New York, 1948) for the history of imaginary voyages to the moon.

Walther von Tschirnhausen.[16] Johann Christoph Gottsched, in the preface to his own translation, also refers to this earlier translation and notes that it was so popular that no copies of it had been available for several years.[17] Gottsched's translation of a later, expanded French edition, supplemented by his own explanatory notes and diagrams, was issued five times between 1726 and 1760.[18]

These dialogues between Fontenelle and a lady of high station are an example of popular scientific literature not directed to scientists or scholars, but intended for the enlightenment of the intelligent, literate laity whose interests can best be aroused by presenting difficult material in an entertaining and even amusing manner. The work was read by Germans in the original and in translation; it was cited and quoted innumerable times in the popular literature. Its influence in Germany as a popular work on science, as a source for the dissemination of the new astronomy was such that it must be considered as one of the very significant popular books of the German enlightenment.

The material is presented in the form of six conversations held in the evening between Fontenelle and a countess to whom he explains the essential facts, theories and speculations of astronomy. In the first evening, Fontenelle explains the Copernican system of the world and how it is an improvement over previous systems. He stresses that the earth is a planet and that the other stars are heavenly bodies like the sun. He amuses the countess by imagining that he is elevated above the earth and sees the whole earth pass by as it turns on its axis. Exercises of the imagination such as these entertain and, at the same time, aid the beginner to grasp what is contrary to sense perception, namely, the movement of the earth.

---

16 See Gottlieb Stolle, *Anleitung zur Historie der Gelahrheit* (Jena, 1727) p. 326; Johann Georg Walch, *Philosophisches Lexicon* (Leipzig, 1733) p. 2026; Zedler's *Universal Lexicon*, Volume 28, (1741) p. 626. In a recent publication, *Tschirnhausen und die Frühaufklärung in Mittel und Osteuropa* (Akademie-Verlag, Berlin, 1960), Ernst Winter offers evidence that Tschirnhausen was the translator. In his examination of the correspondence of the Tschirnhausen circle, Winter learned of a certain Vogel who himself had translated the Fontenelle work and then, as he confessed in a letter to the mathematician Knorr, was informed by the Leipzig publisher Fritsch that a translation had already been prepared "von einem vornehmen und grossen Mathematico aus Sachsen." p. 40.

17 *Gespräche von mehr als einer Welt* (Leipzig, 1730), second edition, preface, leaf 6: "Man hat diese Gespräche des Herrn Fontenelle schon am Ende des vorigen Jahrhunderts ins Deutsche übersetzt; und hier in Leipzig in Duodetz ans Licht gegeben". Neither Gottsched nor his biographers mention the name of the translator. The copy of the 1698 translation which I examined at the library of the University of Göttingen did not name the translator.

18 Ibid., Leipzig, 1726, 1730, 1738, 1751, 1760. Hans Fromm in his *Bibliographie deutscher Übersetzungen aus dem Französischen 1700—1948* (Baden-Baden, 1950—1953) includes Gottsched's translation of Fontenelle's *Auserlesene Schriften* (Leipzig, 1751) but omits the earlier editions of Gottsched's translations of *Gespräche von mehr als einer Welt* as well as of other Fontenelle works. Fromm lists two later German translations of the *Entretiens*, one by the astronomer, Johann Elert Bode, (Berlin, 1780).

The next three dialogues relate the pertinent facts about the moon and the planets of our solar system. He fascinated the lady with the speculation that the moon and the planets are all inhabited by rational creatures. He presents the main arguments that are repeated by many authors during the next century to support the possibility and probability of such inhabitation. There is the argument of analogy between this planet and the others. Since the earth belongs to the same species of heavenly bodies as the planets, one can conclude from circumstances on the earth to those on the planets. Secondly, there is the argument of the purpose of creation. God or nature would not have created such vast bodies uninhabited. If a drop of water or the leaf of a plant is inhabited, all the more reason to expect the planets to be inhabited also. Though he clearly states that this opinion is based on conjectures, it serves as an excellent device to present many of the dry facts and figures about the moon and planets. The entertainment of the instruction is further enhanced by his suggestion that they undertake a "Reise in Gedanken" to the planets and see the cosmos from different points of view. This appeal to the imagination gives the astronomer the opportunity to describe the dimensions, distances and orbits of the planets in our solar system.

In the fifth dialogue the vast cosmos beyond our solar system is described. Fontenelle depicts to the countess the immeasurable space and the innumerable suns and planets of which the telescope can give only an inkling. In the last dialogue, the author supports the material of the preceding dialogues by referring to some of the most recent discoveries by astronomers.

Gottsched's notes to the text go into greater detail in explaining astronomical matters, for which purpose he provides diagrams. For example, in asserting the superiority of the Copernican system, he shows with the aid of a diagram how the apparent retrogradation of planets can be better explained by assuming the motion of the earth; or, he illustrates how the annual orbit of the earth about the sun and the earth's oblique axis cause the seasons. The translator repeatedly refers to Christian Huygens' *Cosmotheoros,* especially on the matter of the inhabitation of the planets which he takes very seriously. The later editions of the translation are further supplemented by references to more recent works and observations of astronomers.

Abbé Antoine Pluche (1688–1761)

According to the French literary historian, Daniel Mornet, Antoine Pluche's *Le Spectacle de la nature* (Paris, 1732–1750) was one of the most influential popular scientific works.[19] Judging by the frequent references to this work by

19 Daniel Mornet, *Les Sciences de la Nature en France au dix-huitième Siècle* (Paris, 1911): "*Le Spectacle de la Nature* est par son influence un des grands livres du

German poets and writers, we can believe that the French original and its German translations[20] extended its influence to Germany as well. The work is divided into eight parts, of which the first four deal with natural history, physics and astronomy, the next three with man and his functions as a social creature and the last part with man's duties to God.

In the preface to the first volume, he makes it quite clear that his orientation is physicotheological. He believes that nature is best designed to cultivate our reason and turn our attention to God. His excursions into teleological explanations do not, however, compromise his scientific material which he has drawn from the works of modern scientists: "Die Schrifften, daraus wir den besten Unterricht gezogen, und die wir am öfftesten anführen, sind die *Memoires de l'Academie des Sciences,* die *Transactions Philosophical* der Englischen Societaet, daraus Lowthorp und John einen Auszug gemacht, die Schrifften des Malpighi, Redi, Willoughby, Leeuwenhoek, Grew, Nieuwentyt, Derham, Vallis-nieri &c" (I, p.b).

One half of the first volume is devoted to insect life. Caterpillars, silkworms, spiders, bees, flies are enumerated and described. He describes the parts of the body, various functions and the habits of individual creatures. There are numerous illustrations. The rest of the volume continues with testaceous animals, birds, quadrupeds and fish. In the last section, he also considers the general structure of plants. However, vegetation is the main subject of volume two. There he describes many individual plants, flowers and fruits. Matters related to vegetation such as gardening, grafting and pruning are also considered in some detail.

The subject of the third book is phenomena associated with the earth, those on the surface, those above it and those beneath it. He discusses pasture and meadow grounds and mountains; he lists different types of bodies of water and the living creatures found there. Then he turns to phenomena above the earth. He explains the properties of air and various phenomena associated with the air such as clouds, mists, dew, snow, rain, lightning, thunder, storms, winds. Of phenomena beneath the earth he considers fossils, oils, salts, stones, metals, enumerating many specific kinds of each.

The fourth book is about the heavens. It is not a formal astronomy but rather a description of the visual aspects of the heavens during which astronomical

XVIIIe siècle. Il rivalise assurément pour le nombre de ses lecteurs avec *l'Histoire Naturelle de Buffon*" (9). In his bibliography (263) he refers to the English, Italian and Spanish but not to the German translations.

20 Wilhelm Heinsius' *Allgemeines Bücher-Lexikon* (Leipzig, 1812) lists the following German translations for the eighteenth century: (1) Wien, 2 Theile, 1747; (2) Nürnberg, 8 Bände, 1760—1770. The following volumes have been available to me: volumes 1 and 2 (Frankfurt und Leipzig, 1760), volumes 3, 4, 5, 6, 7, 8 (Wien und Nürnberg, 1751, 1753, 1754, 1754, 1755, 1755). Therefore, there were at least two, possibly three, German translations of *Le Spectacle de la nature.*

material such as the motion of the planets, eclipses and the propagation of light
are examined. In the same volume, there is a history of scientific observations
and discoveries and the instruments used from the earliest times to the present.

Volume five is devoted entirely to man. Most of the volume describes his
mental faculties and how he uses them to organize his life to his benefit.
Volumes six and seven deal with man as a social being. Social institutions, trade
and commerce, industrial arts and politics and government are considered. It is
interesting to note that throughout these volumes he returns to the very
practical utilitarian activities of man. His treatment of the natural sciences
focuses on what is immediate and pertinent to man's life. Unlike his
countryman, Buffon, he avoids all speculations about cosmogonies, which brings
us to the subject of his other popular work, *Histoire du Ciel* (Paris, 1739).

The title of the German translation of Pluche's *Histoire du Ciel* serves as a
good statement of what this book is about: *"Historie des Himmels, nach den
Vorstellungen der Poeten, der Philosophen und des Moyses betrachtet. Worinne
der Ursprung des poetischen Himmels, der Irrthum der Philosophen in Absehen
des Baues der Himmels- und der Erdkugel, die Gleichförmigkeit der Erfahrung
und der einzigen Naturlehre des Moyses gezeiget wird"*. This work is a history of
the opinions that men have had about the heavens and its origins. Although he
devotes considerable space to explaining the fables and mythology with which
the ancients adorned the heavens, the real point of the book is to reject the
philosophic fables, the cosmogonies that attempt to explain the creation without
recourse to Revelation. He states his purpose as follows:

> Der Schluss dieser Vergleichung unter der heiligen und weltlichen Naturlehre
> gehet dahin, dass wir das Vermögen der menschlichen Wissenschaft auf das
> genauste erkennen, dieselbe so wohl durch die Erforschung der brauchbaren
> Dinge und Verlassung alles desjenigen, was uns verführen kann und unsere
> Kräfte übersteiget nach ihrem Maasse als auf ihren wahren Gegenstand richten
> lernen. Dieses ist der einzige Endzweck dieser Historie. (Preface 4)

Here he maintains that the goal of the book is to demonstrate that the
purpose of human knowledge is to seek out what is useful to man and not to
exceed its limitations. He proceeds to show the folly and superstition of the
ancient poets and the extravagant errors of the cosmogonies of ancient and
modern philosophers such as Aristotle, Empedocles, Epicurus, Leucipus,
Democritus, Descartes and Gassendi. He singles out Newton as a scientist who
remains true to both science and the Bible:

> Hingegen scheinet die Naturlehre des Herrn Newton mit beyden voll-
> kommen übereinzukommen. Er widerspricht der Erfahrung in nichts, da seine
> ganze Naturlehre dahin gehet, eine allgemeine Thätigkeit einzuführen, welche
> die Erfahrung in der ganzen Natur zeigen kann, ohne dass sie die Ursache
> derselben anzuweisen unternimmt. Sie kömmt vollkommen mit der Erzählung

des Moyses überein, weil Herr Newton sowohl als Moyses die Hervorbringung der verschiedenen Elemente und die Bildung des Ganzen von so vielen Befehlen oder Willen des Schöpfers und von keiner physikalischen Ursache herführet. (333)

The true scientist is in harmony with Revelation. He does not try to explain the creation which exists through God's will and is narrated in its final form in the Bible. Instead he uses his senses and reason to understand the natural phenomena about him and how they serve his well being. The attitude toward science that Pluche teaches in this work — positive on the one hand, but cautious about any excessive trust in reason — we find repeated by many German authors.

Georges Louis Leclerc, Comte de Buffon (1707–1788)

In the second half of the eighteenth century, the most popular work in natural history was the forty-four volume *Histoire naturelle, générale et particulière* (Paris, 1749–1804) by Georges Louis Leclerc, Comte de Buffon. The first three volumes containing his controversial "Théorie de la Terre" appeared in 1749; the next twelve volumes on quadrupeds appeared between 1755 and 1767. Between 1774 and 1789 there were seven supplementary volumes including the famous *Epoques de la Nature* (1779). The next nine volumes (1770–1783) were about birds and were followed by five volumes (1783–1788) on minerals. After his death eight further volumes were published about reptiles, fish and cetaceans. The German translations in the eighteenth century were as follows:

(1) *Allgemeine Historie der Natur nach allen ihren besonderen Theilen abgehandelt, nebst einer Beschreibung der Naturalienkammer des Königs von Frankreich.* Mit einer Vorrede von Albrecht von Haller. Bd. 1–11 (Hamburg und Leipzig, 1750–1781); this translation was based on the first French edition (Paris, 1749–1767).

(2) *Allgemeine Naturgeschichte.* Eine freye mit einigen Zusätzen vermehrte Übersetzung, nach der neuesten französischen Ausgabe von 1769, von Friedrich Heinrich Wilhelm Martini. Bd. 1–7 (Berlin, 1771–1775). This is the translation that was available for this study. Martini provides copious footnotes in which he explains and criticizes the text and quotes the opinions of other scientists. The seventh volume includes a bibliography of all writings mentioned by Buffon in the text and by the translator in the notes (VII, 267–285).

(3) *Naturgeschichte der vierfüssigen Thiere,* übersetzt von Friedrich Heinrich Wilhelm Martini und Bernhard Christian Otto. Bd. 1—23 (Berlin, 1771—1801).

(4) *Naturgeschichte der Mineralien.* Frei übersetzt und mit Zusätzen vermehrt von Christian Ernst Wünsch (Leipzig und Frankfurt, 1784).

(5) *Naturgeschichte der Vögel,* übersetzt von Friedrich Heinrich Wilhelm Martini und Bernhard Christian Otto. Bd. 1—37 (Berlin, 1772—1829).

The greater part of this monumental work on natural history appeared in the last three decades of the century. Of interest to us is the translation of the first three volumes which appeared in 1750, with Albrecht von Haller's very pertinent preface, "Vom Nutzen der Hypothesen". In the first three volumes Buffon explains the creation of the planets and the gradual formation of our earth and the reproduction and growth of animals. Natural history as such is not really begun until the succeeding volumes. Most of the references to Buffon in the 1750's are to his reflections on cosmogony in the first volume. After showing the inadequacies of the cosmogonies of his predecessors, especially Whiston, Burnet and Woodward, he explains his own theory according to which the planets were originally fragments of the sun, chipped off by the impact of a comet and at the same time acquiring the impulse of rotation and revolution in the same plane. These fragments gradually cooled off and became inhabitable planets. The stages of the transition from molten masses to inhabitable planets are the subject of his later work, *Epoques de la Nature* (1779). The existence of fossils he explains by assuming that the earth was once entirely covered by water which gradually sank into the interior of the earth through cracks in the earth's crust. This is simply the reverse of Burnet's theory.

In regard to these speculations, Haller's preface to the first volume entitled "Vom Nutzen der Hypothesen" is very pertinent. In regard to hypotheses, he advocates the middle road. He warns against the arbitrary hypotheses of the Cartesians which he calls inventions of the imagination, but also recommends hypotheses as a useful part of scientific method. Among many examples of fruitful hypotheses, he cites the Linnaean system of classification and Newton's belief that the earth was flat at the poles, which he had claimed on the basis of computation, and which was later verified by measurement. Haller concludes his preface by urging the reader to approach Buffon's work "mit einer philosophischen Achtsamkeit" and to heed the qualifications which he had recommended for the use of hypotheses.

François de Salignac de La Mothe Fénelon (1651–1715)

To be considered briefly is a work by Fénelon, who is well known to German literary historians for his *Les aventures de Télémaque* (Paris, 1699). Not as well known was his *Demonstration de l'existence de Dieu, tirée de la connaissance de la nature . . .* (Paris, 1713). The German translation appeared under the title *Augenscheinlicher Beweis dass ein Gott sey, hergenommen aus der Erkenntniss der Natur* (Hamburg, 1714 und 1728) with a preface by Johann Albert Fabricius. Of some pertinence to our study is the second chapter of the first part, "Preuves de l'existence de Dieu, tirée de la consideration des principales merveilles de la nature", in which he surveys natural phenomena from the largest to the smallest without too much scientific detail, always to conclude with the pious reflection that only God could be the source of such marvellous harmony and design. The work belongs to the older tradition of praising God in nature rather than to the more modern physicotheological tradition.

Christian Huygens (1629–1695)

Of the Dutch popular scientific works, we shall begin with a work very similar to Fontenelle's *Conversations,* namely, Christian Huygens' *Celestial Worlds Discovered* which first appeared in Latin in 1698.[21] The catalog of the British Museum lists English translations of 1698, 1722 and 1757 and a French translation of 1718; the catalog of the Bibliothèque Nationale lists in addition, a French translation of 1720. Neither lists a German translation. In Julius Bernhard von Rohr's *Physikalische Bibliothek* a German translation is mentioned: *Weltbeschauer oder weltbetrachtende Mutmassungen* (Frankfurt, 1704) by Johann Philipp von Wurtzelbau, an astronomer.[22] Our discussion is based on the first edition of the English translation, (London, 1698).

The work was often cited and was well known in Germany in the first half of the eighteenth century, though not nearly as well as the one by Fontenelle. It has the same didactic purpose, to disseminate the new astronomy in popular, non-technical literature. That it was the work of a mathematician and astronomer adds to the significance of the work.

In the first part of his book, Huygens vigorously defends the Copernican system and the belief in a plurality of inhabited worlds. As his predecessors of the latter notion, he names Nicolas Cusanus, Giordano Bruno, Johann Kepler

---

[21] *Cosmotheoros, sive De Terris Coelestibus, earumque ornatu, conjecturae* (The Hague, 1698).
[22] (Leipzig, 1754), p. 103; In Zedler's *Universal Lexicon,* volume 28, the title of the German translation is rendered as follows: *Weltbetrachtende Muthmassungen von den himmlischen Erd-Kugeln und deren Schmuck.*

and Bernard de Fontenelle. He refers specifically to Kepler's "Astronomical Dream". His explanation of the Copernican system is quite thorough; he provides diagrams and computations to describe the orbits of the planets, their proportion to one another, the proportion of the planets' magnitudes to one another and to the sun and the time planets require for their orbits. He also explains how these figures were attained and what instruments were used.

As regards the question of the inhabitation of the planets, he argues — and not very convincingly — that there is no reason to believe that the inhabitants and circumstances on the planets are radically different from those on earth. He proceeds to describe our planet and its inhabitants. There is much teleological reasoning to show that things must be the way they are and that this will be the way on the planets too. He maintains that rationality and sociability are part of man's nature and thus would be the nature of the planetary inhabitants also. He examines human arts and sciences, astronomy, geometry, optics, music with the understanding that they are an inevitable expression of human society.

In the second part he leaves the earth and undertakes an imaginary journey to the planets to learn what their arts and sciences are: "And now that we have ventured to place Spectators in the Planets, let's take a journey to each of them and see what their Years Days and Astronomy are" (105). He distinguishes his journey from that of Athanasius Kircher's *The Ecstatic Journey*,[23] who followed the Tychonian system and had recourse to astrology. He intends to work out the astronomy, the perspective of the various planets, on the basis of the latest discoveries of the new astronomy.

How seriously he took the possibility of the planets' inhabitation is an open question. It does, however, serve as an entertaining device to exercise imagination and knowledge of astronomy and to make the layman more familiar with his solar system. He applies the principles of the Copernican system to each planet with the result that the reader not only learns much astronomy but improves his capacity to conceive of different points of view. This was one of the favorite pastimes in the eighteenth century and Huygens' *Cosmotheoros* is surely one of its sources.

Bernhard Nieuwentyt (1654—1718)

A very popular scientific work with a religious purpose and orientation is Bernhard Nieuwentyt's thorough compendium of science, written to persuade atheists and unbelievers of the truth of the Christian faith. Ten years after the publication of the original in 1716, there were already five Dutch editions and five editions of the English translation entitled, *The Religious Philosopher*. The

23 *Itinerarium Exstaticum . . .* (Rome, 1656).

German translation by Baumann was made from the original Dutch text. In the preface we learn that this German translation has remained faithful to the original and, unlike the French translation, has omitted nothing.[24] The German edition is further supplemented by Christian Wolff's preface, a biography of the author, marginal summaries of the content on every page, an appendix of explanations of some 250 foreign words and an index of the Greek and Hebrew words that were used in the text. The twenty-eight plates of diagrams and illustrations were reproduced from the original.

In his preface Wolff praises Nieuwentyt's achievements as a mathematician and lauds his efforts in the present work to use his intellect, sharpened by mathematics, to disseminate science and to demonstrate that the scientific knowledge of nature leads to God. Wolff, furthermore, considers it praiseworthy that Nieuwentyt wrote his work in his native Dutch and adds that he also has used his native language to give the unlearned as well as the learned the opportunity to know God through nature.

In his own preface, Nieuwentyt states that it is the purpose of this text to convince atheists of their folly and show them the wisdom of God in nature. To fulfill this purpose he will rely primarily on observations and experiments and avoid speculative hypotheses. Throughout the text he warns against speculations that foresake observation and experiment.

Unlike most compendiums of science, this one begins with a long and thorough anatomy of the human body. This may be due to the fact that Nieuwentyt was a physician and could write with authority on the subject. His anatomy includes an analysis of sensation, that is, the five senses and more briefly mental and emotional states such as memory, imagination, feelings. The natural phenomena pertaining to our planet are divided, as in all compendiums, according to the four elements. Plants and animals are considered briefly before he turns to the heavenly bodies and the study of astronomy. In the concluding chapters, he considers special problems pertaining to science, scientific laws and the limitations of science.

The scientific validity of the text, for its time, is beyond question. As a physician and mathematician he had a professional's familiarity with his subject matter. True to his purpose, as stated in the preface, he avoids speculations and sticks to observations and experiments. Throughout the text, more than one hundred experiments are described and detailed observations, facts and figures are provided in all sections. By avoiding speculations he also avoids religious controversies. He considers, for example, the possibility of inhabitants on the

---

[24] Bernhard Nieuwentyt, *Die Erkänntnüss der Weissheit, Macht und Güte des Göttlichen Wesens, aus dem rechten Gebrauch derer Betrachtungen aller irrdischen Dinge* ... (Frankfurt und Leipzig, 1732), translated by Wilhelm Conrad Baumann. Another translation was made by Johann Andreas Segner (Jena, 1747).

moon and the other planets, a speculation indulged in by so many of his
contemporaries; he, however, drops the matter on the basis of insufficient
empirical material.

He is also very cautious about the heliocentric system of the universe. He
grants its simplicity but does not consider its truth as certain. Whether he took
this position simply to avoid religious controversy or because of a caution
demanded by scientific method is an open question. He points out that no stellar
parallax has yet been discovered, as one might expect from the earth's annual
orbit, and that though the hypothesis of the earth's motion is convenient for
calculations, that does not suffice to verify its truth. Thus, he believes it is false
to say that when Scripture speaks of the moving sun, it is speaking only
according to the understanding of the unlearned.

In all other respects he is completely modern in scientific matters. His
religious orientation is, on the whole, orthodox. He frequently exhorts his
readers to recognize the wisdom, goodness and might of God in a natural
phenomena either because of the beauty or wisdom of its design or because of
the divine purpose he sees in it. He does not resort to any speculations like those
of Whiston and Burnet to demonstrate that Biblical events can be accounted for
by natural law. In fact he specifically warns against those who pretend to know
the structure of the world in such detail as if they had been present at its
creation and ever since.

However, he does engage in speculations of a different sort. Frequently, in all
sections of the text, Nieuwentyt contends that a recent scientific discovery is
implied in certain Biblical passages whose Hebrew words he analyses with
ingenuity to prove his point. For example, he finds Newton's color theory,
whose validity he does not question, implied in a passage in Job XXXVIII, 24:
"Wo ist der Weg: (allwo) das Licht zertheilet wird, und der Ost Wind sich
zerstreuet auf Erden". His analysis of the Hebrew text leads him to the following
re-translation of the passage: "Welches ist die Weise, wodurch das Licht in
verschiedene Theile zertheilet wird (zerspalten wird) und dessen Aufgang sich
zerstreuet auf Erden". Thus, he concludes, in this single passage are contained
the two most important properties of light, namely, decomposition and
divergence (629—630).

Another example is his attempt to find the force of gravity in a Biblical
passage. He considers Newton's theory very probable and accepts it not as a
speculation, but because experiments point to its validity. He finds this
interplanetary force of attraction implied in the following passage from Job,
XXXVIII, 31: "Kanst du die Strängen (Seiler) des Orions loss mach". After an
examination of the original Hebrew he comes to the following: "Könt ihr die
Bande wodurch der Planet . . . an die Sonne gleichsam angebunden ist, loss
machen? " Furthermore, he believes that the Hebrew translated as "Stränge" or
"Bande" really has the meaning "anziehende" (720—721). Thus, a natural law

only recently discovered by human efforts has been implied by Revelation from the very beginning.

Nieuwentyt is a good example of an enlightened man at the turn of the century who values both the revealed word of God and the results of the new scientific method and thus must bring harmony between the two. It is clear, however, that he looks for a Biblical source for a scientific truth only after its truth has been established by scientific method.

Pieter van Musschenbroek (1692–1761)

The translation of Pieter van Musschenbroek's *Grundlehren der Naturwissenschaft* (Leipzig, 1747) by Johann Christoph Gottsched is another example of the latter's diligence in popularizing the sciences in Germany. In his preface he mentions that he was assisted in the translation by two associates but that he reviewed the work in its entirety. The translation does have the Gottsched touch, for the style is smooth and readable, which cannot be said of many translations of the time.

Gottsched's preface, as usual, is informative and interesting. In this text, Gottsched informs us the author has brought together the scientific achievements of the past century made by the academies of science in Florence, Paris, London, Berlin and Petersburg and by many independent scientists in Germany and the Netherlands. Musschenbroek wrote the work in Latin, for it was intended for university students. In 1743 he revised the first edition of 1734 to include new scientific discoveries. The translation is based on this second Latin edition which, Gottsched says, is more up to date than the German works of Scheuchzer and Wolff and thus justifies his labors. Already in the first edition the author had included many teachings of the Newtonian philosophy, though he claims to be neither a Newtonian nor a Cartesian. The translator furthermore points out that this is a text on experimental physics and omits astronomy and the life sciences which would be required of a comprehensive science of nature.

In his own preface Musschenbroek asserts emphatically that he is primarily an experimentalist and follows no sect. Science is now making such rapid progress because it is no longer confined to the empty products of the imagination but follows observations, experiments and mathematical proofs. He defends his acceptance of an attractive force in all bodies on the basis that he has been persuaded of it by experiment and does not treat it as a hypothesis, that is, a mere speculation. Thus, he rejects the subtle fluid substance that is supposed to permeate all things according to the Cartesians, for there are no experiments to demonstrate it. At the same time, he does not claim to know what the attractive force is and cautions that as long as we are ignorant of such matters we should stick to observations of the effects and experimentation.

The text is what the prefaces by Gottsched and Musschenbroek claimed for it. It is a text book of experimental physics. He describes the standard experiments concerning moving and falling bodies, liquids at rest and in motion, pendulums, levers, optics, dioptrics, catoptrics. The laws derived from these experiments are presented in mathematical form wherever it is required.

Although he does not claim to be a Newtonian, he repeatedly rejects Cartesian explanations. The essential nature of material bodies is not extension, there is no aether, space is empty and light does not consist of impulses transmitted by the all pervading aether from the source to the viewer. He accepts the Newtonian explanation of light and color and, as he had already noted in the preface, the Newtonian attractive force between bodies.

Although this text by a famous experimentalist was intended for university students, in Gottsched's readable German translation it became more accessible to laymen and thus played its role in the diffusion of scientific material.

Jan Swammerdam (1637–1680)

The German translation of Jan Swammerdam's work in entomology will be considered briefly. He was one of the greatest of the early microscopists and spent much time on the study of insects for which he mapped out a natural classification. His papers were published in 1737 by Hermann Boerhaave in Dutch and Latin under the title *Bybel der Natuure* (Leyden, 1737, 1738). The title page of the German translation has the following information: "*Bibel der Natur,* worinnen die Insekten in gewisse Classen vertheilt, sorgfältig beschrieben, zergliedert, in saubern Kupferstichen vorgestellt, mit vielen Anmerkungen über die Seltenheiten der Natur erleutert, und zum Beweis der Allmacht und Weisheit des Schöpfers angewendet werden. Nebst Hermann Boerhaaves Vorrede von dem Leben des Verfassers. Aus dem Holländischen übersetzt. Leipzig, 1752". This 410 folio volume with fifty-three plates is one of many richly illustrated works on subjects of natural history that were appearing by the middle of the eighteenth century.

I shall now discuss the translations of two philosophic poems containing much scientific material and which because of their popularity can be viewed as sources for popular interest in scientific themes.

Charles Claude Genest (1636–1719)

Charles Claude Genest's *Principes de Philosophie* (Paris, 1716) was translated by Barthold Heinrich Brockes, and under the title *Grund-Sätze der Welt-Weisheit des Herrn Abts Genest,* the French and German text appeared in the third part of Brockes *Irdisches Vergnügen in Gott*.[25] Johann Georg Hamann (the Elder), in the preface to the first edition, says those who compare Genest with Lucretius prefer the former "wegen der Gründlichkeit seiner Welt-Weisheit" (Preface 3). Hamann maintains that Genest and Brockes have one and the same purpose, namely, "Die Aufmunterung zur Erkenntniss und Verehrung des Schöpfers, aus der Beobachtung der Creaturen . . ." (Preface 6).

Kurt Feess shows in his dissertation on Genest, that it was his purpose to popularize the Cartesian philosophy and to lead men to God through a contemplation of his works.[26] He says Genest had worked on the poem for thirty years, which means that he and Melchior de Polignac began their anti-Lucretian poems about the same time.

The poem is a versification of Descartes *Principes de la Philosophie,* although he does not follow this text in all respects. He treats the abstract material about the principles of knowledge and material objects more briefly than Descartes does and frequently adds his criticism of the opinions of ancient philosophers in order to show the insufficiency of those systems that do not recognize God as the creator. He follows Descartes rather closely in his presentation of the visible world in the heavens and on earth and in his description of sensation and the organs of sensation.

Though Genest's orientation is Cartesian in many respects, the scientific section of his poem, especially the part on astronomy, conveys much valid scientific material. The five editions of the translation suggest that the poem was not unfamiliar to the German reading public and that it may have served as a model for didactic scientific verse.

Melchior de Polignac (1661–1741)

Melchior de Polignac's *Antilucretius* (Paris, 1747) like Genest's *Principes de Philosophie* is a didactic poem which teaches the new learning within a Cartesian framework. For decades Polignac had worked on his poem which was eagerly awaited by the pious, deist as well as orthodox, as an antidote to what was viewed as the poison of Lucretius. Our discussion of the poem will be based on reviews of the poem in two periodicals edited by Gottsched, where we find, in addition to a summary of the contents, a history of the poem's composition and an account of the translation through which the poem became accessible to the German reading public.

---

25 (Hamburg, 1728). Other editions appeared in 1730, 1736, 1739 and 1747. The third edition of 1736 was available.
26 Kurt Feess, *Charles Claude Genest* (Köln, 1912), p. 97.

The poem was first reviewed in Gottsched's *Neuer Büchersaal*,[27] volume V (387—405), when its first Latin edition (Paris, 1747) appeared and again six months later in the same periodical, volume VI (458—471), when the text was edited in Germany (Leipzig, 1748). The reviewer provides us with a thorough account of the history of the work and its contents.[28] Prompted by a conversation with Pierre Bayle in 1697 on religious matters, the author decided to attack the atheism of the Epicurean philosophy which, sweetened by the poetry of Lucretius, had poisoned the minds of the Romans and was now doing the same to Europeans in the form of French and English translations of the Lucretian poem. Polignac's poem had already been translated into French and the reviewer hopes that a good German philosophical poet will translate the work into German. Although a German translation did not appear until 1760, a German publisher, Breitkopf, issued the Latin text the following year (Leipzig, 1748), together with Gottsched's preface about ancient and modern philosophic poets. The reviewer tells us that although Polignac follows the Cartesian philosophy in his poem, he was an admirer of Newton's mathematical teachings and was the first to bring them to France.[29] In the poem he used Newton's color theory, but rejected the latter's concept of empty space and the theory of an attractive force between material bodies in favor of Cartesian explanations. He also follows Descartes' teaching that animals are mere machines and need souls as little as do plants and minerals. In the section on animals, he also gives a thorough account of the human body which the reviewer considers the most beautiful part of the poem. In his discussion of the cosmos, Polignac deals with the essentials of astronomy in which he emphatically accepts the Copernican system. In both reviews, samples of the poem are rendered into German prose.

When the German translation[30] finally appeared in 1760, it was reviewed in

[27] *Neuer Büchersaal der schönen Wissenschaften und freyen Künste* (Leipzig, 1745—1750), edited by J.C. Gottsched.

[28] For a thorough account of the poem's background and an interpretation of its content see C.A. Fusil's *l'Anti-Lucrèce du Cardinal de Polignac* (Paris, 1918). Fusil notes, for example, that the poet was very familiar with the sciences: "Descartes, Gassendi, Leibniz, Malebranche, Spinosa, Clarke, Newton lui sont des auteurs familiers. La dialectique, la metaphysique et la science proprement dite, mecanique, physique, astronomie, histoire naturelle, pour lui n'ont plus de secrets" (9). For a more recent discussion of the poem see Wolfgang Bernard Fleischmann, "Zum Anti-Lucretius des Kardinals de Polignac," *Romanische Forschungen*, LXXVII (1965), 42—63.

[29] See C.A. Fusil's *l'Anti-Lucrèce du Cardinal de Polignac:* "En 1722, nous le voyons recommencer les experiences de Newton sur les couleurs, à l'aide de prismes qu'il fit venir d'Angleterre, et Newton lui écrivit pour le remercier de sa probite scientifique" (9).

[30] *Antilucrez, oder neun Bücher von Gott und der Natur* (Breslau, 1760). "Nach der Pariser Ausgabe aus dem Lateinischen prosaisch übersetzt, von Martin Friedrich Schäfern, . . ." It should be noted that C.A. Fusil in his *l'Anti-Lucrèce . . .* mentions French, English and Italian translations of the poem, but neither the German translation of 1760 nor the Leipzig edition of the Latin text of 1748; nor are they listed in the catalogs of the British Museum and Bibliothèque Nationale.

Gottsched's *Das Neueste aus der anmuthigen Gelehrsamkeit*.[31] In the review we
learn that the German edition contains in addition to the poem, Gottsched's
essay on philosophic poets, an essay by de Bougainville, the French translator,
on the philosophy of Epicurus and other materialists and an essay on the history
of the *Antilucrez*. The reviewer summarizes the contents of the last five books,
giving samples of the prose translation with which he is well satisfied. Although
he considers this poem a highly significant work in the defense of religion, he
does not fail to point out that the Cartesian philosophy on which the work is
based is no longer acceptable and that many scientific discoveries have been
made since the writing of the poem.

As a summary of the preceding I have arranged the translations according to
the subjects represented. I have indicated the dates of the first editions of the
originals and of the various editions of the translations:

author		*original*	*translation*
	Cosmogonies		
(1635–1715)	Burnet	1681–1689	1693, 1698, 1703
(1628–1705)	Ray *	1693	1698, 1732
(1665–1728)	Woodward **	1695	1744, 1746
(1667–1752)	Whiston	1696	1713, 1753
	Popular Astronomies		
(1614–1672)	Wilkins	1638	1713
(1657–1757)	Fontenelle	1686	1698, 1726, 1730, 1738, 1751, 1760
(1629–1695)	Huygens	1698	1704
	Physicotheologies		
(1628–1705)	Ray ***	1691	1712
(1651–1715)	Fénelon	1713	1714, 1728
(1657–1735)	Derham ****	1713	1730, 1732, 1736, 1741, 1750, 1764
(1657–1735)	Derham *****	1714	1728, 1732, 1739, 1745, 1750, 1765

---

[31] (Leipzig, 1751–1762). The reviews in question are found in 1760: 61–67, 692–703.

Natural History and Physics

(1665–1728)	Woodward ******	1728–1729	1746
(1688–1761)	Pluche	1732–1750	1747–1755, 1760–1770
(1637–1680)	Swammerdam	1737–1738	1752
(1707–1788)	Buffon	1749–1804	1750–1829
(1692–1761)	Musschenbroek	1734	1747

Scientific Poets

(1636–1719)	Genest	1716	1728, 1730, 1736, 1739, 1747
(1661–1742)	Polignac	1747	1760

*	*Three Physico-Theological Discourses*
**	*Essay toward a Natural History of the Earth*
***	*The Wisdom of God Manifested in the Works of the Creation*
****	*Physico-Theology*
*****	*Astro-Theology*
******	*Natural History of the Fossils of England*

B. THE COMPENDIUMS OF SCIENCE

The compendiums of science contributed to the diffusion of scientific knowledge in a very direct way. They were intended for students in schools and universities and the layman in general. They were written by people thoroughly trained in the new sciences, if not scientists themselves. The compendiums encompass the new learning in astronomy, physics, natural history and anatomy of plants, animals and man. They present the details about natural phenomena as pertaining to the heavens, the earth and living beings. The order of the natural phenomena presented in the compendiums is the order found in the short and long surveys of natural phenomena that so often recur in the poets and prose writers of this period. These compendiums were inexpensive, not exceptionally technical and in some instances well written.

For this discussion I have selected the four most popular compendiums, namely, those by Johann Jacob Scheuchzer, Christian Wolff, Johann Christian Gottsched and Johann Gottlob Krüger. I shall consider a few others more briefly. It is interesting to note that these compendiums were used by Goethe in his *Geschichte der Farbenlehre* to tell the story of the acceptance of the Newtonian color theory in Germany. He consulted about twenty compendiums written in the eighteenth century including, in addition to the ones considered here, Latin compendiums and those written in the later decades of the century.[1]

Johann Jacob Scheuchzer (1672–1733)

One of the most widely read compendiums of science in the first half of the eighteenth century was *Physica oder Natur-Wissenschaft*[2] by the Swiss naturalist Johann Jacob Scheuchzer, famous for his work in paleontology and natural history. He defines "Physica" as "eine Wissenschaft dessen, so durch der natürlichen Cörpern Kräffte kan zuwegen gebracht werden" (I, 1). This is a definition of natural science and his two volume compendium of science does include all the natural sciences. In the first volume he takes up the general properties of natural phenomena such as extension, size, elasticity, and in the second volume specific natural phenomena such as stars, mountains, plants.

In the very beginning in comments on scientific method, he warns against following any one school, be it that of Aristotle, Plato, Epicurus, Descartes or Gassendi. The true sources of science are the senses and reason and not the one or the other alone but both together. He warns of the dangers of relying too

---

[1] Goethe, *Naturwissenschaftliche Schriften*, I (Artemis Verlag, Zürich, 1949), pp. 626 – 634.
[2] (Zürich, 1729), third edition; first edition, 1703; second edition, 1711; fourth edition, 1743.

much on either experience or reason and cites Descartes as an example of the latter. Scientific method, he maintains, requires observations, experiments, application of mathematical principles and caution toward hypotheses.

Throughout his discussion in the first volume of the general properties and qualities of natural bodies, he cites the explanations of Aristotle, Descartes, as well as the more modern scientists like Boyle, Bernoulli and Newton. He values especially the opinions of the latter, and his *Optics* and *Principia* are quoted frequently. For example, in the section on light and color the views of Aristotle, Descartes, Boyle and others are recorded. However, an entire chapter of thirty pages is devoted to an explanation and paraphrase of Newton's *Optics* (I, 116–146).[3] It is a thorough discussion of the contents, with the experiments described and the mathematical computations reproduced. In his chapter on motion, several views are presented, but Newton's laws of motion as found in the *Principia* receive special attention. Thus, we have in Scheuchzer one of the earliest advocates of Newtonian thinking in Germany.

The subject of the second volume is no longer general properties and qualities of bodies but the whole, concrete natural bodies as studied by astronomy, the earth sciences and the life sciences.

In the chapters on astronomy, he considers cosmogenic theories, geocentric and heliocentric systems of the universe and offers an impressive array of facts and figures about the planets and stars. He accepts the Copernican system, although he does explain the Ptolemaic and Tychonian systems and gives a detailed account of the arguments both for and against the heliocentric system. His discussion of Kepler's planetary laws, which he finds supported by Newton ". . . in seinem herrlichen Buch *de Principiis Philosophiae Naturalis Mathematicis*" (II, 130), leaves little doubt about his preference.

In his discussion of the planets, the subject of their inhabitation inevitably occurs. Due to the assumed similarity of the planets with the earth, Scheuchzer considers their inhabitation quite plausible. The source he cites for his speculation is Huygens' *Cosmotheoros*. In contrast to Huygens, who had denied a lunar atmosphere, he even argues for the inhabitation of the moon. Another speculation that Scheuchzer indulges in, which was very popular among the poets, is the attempt to picture the universe from the perspective of each of the planets.

From these cosmic themes he turns to the geocosm to consider natural phenomena above, on and beneath the earth. His approach here is more that of the natural historian who describes and classifies a wide range of specific phenomena. There is a natural history of the waters of the earth, a natural

---

3 According to Goethe in his *Geschichte der Farbenlehre*, the chapter on Newton's *Optics* was present in the 1711 edition but not in the 1703 editions: Goethe, *Naturwissenschaftliche Schriften*, I (Artemis Ausgabe), p. 627.

history of winds, a natural history of stones, metals and minerals. The latter is especially thorough and detailed.

His concluding chapters are about the life sciences. In the section on the vegetable kingdom, he points out the advances that have recently been made. In antiquity, he maintains, only 600 species of plants were known, whereas now that figure has risen to 12,000. He discusses the work of Ray, Grew and Malpighi and singles out the *Vegetable Statiks* of Stephen Hales as a fine example of modern experimental philosophy. He concludes by giving Tournefort's classification of plants into twenty-two classes.

The chapters on the animal kingdom are very informative about the structures and functions of animal parts. He divides animals into quadrupeds, reptiles, birds, fish and insects and considers the circumstances of many individual species. He is opposed to the Cartesian contention that animals are mere machines. The concluding chapter on man covers primarily his psychological functions with only a few paragraphs about the structure of his body.

Christian Wolff (1679—1754)

It is well known that Christian Wolff's philosophic system dominated in Germany in the 1720's, 1730's and 1740's. In the 1720's he presented his system of "Weltweisheit" in German works, and in the following two decades he published more elaborate Latin works. The many editions of his German works between 1720 and 1750 testify to their popularity. Ludovici's history of the Wolffian philosophy records its extraordinary success and influence in all spheres of thought.[4]

Wolff's "Weltweisheit" encompasses all fields of learning. It places every discipline on a secular, rational foundation. Revelation is not rejected; it is the capstone of the system. Thus, it completes the system, but the system can stand without it on its own rational foundation. Shifting the function of Revelation from the foundation to the capstone of learning aroused the opposition of the orthodoxy, but it was eagerly embraced by the progressives, the "Aufklärer". Ludovici's list of Wolff's students and supporters is impressive indeed.

Wolff's earliest publications were in mathematics and logic.[5] His application of the rigor and discipline of mathematics and logic to other secular disciplines constitutes the uniqueness of his system. His popularity from the 1720's on was

---

4 Carl Günther Ludovici, *Ausführlicher Entwurf einer vollständigen Historie der Wolffischen Philosophie* (Leipzig, 1738).
5 Christian Wolff, *Anfangs-Gründe aller mathematischen Wissenschaften* (Halle, 1710). There was a sixth edition in 1744. *Mathematisches Lexikon* (Leipzig, 1716). *Vernünfftige Gedancken von den Kräfften des menschlichen Verstandes* (Halle, 1712). The thirteenth edition appeared in 1754.

not as a mathematician but as a metaphysician and moral philosopher. What is usually not emphasized by histories of philosophy is that he fully subscribed to modern scientific method, that he taught science at the University of Halle, and that natural science is an integral part of his system of "Weltweisheit".

His system, as it was presented in the German works, is divided into two parts, a theoretical and a practical part. The theoretical part consists of logic, metaphysics[6] and natural science. The practical part consists of ethics, economics and politics.[7] Of interest to us are his volumes on natural science (Natur-Lehre), which is divided into an experimental part (Versuchs-Kunst) and a dogmatic part (Natur-Wissenschaft).

Experimental science is the subject of his three volumes of *Nützliche Versuche*,[8] which contain numerous standard physical experiments, many of which Wolff used in his university course on experimental physics. He frequently notes that he has repeated these experiments himself, for he accepts nothing as proven until he thinks and works it through himself. The text is accompanied by hundreds of diagrams of instruments which the author explains in detail. He describes the experiments, how they are set up and carried out. He explains that he describes even some very ordinary experiments because he wants to convey not only the results but also the method of experimentation. Thus we have here not only a collection of experiments but a text on scientific method. Considering Wolff's influence on several generations, this commitment to scientific method was certainly a factor in the popularization of science.

The dogmatic or didactic part of his "Natur-Lehre" is further divided into two parts, one part of which presents natural phenomena according to efficient causation and the other according to final causation. The first approach teaches the results of the scientific search for causes and effects in natural phenomena, and the second teaches the purposes for which natural phenomena exist. The former is treated in his *Vernünfftige Gedancken von den Würkungen der Natur*[9] and the latter in two volumes, *Vernünfftige Gedancken von den Absichten der natürlichen Dinge*[10] and *Vernünfftige Gedancken von dem Gebrauche der Theile in Menschen, Thieren und Pflanzen*.[11]

---

6 His German work on metaphysics is *Vernünfftige Gedancken von Gott, der Welt und der Seele des Menschen* (Frankfurt and Leipzig, 1719). There was a seventh edition in 1738.

7 These subjects were treated in *Vernünfftige Gedancken von der Menschen Thun und Lassen* (Halle, 1720) and *Vernünfftige Gedancken von dem gesellschaftlichen Leben der Menschen* (Halle, 1721).

8 *Allerhand nützliche Versuche, dadurch zu genauer Erkäntniss der Natur und Kunst der Weg gebähnet wird*, 3 Bände (Halle, 1721–1723). There was a third edition: 1745–1747).

9 (Halle, 1723). A fifth edition appeared in 1746.

10 (Halle, 1724). A second edition appeared in 1726.

11 (Frankfurt and Leipzig, 1725). A third edition appeared in 1737 and another in 1753.

His *Vernünfftige Gedancken von den Würkungen der Natur* can by itself be considered a compendium of science. As is customary in compendiums, he begins with considerations of the general qualities of material bodies, then comes astronomy, then the circumstances on the earth and finally the living beings on earth, plants, animals and man.

In the first section, in discussing the physical properties of bodies, he comments on the divisibility of matter into minute particles. All the spaces or pores between these particles are filled and matter is constantly in motion permitting changes in material objects to take place. He explains the nature of such properties as density, hardness, fluidity, softness and how changes in these properties can happen.

In the next section on the cosmos, the pertinent facts of the new astronomy are narrated. He fully accepts the Copernican theory and its extension that every star is a sun and thus also the center of a solar system. The earth is a planet and the other planets resemble it in many respects among which might be their inhabitability. Comets are heavenly bodies like the planets and have regular predictable orbits. In his discussion he refers to the works of many modern astronomers, Galileo, Huygens, Cassini, Hevel, Kepler, Marius, Halley and Newton. Newton's gravitational theory is not considered until the third part, on the earth.

In the next section he considers the earth's annual and diurnal motions and its figure. The phenomena on the earth he divides according to the elements to which they belong, air, water or earth. Among air phenomena he considers various light phenomena, winds, fog, clouds, dew, snow, frost, hail, the rainbow and others. In discussing the rainbow, the Newtonian color theory is fully accepted. Among water phenomena he considers rain, rivers, lakes and the sources of these phenomena. In discussing tides, he considers the explanations of Descartes, Kepler and Newton and accepts the latter fully. He explains the moon's gravitational pull on the earth and that according to Newton all heavenly bodies exert such attraction on one another. He believes that such a gravitational attraction has been experimentally verified but denies that its cause is known: "Wir nehmen diese Schweere der Planeten gegen einander, oder ihre magnetische Krafft an als eine Sache, die in der Erfahrung gegründet ist, aber eine uns zur Zeit noch nicht völlig bekandte Ursache hat, die wir zu weiterer Untersuchung ausgesetzet seyn lassen. . ." (556). As part of earth phenomena, he considers mountains, fossils, volcanoes, earthquakes, stones, metals and minerals.

In the last section on living beings, he begins with the parts of plants such as had been discovered by scientists like Malpighi, Grew and Leeuwenhoek. He discusses the nourishment and reproduction of plants; in connection with the latter he examines the difficulties involved in the preformation and encapsulation theories. In his discussion of animals and man, he confines himself to an examination of basic functions such as nourishment, digestion, circulation of the blood and procreation. Here he is concerned only with what living beings have in common not with the uniqueness of individuals and species, which is the task of the natural historian.

Now let us turn to the two volumes that deal with final causation of natural bodies. His first work, *Vernünfftige Gedancken von den Absichten der natürlichen Dinge*, is a physicotheology. Following the order of the previous compendium of science, he surveys the properties of natural bodies, the heavens, earth phenomena and living beings, pointing out the use to man of the specific phenomena and showing how the phenomena are evidence of God's wisdom, goodness and power. Like all physicotheologies, this one teaches much science, to be sure, not as much as the preceding compendium, because its main purpose is to show the value of natural phenomena to man, their influence on his personal and social existence.

This second work, *Vernünfftige Gedancken von dem Gebrauche der Theile*, is not a physicotheology though it too deals with purpose. Here the purpose of specific parts and functions of living beings are examined; but the purpose sought is not in relation to something extraneous. Since God created all living beings, he intended them to thrive, to live. Each part and function of any living being was designed by God to contribute to the preservation of that living being. So, when the author seeks the purpose of an organ, for example, he seeks what it contributes to the preservation of the whole. The text, therefore, is primarily an anatomy of living organisms in which the explanations of structures and functions are in terms of the life of the organism. This work, therefore, unlike the previous one, avoids an anthropocentric teleology and can be considered a popular medical text.

Thus, of the six volumes of the "Natur-Lehre" part of his system, three contain experiments and teach scientific method, one is a compendium of science, one is a popular medical text and only one is a physicotheology with the teleological speculations that are usually cited as examples of Wolff's approach to nature.

Johann Christoph Gottsched (1700–1766)

Christian Wolff's systematic presentation of "Weltweisheit", which had been widely disseminated in Germany in the 1720's through his German works, received a new and simplified form in Gottsched's *Erste Gründe der gesammten Weltweisheit*.[12] The latter states clearly that his work is intended as an introduction to and preparation for a study of Wolff's work; he intends to

---

12 Two volumes, sixth edition (Leipzig, 1756). Other editions: 1731 (1), 1735 (2), 1739 (3), 1742 (4), 1748 (5), 1756 (6), 1762 (7), 1766 (8).   .

prepare for the more elaborate, extensive and technical works of Wolff.

Following Wolff, Gottsched divides "Weltweisheit" into a theoretical and a practical part. The former includes logic, metaphysics and natural science; the latter, ethics, political science and economics. Our concern is with the two-hundred-page section on science, which is a compendium of the sciences of the time. A comparison of the second, fifth and sixth editions of the work reveals few significant changes. There are frequent changes in style of which Gottsched was very conscious. In the fifth edition a chapter on electricity was added. In the later editions, there are references to more recent writings and observations.

Gottsched's arrangement is that of most compendiums of the time. It is divided into four parts: the first deals with general properties of natural bodies; the second with heavenly bodies, that is, astronomy; the third, with the earth and the phenomena pertaining to it, that is, the earth sciences; and the final part is about plants, animals and man, the life sciences.

In the first part, he discusses the divisibility to which all material bodies are subject. He examines the nature of the constituent parts of material bodies and how they differ from one another to cause the many different composite objects. He also considers — as most physicists of the time did — the problem of the spaces between the minute particles, the pores of the bodies and whether they are empty or filled with some substance. In this connection he challenges Lucretius who believed in an emptiness between the particles. Gottsched, however, maintains that all crevices between these particles must be filled with some substance like water, air, light, heat or magnetic material. Many further properties of natural bodies are explained in terms of these minute particles, according to their arrangement, interrelation and the substances filling the spaces between them. It is interesting to note that in explaining the physical property, hardness, he refers to the attractive power which, he says, the English attribute to the particles, Gottsched, however, does not believe it necessary to assume such an unlikely attractive power, especially since there are more plausible, that is, mechanical explanations, available.

The chapters on astronomy offer the facts and figures about sizes and distances of heavenly bodies according to the observations and discoveries of the most recent astronomers. Gottsched, with his sense for history, is acutely aware of the improvements the moderns have brought into astronomy. He explains the Ptolemaic and Tychonian world systems, as well as the Copernican, but emphatically defends the latter. As always, he stresses the contributions of German scientists: Simon Marius discovered the four moons of Jupiter in 1609 one year before Galileo; Johann Fabricius and Christoph Scheiner observed the sun spots with telescopes in 1611, again one year before Galileo; and Georg Samuel Dörfel proved, in a publication of 1681, that comets have orbits subject to the same laws that Kepler discovered for the planets.

In the chapter on the sun, the nature of light and color is discussed. He presents both the Cartesian and Newtonian points of view and each time selects the latter. Descartes maintains that light is propagated instantaneously, but Gottsched agrees that Newton demonstrated that light requires time to traverse space. He considers the Cartesian notion of space filled completely with round spheres as the medium for the transmission of light, as too speculative and adheres to the Newtonian theory that light is an actual out-pouring of substance from the sun to the planets. He also accepts Newton's explanation of color and describes his experiments. In the chapter on comets, he also refers to Newton's theory of gravity as follows:

> Neuton hat aus der Erfahrung erwiesen, dass alle Weltkörper gegen einander eine magnetische Kraft haben. Die Beobachtungen der Sternseher bestätigen solches: obwohl man die Ursachen davon nicht anzugeben weis. Ein jeder Planet wird also von der Sonne angezogen; damit er nicht aus seiner runden Bahn in einer geraden Linie davon fliege. Ein jeder Hauptplanet zieht seine Trabanten oder Monden eben so an sich: und überhaupt zieht auch ein Planet den andern; doch stärker oder schwächer, nachdem er näher oder weiter von ihm steht, grösser oder kleiner ist. Diesem zufolge ziehen denn auch die Cometen, als grosse Weltkörper, diejenigen Planeten nach sich, denen sie in ihrem Laufe etwas zu nahe kommen. (344—345)

In the chapter on the moon and the planets, he shows how, on the basis of telescopic observations, one can conclude that the moon and the planets are heavenly bodies that do not have a light of their own but reflect the sun's, that there are mountains and valleys, seas and oceans on their surfaces, that they have an atmosphere and divisions into day and night. From this similarity between the earth and the planets, Gottsched, as well as many of his contemporaries, concludes that the planets are inhabited. He adds that there is no need to suppose that these inhabitants resemble man in detail: "Die Natur verändert ihre Werke tausendfältig" (326) and thus the inhabitants may indeed be quite different from man in appearance.

In the last section on astronomy, he turns to the fixed stars and notes the immense numbers, sizes and distances involved. Thus, the heavens acquire an immeasurable depth and extension. Furthermore, everyone of these is a sun, possibly even larger than our own, and thus most likely the center of a planetary system. Finally, he considers the appearance and disappearance of stars, as had been observed by Tycho in 1572. He speculates that since life on planets is dependent on the sun, such an appearance and disappearance of a star signifies the creation and destruction of inhabited worlds.

The third section of the compendium, consisting of ten chapters, considers a multitude of phenomena pertaining to the earth. In the beginning he raises the question of the figure of the earth. Picard and Cassini, he points out, had concluded from their measurements that the earth was eggshaped. However, Maupertuis had been able to prove by his journey to Lapland that the earth is flat at the poles, even flatter than Huygens and Newton had expected.

He proceeds to a discussion of the origin of the earth. He cites the theories of Descartes, Detlev Clüver, Thomas Burnet and William Whiston and maintains that the latter had developed a theory which contained the best features of the others and at the same time was in harmony with Scripture. Gottsched then discusses Whiston's theory at length, repeatedly giving his approval, though only as a theory and not as an article of faith. His account in this work of the Whistonian speculations concerning the cometary origin of the earth and the Flood undoubtedly is one of the sources of their popularity in Germany for the next few decades.[13] All this material is present in the second edition of 1735. In the later editions he also refers occasionally to Johann Heyn's tract on comets, which includes an elaborate restatement of Whiston's theories, as well as a preface by Gottsched on the history of cometary theory.[14]

In the remaining chapters, the most significant facts of the earth sciences are related. This vast array of natural phenomena is arranged according to the four elements, water, air, earth and fire.

In the chapter on water phenomena his remarks on the cause of tides are of interest to us. He rejects the Cartesian explanation of the moon pressing on the aether which in turn presses on the earth's water, in favor of, ". . . was Kepler und die neuern Sternseher von der anziehenden oder magnetischen Kraft aller himmlischen Körper lehren" (384).

Air phenomena are divided into plain air phenomena such as winds, vapors and the atmosphere; watery air phenomena such as dew, fog, clouds, rain, frost, snow and hail; shining air phenomena such as the rainbow, solar and lunar coronas and the northern lights; and finally, fiery air phenomena such as lightning and will-o'-the wisps.

In the section on earth phenomena he enumerates salts, metals and stones and discusses their physical properties and chemical properties such as solubility and inflammability. In connection with stones, he also examines theories concerning fossils, such as Johann Jakob Scheuchzer's contention that they were caused by the Flood and a more recent theory which he attributes to Emanuel

---

13   Andrew D. White in *A History of the Warfare of Science with Theology* claims that the acceptance of Whiston's theory in Germany was "mainly through the all-powerful mediation of Gottsched" (Dover reprint of 1960, Vol. I, 206). There is no evidence that Gottsched used his influence in favor of Whiston. In fact there were many who supported Whiston's theories quite independently of Gottsched; for example, Johann Jakob Bodmer used much of Whiston's speculations in his *Der Noah* (Zürich, 1752) and it is not likely that he did so to accomodate Gottsched.

14   Heyn's first publication, which includes the preface by Gottsched, was *Versuch einer Betrachtung über die Cometen, die Sündflut und das Vorspiel des jüngsten Gerichts, nach astronomischen Gründen und der heiligen Schrift angestellet* (Berlin, Leipzig, 1742).

Swedenborg, according to which the outer form of the earth changes gradually so that what is now land may once have been beneath the sea. Gottsched considers this theory the more plausible and maintains that it is finding more and more support among scientists. The magnet, as a special stone, receives an entire chapter, in which its unique properties are described. Gottsched favors the theory that views the entire earth as a magnet as a means of explaining the stone's qualities.

In the sections on fire phenomena, there are several points of interest. Heat he considers as caused chiefly by the activity of a subtle substance which permeates all bodies. When the movement of this substance is accelerated through the rays of the sun or friction, then the warmth of the body is increased until the movement of the particles is so rapid that parts of the body fall off or the body turns into a liquid. Should certain sulphuric particles be present, then a flame is ignited.

Another point of interest is his belief in the existence of subterranean fire which he also links with earthquakes. The latter are caused by the presence of sulphuric and other combustible substances in the hollow caverns beneath the surface of the earth. Once these are ignited they naturally seek an outlet, thereby causing either volcanic eruptions or tremors if the earth's crust is very thick.

The last part of the compendium deals with the life sciences, the study of plants, animals and man. In the chapter on plants, he describes the inner parts of plants and their outward appearances, drawing on Leeuwenhoek and Malpighi for the former and on Tournefort and Rivinus for the latter. Of plant functions, he considers especially the nourishment and reproduction of plants. He maintains that plants draw their nourishment primarily from water which, however, is not pure but carries with it elements such as salt and sulphur. As far as the propagation of plants is concerned, he accepts the preformation and encapsulation theories as the most likely.

In his two chapters on animals, he considers several subjects of interest. He divides animals into four classes: insects, animals living in the water, animals that have the capacity to fly and those that are earth-bound. He comments on the thousands of species that have already been discovered in each class and that there is reason to believe that many thousands more are as yet unknown.

He discusses at considerable length the reproduction of animals. Modern scientists, he maintains, follow Harvey in believing that all animals originate from eggs. He raises the question whether the organism, which is to develop, already exists in the egg as the preformation theory contends in the case of plants. He follows instead the theory of Leeuwenhoeck according to whom the organism exists in the male sperm which then needs the egg simply for nourishment and development.

He briefly examines other functions of animal organisms such as nourishment, digestion, the circulation of the blood, locomotion and the parts of the body that are involved. He also discussed in some detail the anatomy of the sense organs, eyes, ears, nose, tongue, and skin. Since much of what he has explained about the functions of animals applies also to man, he confines himself in the final chapter on man to anatomical descriptions of the main parts of the human body.

Johann Gottlob Krüger (1715–1759)

Johann Gottlob Krüger was one of the many physicians and scientists of his generation who came under the influence of Christian Wolff's system of "Weltweisheit". Like his predecessors, Wolff and Gottsched, he was an "Aufklärer". He used German in his numerous scientific works and succeeded in attaining a good literary style. As a professor of medicine and member of several scientific societies, he was well equipped to write his *Naturlehre,* the first part of which is a compendium of science.[15]

An interesting preface to the work was written by the famous professor of medicine at Halle, Friedrich Hoffman, Krüger's own teacher at the university. Hoffman stresses the limitations of reason in face of the fundamental questions about God and man. He undertakes two surveys of natural phenomena; one to show how much we know and one to demonstrate our ignorance. The purpose of the paradox is to encourage scientific studies and at the same time to warn against attempting to exceed the limitations of reason and scientific method.

Let us now turn to the text itself. The subject matter as the title indicates is "Naturlehre" which he defines as "eine Wissenschaft dessen, was durch die Kräfte der Cörper möglich ist" (1). It amounts to physics in a broad sense to include such matters as astronomy, meteorology, optics and even the anatomy of plants and animals. It meant experimental science, examination of cause and effect in natural phenomena by means of experiment and generalizations based on those experiments.

The 790 page text is divided into fourteen chapters of which the first five deal with the properties of material bodies, the following five with phenomena associated with the four elements and the remaining with light, atmospheric phenomena, the cosmos and plants and animals, respectively. We shall now follow through the chapters summarizing and selecting significant points.

---

15 (Halle, 1740). In 1770 the fourth edition appeared. The second part on physiology had three editions between 1743 and 1777; the third part on pathology had three editions between 1740 and 1765. A simplified version of this compendium appeared under the following title: *Die ersten Gründe der Naturlehre auf eine leichte und angenehme Art zum Gebrauch der Jugend und Anfänger* (Halle, 1759).

In the first chapter he discusses scientific method. Prior to reasoning about nature, experience is necessary. Experience, he says, is either by observation of things that happen or by experiment where one arranges phenomena according to design. Both are needed in science and it is in this respect that the ancients were deficient and that moderns have gained the advantage. The rest of the chapter deals with natural bodies, their composition and qualities, with many references to microscopic observations to demonstrate the subtlety and minuteness of material bodies.

The second chapter is a discussion of force and the laws of motion which gives Krüger an opportunity to state his faith in the orderliness of nature: "Die Natur einer Unordnung beschuldigen, heisst dieselbe nicht kennen. Wer aber ordentlich handelt, handelt nach Regeln. Es giebt demnach gewisse unveränderliche Gesetze der Natur, welche die Cörper bey ihrer Bewegung beständig in acht nehmen" (18). In this chapter Newton is mentioned several times and in discussing Newton's first law of motion he quotes from the *Principia*. The chapter contains many experiments and mathematical demonstrations to explain the laws of motion and specific problems raised by moving bodies.

The third chapter, "Von der Schwere", deals with gravity as a quality of all material bodies since they all tend to the center of the earth and again many examples are adduced to demonstrate the operation of this force, though he leaves it to a later chapter to discuss gravity as a cosmic force in the Newtonian sense.

The fourth chapter discusses bodies in liquid form and the physical and chemical properties of material bodies in general. Both chapters are generously provided with examples and experiments. In the beginning of the fifth chapter, he maintains that between all bodies there is a constant attractive power and thus matter is not dead or at rest but constantly in an active state: "Weil man nun die Würckung eines Cörpers als eine Sache anzusehen hat, welche sich von seiner Kraft nicht trennen lässt: so müssen die Cörper in der Welt beständig in einander würcken. Alles ist belebt, alles ist, so zu sagen, beseelt. Und auf diese Weise ist die Naturlehre ziemlich lebendig geworden; da sie hingegen ganz todt war, so lange man sich überreden konte, dass der Cörper ein todtes und blos leidendes Ding sey" (196).

With chapter six, "Von dem Feuer", he begins to study the qualities of specific natural phenomena rather than those of natural phenomena in general as he had done in the first five chapters. His subject in this chapter is fire which he defines as that material body which causes the sensation of heat. He also considers both heat and light as effects of fire and necessary for the preservation of life. Fire, too, is subject to law, for nature is an orderly law giver: "Die Natur ist eine viel zu ordentliche Gesetzgeberin, als dass sie sollte unterlassen haben, dem Feuer Regeln vorzuschreiben, nach welchen es seine Bewegung hervorbringet" (292). The chapter is again supplied with many examples to demonstrate the various circumstances and conditions under which bodies attain heat.

In the seventh chapter, "Von der Luft", the familiar experiments by Guericke, Torricelli and Boyle are recounted with most space granted to the German Guericke. In this chapter there is a pertinent comment on Krüger's conception of scientific method: "Die Luft hat man erst im vorigen Jahrhundert besser kennen lernen, nachdem man angefangen Experimente anzustellen, und dadurch die Natur zu zwingen, dasjenige zu zeigen, was sie sonst vor unsern Augen zu verbergen gewohnt ist" (341). It is quite a modern understanding of the scientific experiment as an attempt to wrest from nature secrets she keeps concealed.

In the subsequent chapter he takes up sound as a specific case of the previously considered air phenomena and in the ninth chapter the qualities of water are analyzed.

The tenth chapter "Von der Erde" is a very lengthy one dealing with those phenomena associated with and found on the earth. He raises the question of the different earth strata which he says must have arisen through floods. He maintains that the Biblical deluge could not alone have caused all the various strata. Thus there must have been many floods and transformations on earth of which we have no record.

In connection with floods and the transformations caused by them, he takes up the subject of fossils which he considers among the treasures of nature: "Der Erdboden ist die rechte Schatz- und Kunstkammer der Natur. Denn ausser denen Metallen begreift er eine solche Menge gebildeter Steine von allerhand Arten in sich, dass man sich billig darüber verwundert. In den grösten Tiefen findet man in Stein verwandelte Muscheln, menschliche Gerippe von ausserordentlicher Grösse, Pflantzen und Fische, welche ihre Gestalt den härtesten Steinen eingedrückt haben" (472). He is convinced that fossils are not tricks or games of nature, but that they were originally natural phenomena which in the course of time have acquired their present fossilized state. Here also he grants that the Biblical deluge was undoubtedly the cause of some fossils, but since it lasted only one year it could not suffice as an explanation of all fossils. In the rest of the chapter, he takes up other treasures of the earth such as salts, metals, precious stones, the magnet, electricity and earthquakes.

The eleventh chapter, "Von dem Licht und den Farben," is an account of the laws of optics, such as those connected with the reflection and refraction of light. He also describes instruments and optical equipment such as lenses, mirrors and magnifying glasses. As far as colors are concerned, he follows the Newtonian account giving ample experiments and examples. In the twelfth chapter, "Von den Lufterscheinungen," he takes up individual atmospheric phenomena such as winds, fog, clouds, rain, snow, frost, hail, dew, rainbows, thunder, lightning and others.

The thirteenth chapter "Von dem Weltgebäude" is the longest chapter in the
text. He proceeds in the customary manner starting with the sun and the planets
of our solar system, taking them up individually, then the comets and the
number of fixed stars each of which he considers to be a sun and center of a
solar system. Many themes are taken up in detail: the size of each heavenly
body, distances from the sun, number of satellites, the earth's diurnal and annual
movements, the shape of the earth and one of the favorite topics of the
astronomers of this time, namely, the inhabitation of the planets. Like most of
his contemporaries, he argues for the inhabitation of planets by analogy between
our planet earth and the others. Another argument as popular is the reflection
that the resourcefulness and plenitude of nature demand the inhabitation of
these huge earthlike heavenly bodies:

> Man muss sich von der Natur eine viel edlere Vorstellung machen. Sie bringt
> nicht ein Stäubgen vergebens hervor: wie vielweniger wird sie Cörper von
> solcher erstaunlichen Grösse ohne allen Zweck, ohne alle Absicht um die
> Sonne herumlauffen lassen? Jupiter und Saturn sind bey nahe 1000 mal
> grösser als die Erde. Die Erde ist mit so vielen Pflantzen und Thieren besetzt,
> dass es schon eine Verwegenheit heisst, wenn man sich nur die Anzahl aller
> der Arten zu bestimmen untersteht. Jupiter und Saturn aber solte gantz leer
> seyn, man solte daselbst nichts als grosse Wüsteneyen und unbewohnte
> Länder antreffen? Gewiss, dies wäre ein Gedancke, der bey der sonst
> bekannten Geschicklichkeit der Natur recht seltsam erschiene. (718)

Thus, the argument by analogy intends to support the likelihood of the
inhabitation of planets whereas the latter argument intends to show the
unlikeliness of their uninhabitability. However, he is not as dogmatic about this
matter as others and admits that we cannot come to any conclusions about the
nature of those inhabitants of other planets as, for example, Huygens tried to
do.

In discussing the causes of planetary motion, he follows Newton's law of
gravitation: "Dass die Schwere dergestalt abnehme, wie das Quadrat der
Entfernung von dem Puncte, gegen welchen die Schwere gerichtet ist, zunimmt,
hat Newton zuerst gefunden. Es liegt darinnen der Grund von denenjenigen
Regeln, nach welchen die Planeten in unsrer Weltordnung ihre Bewegung
verrichten" (721). Kepler's laws of planetary motion are also mentioned in the
discussion of the Newtonian system. The nature of comets is discussed and in
this connection Whiston's theory is examined. He speaks favorably of Whiston's
theory of a cometary cause of the Biblical deluge. However, Krüger grants that
the theory is no article of faith and can be accepted or not. He concludes the
chapter with another popular theme of the astronomy of the time, namely, the
speculation that every star is a sun surrounded by planets and that the solar
systems are unlimited in number.

The concluding fourteenth chapter "Von den Pflantzen und Thieren" is quite brief, considering the subject matter. He does not approach it with the natural historian's interest in individual species, but from the point of view of the philosopher who seeks general statements. Thus, he considers only what plants have in common, namely, their parts and functions. He also gives a clear statement of the encapsulation theory to which he subscribes fully. Finally, in the few remaining pages of the compendium he presents a brief anatomy of the human body and just a few remarks about the orderly structures of animals.

Another compendium of science I shall briefly examine is *Physica Generalior, oder kurtze Sätze von denen natürlichen Cörpern* (Regensburg, 1724) by Johann Matthaeus Barth, a theologian and a Cartesian. The text is supplemented by copious footnotes which present the opinions of contemporary non-Cartesian scientists like Newton, Leibniz, Huygens, Boyle and Wolff. Nevertheless, the author consistently resorts to Cartesian explanations of natural phenomena and for that reason the compendium is of interest to us.

In the preface Barth explains that his work is directed toward beginners in scientific studies and those who are not fluent in Latin and the reading of philosophic works. He maintains that Wolff's German works are too complicated, lengthy and mathematical. Moreover, as a theologian, he realizes how important it is to learn to see God in His works and how easily the Christian, who is ignorant of scientific matters, plays into the hands of the atheists.

The text is divided into four chapters: The first is about physical bodies in general, their properties and qualities; the second chapter deals with heavenly bodies; the third with atmospheric phenomena such as light, colors, heat; and the fourth chapter with matters pertaining to the earth. Throughout the work he relies heavily on the aether which seems to be the very soul or spirit of matter. Matter itself is extended and totally passive. All matter has pores of varying numbers, sizes and shapes; the aether particles penetrate through these pores and thereby all the observable properties of bodies can be explained. That is why he rejects any force of attraction between bodies that is not a pushing-pulling variety: "Nur ist allhier noch zu erinnern / dass kein *motus attractionis* oder Ziehung zu statuiren nöthig / noch auch deutlich könne erklärt werden / sondern es geschiehet alles durch die pulsion oder stossen und schieben". (39—40)

In the second chapter, he explains the Copernican system of the world retaining the Cartesian vortices. In the third chapter he uses the Cartesian explanation of light, that it is a movement precipitated by the sun's rotation and transmitted almost instantaneously through the aether. In a long footnote he explains Newton's theory of color and maintains that it is compatible with his theory of light. In the fourth chapter he gives the Cartesian account of the tides, namely, that the moon exerts pressure on the aether which in turn is transmitted to our atmosphere and from there to the water of the oceans. In a footnote he explains the Newtonian theory of gravity as an explanation of the tides, but rejects it because he believes there is insufficient evidence to accept the existence of such a force.

Kurtze Fragen von den natürlichen Dingen (Halle, 1719) by Johann George Hoffmann is a compendium of scientific knowledge in the major fields intended for use in the schools.[16] It is a science-for-the-layman text in which great care is taken to present the material in a religious context. A long preface by the theologian and friend of August Hermann Francke, Johann Daniel Herrnschmidt (1675—1723), is of interest because of his objective account of modern scientific method and liberal theological attitude toward that scientific method.[17]

In his introduction Hoffmann indicates that the sciences will be presented within a religious context. Revelation provides for man's salvation and knowledge of spiritual matters, yet a right understanding of natural objects to which the Bible exhorts us also leads to God and right action. Throughout the text Hoffmann presents his knowledge of natural objects with repeated praises of God in nature, quotations from the Bible and reminders of man's duty to God. He presents his subject matter in seven chapters. The first three chapters deal with astronomy, physics and meteorology. Chapters four, five and six deal with the life sciences, botany and biology, and the last chapter concerning the soul deals with psychological matters.

Though the text contains numerous pious exhortations and warnings, we find an authentic appreciation of science and scientific method and an informative popular scientific text. Since this text with its many editions was intended for the schools, it must have contributed to disseminating an enlightened approach to science.

Another popular scientific compendium was *Einleitung in die Naturlehre* (Göttingen, 1746) by Johann Andreas Segner (1704—1777), professor of mathematics at the University of Göttingen and translator of Nieuwentyt's *Rechter Gebrauch der Weltbetrachtung zur Erkenntniss . . . Gottes* (Jena, 1747). The work was very favorably reviewed in the learned journals of the time and can certainly be ranked on a level with those of Wolff, Gottsched and Krüger.

Johanne Charlotte Unzer's (1724—1782) *Grundriss einer Weltweisheit für das Frauenzimmer* (Halle, 1751) includes a compendium of science. The author was the wife of the physician Johann August Unzer, the editor of several popular scientific periodicals, and the niece of Johann Gottlob Krüger who wrote the introduction to the text. The work is a simplified version of Gottsched's *Erste Gründe der gesammten Weltweisheit*. The more complex material is omitted and throughout the text there are selections of poems by contemporary authors like

---

16   The sixth edition (Halle, 1770) was available for this study. A ninth edition appeared in 1790.

17   Herrnschmidt's preface to the first edition is dated 1719.

Brockes and Haller. The scientific part was also published separately under the title, *Grundriss einer natürlichen Historie und eigentlichen Naturlehre für das Frauenzimmer* (Halle, 1751).

Finally, I should like to refer to *Erste Gründe der Naturlehre* (Halle, 1753)[18] by Johann Peter Eberhard (1727—1779), a physician and professor of mathematics and physics at the University of Halle. The fourth edition of 1774 is more specialized than the other compendiums of science, concentrating primarily on general and specific properties of material bodies. It could be called a physics text book rather than a compendium of science. In the preface to the third edition he comments on the daily increase of scientific knowledge and this text might, thus, be an example of the growing need of specialization.

---

18 The fourth edition (Halle, 1774) was available for this study.

C. PHYSICOTHEOLOGY AND BIBLICAL SCIENCE

The relationship between religion and the new sciences is one of the very significant chapters in cultural history of the last four centuries. It is also relevant to this study's interest in the popularization of science in Germany in the eighteenth century. Orthodox and deist apologists for the Christian religion made use of science in their campaign against the various manifestations of atheism and thereby aided the diffusion of the new learning. This cooperation between science and religion took various forms. There were the cosmogonies that sought to find natural explanations for Biblical events, there was edifying literature in which God's glory was readily seen in any natural phenomena and then there were the physicotheologies and Biblical science; the former justified God in nature, the latter justified him in the Bible.

As far as the cosmogonies are concerned, those of Burnet, Ray, Woodward, Whiston and Buffon, which were discussed in the section on translations, tried to explain the Biblical story of the creation, the flood and the final conflagration by using principles derived from the new sciences.[1] These cosmogonies are examples of the attempt to harmonize science and religion. Possibly, these attempts to find a natural, rational explanation of these fundamental Biblical events were encouraged by the success other authors had in proving that the Copernican system was not incompatible with the Bible. John Wilkins' *Vertheidigter Copernicus,* which we have already discussed, is one example. A German example of this type of literature is *Astronomischer Beweissthum des Copernicanischen Welt-Gebäudes aus Heiliger Schrifft* (Frankfurt und Leipzig, 1691) by Johann Jacob Zimmermann (1644—1694), the translator of Burnet's *Sacred Theory of the Earth.* Zimmermann presents numerous arguments and proofs that the Copernican theory is in harmony with Scripture. In the course of interpreting Biblical passages involving heavenly bodies, the author, an astronomer, manages to teach the main aspects of the new astronomy. Johann Georg Hagelganss has the same purpose in his *Kurtze doch Gründliche aus der Übereinstimmung des Lichts der Natur und Offenbahrung geleitete Vorstellung des Welt-Gebäudes* (Frankfurt, 1736). He first considers the system of the world as taught by reason, that is, the Copernican system, and then turns to the Bible to select those passages that support the system and to explicate those that could be construed as anti-Copernican.[2]

A bibliography of the edifying literature in antiquity, the middle ages and modern times which sings the praises of God in nature can be found in Johann

---

[1] For a thorough account of cosmogonies in the seventeenth and eighteenth centuries see Katherine Brownell Collier's *Cosmogonies of our Fathers* (Columbia University Press, 1934).

[2] See Ernst Zinner's *Entstehung und Ausbreitung der Copernicanischen Lehre* (Erlangen, 1943) for an account of the controversy over the Copernican theory in Germany.

Albert Fabricius' preface to his translation of William Derham's *Astrotheologie* (1728). Some of the modern examples of this literature in the German language are the fourth book of *Vom Wahren Christentum* (1605—1609) by Johann Arndt (1555—1621), *Gottholds Zufälliger Andachten* (1674) by Christian Scriver (1629—1693), *Amadei Creutzbergs Seelen-erquickende Himmels-Lust auf Erden* (1728) by Philipp Balthasar Sinold (1657—1742) and *Die merckwürdigen Wercke Gottes in denen Reichen der Natur* (Dresden, 1724) by Valentin Ernst Löscher (1673—1749). In these works there is relatively little scientific material in the reflections on natural phenomena. A natural object is usually only an occasion for pious thought, and when there is appreciation expressed for the world of nature, it does not involve science to any significant degree.

Physicotheology, generally speaking, can include any type of literature in which the author demonstrates the existence of God and His qualities from the design in nature or in which God simply is praised in His works. Bibliographies of physicotheological literature usually understand this type of literature in a very broad sense and may include sermons, poems, cosmogonies, scientific compendiums, in fact, any work that intends to show harmony between science and religion. Compiling bibliographies was quite common in eighteenth-century Germany and there are several bibliographies of physicotheological literature written by physicotheologians themselves. The most elaborate is the one by Johann Albert Fabricius, mentioned above. Another valuable contemporary source for this type of literature is *Bibliotheca Theologica* by the scholar and bibliographer Johann Georg Walch.[3] Of later studies, Otto Zöckler's little known *Geschichte der Beziehungen zwischen Theologie und Naturwissenschaft* is the best introduction to the history of the relations between science and religion in Germany and provides a sympathetic and thorough survey of the efforts to harmonize science and religion in the eighteenth century.[4] Lois Westen in her dissertation on bee literature in the eighteenth century offers a bibliography of physicotheologies including poems, essays, books and sermons in which natural phenomena are used for the glory of God.[5]

By far the most extensive study of physicotheology, its history and its implications was undertaken by Wolfgang Philipp in *Das Werden der Aufklärung*

---

[3] Four volumes (Jena, 1757—1765), Vol. I, pp. 700—705.

[4] Two volumes (Gütersloh, 1877—1879). Zöckler's contemporary, Andrew D. White, ignored the physicotheological tradition in his well-known study, *A History of the Warfare of Science with Theology* (New York, 1896). Zöckler's history should be taken as a necessary corrective to White's tendentious approach to the relation between science and religion. Zöckler was familiar with White's earlier work, *The Warfare of Science* (London, 1876), and charges White with bias, ignorance and historical inaccuracies (Vol. I, pp. 12—13).

[5] Lois Armour Westen, *"Melitto-Logica" the Mythology of the Bee in Eighteenth-Century German Literature* (Diss. University of Illinois, 1952), pp. 64—84.

in theologiegeschichtlicher Sicht.[6] With great erudition he demonstrates the vastness and duration of the physicotheological movement. It is beyond the scope of the present study to evaluate Philipp's claims for the theological significance of this movement. The relevance of Philipp's book lies in its presentation of overwhelming evidence that the physicotheological orientation inspired a popular literature that contributed extensively to the diffusion and acceptance of the new sciences.

A special distinction within the physicotheological literature must be made which the above mentioned bibliographies omit, with the exception of Otto Zöckler. He distinguishes what he calls a "specielle Physikotheologie" from the rest.[7] What distinguishes the works that belong to this category is the quantity and quality of the scientific material they contain. This special type of physicotheology had its beginning with William Derham's *Physico-Theology* (1713) and *Astro-Theology* (1714) which we have already discussed in the section on translations. There we indicated that these works were serious popular scientific texts within a religious framework. We also indicated the popularity of the German translations of these works: from 1728 to 1765 there were six editions of *Astrotheologie* and from 1730 to 1764 there were six editions of *Physicotheologie*. During approximately the same period this special type of physicotheology flourished in Germany as in no other nation. The following list of short titles of German physicotheologies, divided into earth and life sciences, shows the extent to which this type of popular literature embraced the subjects of natural history within a religious framework:

The earth sciences

(Fabricius)	Pyrotheologie, 1732
(Fabricius)	Hydrotheologie, 1734
(Lesser)	Lithotheologie, 1732, 1735, 1751
(Heinsius)	Chionotheologie, 1735
(Ahlwardt)	Brontotheologie, 1745, 1747
(Lesser)	Heliotheologie, 1753
(J.C. Wolf)	Orotheologie, 1756
(Preu)	Sismotheologie, 1772

---

[6] Göttingen, 1957. See also Philipp's article "Physicotheology in the age of Enlightenment: appearance and history," *Studies on Voltaire and the Eighteenth Century,* ed. Theodore Besterman (Genève, 1967), Vol. LVII, pp. 1233—1267. John Dillenberger's *Protestant Thought and Natural Science: A Historical Study* (New York, 1960) would have benefitted from the work of both Zöckler and Philipp, for his treatment of the physicotheological movement, especially in the eighteenth century, is inadequate.

[7] *Geschichte der Beziehungen,* Vol. II, pp. 87, 251.

The life sciences

(Lesser)	Insectotheologie, 1738, 1740, 1750
(von Rohr)	Phytotheologie, 1740, 1745
(Zorn)	Petinotheologie, 1742–1743
(Lesser)	Testaceotheologie, 1744, 1756, 1770
(Rathelf)	Akridotheologie, 1748–1750
(Richter)	Ichthyotheologie, 1754
(Chemnitz)	Testaceotheologie, 1760
(Schirach)	Melittotheologie, 1767

Though most of these titles are mentioned by the authors who have studied the physicotheological movement, these elaborate compendiums have not received the attention they deserve. As popular scientific works, written with the didactic intent of communicating instruction in both science and religion, they played a role in the diffusion of science. We have selected several of these texts for closer examination.

Johann Albert Fabricius' Hydrotheologie

Johann Albert Fabricius, translator of the popular works of William Derham, followed in the latter's footsteps by writing the first German physicotheologies, namely, Hydrotheologie[8] and Pyrotheologie.[9] Both of these works had already been planned but not worked out by Derham. The polyhistorian Fabricius is much more of a scholar and bibliographer than a scientist; in his Hydrotheologie he very ably compiles, from the scientific works of the time, an impressive array of facts about water.

The work is divided into three books. The first book deals solely with the general qualities of water such as its density, weight, viscosity. Water is looked at from every conceivable point of view. The explanations are not very technical, but nevertheless are documented by the scientific works from which he drew. The list of these scientific sources is quite impressive: Wolff, Hartsoeker, Boyle, Musschenbroek, Fahrenheit, Derham as well as the Philosophical Transactions, the Memoires de l'Academie des Sciences, the Acta Eruditorum and many others.

---

[8] Hydrotheologie oder Versuch durch aufmerksame Betrachtung der Eigenschaften, reichen Austheilung und Bewegung der Wasser die Menschen zur Liebe und Bewunderung ihres ... Schöpfers zu ermuntern (Hamburg, 1734). There was a French translation (La Haye, 1741; Paris, 1743).
[9] Pyrotheologie oder Versuch durch nähere Betrachtung des Feuers, die Menschen zur Liebe und Bewunderung ihres ... Schöpfers anzuflammen (Hamburg, 1732).

The second book is about the distribution of waters throughout the world. He enumerates the different types of water that exist and describes some of the well-known ones in various parts of the world. This section could be called a natural history of water. He begins by considering water on the planets, on our moon and in the atmosphere of the earth. Then he descends to the earth and considers the various bodies of water found there, such as oceans, bays, rivers, lakes, ponds, brooks and springs. He also examines the many devices man uses to control and use water such as canals, dams, harbors and many vessels with which he navigates the waters. Finally, he considers the indispensability of water in plants, animals and man.

In the third book he looks at water in a state of motion and the different circumstances that cause motion. Tides, floods, the flow of rivers, whirlpools, waterfalls are examined. He considers the mobility of water essential to the earth and compares it to the circulation of the blood in an animal organism.

Though *Hydrotheologie* is not an original scientific treatise, its compilation and orderly arrangement of a vast number of facts about water make it a useful and informative contribution to popular science. Fabricius further enhances the value of his book by providing bibliographies on a variety of subjects, relevant to the subject of water. The longest one is a list of writings on statutes pertaining to the sea. There are also bibliographies of books about Noah's ark, about the tides and about the Nile river.

The religious element plays as much of a role here as in Derham's works, again without invalidating the main factual body of the book. The religious theme appears in the form of Biblical quotations and teleological considerations. However, Fabricius never resorts to the Bible as an authority to validate or explain any statement of science. Nevertheless, in one of the teleological passages, our author asserts that the recognition of purpose and design in natural phenomena is the best part of science, and only thereby does his work on water become a "Hydro-Theologie" (82). The text is furthermore embellished by occasional selections from the poetic works of Brockes, the favorite poet of the physicotheologians.

Christian Friedrich Lesser's Insecto-Theologia

Christian Friedrich Lesser (1692–1754), a clergyman and a member of the Academia Naturae Curiosorum, was the author of three physicotheologies, *Insecto-Theologia, Testaceo-Theologie* and *Lithotheologie,* in which he demonstrated God and His qualities in the world of natural history and in the world of the microscope. By far the best known was his *Insecto-Theologia*,[10] with its three German editions and translations into French and Italian.[11]

In the introduction to his *Insecto-Theologia*, he feels obligated to justify his detailed treatment of the insect world. Man tends to neglect the tiny, insignificant creatures of the insect world. Yet, he maintains, they, too, mirror the wisdom of God and in their intricate and subtle structures, they surpass the best that man could do with his art. To be sure, man's intellect is capable of loftier contemplation and he doesn't wish to defend the mere "Naturalien-sammler". Yet a theologian should be well acquainted with all the sciences, and so he studies the book of nature not only in the vast heavens but also in the insect world; the world of the microscope draws his attention, no less than the world of the telescope.

> Die auf der Erde hin und wieder zerstreute Insecta von so vielerley Farbe und Gestalt, die im Meer schwimmende See-Sterne und Würme ziehen meine Gedancken nicht weniger an sich, als die am Himmel zerstreute Gestirne die Stern-Forscher. Wenn diese mit ihrem Fern-Glass den Himmel, als einen blauen Atlas, und die Sterne, als so viel hierauf funckelnde Demante ansehen, so sehe ich mit meinen Vergrösserungs-Gläsern nicht minder an denen Insecten unerforschliche Wunder, als jene an denen Gestirnen. (14)

In this introduction he also follows the example of a fellow physico-theologian, Johann Albert Fabricius, by providing an extensive bibliography of those who have studied the insect world. He divides them into various groups: those who have collected insects, those who have studied insects through the microscope, those who have studied their characteristics, those who have dissected them and those who have painted them according to real life.

His own work, he maintains, is based on many years of study of the insect world both with and without the microscope. It is impossible, however, to exhaust the subject, for many insects are daily revealed to us in newly discovered lands, in the oceans and through microscopic studies. He has written his work in German, for there are many "Curiosi" and other interested people who do not know Latin and may wish to read this work to praise God in nature and enlighten themselves about the world of insects. Finally, he cautions that the book of nature is not a substitute for Scripture but is intended to lead the reader to Scripture.

---

[10] *Insecto-Theologia, oder Vernunfft- und Schrifftmässiger Versuch, wie ein Mensch durch aufmercksame Betrachtung derer . . . Insecten zu . . . Erkänntniss . . . der Allmacht, Weissheit, der Güte und Gerechtigkeit des grossen Gottes gelangen könne* (Frankfurt und Leipzig, 1738). There was a second edition in 1740 and a third in 1758; all references are to the second edition of 1740.

[11] French by P. Lyonnet (La Haye, 1742; Paris, 1745); Italian (Venezia, 1751).

As is characteristic of physicotheologies, the *Insecto-Theologia* is a compendium, a compilation of facts and information about insects. The work is divided into two parts. The first considers insects as the subject matter of science and the second views the function and purpose of insects in the world, primarily in human society.

In the first part we learn about the classification of insect species, about the various functions of insects such as movement, nourishment, reproduction, metamorphosis, about their inner and outer parts, their senses and other qualities peculiar to them. The scientific material is separate and distinct from the religious material of which there is not very much. The latter can be divided into two types. There are the pious comments, usually at the end of a chapter, in which the author praises God in some specific natural phenomena under discussion, or he cites Biblical quotations to demonstrate the correspondence between science and Scripture.

The first part is much more of a scientific treatise than a theological one. Of special interest is the fourteenth chapter, "Von dem Witz derer Insecten", in which he describes the social and constructive instincts of such insects as bees, wasps and ants. This was one of the popular interests shared by scientists and laymen.

The second part of the work on the functions and purposes of insects in human life is peripheral if not entirely irrelevant to a scientific study of insects, yet it does belong to the total, encyclopedic approach of the physicotheologies. He discusses in some detail both the benefit and harm that insects cause to humans, and out of both manages to draw evidence for the justice, wisdom and goodness of God. As in the first part, there is religious material in the form of pious sentiments and Biblical quotations, though it is decidedly subordinated to the subject matter.

Summing up, the *Insecto-Theologia* is a compendium of information about insect life placed within a religious framework. The scientific material, based on the author's own investigations and the work of contemporary scientists, is presented in a simplified form to be readily grasped by the layman. Religious material is scattered throughout the text but does not compromise the validity of the scientific material.

Finally, it is of interest to this study that the author quotes verses from three physicotheological poets, Brockes, Triller and Zell.

Christian Friedrich Lesser's Testaceo-Theologia

The construction of Lesser's *Testaceo-Theologia*[12] is similar to that of his *Insecto-Theologia* in most respects. In his long introduction he again justifies his interest in these apparently insignificant creatures. He insists that all men and especially theologians should study all the realms of nature. Even the most contemptible animal is a "natürliches Wunderwerk" (8), and a sure sign of a wise and mighty creator. The intricate structure of mollusks with their complicated structures and functions is clearly beyond the power of any man to duplicate; these creatures are evidently products "des allmächtigen Künstlers" (14).

As he had done in the previous work, here too he presents a bibliography of investigations of mollusks (22—65). He maintains that the moderns have been much more successful in these studies:

> Es ist unter die Glückseligkeiten der neuern Zeiten auch dieses zu rechnen, dass sie weit fruchtbarer, als die ältern an solchen Männern sind, welche theils durch eine Lobens-würdige Neugierigkeit, theils durch eine untadelhafte Liebe zur Wahrheit in Italien, Frankreich, England und Teutschland erwecket worden, mit allem ersinnlichen Fleisse dahin zu sehen, nach dem Probier-Steine der Wahrheit zu untersuchen, was die Verfasser der natürlichen Dinge in Schriften hinterlassen, und dasjenige hinzu zu thun, was jene aus Mangel mehrerer Nachrichten und Erfahrungen aussengelassen. (21—22)

The bibliography is divided into several sections. First he discusses the works of about thirty authors from England, Italy, France, Germany, Holland and Switzerland, written during the sixteenth and seventeenth centuries. Then he enumerates those works that are illustrated by woodcuts and engravings. Since it is even better to see natural objects themselves, he lists private collections of natural objects which contain mollusks. With this bibliography alone, he has performed a service to conchology.

He concludes his introduction by again justifying his use of the German language. He explains that many of the unlearned, that is, those who have not attended a university, are interested in the works of nature and recognizing God in those works.

The text itself again has a structure similar to the preceding one. The book is divided into two parts. The first presents the scientific material about the structures and functions of mollusks and the second part discusses their usefulness to man and to other animals.

There are religious comments and Biblical quotations throughout the text. Typical of these is his lengthy consideration at the end of chapter 1, book 1

---

12 *Testaceo-Theologia, oder gründlicher Beweis des Daseyns und der vollkommensten Eigenschaften eines göttlichen Wesens, aus natürlicher und geistlicher Betrachtung der Schnecken und Muscheln* . . . (Leipzig, 1744), 2nd ed., 1756; 3rd ed., 1770.

where he contends that due to the extraordinary complexity of mollusks, the sufficient reason for their existence could not be man or any spirit but must necessarily be God. Here again, we can safely say that these pious comments and the Biblical references do not detract from the factual, scientific material of the book.

Christian Friedrich Lesser's Lithotheologie

Lesser's *Lithotheologie* in its final form is the lengthiest of his physicotheologies though not the most popular.[13] The preface constitutes a fine statement of purpose of Lesser, the theologian, the scholar and the amateur scientist. He makes it clear that the Book of Nature is subsidiary to the Bible since it cannot give us salvation. Nevertheless, it is our duty to praise and recognize God in nature. To do so we must learn to use our eyes and acquire the habit of observing what nature places before them. There is no doubt about his status as an amateur scientist who enjoys the pleasures that first-hand observation and discovery bring, when we read the following:

> Ich habe von Jugend auf die Gewohnheit gehabt, wenn ich etwas in der Natur gesehen, dass ich meine Gedancken darüber gehen lassen. Und nachdem ich die Physic auf Universitaeten mit studiret, hat mich dieses angetrieben, noch mehr natürlichen Dingen nachzusinnen, um desto mehr aus denen Geschöpffen den Schöpffer zu erkennen, und dessen Allmacht, Güte und Weissheit zu preisen. Ich habe dannenhero, was nur aus dem dreyfachen Reiche der Natur sonderliches, so wohl auf Reisen, als auch bey Besichtigung Königl. Fürstl. und Privat-Personen Cabineten vor Augen kommen, fleissig angemercket.
> ....
> Bisweilen habe ich zu Fusse in der Nachbarschafft hohe Berge bestiegen, niedrige Thäler durchwandert, und tieffe Höhlen und Klüffte durchkrochen, da ich denn so glücklich gewesen, viele curieuse und von keinem vor mir in dieser Gegend attendirte Steine zu entdecken, ... (XXIV—XXV)

In the preface we also have a bibliographical essay where he shows his familiarity with the physicotheological tradition. Though there is no biblio-

---

13 The first version appeared under the following title: *Kurzer Entwurf einer Lithotheologie, oder eines Versuches, durch natürliche und geistliche Betrachtung der Steine, die Allmacht, Güte, Weissheit und Gerechtigkeit des Schöpffers zu erkennen, und die Menschen zur Bewunderung, Lobe und Dienste desselben aufzumuntern* (Nordhausen, 1732). The first completed version was entitled as follows: *Lithotheologie, oder naturhistorische und geistliche Betrachtung der Steine* (Dresden, 1735). The later edition (Hamburg, 1751), which was used for this study, is unchanged in its structure but has a total of 1488 pages of text compared to 1300 pages in the 1735 edition.

graphy of books on stones as such, throughout the text scientific works on stones are constantly cited in the footnotes.

Lesser divides his text into nine books, the substance of which, however, can be structured into three categories. The one category is the scientific part, in which he describes the nature of stones, their different qualities, appearances and physical and chemical properties. He explains the origins and development of stones and provides an elaborate classification of stones. The second category can be called a sociology of stones, namely, a study of the use and misuse of stones in various areas of human endeavor. Finally there is the religious part in which repeated demonstrations of God's qualities are derived from these reflections about stones. The text has many Biblical quotes partly because they refer to stones and partly as illustrative pious comments. As a compendium of science it is informative, systematic and comprehensive. Undoubtedly, in this book he says everything that could possibly have been said about stones at that time.

Julius Bernhard von Rohr's Phyto-Theologia

Phyto-Theologia[14] by Julius Bernhard von Rohr (1648–1742) is a fine example of this species of literature. His work is an encyclopedia of facts about the subject he has chosen to discuss in praise of the Creator, namely, plant life. The religious material in the book once again is not presented in such a way that it interferes with the scientific or factual value and validity of the work.

In the introduction von Rohr places himself in the physicotheological tradition of Boyle, Ray, Derham and his countrymen, Fabricius and Lesser. He finds pleasure in physicotheological works, for they show how natural science and natural theology are connected.

In his present work, von Rohr points out, he has relied heavily on travel journals and scientific works, of which those by Christian Wolff have been especially valuable. Indeed, the scientific works of Wolff are cited as a source some forty times. Further sources are the German and Latin works of some thirty German and foreign scientists. Fifteen travel reports, mostly by Germans, are the remaining sources. Von Rohr himself clearly is not a scientist and he does not refer to his own observations and experiments as does Derham, for example. It is all the more remarkable that this scholar and clergyman has examined a vast literature on his subject and compiled therefrom a storehouse of information for popular consumption.

---

14 *Phyto-Theologia, oder Vernunfft- und Schrifftmässiger Versuch, wie aus dem Reiche der Gewächse die Allmacht, Weisheit, Güte und Gerechtigkeit des grossen Schöpfers und Erhalters ... erkannt ... werden möge* (Frankfurt und Leipzig, 1740). There was a second edition (Frankfurt und Leipzig, 1745).

The work is divided into three books, each taking up different phases of plant life. In the first book, von Rohr examines the parts of plants, their structures and outer forms. Here, he is more concerned with what plants have in common than in an enumeration of species and individual plants in the manner of the natural historian. At the same time, throughout the entire text he refers to rare and unusual plants, for which he draws on the travel reports.

The second book begins with an interesting treatment of the plant in relation to its environment. This subject is considered from various points of view. He discusses plants' capacity to exist and perpetuate themselves under the most extraordinary circumstances. He considers the ability of so many plants to flourish after being transplanted into foreign soil. In this connection he also takes up man's attempts to improve plants by controlling the environment as he does in agriculture and horticulture.

In this section he also considers the role of plant life in human culture, the impact that plants have on man by appealing to his various senses and by contributing to his arts and sciences. This leads him to a discussion of man's study of plant life and the recent successes in that field of study. While the Aristotelean and scholastic philosophies ruled in Germany, he says, little was accomplished in botany or the other sciences. Then Descartes began to improve the sciences, the microscope was invented and in Germany, Christian Wolff improved even on Descartes. In the concluding chapter of the book, he raises the problem of nomenclature in botany and makes suggestions for a more natural system. He again asserts that botany is now flourishing in all of Europe and especially in Germany.

The last book concentrates on the utility of plants especially for man, but also for animals and insects. He goes into this matter with considerable detail and, though he belabors the point, conveys many facts and much information.

Religious themes, of course, pervade the text; it is, after all, a physico-theology. There are praises of God at the end of most chapters, constant references to God's design and attempts to see a divine purpose in practically every natural phenomena. This theology, however, provides no more than a frame and the text can indeed stand on its own merits as a work of popular science.

The poet of physicotheology, Brockes, has a place in this text also, and in fact von Rohr calls him the greatest poet of the times (130). Von Rohr himself makes an attempt at physicotheological poetry with a seven stanza poem on insects (530—531).

Johann Heinrich Zorn's Petinotheologie

From the preface and the introduction to Zorn's *Petinotheologie* it becomes clear that the author was as much an amateur scientist as he was a clergyman.[15] In the preface by Johann Peter Reusch, a professor of philosophy at Jena, Zorn is praised for his skill in observing nature and for his diligence in collecting specimens. Zorn, himself, declares in his introduction that God reveals himself to man through his senses and reason if only he will learn to use them correctly.

Zorn uses the introduction to clarify his reasons for preparing this voluminous study on birds. He wishes to lead men to a recognition of God, to combat atheists and also to teach science to the layman: "Meine Haupt Absicht ist, nicht nur Gelehrten, sondern auch Ungelehrten zu schreiben, und auch diese durch nähere Betrachtung der Vögel, auf eine leichte und begreiffliche Art, zum Schöpffer anzuführen, und also hauptsächlich bey der Natur-Lehre zu bleiben, so ferne dieselbe einem jeden begreifflich ist" (27). He is quite emphatic when he asserts the value of books of this kind for the dissemination of science: "Es ist gewiss, dass Bücher dieser Art in gewissem Verstande mehr zur Ausbreitung der Wissenschafften beytragen, als die, welche nach der schärffesten mathematischen Lehr-Art geschrieben sind" (27).

The bulk of the seventy page introduction consists of a bibliography of 165 books about birds from antiquity to the present. The majority of the works were written during the preceding 200 years. Most of the titles are in Latin, German titles are second in frequency, with a few English and French titles. With some of the rarer, inaccessible works he gives a table of contents with explanatory comments. Throughout these two volumes, encompassing 1350 pages, there is ample evidence that the author used his own first-hand observations and consulted the best scientific works available.

As an introduction to ornithology for the layman Zorn's efforts are undoubtedly highly successful. The classification and presentation of the subject matter are clear throughout and easy to follow by a beginner in the discipline. The first volume deals with the more general properties and circumstances of birds, whereas the second volume concentrates on individual species. In the first volume we read about the instincts of birds: the reproduction of species, the building of nests, migratory habits. He examines the structure of birds, the parts of their bodies and their functions, such as digestion, reproduction, flying. One of the longest sections is devoted to a study of chick embryos, with the differences of each day noted with precision and detail. Embryologists such as Harvey and Malpighi are cited frequently. In volume two he goes into detail about the differences between the species. He enumerates the differences

---

15 *Petino-Theologie, oder Versuch die Menschen durch nähere Betrachtung der Vögel zur Bewunderung, Liebe und Verehrung ihres Schöpfers zu ermuntern.* Two volumes (Vol. I, Pappenheim, 1742; Vol. II, Schwabach, 1743).

according to exterior and interior parts of birds; he notes different habits, ways of singing, building nests etc. He also devotes detailed attention to bird species native to Germany, covering over one hundred species. Beyond a doubt, the work's importance lies in the quantity and quality of its scientific material. As in most physicotheological compendiums we find here also a sociological section, namely a study of the uses and misuses of birds by man and the functions of birds in the pagan, Jewish and Christian religions. Naturally, Biblical quotations abound, attention is called to birds mentioned in the Bible and physico-theological reflections reappear frequently. The work concludes with a passage from a Brockes poem.

Johann Gottfried Ohnefalsch Richter's Ichthyotheologie

Ichthyotheologie, oder Vernunft- und Schriftmässiger Versuch die Menschen aus Betrachtung der Fische zur Bewunderung, Ehrfurcht, und Liebe ihres grossen, liebreichen und allein weisen Schöpfers zu führen (Leipzig, 1754) is by Johann Gottfried Ohnefalsch Richter (? —1765), a clergyman. The preface by J.D. Titius, Professor of "Weltweisheit" at the University of Leipzig, contains several pertinent comments about the author and physicotheological writings in general. He lists the many natural phenomena that have already been treated by physicotheologies and commends Richter for adding fish to this list. These physicotheological writings, Titius maintains, increase our knowledge of natural phenomena. Nor is the teleological approach incompatible with scientific method; the search for final causes simply supplements our search for efficient causes. Finally, as regards Richter's labors, his many years of devoted study of water creatures, he raises the question whether a clergyman should not rather concern himself with philology than with science. He answers, "Die Philologie lehre uns die Worte in der Bibel, die Physik aber die wichtigsten Sachen in derselben verstehen" (preface 5). He points out that Richter's sources for the work are his own observations of fish, the writings of the best ancient and modern authors on the subject and the assistance he received from German and foreign scientists through an active correspondence.

The text is divided into a general and a specific part. The general part considers the structure and functions of fish, the uses of fish to man, the role fish play in the life and thought of man and the divine purposes that can be noted in the study of fish which then lead to recognition of God. He provides a list of all fish in oceans, seas and rivers that have come to his attention. In his theological reflections, he considers all the Biblical passages pertaining to fish. In the second part he considers twenty-five fish in detail. He describes their inner and outer appearance, indicates where they can be found, in which waters and areas of the world and discusses their individual and social habits. Finally, every fish receives the honor of a poetic description composed by Richter himself.

Several other physicotheological compendiums that follow patterns similar to those discussed above deserve to be mentioned. *Akridotheologie* by Ernst Ludwig Rathelf (1709–1768), a clergyman, was sufficiently well-known that it was translated into Dutch[16] and reviewed in Bodmer's *Freymüthige Nachrichten* of 1749.[17] In the preface the author reports that what prompted him to write this physicotheological study were the many reports of the invasions of locusts in Hungary, Poland, England and Germany. In the historical and scientific part of the work Rathelf relied on material drawn from ancient and modern authors who have described the location, movement and propagation of locusts. There are many physicotheological reflections and Biblical passages concerning locusts are explained.

Peter Ahlwardt (1710–1791), a professor of logic and metaphysics at the University of Greifswald wrote *Bronto-Theologie, oder vernünftige und theologische Betrachtung über den Blitz und Donner, wodurch der Mensch zur wahren Erkenntniss Gottes ... geführet werden kann* (Greifswald, Leipzig, 1745). The first part of the text presents what is known about thunder and lightning in forty-six paragraphs. The second part carries out the physicotheological design. The work was reviewed in the *Göttingische Zeitung von gelehrten Sachen* of 1745 (517–519), where we learn that the author had already written an academic publication on the subject of thunder and lightning, but an unusually heavy thunderstorm on April 12, 1744 had led him to present his knowledge of the subject within a physicotheological framework.

A sequel to Lesser's *Testaceo-Theologia* is *Kleine Beyträge zur Testaceotheologie, oder zur Erkenntniss Gottes aus den Conchylien* (Frankfurt, Leipzig, 1760) by Johann Hieronymus Chemnitz (1730–1800). He was a clergyman but also sufficiently well-known for his work in natural history to be elected to membership in the "Kaiserliche Akademie der Naturforscher". The text of this physicotheology is in the form of five letters, four of which are devoted entirely to the subject of conchology with one, the third letter, presenting the religious justification of the work in the form of physicotheological arguments. The fourth letter is a bibliography of books on conchology by German and foreign authors and the fifth is an account of collections of natural curiosities. The work

---

[16] *Akridotheologie, oder historische und theologische Betrachtungen über die Heuschrecken.* Two volumes (Hannover, 1748, 1750). The Dutch translation was by Peter Adrian Verwer (Amsterdam, 1750).

[17] *Freymütige Nachrichten von neuen Büchern* (Zürich, 1744–1763), edited by Johann Jakob Bodmer, pp. 369–370.

was reviewed with high praise in 1760 in *Briefe, die neueste Literatur betreffend.*[18]

Adam Gottlob Schirach's (1724–1773) *Melitto-Theologia, die Verherrlichung des glorwürdigen Schöpfers aus der wundervollen Biene, nach Anleitung der Naturlehre und Heiligen Gottesgelahrheit* (Dresden, 1767) is discussed by Lois Westen in her dissertation on the mythology of the bee.[19] In Schirach we once again have a clergyman who was also highly esteemed as a natural historian. According to Westen he was "one of the most ardent beekeepers of his day and not only wrote prolifically on the subject, but also founded the Upper Lusatian Beekeepers' Association and edited a journal on the subject" (22). His physicotheology received sufficient attention to be translated into French (La Haye, 1771) and into Italian (Brescia, 1774).

In Johann Samuel Preu (1729–1804) we have another clergyman who is as committed to modern science as he is to his religion. In his *Versuch einer Sismotheologie, oder physikalisch-theologische Betrachtung über die Erdbeben* (Nördlingen, 1772) he gives a historical account of opinions about the causes of earthquakes from the Babylonians to the present time. He leaves no doubt about his belief in the superiority of modern scientific method: "Nur die vielen Experimente und die durch richtige Induktion rechtmässig erworbenen allgemeinen Sätze von den Eigenschaften und Würkungen der Körper, setzte die spätern Naturlehrer in den Stand, solche Ursachen von der Erzeugung und den Folgen der Erdbeben anzugeben, welche die Probe der Untersuchung aushalten" (22). As in other physicotheological compendiums we find an extensive bibliography of books on his subject, a presentation of what he believes are the best scientific explanations, and physicotheological assurances — especially necessary in the case of earthquakes — that the discoveries of science reinforce our faith in a wise and good Creator.

A few final summarizing comments about these physicotheological compendiums and their authors. The subject matter is usually treated from three different points of view. First, there is the scientific point of view in which the authors present their own observations and those of other scientists; this is the part that contributed most to the diffusion of science. Secondly, there is the role that the natural phenomena in question play in human culture — what men think and imagine about it, how they use and misuse it. Thirdly the authors show how a contemplation of the specific natural phenomena leads to a recognition of God and His qualities. The first is the empirical search for efficient causes, and the second and third represent the teleological quest for final causes, for purpose in nature.

---

[18] (Berlin, 1759–1765), edited by Lessing, Mendelssohn, Nicolai. The review is letter 120, pp. 65–80.
[19] Westen, op.cit., pp. 262–266.

Some of the physicotheologians were amateur scientists who relied on their own observations, as well as the scientific literature: Lesser, Richter, Ahlwardt, Zorn, Schirach and Chemnitz. Others amassed their facts primarily from their voluminous reading: Fabricius, von Rohr and Rathelf. Most were clergymen: Lesser, Richter, Rathelf, Zorn, Schirach, Chemnitz, Heinsius and Preu. Others were scholars and university professors: Fabricius, von Rohr, Ahlwardt. Most of them supplement their works with bibliographies of scientific works on their subject. Most quote physicotheological poets, Brockes, Triller and Zell — expecially Brockes. A few make their own attempts at physicotheological poetry.

Now let us turn to Biblical science, a type of literature whose primary purpose is to demonstrate that Biblical passages pertaining to nature are in accordance with the findings of science. It has already been noted that physicotheology justifies God in nature and Biblical science justifies Him in the Bible in regard to the teachings of the new sciences. In the physicotheologies there were, of course, many references to Biblical passages involving natural phenomena. However, Biblical science seeks to explain these passages systematically and exhaustively.

Four works will be considered, two by the Swiss scientist, Johann Jacob Scheuchzer (1672–1733) and two by Johann Jakob Schmidt (1691–?), a clergyman. Scheuchzer handles his subject chronologically, that is, he provides a chapter by chapter commentary on the natural phenomena as they occur in the text. Schmidt, on the other hand, proceeds thematically, selecting a subject like physics or astronomy to deal with all Biblical passages belonging to that field.

Scheuchzer's Hiobs Naturwissenschafft

Johann Jacob Scheuchzer's first work on Biblical science is *Jobi Physica Sacra, oder Hiobs Natur-Wissenschafft verglichen mit der Heutigen* (Zürich, 1721). In the preface he considers the possibility of organizing his commentary systematically as it is done in the compendiums of science, according to the main fields such as astronomy, physics, natural history and anatomy; for, in Job a wide spectrum of natural phenomena is represented. However, he prefers the method of the running commentary to illuminate passages that mention natural phenomena as they occur.

Several examples can be given that illustrate Scheuchzer's method and show the kind of scientific information that a reader would learn from this book. Job XII, 8: "Oder / frag das Stäudlein der Erden / so wird es dich lehren . . ." brings Scheuchzer to reflect about plants in general, their reproductive functions and their anatomy. In regard to the latter, he refers to the work of Malpighi and Grew with the microscope: "Wer die Mühe nimmet / und insonderheit mit

Vergrösserungs-Gläseren nach einem Malpighio und Grew betrachtet die unvergleichlich künstliche Gestalt aller und jeder Theilen ins besonder / der Wurzeln / Stengeln / Stämmen / Ästen / Augen / Rinden / Blätteren / Blumen / Früchten / Nahrungs-und Lufft-Gefässen / der wird bald sehen / dass die Pflanzen ohne Ausnahm / so auf dem trockenen Land / in Bergen und Thäleren / in dem Meer / Seen / Flüssen / Brunnen / seyen ein ohnmittelbares Werk Gottes . . .? " (88)

The new astronomy is the subject of his commentary to Job XXII, 12: "Ist nicht Gott in der Höhe des Himmels? Siehe doch das Oberste der Sternen / wie sie so hoch stehen? " He explains many of the results of the astronomers' telescopic observations, as for example, the vast distances that the Copernican astronomers attribute to the stars:

Nun ist diese bisherige Rechnung nichts gegen der Weite der Fixsternen. Weilen diese sich in ihrer Situation, oder Grösse / nichts abänderen / die Erde mag in ihrem Jahrkreiss seyn / wo sie immer wil / so folget / dass dieser *orbis magnus* der Erde kaum als ein Pünctlein zurechnen gegen dieser ohnermesslichen Weite der Fixsternen / und kommen alle heutigen Copernicanischen Astronomi darinn überein / insonderheit nachdeme sie die Sternen durch gute Telescopia deutlich abgeschnitten gesehen / dass man sie wol halten könne vor so viel Sonnen / und zwahren / dass sie nicht in einem Umkreiss stehen / wie ehemahlen geglaubt worden / sondern je einer über den anderen / so dass wol Fixsternen seyn können / die so weit über den uns nächsten Sternen erhoben / als dieser von der Sonn selbst abstehet. (142—143)

His commentary to Job XXVII, 3: "Er setzet der Finsternuss ein Ende" is quite interesting. He interprets the passage historically by suggesting that the seventeenth century with its many inventions and discoveries has put an end to the preceding darkness. On the next two pages (181—182), he lists some of the outstanding scientists of the seventeenth century and their discoveries. Represented are: Galileo, Descartes, Leibniz, Newton, the Bernoullis, Cassini, Huygens, Hevel, Leeuwenhoek, Tschirnhausen, von Guericke, Torricelli, Pascal, Borelli, Boyle.

He uses Newton's color theory to explain Job XXXVIII, 24: "Durch welchen Weg das Liecht ausgetheilet / oder der Ostwind auf der Erden zertheilet werde? " He explains the dispersal of light in space according to Newtonian principles as he does the relationship of color to light:

Gehet die in meinem Text befindtliche Zertheilung des Liechts auf die Verschiedenheit der Sonnenstralen / und deroselben Beschaffenheiten / so öffnet sich insonderheit nach der neuesten Philosophie des Neuton ein Meer voller Wunder : da sehen wir / dass die Sonnenstrahlen nicht alle von gleicher Art / sondern unter sich ungleich / so zureden / gefärbet / und auf ungleiche Weise gebrochen und reflectiert werden; dass die / so stärker gebrochen werden / auch stärker zurückprellen; dass also das Sonnen-Licht bestehe aus rohten / gelben / grünen / blauen Stralen / nämlich in philosophischem Verstand; dass die Lichtstralen vielfältig zertheilet / gebrochen / und reflectiert werden in der inneren Substanz der Cörperen . . . (353).

Newton is again referred to in his commentary on Job XXXVIII, 33: "Bist du auch des Himmels-Lauff berichtet / dass du seine Ordnung auf Erden aufrichtest?" Here he directs himself against the writers of cosmogonies, especially the Cartesians, who explain the creation by mechanical causes. He claims the support of Newton by quoting a passage from his *Principia,* where Newton denies that the laws of gravitation which sustain the planets in their orbits were sufficient to put them there in the beginning (368).

In his preface he had alluded to a larger work he had practically finished, ". . . einen ganzen Commentarium über die Physicalischen und Mathematischen Texte H. Schrifft / Alten und Neuen Testaments . . ." (preface 4). That was undoubtedly his *Physica Sacra* to which we shall now turn.

Johann Jacob Scheuchzer's Physica Sacra

Kupfer-Bibel, in welcher die Physica Sacra, oder geheiligte Natur-Wissenschaft derer in Heiliger Schrifft vorkommenden natürlichen Sachen deutlich erklärt und bewährt (Augsburg, Ulm, 1731—1735), is Scheuchzer's masterpiece about Biblical science. The work consists of six large folio volumes elaborately illustrated, of which the first five deal with the Old Testament and the last with the New Testament. The task Scheuchzer set himself in this work was to explain all natural phenomena referred to in the Bible according to the findings of modern learning. This included material pertaining to astronomy, physics, natural history, history, geography, architecture. As he had done in his earlier work, he proceeds through the Bible, verse by verse, explaining each phenomenon in turn.

A summary of the work in verse is given by Johann Martin Miller, a clergyman. He asserts Scheuchzer's intention to enlighten readers of the Bible, to illuminate passages they might misconstrue and generally to teach his readers to use their senses and reason to get a better grasp of God's wisdom in the Bible. To achieve this goal, Scheuchzer's immense learning will be applied, which Miller describes as follows:

Er hat sich gross bemüht, drey Reiche durchzuwandern,
Kennt Pflantzen, Mineral und Thiere eins vom andern.
Die Medicin belehrt den Abdruck Gottes kennen,
Kranckheiten samt der Cur mit eignen Namen nennen.
Mathesis zeigt die Stern, des Himmels Krafft und Lauf,
Die Zahl- und Messe-Kunst lösst Zweifel-Knoten auf.

Die Bau-Kunst stellet er Grund-mässig für die Augen,
Die Werckzeug-Regeln, so zu gröster Würckung taugen;
Das Zeit-Buch der Geschicht von alt- und neuen Sachen,
Kan sein Erklärungs-Fleiss uns allen nutzbar machen.
Die Quell und Eigen-Art der Sprachen weiss er richtig,
Und bringet den Verstand zu Bibel-Texten tüchtig.

Scientific explanations are especially frequent in his commentary to Genesis. He explains the Copernican and Ptolemaic systems and clearly decides for the former. Diagrams are provided and the relative sizes and distances of heavenly bodies lead to frequent digressions in the area of natural history. He enumerates metals, stones, plants and animals; there are elaborate copper plates of insects, birds, mollusks. In discussing Noah's flood, he mentions Burnet's theory and gives an account of Whiston's cometary theory, but maintains that the flood was a miracle and cannot be explained by natural causation. As evidence of the flood, he discusses fossils at length.

Though the work was too expensive to be owned by many people, it was known and respected among the learned. With this work, Scheuchzer placed his reputation as a scientist and theologian in support of attempts to harmonize the traditional religion and the new learning, thereby defending the new learning against the attacks of the orthodox.

Johann Jakob Schmidt's Biblischer Physicus

Johann Jakob Schmidt states the purpose of his *Biblischer Physicus*[20] in the preface to the work. Natural science is useful and necessary as are the other sciences for the explication of Scripture. The explicator of the Bible must have at least a moderate familiarity with scientific matters to avoid false explanations. In this book the author intends to illuminate many verses of Scripture pertaining to natural phenomena. He does not intend to teach science from the Bible or derive scientific principles from the Bible. He does, however, provide explanations of natural phenomena according to the newer philosophy and its experiments and observations, though only as much as is necessary to explain the passages in Scripture.

He distinguishes his work from physicotheologies and works that lead readers to God through nature. Though these works also cite Biblical passages, they are not nearly as comprehensive and encyclopedic as the present work. It is

[20] *Biblischer Physicus oder Einleitung zur Biblischen Natur-Wissenschaft ... zur Erkänntniss und Preiss des Schöpffers und zum rechten Verstande der Heiligen Schrift, sofern dieselbe irgendwo von physicalischen Dingen handelt, aus dem Grund-Texte ... vorgetragen, auch mit der heutigen gründlichsten Philosophie verglichen ...* (Leipzig, 1731). A second edition appeared in 1748.

Schmidt's intention to list all or most natural phenomena that occur in the Bible organized according to the structure of scientific texts and compendiums. This is what he means by Biblical science. Furthermore, Biblical science is to lead to a better understanding of both Scripture and science and a demonstration that the two are not at variance.

He begins with Biblical passages pertaining to the properties of nature in general, then those dealing with the creation of the world and the heavenly bodies, the latter rather briefly since astronomy is covered thoroughly in his *Biblischer Mathematicus*. After cosmic matters, he turns to the earth and examines Biblical passages involving natural phenomena above, about, in and on our planet earth and finally those that deal with the life sciences, that is, plants and animals.

He carries out his purpose as stated in the preface with consistency. Brief accounts of each natural phenomenon are given, followed by lengthy enumerations of the Biblical passages in which that phenomenon occurs.

In the section dealing with the earth sciences, he shows his modernity by giving an elaborate Newtonian account of rainbows complete with diagrams. Newton is referred to as the "scharfsinnige und grundgelehrte Naturkundiger" (108). However, he rejects completely the speculations of Burnet and Whiston who try to explain or clarify by natural causes acts of God such as the creation and the flood. He follows the orthodox position by neither accepting Whiston's theory that the Genesis account of creation applies only to the earth, nor Burnet's theory that the original figure of the earth was radically different from what it is now, nor attempts to explain the flood by natural causes such as the passage of a comet or a sudden cessation of the earth's diurnal rotation or a subterranean fire. He is generally cautious about speculative physical theories. In his discussion of tides, he avoids both the Cartesian and Newtonian explanations and contends that the cause is unknown though it has been established that there is a correspondence between tides and the moon's orbit.

In the preface he had commented that he considers the present work as a complement to his previously published *Biblischer Historicus*,[21] for there he had not considered natural history. Indeed, more than two thirds of *Biblischer Physicus* is a natural history of stones, gems, metals and minerals, plants and animals found in the Bible. He lists twenty-five precious stones mentioned in the Bible, comments on their appearance and their locations according to the natural historians and lists the Biblical passages where they occur. By far the largest part of the book deals with plants and animals. He refers to the studies on plant anatomy of Malpighi, Grew and Leeuwenhoek with their microscopes, briefly discusses parts and functions of plants and then gives a lengthy enumeration of plants mentioned in the Bible. Even more extensive is the section on animals. He

---

21 *Biblischer Historicus* (Leipzig, 1728; second edition, Leipzig, 1740).

again discusses parts and functions of animals and then turns to specific animals in the Bible. The result is a surprisingly long natural history of animals, subdivided into quadrupeds, birds, worms and snakes, insects and fish. The perspective, presented by this text, over the number and variety of species of stones or plants or animals found in the Bible, is striking and illuminates this aspect of the Bible very well.

Johann Jakob Schmidt's Biblischer Mathematicus

Biblischer Physicus was followed by *Biblischer Mathematicus*[22] in which Schmidt assembled all the Biblical passages that in any way involve mathematics or mathematical principles. He follows the mathematicians of his time in dividing his subject into seven areas: "Biblische Arithmetica", "Biblische Geometrie", "Biblische Statica", "Biblische Architectur", "Biblische Astronomie", "Biblische Horographie" and "Biblische Optica". In the first of these, for example, he solves more than a dozen numerical problems such as "Wie die Kinder Israel die kurtze Zeit in Egypten sich so vermehren konnten, dass sie von 70 Seelen, auf 600000 Man angewachsen? Exod. 12, 37. coll. Gen. 46, 27" (39). The "Biblische Architectur" presents most interesting conjectures, based on the Biblical text, concerning structures such as Noah's ark, the tower of Babel, Solomon's temple with illustrations and diagrams to prove their architectural feasability.

Of primary interest to this study is the section on astronomy, a subject which Schmidt had only touched in his *Physicus*. Next to architecture, he tells us, astronomy is the field of mathematics that occurs most frequently in the Bible. Indeed, his discussion of astronomy in the Bible once again illustrates the richness and variety of its subject matter.

In this section he again follows the order prevalent in the science books. He begins with general considerations about the universe, then the sun, moon, planets, fixed stars, new stars, comets, and eclipses are taken up. In each chapter he presents the views, facts and figures of modern astronomers and discusses the Biblical passages where the specific subject is mentioned.

The picture of the universe he presents is entirely modern with the one exception that he does not consider the Copernican system as fully demonstrated. At the same time, he describes it at length, grants its advantages over other systems and does not believe it contradicts Scripture. Thus his position is one of caution in regard to both religion and science.

In all other respects he shares the opinions of his contemporaries. He is

---

[22] *Biblischer Mathematicus oder Erläuterung der H. Schrift aus den Mathematischen Wissenschaften* ... (Züllichau, 1749). The first edition appeared in 1736.

especially eloquent in describing the enormous distances between heavenly bodies, their sizes and numbers. Each of the vast number of stars is a sun about which planets like ours orbit and which most likely are inhabited by living creatures. Through the telescope we constantly perceive new stars; we see, for example, that the milky way, "Galaxia," is nothing more than a collection of countless stars densely grouped together.

In his discussion of the sun, he pauses over the implications of sun spots, he marvels at the speed of light and decidedly rejects Descartes' opinions about light and heat. In regard to the moon, he again follows his contemporaries by deducing the presence of mountains, valleys, seas and an atmosphere on the moon from the way light is reflected and refracted. All this assures him of the likelihood of the moon's inhabitation. He grants that Scripture says nothing about this, but the Bible, he adds, is silent about many things which are apparent to our senses.

Schmidt wrote altogether five works on Biblical science. In addition to those already mentioned, namely, *Biblischer Physicus, Biblischer Mathematicus, Biblischer Historicus,* he also wrote *Biblischer Geographus* (Züllichau, 1740) and *Biblischer Medicus* (1743).

This concludes the discussion of Biblical science. Though Biblical science did not contribute as much to the diffusion of science as physicotheology, it did serve to legitimatize the new science in the minds of the pious and orthodox by demonstrating repeatedly that the Bible was in accord with the new learning.

The physicotheological literature, taken now in its broadest sense to include the various types of works discussed in the section, played a role in the religious apologetics and polemics of the time against atheists, naturalists and deists who questioned the transcendence of God and the divine authorship of the Bible and asserted the autonomy of nature. Yet it is doubtful that this literature was highly effective in this respect. Philosophically these writings are not very convincing; nor do they add anything new to theological arguments. After all, praising God in nature goes back to the Old Testament. Moreover, in attempts to harmonize science and religion, it was often God's wisdom and the Biblical text that were adjusted to the scientific principle in question. Rather, the physicotheological works were most effective and successful as popular didactic literature. This didacticism is an expression of the well-known optimism of the eighteenth-century enlightenment. Physicotheological literature is essentially optimistic. The authors have the utmost confidence in their enterprise. They know they are participating in a venerable and theologically acceptable tradition, and they know that the rapid development of the empirically oriented study of nature is making a nature accessible that is real, visible and beyond verbal and logical dispute. The layman, inadequate in the arena of philosophical and theological controversy, was eager to accept instruction and enlightenment that enhanced his dignity and did not conflict with his religious conscience. The physicotheological movement strengthened the Enlightenment and contributed to making the new learning accessible and acceptable to both the uneducated and the educated.

D. THE PERIODICALS

The discussions and bibliographies of eighteenth-century periodicals by Joachim Kirchner,[1] David A. Kronick[2] and Wolfgang Martens[3] demonstrate the extraordinary abundance of German periodicals in that century. Aside from the moral weeklies of which there were 180 in Germany by 1740,[4] there were literary, technical, scholarly and scientific journals of great variety. This profusion of periodicals existed in all parts of Germany. Quite a few journals were published at centers of learning like Leipzig, Berlin and Halle. Many, on the other hand, especially the review journals, had only a regional circulation. Many of them lasted only a few years, many had a small reading public and some were of doubtful literary quality. Nevertheless, they disseminated learning to all German speaking areas of Europe and must be considered one of the potent instruments of the Enlightenment in Germany.

Of interest to this study is the role that the periodicals played in the dissemination and popularization of the natural sciences. Of the many technical and specialized scientific journals in Germany in the eighteenth century, so ably discussed by Kronick, most appeared after 1750. Even before 1750, however, the number of these journals in Germany relative to England and France was considerable also. One example is Johann Kanold's *Sammlung von Natur und Medizin* . . . (Breslau, 1718–1736). It was a collaborative effort by several physicians, members of the Academia Naturae Curiosorum, to report observations of weather, agriculture and epidemics, to report medical and scientific discoveries and announce news of scientific societies.[5] However, it is not the technical specialized scientific journals we should like to discuss, but rather those journals that were directed toward the educated layman and which include scientific subject matter for the non-scientist, as well as the scientist. Of these I shall consider first several of the longer review journals whose purpose was to inform the reading public of the latest developments in the fields of learning including the natural sciences and, secondly, I shall consider at length several popular periodicals by men of letters who were interested in science and in teaching science to the layman.

Of the general review journals, I have examined the *Deutsche Acta Eruditorum* (Leipzig, 1712–1739),[6] its successor the *Zuverlässige Nachrichten*

[1] *Die Grundlagen des deutschen Zeitschriftenwesens* I (Leipzig, 1928) and II (Leipzig, 1931).
[2] *A History of Scientific and Technical Periodicals* (New York, 1962).
[3] *Die Botschaft der Tugend* (Stuttgart, 1968).
[4] According to Beck's "Verzeichniss der in deutscher Sprache herausgekommenen sittlichen Wochenschriften" in *Das Neueste aus der anmutigen Gelehrsamkeit* (Leipzig, 1761), pp. 829–841.
[5] See Kronick, pp. 78–80.
[6] Edited by Justus Gotthard Rabener, Christian Schöttgen and Johann Georg Walch.

(Leipzig, 1740–1757), the *Neue Zeitungen von gelehrten Sachen* (Leipzig, 1715–1784)[7] and the *Göttingische Zeitung von gelehrten Sachen* (Göttingen, 1739–1752).[8] I have also examined the theological review journal, *Unschuldige Nachrichten*,[9] and Johann Jakob Bodmer's *Freymütige Nachrichten*[10] which contain numerous reviews of popular scientific works. These review journals have been examined to see what kind of scientific works were selected and how they were reviewed. This has provided a picture of what the interested layman would learn of popular scientific literature from a consistent reading of the review journals.

Of German scientific writings reviewed there are the mathematical and astronomical works of J.B. Wiedeburg, J.G. Doppelmayr and A.G. Kästner and the popular astronomy works of J. Heyn and E.C. Kindermann; there are the medical works of L. Heister, G.E. Stahl and A. von Haller; in natural history we have the works of C. Mylius, J.L. Frisch, J.D. Denso, J.A. Rösel von Rosenhof, G.W. Knorr, M.F. Ledermüller, H.S. Reimarus and J.G. Sulzer; compendiums of science of C. Wolff, F. Maurer, J.J. Scheuchzer, J.C. Gottsched and J.A. Segner are reviewed; finally, the physicotheological works of J.B. von Rohr, F.C. Lesser, J.H. Zorn, J.G.O. Richter, E.L. Rathelf, J.J. Schmidt and J.G. Walpurger are also represented.

The works of the following non-German scientists were reviewed: in the field of natural history there are Swammerdam, Boerhaave, Trembley, Réaumur, Buffon, Grew and Needham; in mathematics and physics we have Newton, Huygens, Musschenbroek, Swedenborg, Bion, Gravesande, Nollet, Fay and Maupertuis; and of the popular writers, there are Whiston, Woodward, Derham, Nieuwentyt, Algarotti and Pluche.

This is by no means an exhaustive list, but it represents the authors who were relatively well known and whose works were reviewed repeatedly. With the exception of controversial writings like those of Whiston, Heyn and Kindermann, the reviews are positive. The reviewers, without an exception, subscribe to the methods and prospects of modern science. There is no cultural pessimism in the form of doubts as to the value of science and experimentation.

Review journals of this sort were found throughout Germany as, for example, at Altona (1745–1789), Erlangen (1749–1789), Dresden (1749–1801), Erfurt (1754–1796), Halle (1729–1810), Frankfurt (1736–1790) and Jena

---

7   Edited by Johann Gottlob Krause, from 1735 by Johann Burckhard Mencke and later by Otto Mencke.
8   Continued from 1753 to 1801 as *Göttingische Anzeigen von gelehrten Sachen* and 1802–1916 as *Göttingische Gelehrte Anzeigen.*
9   *Unschuldige Nachrichten oder Sammlung von alten und neuen theologischen Sachen, Büchern, Urkunden* (Leipzig, 1702–1761), Hrsg. von Valentin Ernst Löscher, ab 1751: von Joh. Elias Kapp und Joh. Rud. Kiessling.
10   *Freymüthige Nachrichten von neuen Büchern und andern zur Gelehrtheit gehörigen Sachen* (Zürich, 1744–1763).

(1749–1786).[11] We can expect, therefore, that through these journals, which frequently give very thorough and objective accounts of the books reviewed, information about scientific publications was disseminated in many parts of Germany.

Of popular periodicals by men of letters, those of the Gottsched school between 1740 and 1760 contain much significant scientific material. These periodicals were of good literary quality, they were edited by well-known men of learning and their reading public and influence were more than local. Included in this group are Schwabe's *Belustigungen*, Gottsched's *Neuer Büchersaal* and *Das Neueste aus der anmuthigen Gelehrsamkeit*, Kästner's *Hamburgisches Magazin* and Mylius' *Der Naturforscher* and *Physikalische Belustigungen*. We shall consider these periodicals at length, for they are excellent examples of the attempts that were being made during our period to assimilate the natural sciences into liberal or humane learning.

Belustigungen des Verstandes und des Witzes

Belustigungen des Verstandes und des Witzes (Leipzig, 1741–1745) edited by Johann Joachim Schwabe (1714–1784) is a periodical mentioned in every history of German literature because of the role it played in the controversy between Gottsched and Bodmer and Breitinger. As an organ of the Gottsched circle, it contains contributions from his students and followers. My concern is not with the literary controversy between Gottsched and the Swiss, but with the large quantity of popular science material whose presence in the periodical has not been given proper attention. There are thirteen rather lengthy didactic or reflective poems and twelve essays of literary merit, containing a variety of scientific themes and subjects. I shall consider first the poems and then the essays, indicating briefly the scientific material in each.

In the January, 1742 issue there is Christoph Friedrich Neander's (1724–1802) "Grösse des Schöpfers in dem Weltgebäude", a didactic poem of ninety lines in which the youthful author exhorts his readers to recognize God in the works of nature. To do so one should first rise beyond the limitations of our perspective on earth and with our thoughts attain a cosmic perspective of the millions of suns and worlds. This reduces our planet and its inhabitants to insignificance, yet helps us to conceive of God's greatness. From this vast perspective he turns to our solar system and marvels at the sun, "O güldner Mittelpunct! du Herz von jenen Kreisen, / Worinn in steter Flucht sich sieben Welten weisen" (40). The sun is the heart of the universe and through its light transmits life to every corner:

11 See Kronick, p. 160.

Wer hat in deinen Stral die Zeugungskraft gesenkt,
Und Wärme, Farb und Licht in ihm so schön vermengt?
Ja, wie erstaunt sieht man ihn durch viel tausend Meilen
Und fast im Augenblick zu dunkeln Körpern eilen? (40)

In the last two lines we have an example of the modern view of light, a substance traversing space, having supplanted the Cartesian view of light as impulses transmitted through the aether. In the concluding lines, he turns to natural phenomena on earth, all evidence of God.

In the anonymous "Philosophische Gedanken" (February, 1742), God is recognized as the source and preserver of all things. The smallest creature on earth, as well as the vast heavenly bodies are examples of God's wisdom. Only after death will our science be complete and only then will we grasp the true relationship of things.

In the April, 1742 issue, there is a two hundred line poem by Johann Elias Schlegel addressed to Kästner, "Dass die Mathematik einem Dichter nützlich sey". Mathematics and poetry have much in common as Leibniz understood very well:

Mein Kästner, jener Geist, den England selbst verehrte,
Und der den kleinsten Theil unendlich theilen lehrte,
Selbst Leibniz hielt für sich die Dichtkunst nicht zu klein,
Und pries den Phosphorus in prächtigem Latein,
Verliess die Algebra mit Wurzeln und Potenzen,
Und fühlte Gluth und Gott, und mass der Verse Grenzen. (337)

Nevertheless too many believe, "Wer die Eklipsen kennt, den kennt Apollo nicht" (337). He offers several examples to show that similar rational principles underlie both poetry and mathematics. Furthermore, the poets must know mathematics, that is, astronomy, to avoid the mistakes of the ancients who did not know the true order of the cosmos:

Wer vom Saturnus spricht, muss wissen, was er nennt;
Und niemand denket gut und richtig von den Sternen;
Er muss die Wissenschaft der Himmelskörper lernen. (341)

By asserting the rational common denominator of poetry and mathematics, he emphasizes the rationality of poetry in the spirit of the Gottsched school. Also in the spirit of Gottsched is that the poet be aware of the latest discoveries, so that he can use his images taken from nature correctly.

In "Die engen Schranken der menschlichen Wissenschaft" (September, 1742), an anonymous poet surveys the sciences, astronomy, the earth sciences and the life sciences to show that man has no real knowledge of the fundamentals. He begins with the heavenly bodies:

Bestimmt die Zahl von jenen Sternen!
Wir möchten mit Gewissheit lernen,
Was für ein Triebwerk sie bewegt?
Was sie im Luftraum schwimmend trägt?
....
Erzählt uns der Kometen Menge!
Zeigt ihren Nutz, bestimmt die Länge,
In der ein jeder seine Bahn
So ordentlich durchlaufen kann. (196)

Perhaps knowledge is possible only when it is confined to our immediate earth. But do we really understand the nature of gravity, light, fire? Do we know how stones and metals come to be and how the magnet has its mysterious qualities? Then he turns to animals and asks whether we understand their ways:

Wollt ihr sie bloss Maschinen nennen?
Wird sie ein Trieb so lenken können?
Wie oder wirkt allhier Verstand?
Das alles ist euch unbekannt. (198)

He concludes that since man knows so little of the world about him and of himself, he should recognize that it is his first duty to know God and practice virtue.

"Die Gränzen der menschlichen Vernunft" by M.G. (December, 1742) in contrast to the previous poem does not emphasize the insufficiency of human science. Man indeed has discovered natural laws in the heavens and on earth and can be justly proud. It is also within the capacity of reason to deduce the existence of God from a contemplation of nature. Man, however, transcends his limitations if he tries to understand why and how God created the world.

In "Der Mangel der Gründlichkeit in den Wissenschaften" (January, 1743), Carl August Gebhardt grants the success of human reason in disproving false teachings and superstition:

Wenn ein geübter Geist der Welten Bau erklärt,
Und unsre Sonne nicht mit fernerm Lauf beschwert,
Den Aberglauben tilgt, beweist, dass die Cometen
Aus ihres Wirbels Luft verirrte Planeten,
Nicht Drohungszeichen sind . . . .(66)

The new astronomy with its heliocentric system in which comets are heavenly bodies with calculable orbits is used here as representative of the progress of modern science. He regrets that these successes have led to doubts about matters of faith. Though man has made many discoveries, his knowledge will always be limited. Therefore, he should not overestimate the value of science and should not allow false pride to deflect him from faith and virtue.

By the same poet we have "Gedanken bey der Anschauung vieler Welten", (April, 1743), in which the contemplation of the plurality of inhabited worlds reminds the author of the insignificance of man and the folly of believing that God created all solely for man. This insight should lead man to God and to the further recognition that our knowledge of the world will be complete only after death.

In J.G. Harrer's "Einige Gegenstände der neuen Dichtkunst" (February, 1743), modern poets are exhorted to strive for the greatness attained by the ancients, by taking inspiration not from Gods and heroes but from nature and truth. The poet should rise to the vast spheres and see the many worlds and the possibility of even more. Of these things the modern poets should sing.

Christian Friedrich Zernitz (1717–1744), in his "Philosophische Gedanken über die göttliche Weisheit bey dem Sterben der Menschen" (April, 1743), demonstrates with many examples the balance and conservation in nature such that death is appropriate and a part of God's wisdom. His description of nature's processes is significant and will be discussed further in part II.

In March and May, 1744, appeared two long didactic poems by A.G. Kästner and Christlob Mylius on the subject of comets and their inhabitation. In his poem "Philosophisches Gedicht von den Kometen", Kästner explains the modern teaching concerning comets. He describes the views held about comets in antiquity and rejects them, as well as superstitious fears that comets bring misfortune. He begins his exposition of the modern teaching with a praise of Newton:

> Du, der unendlich mehr, als Menschen sonst gelang,
> Ins Innre, der Natur mit kühnen Blicken drang,
> O Newton! möchte doch, erfüllt von deinen Sätzen,
> Mein Lied der Deutschen Geist belehren und ergötzen. (280)

The basis of the modern cometary theory is Newton's universal gravitational force which applies also to planets:

> Dass sechzehn Welten stets in unverrrückten Kreisen,
> Im weiten Himmelsraum, um ihre Sonne reisen;
> Dass ein geworfner Stein, der durch die Lüfte dringt,
> Im Bogen aufwärts steigt, im Bogen wieder sinkt;
> Macht beydes eine Kraft . . . .(280–281)

The true orbit of comets was discovered by Newton, though it had already been measured earlier by the German, Samuel Dörfel:

> Des Sternes wahre Bahn blieb Keplern noch versteckt;
> Den Britten hat zuerst ein Newton sie entdeckt;
> Noch vor ihm hatte sie ein Deutscher schon gemessen:
> Doch Newton wird verehrt, und Dörfel ist vergessen. (281)

Kästner, however, rejects the possibility that comets are inhabited. He also considers the theories of Whiston and Heyn as possible but unconvincing. Mylius, on the other hand, affirms both the inhabitation of comets and Whiston's theory. The inhabitation of comets is the main subject of Mylius' "Lehrgedicht von den Bewohnern der Kometen" which we shall consider in part II with his other scientific poems.

In "Der Geist der Religion" (December, 1743), Johann Daniel Overbeck describes the sorry state of the Christian religion before Luther, and compares Luther's reformation of religion with the reformation Newton brought into science:

Wie Newtons heller Geist Welt, Körper und Natur
Weit klärer aufgedeckt, als die, die auf der Spur
Gelehrter Dichtungen, eh er dazu gekommen,
Sich durch diess weite Feld zu wandern vorgenommen;
Wie er manch Vorurtheil und übereilten Wahn
Und Schlüsse sonder Kraft behutsam abgethan,
Der Schulgelehrsamkeit aus klugem Rath vergessen,
Selbst allem nachgeforscht, selbst alles ausgemessen,
Bis er es überall im Dunkeln licht gemacht,
Und so der Wahrheit Grund recht in den Stand gebracht:
So macht es Luther dort . . . .(519)

Our poet emphasizes Newton's reliance on his own experimentation and measuring in his overthrow of the falsehoods of the past.

Finally, there is Christian Gottlieb Istrich's "Von der Nothwendigkeit der Messkunst in der Weltweisheit" (September, 1744). He demonstrates with several examples the importance of precise measurements to the philosopher's knowledge of the world. It is indispensable especially in astronomy:

Die Messkunst macht diess klar. Sie weis allein die Zeiten,
Die aller Umschwung braucht, untrüglich anzudeuten,
Lehrt, wenn ein Irrstern nicht, und wenn er völlig glänzt,
Und zeigt des Himmels Feld, das seine Bahn umgränzt. (196)

Now let us turn to the essays which contain scientific material. In the October, 1741 issue, we have the anonymous "Philosophische Muthmassungen von dem Aufenthalte der abgeschiedenen Seelen". The author entertains reflections on this question because, since the old Ptolemaic system of the world has been abandoned, there has been confusion as to the abode of departed souls. He maintains that after death the human being will undergo a metamorphosis such as can be seen in many animals and which takes place in man himself in the transitions from the invisible sperm to the fully grown person. In this new form, he will be able to move through space with the speed of light. It is not improbable, he says, that the vast areas between suns and inhabited planets will be the abode of these more perfect beings. Especially those who have lived a contemplative life like scientists and astronomers will rise to those heights and delight in seeing wholly what they previously saw only in part. The anonymous author believes he will be one of those, for throughout his life he has taken great joy in contemplating the universe according to the new discoveris of Copernicus, Kepler, Newton and Whiston.

In his essay in the March, 1744 issue, "Von dem Nutzen der zeitigen Erlernung der Naturlehre wider den Aberglauben", J.G.J. Breitkopf expresses his conviction that the best way to destroy superstition, which is simply based on ignorance of true causes, is by science. In this respect, Breitkopf maintains, we have an advantage over the ancients who were as children in the sciences. Future generations, building on our achievements, will be so advanced that they might even be able to contact other inhabited worlds and learn from their scientific achievements. In the essay, the author describes many superstitions and their harmful influences. He concludes with a plea to introduce science into the schools, for the earlier a child learns the true causes of things, the easier it is to eradicate superstitions.

In September, 1744, there is a satire, "Das Lob eines wildgewachsenen Baumgartens, in der Gesellschaft redlicher Verehrer der Natur" by "Sylvius, Freyherrn von Verwildern". It is a satire on the worshippers of nature who maintain that the spontaneity of nature in plants, animals and men should not be tampered with by human art. The speaker shows the absurdity of nature left to itself, especially in human society.

There are five essays with scientific subject matter by the young Abraham Gotthelf Kästner (1719–1800), whose fine literary style, clarity and wit seem already fully developed. In "Abhandlung von dem Einflusse der theoretischen Philosophie in der Gesellschaft" (July, 1742), he demonstrates the practical value of mathematics and science to human society. In his "Brief über den leeren Raum, bey Zurücksendung der Naturlehre der Marquise von Chatelet" (April, 1743), he shows that she followed Christian Wolff to a considerable degree. In this connection he taunts Voltaire who considered her a disciple of Newton. Kästner's wit is evident throughout the essay when he takes Voltaire to task for a number of things such as excessive reverence for Newton and disrespect for Wolff and the Germans in general. In his "Gedanken über eine neu angegebene Ursache von Newtons allgemeiner Schwere" (January, 1744), he reviews the work of George Andreas Müller who had attempted to explain the attractive force between two material bodies as being caused by an elastic, all pervading heavenly substance. Kästner rejects the author's thesis with a formidable display of wit. Another satirical essay by Kästner is his "Nachrichten aus der philosophischen Historie. Das ist: Thaten einiger Mondregentinnen." (November, 1744). He tells the history of philosophy from Aristotle to his own time with this allegorical tale of moon queens named, in the order of their appearance, Stagire, Fancyful, Monade and Atome. Stagire ruled over the empire Reasoning for a very long time until Fancyful, brought up in the province Measuring, took over the government. In this vein he continues his fable, which he placed in the moon because Ariosto had said that everything lost on earth, especially reason, can be found on the moon. In his essay "Gedanken über die Hypothesen in der Naturlehre" (May, 1745) on scientific method, he distinguishes between valid and invalid hypotheses. He is very much aware that the misuse of hypotheses, as in the case of Descartes, can impede science, and their proper use benefit it. As a useful hypothesis he cites Kepler's conjecture that the orbits of planets are elliptical. His discussion of hypotheses is quite modern. Yet, in his last example, electricity, he violates one of his own principles, namely, hypothesizing before sufficient observations have been made.

Finally, there are three essays with scientific themes by Christlob Mylius, which shall be discussed at greater length in part II. There is his "Betrachtung über die Majestät Gottes . . ." (November, December, 1743) in which he surveys the kingdoms of nature and stresses the necessity of science for a recognition of God in nature; there is his "Untersuchung, ob die Thiere um der Menschen willen geschaffen sind", (October, 1744) in which he describes the richness and manifoldness of the animal kingdom; and then his "Gedanken von dem Zustand der abgeschiedenen Seelen" (January, 1745), where he develops the popular theme of the ascent of souls to other heavenly bodies after death.

With this large quantity and variety of scientific themes and subjects in prose and poetry, the *Belustigungen des Verstandes und des Witzes* is unique as a literary periodical. It undoubtedly reflects the perspective of Gottsched according to whom the natural sciences receive full membership in the community of liberal learning and who, furthermore, sees a rational basis common to the arts and the sciences.

Now let us turn to Gottsched's periodicals. We have already seen some of Gottsched's efforts as a popularizer of science in his translations and his very popular compendium of science. What has been overlooked by all his biographers is that he continued his efforts as a popularizer of science in the 1740's and 1750's as editor of *Neuer Büchersaal der schönen Wissenschaften und der freyen Künste* (Leipzig, 1745—1750) and *Das Neueste aus der anmuthigen Gelehrsamkeit* (Leipzig, 1751—1762). In his earlier periodicals, *Die Vernünftigen Tadlerinnen* (Leipzig, 1725—1726) and *Der Biedermann* (Leipzig, 1727—1728), there are only occasional references to scientific themes. It is in the later periodicals that he makes a conscious effort to present scientific material as an integral part of liberal learning.

Neuer Büchersaal der schönen Wissenschaften und der
freyen Künste

In the preface to his *Neuer Büchersaal,* Gottsched justifies his new periodical. Due to the tremendous increase and expansion in all fields of learning, monthly journals, in increasing numbers, have been founded to enable the learned to keep abreast of the latest works in their respective fields. In addition to medical, theological and juridical periodicals there have been "critische, exegetische, homiletische, öconomische, chymische, moralische und viele andere Monatschriften . . ., deren Anzahl fast nicht zu bestimmen ist" (4). Gottsched grants the necessity and value of these specialized journals; yet he believes there is room for the present one which does not specialize in any one area but devotes itself to "die schönen Wissenschaften und freyen Künste" which include "ausser der Dichtkunst und Beredsamkeit, auch die Geschichte, die Alterthümer, die Musik, die Malerkunst, ja selbst die Sprachkunst" (7). This periodical is directed toward those whose interest in learning is not professional, who pursue their interests purely for the sake of amusement and enlightenment. Therefore, the periodical will discuss subjects and books from many fields and many countries. It is of significance to this study to note the many scientific subjects that appear in a periodical of this sort. It is evidence of the extent to which the sciences were being assimilated into the community of letters.

In this periodical, as well as the one that superseded it, Gottsched shows much interest in scientific societies and their publications. His comments are especially interesting because of his sense for the history of institutions, his interest in the spread of science and in the contributions of German scientists.

In 1746 (Vol. III, 72–81, 209–219) of the *Neuer Büchersaal,* he reviews the *Histoire de l'Academie Royale des Sciences et des belles Lettres de Berlin Année 1745* (Berlin, 1746). Gottsched discusses the history of this Berlin Academy from its beginnings to its decline and subsequent rejuvenation in 1744. He criticizes the use of French for the current proceedings of the academy. Latin had been the language of the academy's previous publications, but now French has been substituted, because it is claimed that French has become the language of learning and that all good books are translated into French. Gottsched disputes this emphatically. In the northern countries and Poland, French is by no means so widespread among the learned. Moreover, many good English, German, and Italian books have not been translated into French. He hopes at least that these proceedings will find a German translator in the near future. In the second part of the review (Vol. III, 209–219) he discusses the academy's scientific experiments and contributions, most of which were by German scientists such as Johann Nathanael Lieberkühn (1711–1756), Christian Friedrich Ludolff (1707–1763), Johann Theodor Eller (1689–1760), Leonhard Euler (1707–1783), Johann Kies (1713–1781), Johann Heinrich Pott (1692–1777), and Andreas Sigismund Marggraf (1709–1782). Gottsched, always eager to point out German scientific achievements, asserts in his summary of Kies' work on cometary orbits, that it was a German, Georg Samuel Dörfel (1643–1688) who first discovered the true orbits of comets, several years before Newton.

In 1748 (Vol. VII, 99–117) and 1750 (Vol. X, 99–109) of the periodical, he reviews the work of the Berlin Academy for the years 1747 and 1748, again pointing out that most of the contributions in the science and mathematics sections were by Germans.

In 1748 (Vol. VII, 291–305), he reviews the German translation of the scientific sections of the Royal Academy of Sciences in Paris for the years 1692, 1693, 1699, 1702.[12] He considers the translation of the proceedings of a scientific academy an especially worthwhile activity. He refers to the many scientific societies in existence and maintains that this eagerness for the sciences is a characteristic of the times and distinguishes the moderns from the ancients. He does not fail to mention the role of science in Germany: "Nun hat es zwar in Deutschland, seit mehr als einem Jahrhunderte, an gelehrten Naturforschern auch nicht gefehlet. Allein man weiss wohl, dass die wenigsten dieser gelehrten Männer sich bisher auf ihre Muttersprache geleget haben" (295). He regrets that the *Acta Academiae Naturae Curiosorum* were written in Latin, while the proceedings of the societies in Italy, London and Paris were published in their native languages. He hopes that the example of Sturm, Tschirnhausen and Wolff, who wrote scientific works in German, will be followed more and more.

His discussion of the Danzig Academy of Sciences in 1748 (Vol. VII, 387–406) is of interest. Already in 1670 Danzig scientists formed a society which, however, lasted only a few years. In 1720 another attempt was made and finally in 1742 the present society was founded. They immediately began to gather their scientific equipment and started with regular meetings in 1743. Most of the fifteen scientific treatises in the first volume of the society's proceedings were by well known Danzig scientists, such as Heinrich Kühn (1690–1769), Jacob Theodor Klein (1685–1759), Michael Christoph Hanov (1695–1773) and Daniel Gralath (1708–1767). Gottsched expresses satisfaction that this society published its proceedings in German.[13] In this review he also mentions that the "alethophilische Gesellschaft" in Stettin has exerted great efforts to accumulate scientific equipment for the purpose of conducting experiments.

Of interest are also the reviews of scientific works. In 1746 (Vol. III, 314–328) there is a discussion of Gerhard Andreas Müller's *Untersuchung der wahren Ursache von Newtons allgemeiner Schwere,* (Weimar, 1743). Müller has a

---

12 *Der Königlichen Akademie der Wissenschaften in Paris, physische Abhandlung, erster Theil,* "welcher die Jahre 1692, 1693, 1699, 1702 in sich hält, aus dem Französischen übersetzt von Wolfgang Balthasar Adolph von Steinwehr" (Breslau, 1748).

13 *Versuche und Abhandlungen der naturforschenden Gesellschaft in Danzig* (Danzig, 1747).

unique conception of the aether, considering it denser than mercury but with a fluid elasticity such that the movements of bodies are not impeded. The reviewer gives a thorough and sympathetic account of these speculations, but makes it clear that he does not subscribe to them.

In 1747 (Vol. IV, 31—45) there is a review of Anton-Lazzaro Moro's *De Crostacei et degli altri marini corpi . . .,* (Venice, 1740).[14] In this work Moro maintains that marine animals and plants found as fossils on many mountains originally lived in the sea and became petrified when they were forced into their present locations by mountains rising out of the sea. He also tries to show the harmony between his explanation of the creation and the Genesis account. The reviewer describes the work in detail and concludes that it was a new cosmogony worthy to be placed next to those of Descartes, Burnet, Whiston and Woodward.

In the same volume (176—177), there is a description of a recent artificial model of the Copernican system by a German professor of mathematics, Jacob Woyten. Gottsched also reviews (325—335) an anonymous French work of 1745 which tries to refute the Copernican system. He expresses his surprise that such a book has been published, in view of the fact that the Copernican system has been taught for some time by astronomers in and out of Europe and has been accepted as the true system by the academies of sciences in Berlin, London, Paris and Petersburg. It is of interest to read his emphatic rejection of the author's contentions that Thorn, the birthplace of Copernicus, was in Poland:

> Der andre Fehler ist, dass er Thorn in Polen suchet, darinn es doch eben so wenig gelegen ist als Danzig, oder Elbing. Thorn ist vor fünfhundert Jahren, auf dem den alten Preussen zuständigen, und den Polen nicht unterworfenen Grunde und Boden, von lauter deutschen Colonien erbauet worden; allezeit, bis auf diese Stunde von lauter deutschen Leuten bewohnt, nach dem kulmischen, das ist einem ursprünglich in deutscher Sprache abgefassten Rechte regieret worden; und nur durch das Bündniss einiger Städte, die sich wider den deutschen Orden aufgelehnet, unter polnischen Schutz gerathen. Heisst denn das in Polen liegen? (335)

In 1747 (Vol. V, 155—199) Gottsched published two letters concerning Whiston's cometary theory as expounded by Johann Heyn. The correspondence is between Heyn and Georg Wilhelm Wegner, both clergymen, on the former's contention that a comet could come so close to the earth as to cause radical changes on its surface. Wegner joins Wiedeburg and Guttmann, the best known of Heyn's adversaries, as well as a host of others, in rejecting Heyn's astronomy and his attempt to find Biblical corroboration for it. Heyn replies, as usual, with much rhetoric, ingenuity and utmost conviction.

---

14 A German translation appeared under the following title: *Untersuchung der Veränderung des Erdbodens* (Leipzig, 1751).

In 1747 (Vol. V, 50–57) there is also a review of the German translation of 1746 of a Latin work on the origin of rivers by the German scientist from Danzig, Heinrich Kühn. In 1748 (Vol. VI, 114–119) there is a review of a French translation of John Needham's, *New Microscopical Discoveries* (London, 1745). The reviewer speaks of the microscopic world as a new world whose bounds we do not yet see. In this volume there is also a review of Jacob Theodore Klein's natural history of fish.

Of pertinence are the reviews of Melchior de Polignac's Latin poem, *Anti-Lucretius,* because of the considerable amount of scientific material it contains. The first Latin edition (Paris, 1747) was reviewed in 1747 (Vol. V, 387–405) and the German edition by Gottsched (Leipzig, 1748) in 1748 (Vol. VI, 458–471). The contents of these reviews have already been discussed in the section on translations.

The periodical also has one long anonymous poem, "Die Gottheit", containing some scientific themes. The poem, which appeared in 1746 (Vol. III, 513–520), resembles many of the poems of Brockes and his school. The poet tries to conceive God's qualities by contemplating His works, the largest and the smallest. The millions of suns in the heavens can not be counted nor the space in which they exist fathomed. But God, who created these immeasurable natural objects, is even more unfathomable. God's power and wisdom are also recognized in the intricate structures of His smaller works. The smallest creature, as well as the vast heavenly bodies, is a masterpiece and arouses amazement. This transition from the world of the telescope to that of the microscope is a favorite theme of the poets of the Enlightenment.

From this discussion of scientific material in *Neuer Büchersaal,* a periodical devoted to the liberal arts, we can see that for Gottsched the new sciences had been assimilated as a part of liberal learning and general education. The periodical also shows Gottsched's consistent efforts to enlighten the public on current developments in the world of science and encourage the cultivation of the sciences in Germany.

Das Neueste aus der anmuthigen Gelehrsamkeit

"Anmuthige Gelehrsamkeit" is the same area of learning that Gottsched described in his preface to *Neuer Büchersaal.* It includes books and interests that do not fall within the domain of the three faculties of learning at the universities. It also refers to the point of view of the reader for whom this periodical is intended. His interests are not professional. He seeks entertainment and amusement but at the same time enlightenment. The subjects covered in the periodical are, therefore, those that would interest an enlightened, educated man of the time. It is our task again to gather together the scientific material that is scattered throughout the twelve volumes from 1751 to 1762.

In these twelve volumes there are fifty items of scientific subject matter. There are reviews of German translations of scientific works and reviews of the proceedings of scientific academies, a few reports of scientific discoveries and observations and several poems with scientific content. These items will be discussed in that order with a focus on Gottsched's reflections, since his comments on the history and diffusion of science are of relevance to this study.

In 1751 (21–33) Gottsched reviewed the German translation of the first part of Buffon's *Histoire Naturelle* . . . (Paris, 1749).[15] Gottsched considers this one of the most important French works of the last twenty-five years, in view of the many wretched novels, tales and comedies that have come out of France in that time. He considers the German translation superior to the original, since the translator, in his notes, corrects the author's errors, among them a false evaluation of the classification of Linnaeus. He passes over Buffon's criticism of the systems of Whiston, Burnet and Woodward and notes only that Buffon's "nagelneue Hypothese", in which the origin of the planets is explained by a comet's impact on the sun, is hardly an improvement. He considers the translation beautiful and clear.

In 1756 (892–897) there is a report of a German translation of a work by Perrault, Charas and Dodart, whose German title is *Abhandlung der Naturge-schichte der Thiere und Pflanzen* (Leipzig, 1756). The reviewer praises the scientific study of nature as the most useful and entertaining occupation. Because no other study has found more enthusiasts than the study of nature, it has attained today's heights. Another reason for its success has been that scientists, as members of academies, have begun to specialize, as is the case with the authors of the present work. Perrault has focused on the description and dissection of animals and Dodart on the natural history of plants.

Of the many scientific works reviewed in these twelve volumes, only three more are by non-German authors. In 1752 (85–90) there is a review of *Philosophia Britannica. Or a new and comprehensive System of the Newtonian Philosophy* . . . (London, 1747) by B. Martin. Gottsched objects to the idea of attaching a philosophy to any particular nation. Always ready to stress German achievements, he cites the many German contributors to modern science.

The subject of German contributions to science is also discussed in the review (1752, 678–691) of an anonymous French work, *Progrès des Allemands dans les sciences, les belles lettres & les arts* . . . (Amsterdam, 1752). He agrees with the author that one important reason why German learning is not well known is because of the practice of writing in Latin, a fact which he regrets.

---

15 *Allgemeine Historie der Natur, nach allen ihren besonderen Theilen abgehan-delt,* . . . *Erster Teil* (Hamburg, Leipzig, 1750).

In the same year (748—764) there is a discussion of an unusual work which had become popular in France, *Telliamed, ou Entretiens d'un philosophe indien* . . . (Basel, 1749) by Benoît de Maillet. It is another cosmogony, the reviewer says, after those of Descartes, Burnet, Whiston, Woodward, Moro and Buffon. Among many other things, de Maillet maintains that fossils are due to the gradual evaporation of water, and that all land animals originally lived in the sea, which they left long ago as more and more water evaporated exposing more land. Under the mask of an Indian philosopher, he can ignore the Biblical account of the creation.

Of the fifteen German scientific works, ten belong to the field of natural history. In 1756 (218—226) there is a review of *Sämmtliche physikalische Beobachtungen* (Regensburg, 1753) by Jakob Christian Schäfer, a clergyman. Gottsched praises the author for having devoted his leisure hours to a study of nature. He praises this work on insects for its useful observations and beautiful German writings.

In 1755 (754—763) there is a consideration of *Kurzer Entwurf der königlichen Naturalienkammer in Dresden* (Dresden, Leipzig, 1755). The reviewer judges this collection the most remarkable one in Europe after the Paris collections. It contains specimens from all the realms of nature. He is also pleased that this report concerning the collection is written in German, since only very few are served by Latin works these days.

In 1757 (237—240) there is an announcement of a forthcoming botanical work, *Geschichte der Pflanzengattungen,* by Johann Gotthilf Müller. The announcement describes the paintings and engravings of plants that illustrate the text.

In 1758 (772—779) there is a vigorous defense of Martin Frobenius Ledermüller's essay on spermatozoa, *Versuch zu einer gründlichen Vertheidigung derer Saamenthiergen* (Nürnberg, 1758). Ledermüller (1719—1769), a lawyer by profession and a microscopist by avocation, had found that his microscopic observations supported Leeuwenhoek's discovery of the existence of seminal animalculi, which the French naturalist Buffon had attempted to refute. Equipped with his own observations and extensive knowledge of the microscope, Ledermüller was able to show that Buffon's opinions were based on an improper use of the microscope. Gottsched emphasizes Ledermüller's amateur status and delights in supporting him against the famous Buffon.[16] The following year Ledermüller began issuing monthly installments of his *Mikroskopische Gemüths-*

---

16 For a thorough account of Gottsched's relationship and correspondence with Ledermüller, see Emil Reicke, *Neues aus der Zopfzeit. Gottscheds Briefwechsel mit dem Nürnberger Naturforscher Martin Frobenius Ledermüller*.... (Leipzig, 1923). For an evaluation of Ledermüller's contribution to microscopy see Friedrich Klemm's "Martin Frobenius Ledermüller: Aus der Zeit der Salon-Mikroskopie des Rokoko," *Optische Rundschau,* Sonderdruck aus Nr. 45 bis 48, Jahrg. 1927 (Schweidnitz, 1928).

und Augenergötzungen (Nürnberg, 1760–1765), sections of which were reviewed in Gottsched's journal.[17] In welcoming the appearance of this work, the reviewer notes the growing current interest in natural history among both men and women and in all classes of society (1759, p. 56).

In 1759 (405–413) there is a review of *Sammlung von Muscheln, Schnecken und andern Schaalthieren* (Kopenhagen, 1758). This work was done on commission from the Danish king. Illustrations of the specimens were painted and engraved by Franz Michael Regenfuss. The text includes a bibliography of writings on conchology from the ancients up to 1758. There is also a list of Danish collections of mollusks and other natural curiosities. The reviewer expresses his surprise that there are so many people in Copenhagen with interest in this branch of natural history.

In 1760 there is a review of Hermann Samuel Reimarus' *Allgemeine Betrachtungen über die Triebe der Natur . . .* (Hamburg, 1760). In 1754 there had been a review of his work on natural religion in which, among other things, he examines God's design and intentions in the animal kingdom. In his later work, the animal world became the main subject. The reviewer notes Reimarus' care in accepting as valid only observations of animals in their natural habitat. He rejects studies of tame or captive animals. Thus the work is based on careful observations of the behavior of animals as they appear in nature. Much must still be done in studies of this sort, our reviewer says, and every interested person can make his contribution. Works such as these, the reviewer maintains, will soon force foreigners to learn German.

In 1761 (851–859) we have *Praktisches Mineralsystem* by Rudolf Augustin Vogel, a physician and member of several German and Swedish scientific societies. The reviewer praises the work for its good German writing and thorough systematic presentation of mineralogy.

In 1762 there is a discussion of Joseph Gottlieb Koelreuter's *Vorläufige Nachricht von einigen das Geschlecht der Pflanzen betreffenden Versuchen und Beobachtungen* (Leipzig, 1761), an important work on the sexual characteristics of plants.

Of German scientific works not dealing with natural history, we have Johann Christian Müldener's *Astronomischer und geographischer Begriff, von dem natürlichen Zustand unserer Welt- und Erdkugel,* reviewed in 1753 (289–295). In this work, which the author had published in 1729 under the pseudonym Geander von der Oberelbe, he teaches the fundamentals of astronomy, physics and natural history to a lady of high station.

In 1755 (358–365) there is a review of Kästner's *Vermischte Schriften* (Altenburg, 1755). The reviewer praises Kästner's industry in philosophy,

---

17 *Das Neueste aus der anmuthigen Gelehrsamkeit,* 1759 (154–158, 472–474); 1760 (85–91, 334–341, 654–662, 915–920); 1761 (574–582), 1762 (742–751).

mathematics and poetry. He considers his poem on comets especially good. It presents cometary theory in such a way that any layman can grasp it, and that is the task of poetry. As the reviewer puts it, "Das ist nun aber das Amt der Poesie, dass sie die Philosophie der grossen Welt werden . . . soll" (360). In 1758 there is also a review of a mathematics text for students by Kästner, which is to replace those of Christian Wolff in use during the past fifty years.

As in *Neuer Büchersaal,* the histories and proceedings of scientific academies are reviewed here also. It is again interesting to note the number of scientific contributions by Germans, which Gottsched does not fail to mention. We learn that German members of the Royal academy of sciences at Berlin made most of the contributions in science for the year 1748. Of the twenty-one scientific and mathematical contributions in the second volume of the proceedings of the Petersburg Academy of Sciences of 1751, the majority were made by German-born scientists (1753, 120–128). Part II of the scientific society at Danzig shows that the contributors were German speaking natives of the city (1754, 885–892).

There are also several reports of astronomical observations. In 1753 (375–377) there is a discussion of the anticipated transit of the planet Mercury in front of the sun on May 6, 1753. The reviewer lists the previous occasions when such a transit was observed in Germany. In 1631, 1661, 1677, 1697, 1707, 1723, 1736, 1743 transits of Mercury were observed in fifteen German cities. The May 2, 1743 transit of Mercury, he points out, was observed only by Prof. John Winthrop in New England. There are also several reports of comets sighted by German astronomers.

An astronomical event that aroused great popular interest was the transit of Venus on June 6, 1761. Gottsched reviewed three published works before the event and afterwards reported observations from Leipzig, Halberstadt, Magdeburg, Meissen, Frankfurt, Wittenberg, Dresden, Stockholm, Warsaw and Amsterdam. Of the three published works he reviewed, two were by Germans and one by the Englishman, James Ferguson. His review of the latter's work, *A Plain Method of determining the Parallax of Venus* (London, 1761), which he says had already been translated into German, is especially interesting. He uses the occasion to make a plea for the study of astronomy by all scholars. Since Fontenelle, he maintains, astronomy has become an essential part of "anmuthige Gelehrsamkeit". Therefore, since laymen and even the ladies are now familiar with this science, scholars can no longer neglect it. He then explains the fundamentals of astronomy in very simple terms, so that all will understand the anticipated transit of Venus: "Wir schreiben nicht für Astronomen, die solche Schriften selbst lesen, oder aus den lateinischen *Actis Eruditorum* einen weit genauern Auszug davon bekommen werden. Wir schreiben für Liebhaber der schönen Wissenschaften, die, da alle Zeitungsblätter von dem Durchgange der Venus durch die Sonne reden, doch gern einen deutlichen Begriff davon haben

wollen" (413). The explanation that follows is a good example of Gottsched's
attempt to teach science to the layman.[18]

In the periodical, there are also poems to be found occasionally, some of
which contain scientific material. The most interesting of these occurred in 1761
(417–420), when the editor was concerned with the transit of Venus. The title
of the poem is, "Warum die Vereinigung der Venus mit der Sonne nicht sichtbar
gewesen? Eine Fabel". In his report of the observation of the transit of Venus at
Leipzig, which was marred by poor visibility, the reviewer had said, "Ein
poetischer Beobachter, der die ersten zwo Stunden durch, vergeblich auf diese
Erscheinung lauerte, rächete sich an derselben durch folgende Fabel" (p. 417).
The fable, seventy lines in verse, is as follows: Apollo and Venus conceived a
passion for one another. Apollo was undaunted by the embarrassing episode
when all the Gods found Venus in the arms of Mars. As Apollo was about to
take Venus into his arms he noticed an intruder. This time it was neither Vulcan
nor any of the other Gods, but the prying eyes "des Prometheus Brut" in the
form of the English astronomer Jeremiah Horrox:

> Auch diessmal war Horocc, ein Sohn der kühnen Britten,
> Mit schlauer Neubegier der Venus nachgeschritten.
> Er hatt' es wohl bemerkt, dass Phöbus ihr gewinkt:
> Indem sie nun verliebt in seine Flammen sinkt,
> Wirds dieser Gott gewahr: dass mit verruchten Blicken
> Ein Sterblicher sich wagt auch Götter zu bestricken.
> So gleich entzieht er sich der Neugier schnöder Art
> So dass des Frevlers Blick beschämt zu Schanden ward. (419)

Horrox (1619–1641) was the first to observe a transit of Venus in 1639. The
poet tells us in a footnote that just as Horrox was about to observe the beginning
of the transit, the sun set. Nevertheless, the poem continues, Horrox saw and
told the entire world. Ever since, mortals have been spying on Venus and now
they have even prophesied that soon the lovers will meet; but Apollo, on his
guard, once more eludes observation with the help of a cloud:

> Man prophezeiht so gar, als ob man alles wüsste,
> Dass diess verliebte Paar, die kaum genossnen Lüste
> Bald wiederholen wird; dass Phöbus dann und wann
> Der Liebesgöttin Kuss von neuem ärnten kann:
> Sie hab ihm den Besuch in nächst verwichnen Wochen,
> Früh, auf den sechsten Tag des Brachmonds, fest versprochen.
> Nun lauscht der halbe Kreis der ehrvergessnen Welt,

---

[18] For a study of the significance of the transits of Venus in 1761 and 1769 and the
impact of these events on European science see Harry Woolf, *The Transits of Venus. A
Study of Eighteenth-Century Science* (Princeton, 1959).

Ob wirklich Phöbus sich die Schöne hinbestellt?
Allein der schlaue Gott lacht ob dem kühnen Volke,
Und deckt, als Venus kömmt, sein Fest mit einer Wolke. (420)

This fable signed G., presumably Gottsched, is indeed one of the most delightful examples of science in literature.

Of other poems with scientific themes, there is "Die beste Welt" an ode in twenty-seven stanzas, appearing in 1754 (109–114). In it there are many references to the vast cosmos and the millions of spheres that constitute the best world. In 1755 (591–593) there is a poem entitled, "Die unvergleichliche Aloe des grossbosischen Gartens zu Leipzig", in which the unusual characteristics of this "Fürstinn der Pflanzen" are described. In 1756 (270–279) there is "Betrachtung der immerwährenden Fürsorge und Regierung eines majestätischen Schöpfers" by A.G.F. Koltitz. The poet demonstrates that God's providence can be recognized in all the works of nature, but especially in the regular orbits of thousands of heavenly bodies in the vastness of space. "Die Wissenschaften" by Johann George Scheffner describes the origin and the growth of the arts and sciences in general, and in Germany and Danzig in particular.

In 1761 (441–451) there is a forty-seven stanza poem praising God in nature, "Ode auf die Betrachtung der Natur". In the beginning the poet contemplates nature in a garden. Then he turns to the heavens and with amazement and fright describes the vast boundless oceans of space and the stars and planets that follow their prescribed paths. Just as God is the cause of order in boundless space, so is He also the source of order on earth. The poet describes the regular transitions of the seasons of the year and the orderly reproduction of plants and animals always according to their own kind. His conclusion is that the presence of order in nature, as shown by astronomy and natural history, is proof of God, the Creator.

In 1758, two long didactic poems with scientific material are reviewed; the one (5–15), teaches the Cartesian system and the other (235–236), the Newtonian. In the former, an anonymous Italian poem, L'Adamo, overo il Mondo Creato, Poema filosofico, (Rome, 1737) an angel teaches Adam the entire Cartesian system of the physical world. The reviewer considers this enterprise fanciful, but finds that the didactic intent is carried out with some poetic talent. The other poem, written in Latin, is here given the German title, Die neueste Weltweisheit, in Verse gebracht, (Rome, 1756). It was by Benedict Stay, with notes by the famous Jesuit scientist R.G. Boscovich. The reviewer suggests that the reason why this work is not poetically as successful as Stay's earlier poem on the Cartesian system is that the fanciful qualities of the latter are more conducive to poetic exuberance than the natural truths found in the Newtonian system.

Finally, I should like to refer to the review in 1760 (61–67, 692–703) of the

German translation of Polignac's *Anti-Lucretius,* another long didactic poem
containing scientific material. In the section on translations, I discussed this
review, as well as those of the Latin editions which had appeared in *Neuer
Büchersaal* of 1747 and 1748.

Hamburgisches Magazin

Abraham Gotthelf Kästner, the editor of the *Hamburgisches Magazin,*[19]
belonged to the Gottsched school, though with considerable independence of
thought and judgment. Haller, for example, who was not favored by the
Gottsched people, was his favorite poet. This, however, did not cause a break
between the two men. When Kästner moved to Göttingen in 1756, he continued
to correspond with Gottsched. After the latter's death, he defended his former
teacher against his Swiss critics; his "Betrachtungen über Gottscheds Charakter"
was one of the few objective evaluations of the man and his work.[20]

During the 1740's in Leipzig, Kästner came under Gottsched's influence and
his literary activity then and afterwards was in the Gottsched spirit. That is true
of his didactic poems, his prose essays, his numerous translations of scientific
works,[21] his emphasis on the use of German in scientific writings and his stress
on German contributions to science. Like Gottsched, he is one of the great
popularizers of science in the Enlightenment.[22]

The *Hamburgisches Magazin* is one of the best examples of his work as a
popularizer of science. In the preface to the first volume, he refers to the
popularity of Schwabe's *Belustigungen* and the many other periodicals which
intend to amuse and enlighten: "Wie sehr hat man nicht seit einigen Jahren den
Verstand und Witz belustiget!" (2) This has moved him to a similar undertaking
but one in which the study of nature will be the central subject. Knowledge of
nature's ways, he maintains in the following passage, is the source of poetry,
mathematics and even virtue and piety:

[19] *Hamburgisches Magazin, oder gesammlete Schriften zum Unterricht und Vergnügen
aus der Naturforschung und den angenehmen Wissenschaften überhaupt* (Hamburg und
Leipzig, 1747—1767).

[20] *Neue Bibliothek der schönen Wissenschaften und freyen Künste.* 6. Band, 1. Stück,
pp. 208—218.

[21] Kästner translated scientific works from English, French, Dutch and Swedish. Most
noteworthy is his translation of all except the first two volumes of *Der Königl.
Schwedischen Akademie der Wissenschaften Abhandlungen aus der Naturlehre, ... auf die
Jahre 1739—1779* (Leipzig, 1742—1779).

[22] There is no complete bibliography of Kästner's translations and essays scattered in
various periodicals. For the best bibliographies see Meusel's *Lexikon der von 1750—1800
verstorbenen teutschen Schriftsteller,* VI, pp. 369—382 and Carl Becker's edition of
Kästners Epigramme (Halle, 1911).

... Ihre unwandelbare Ordnung erwecket unsere Aufmerksamkeit, und gewöhnet unsere ausschweifende Dichtungskraft zu einer gewissen stand-haften Reihe von Gedanken, die der Natur ähnlich ist. Diese unvergleichliche Ordnung ist es, die zu der Mathematik Anlass gegeben hat; einer Wissenschaft, dadurch das menschliche Geschlecht mehr als einmal, gegen den gänzlichen Verfall in eine fast viehische Unwissenheit, ist verwahret worden. Wie sehr reizt nicht das Versteckte in natürlichen Dingen die Neugier der Menschen und wie entzückend belustiget nicht die Mannigfaltigkeit und Schönheit derselben. Ja wir getrauen uns sogar zu behaupten, dass die Erkenntniss der Natur es ist, die den Menschen gottselig, tugendhaft und gottgefällig machet.

Since all Europe has been engaged in the scientific study of nature for almost a hundred years, the editor will select scientific works from various European nations written in languages mostly foreign to Germans. Furthermore, selections will be made from the many scientific treatises found in the writings of scientific societies in all parts of Europe (4).

The twenty-six volumes of the periodical admirably fulfill the editor's purpose. Contributions to the English, French, Danish, Swedish and Russian academies are presented in German translations. There are translations of scientific treatises or reports of the contents of such treatises by Needham, Nollet, Euler, Maupertuis, Trembley, William Watson, Stephen Hales, Réaumur, Boerhaave and Buffon. John Hill's accounts of his microscopic experiments are translated and issued in the periodical between the years 1753 and 1757. The highly interesting essay by Thomas Wright, *An Original Theory or New Hypothesis of the Universe,* (London, 1750), appeared in a German translation in volume X (151–180) in the year 1752.[23] This was the work mentioned by Kant in his 1755 essay on the same subject.

Although most of the periodical consists of translations, there are also interesting German contributions. There are the editor's own numerous essays, always readable and informative. His "Lob der Sternkunst" in volume 1 is one of his best didactic essays. He reviews the main discoveries in astronomy; he discusses Newton's synthesis at length but also mentions German contributions to astronomy. In his "Betrachtung über den Einfluss der Naturlehre in die Metaphysik" (IV, 306–332), he asserts that science does not need metaphysical principles, but that metaphysics, that is, the soul's conception of the world and knowledge of God is certainly aided by science. Other German contributors are Christlob Mylius, Johann August Unzer und Johann Georg Krüger in the earlier years of the periodical. In the later volumes there are works by members of the

---

[23] The German title is: *Neue Theorie des Weltgebäudes auf die Gesetze der Natur gegründet, darinnen die allgemeinen Erscheinungen der sichtbaren Schöpfung und besonders der Milchstrasse aus mathematischen Gründen erkläret werden. In 9 Briefen von Thomas Wright von Durham.*

Berlin Academy and by professors of the University of Göttingen, where Kästner was since 1756. In the 1750's there were many essays by Germans on electricity and also on earthquakes after the Lisbon earthquake in 1755.

Thus, the primary role of the *Hamburgisches Magazin* is that of a collection of original scientific treatises by foreign and German scientists. There are only a few didactic essays and only several reviews of scientific works. The periodical, therefore, was of service to the layman with serious interests in science. A further characteristic of the periodical is that it was not for specialists in any one branch of science. Its selections come from all the kingdoms of nature and from all the disciplines through which man studies those kingdoms.

Finally, two periodicals by Christlob Mylius (1722–1754) shall be considered. Mylius, a cousin of Lessing, had in his brief life begun a promising career in both the arts and the sciences. He had studied medicine, the natural sciences and mathematics at the University of Leipzig and was generally recognized as an astute observer in both natural history and astronomy. He had shown talent in his poetry, dramas and prose works, and in his scientific essays he combined his love of science and his literary ability. Lessing thought highly of his cousin's literary talents and upon his death edited his works. In the second part of this study I shall consider the scientific themes in his poetry and literary essays. Here, however, I am concerned with his two periodicals, *Der Naturforscher* and *Physikalische Belustigungen,* both conceived with the purpose of teaching science to the layman.

Der Naturforscher

For the purpose of this study, *Der Naturforscher, eine physikalische Wochenschrift* (Leipzig, 1747–1748) is most significant. It was a weekly periodical with seventy-eight numbers, appearing over a period of eighteen months from July, 1747 to December, 1748. In the first number he states his purpose, which is to write science for the layman, to open his eyes to the beauties of nature and to teach him what the observations, experiments and reflections of scientists have discovered. Interspersed through the 612 pages of text are forty-five poems by Mylius and Lessing, several of which have scientific themes. Thus, the intention of the periodical is to teach science and at the same time amuse and edify. An interesting description of *Der Naturforscher* appeared in Johann Jakob Bodmer's *Freymüthige Nachrichten* of 1748:

> Der Herr Verfasser dieser Schrift, der Hällische Tadler Mylius in Leipzig, der sich bisher rühmlichst bemühet hat, die Natur fleissig zu betrachten, um sich ihre Wunder bekannt zu machen, verlässt in diesem Blatte die gewöhnliche Bahn der wöchentlichen Schriftsteller. Statt der Moral wählet er die

Naturlehre, und will die Menschen erinnern, dass sie in der Welt sind, d.i. sie
sollen lernen, dass sie fünf Sinne haben; dass sie aber selbige mit der Vernunft
vereinbaren müssen, wenn sie die Vorrechte der Menschheit behaupten
wollen. Es ist dieses Blatt gar nicht für Naturforscher geschrieben, sondern
nur physicalischen Layen gewiedmet. Aber wie gross ist die Anzahl nicht, die
zu dieser Classe gehöret? So viel uns bekannt, so ist der Herr Verfasser der
erste, der ein Wochenblatt von dieser Art schreibet, . . .(161)

A variety of scientific subjects is discussed in the course of the periodical.
Scanning the index we can find that most of the significant topics in the fields of
astronomy, the earth sciences and the life sciences are included. The periodical is
a compendium of science in the form of well written, entertaining essays that
frequently begin in a light conversational tone and then gradually turn to the
more complex scientific materials. The periodical has no book reviews and only
several short translations. Most of the periodical, then, consists of Mylius' prose
essays of high literary quality on the subject of the scientific study of nature. We
shall here confine ourselves to a discussion of several of the more interesting
essays. It is noteworthy that the editor frequently tries to correlate the poems,
which he calls "Intermezzos", with the essays that precede them according to
theme. Thus, the poem, "Die lehrende Astronomie" follows the essay on
astronomy in number seventy-four.

On the subject of astronomy there are a dozen essays of which the most
significant appear in numbers thirty to thirty-three of the periodical. He begins
the first essay with a description of the beauties of heavens on a clear night. He
describes the planets and constellations of stars as they appear to the view. Then
he turns to the serious business of astronomy with the remark that these
heavenly bodies are even more beautiful if one beholds them with the mind, as
well as with the senses. From here he proceeds to teach the fundamentals of
astronomy. He explains the true sizes and distances of the heavenly bodies and
emphasizes the motions of the planets, especially those of the earth, to
demonstrate that a right understanding of nature requires a combination of sense
perception and reasoning. After a thorough discussion of our solar system, he
turns in number thirty-three beyond it to the stars. He divides the visible stars
into six magnitudes according to their distances from the sun. He explains the
tremendous distances of the stars from the earth and from one another. He
speaks of the thin clouds in the heavens which through powerful telescopes are
seen to be a mass of stars, and which are called "neblichte Sterne", nebulae. He
explains that the Milky Way, which we see as a luminous band, actually consists
of innumerable stars. These considerations lead him to the reflection that the
universe may very well have no limits and that the number of stars may not be
finite:

Wer gibt uns aber die Versicherung, dass nicht eine noch viel grössere Menge
Sterne, aller unsrer besten Ferngläser ungeachtet, vor unsern Augen gänzlich
verborgen ist, als wir ihrer mit blossen und bewaffneten Augen wahrnehmen?
Wo sollen wir also dem sämtliche Weltbaue seine Grenzen setzen? Doch hat
er auch Grenzen?

....

Wer weis, wieviel 100,000 Sterne binnen hier und tausend Jahren entdecket
werden? Wer weis, wie viel Millionen derselben stets unentdecket bleiben
werden? Ja wer weis, ob ihre Anzahl endlich ist? (257)

Furthermore, all these stars are suns about which planets revolve such that
every star represents a solar system like ours. He concludes with a discussion of
comets, in which he emphasizes that they are heavenly bodies with enormous,
yet regular orbits.

In number thirteen of the periodical, he explains how the seasons of the year
are caused by the revolutions of the planets about the sun; in number forty-one
he explains the phases of the moon, Mercury and Venus; in numbers fifty-four
and fifty-five, he explains lunar and solar eclipses; in sections fifty-eight to sixty,
he reports his observations of a solar eclipse made in the company of
astronomers in Berlin.

In sections seventy-four and seventy-five, he turns to one of the favorite
speculations of the time, namely, the inhabitation of the planets. He presents the
usual arguments in support of this speculation. The earth is one of the planets
and the planets resemble the earth, since it is likely that on them also there exist
an atmosphere, mountains, valleys, lakes. Since the primary purpose of the earth
is man's inhabitation of it, the same must apply to the planets. As to the nature
of these inhabitants, he stresses that nature loves variety: "Gott und die Natur
lieben die Mannichfaltigkeit, und obgleich die Möglichkeit der Arten der
lebendigen Geschöpfe schon auf unserm so kleinen Puncte der Erde, erschöpfet
zu seyn scheinet, so ist doch nicht zu zweifeln, dass ihrer auf manchem Planeten
eben so vielerley und auf manchem noch viel mehrerley anzutreffen sind." (592)
He considers the various possibilities for these inhabitants. Some may have more
reason than we have and some less, some may be able to fly, others may be able
to swim, some may even have more senses than we do. Furthermore, weather,
temperature, seasons, length of the year, the quantity of sun light — all these
circumstances on the planets of this or any other solar system may contribute to
the variations of their inhabitants. He strengthens the likelihood that such
variety exists with the familiar image of the chain of beings: ". . . . die an sich
selbst sehr lange Reihe der lebendigen Geschöpfe auf unsrer Erdkugel ist ohne
Zweifel nur ein unendlich kleines Glied von der unendlich langen Kette der
beseelten Geschöpfe". (592). He concludes with the assertion that space travel
would be the surest means of verifying the existence of such creatures, but

grants that the obstacles seem insurmountable: "Am allergewissesten würden wir von der Wirklichkeit der Planetenbürger versichert werden, wenn wir auf Luftschiffen dahin reisen können,. . . . Es ist längst erwiesen worden, dass Luftschiffe an sich möglich sind, aber auch zugleich dieses, dass es eine unüberwindliche Schwierigkeit ist, selbige zu Stande zu bringen und drauf zu schiffen" (595).

Natural history is another frequent subject of the essays. In numbers four and five, he discusses the plant and animal kingdoms respectively and gives a lengthy outline of a classification of the realms of nature from stones to animals. In numbers forty-nine and fifty, he exhorts his readers to learn to contemplate the world of plants. He offers an anatomy of plants in discussing their parts and functions. In number fifty-two, the subject is insects. He cites Réaumur's work on insects, as well as the work of the entomologists, Frisch and Rösel. In the essay, he describes the metamorphosis of caterpillars, which he maintains is typical of many other insects.

Mylius was a passionate collector of natural curiosities, and several times in the periodical he defends this activity against the critics who do not see its value. In number twelve, he describes his own collection, and with much wit characterizes his friends and neighbors who have no sympathy for his spiders and bugs. In numbers fifty-one and sixty-three, he demonstrates the value of "physikalische Reisen" for the purpose of collecting specimens from distant lands.

Another subject that recurs in the essays is fossils. Numbers seventeen and forty attempt to explain what fossils are, how they are formed, that is, how natural objects become petrified and how they got where they are found. He speaks of cataclysmic events in the past, whereby fish and sea shells were brought to mountains and whereby Asian, African and American animals were brought to Europe and there, in the course of time, became petrified. He suggests that this was caused by a universal flood like the one recorded in the Bible, or a series of inundations occuring at different times. In numbers seventy-six and seventy-seven, he presents his translation of an essay on fossils by Voltaire, "Abhandlung von den Veränderungen, welche auf unsrer Erdkugel vorgegangen sind, und von den Versteinerungen, welche man für noch davon vorhandenen Zeugnisse ausgiebt", in which Voltaire denies that fossils are petrified natural objects, that they are signs of a past devastation of the earth, that the Biblical deluge completeley inundated the earth and that the speculations of Burnet and Woodward are at all valid. In thirty-one footnotes to the text, Mylius expresses his disagreement with Voltaire, point by point. He defends the view that fossils are natural bodies that had become petrified and not products of playful nature. He also defends the theory that violent changes took place on the earth in the past, but suggests that there may not have been just one flood but several and at different times.

Other scientific subjects in the periodical are weather phenomena which are treated in six essays, the anatomy of the human body in number thirty-seven, earthquakes in number twenty-five and the problem of scientific method in numbers nineteen and twenty-nine.

Physikalische Belustigungen

Mylius edited his last periodical, the *Physikalische Belustigungen,* in the years 1751 and 1752. In 1753, when Mylius began his "physikalische Reise" which was intended to take him to America, Kästner took over the editorship.[24] In his preface to the first volume, he explains what kind of a periodical he intends with his *Physikalische Belustigungen:*

> Wenn man vor einigen Jahren jemanden einen Begriff von einer neu heraus kommenden witzigen Monatschrift machen wollte, so sagte man: "Sie ist wie die Belustigungen". So beliebt und bekannt sich sonst die Belustigungen des Verstandes und Witzes unter den Liebhabern der Dichtkunst und der witzigen Prosa gemacht hatten, eben so ein allgemeines Vergnügen haben die Freunde der Natur und natürlichen Historie seit zwey Jahren an dem Hamburgischen Magazin gefunden. Da ich itzo meinen Lesern eine neue physikalische Monatschrift ankündigen will, so kann ich ihnen keine kürzere Beschreibung davon machen, als wenn ich sage: "Sie wird seyn, wie das Hamburgische Magazin". (3)

The periodical certainly resembles the *Hamburgisches Magazin* more than his previous *Der Naturforscher,* which contained mostly didactic scientific essays. The current periodical consists of translations of very recent scientific essays mainly from French and English sources and original scientific contributions by German scientists. The large number of the latter distinguish it from the *Hamburgisches Magazin* which consisted of translations to a far greater extent. The periodical contains no book reviews because, as Mylius puts it, when a book has been reviewed fifty times one can dispense with the fifty-first review.

It is interesting to note that in his preface to the first volume in 1751, Mylius praises his countrymen for their interest in the natural sciences which he says has been growing rapidly. Kästner, in his preface to the third volume two years later, maintains the same. He attributes the growth of popular interest in science to the increased use of German in scientific writings. Whereas other disciplines are cultivated by a few, natural science is useful and entertaining to all and so should

---

[24] *Physikalische Belustigungen* (Berlin, 1751–1757): Volume I, Nos. 1–10, 1751; Volume II, Nos. 11–20, 1752; Volume III, Nos. 21–24, 1754; Nos. 25 and 26, 1755; Nos. 27 and 28, 1756; Nos. 29 and 30, 1757.

be open to all. However, the professional scientist should, Kästner cautions, learn Latin and other foreign languages in order not to have to rely on translations.

There are no poetic "Intermezzi", as was the case in *Der Naturforscher,* with the exception of a fable in verse at the very beginning entitled, "Der Seidenwurm und die Spinne. Eine Fabel". The silk worm taunts the spider for its useless activity. Its art is wasted compared to that of the silkworm who provides comfort and pleasure to man and thus is cared for by him. The spider, however, is not dismayed and replies that its art demonstrates the existence of a wise creator and though the silkworm's function is of use to man now, will it be so one hundred years hence. The moral:

Sucht und erforscht mit gleicher Stärke
Des Schöpfers grösst' und kleinste Werke,
Ihr weisen Söhne der Natur!
Ein Theil davon nützt euren Zeiten,
Die Nachwelt wird den Rest erbeuten,
Und jedes zeigt des Schöpfers Spur! (1−2)

The main purpose of the periodical, he says later, is "Das Nützliche" . . . At the same time, as in the case of the fable, he justifies contemplations of nature even such as do not contribute anything of immediate utility, for they may do so in the future (4).

The translations are of a wide variety, some only a few paragraphs in length, others extending over several issues of the periodical. They are primarily by French and English authors with many of the shorter ones taken from the *Philosophical Transactions* and from English magazines like the *Gentleman's Magazine.* The subjects of these essays, as well as those by German authors, touch on many subjects, most of which belong to the broad area of natural history rather than astronomy or physics. We shall consider only a few with popular scientific subject matter.

In the fourth issue of the periodical, there is a translation of an exchange of letters between Pierre Lyonnet and Mylius on the subject of Leeuwenhoek's controversial discovery of spermatozoa. Lyonnet had challenged this discovery in a footnote in his French translation of Lesser's *Insectotheologie.* Mylius in an earlier writing to Lyonnet had defended Leeuwenhoek's discovery. The controversy is continued in the letters translated here.

In the eleventh issue of the periodical, there is a translation of a letter, dated February 27, 1752, by Carl Linnaeus to the editor Mylius. He reports that he has been occupied with a description of the queen's collection of natural curiosities, especially the conchae which he has classified according to a new method. He is also working on new classification of plants. He then describes several "physikalische Reisen", being undertaken by students and associates, to Canada,

China, Egypt, Palestine and Spain. Linnaeus expresses the hope that someone will soon travel to Jamaica to study the vast number of plants there.

In the twenty-eighth issue, Mylius reports of a recent German prose translation of a botanical poem in Latin by de la Croix. He praises the poetic quality of the work, *Die Vermählung der Pflanzen,* but points out that since the poem was composed in 1728 the botany is pre-Linnaean.

Of the many contributions by German scientists, four are by Friedrich Christian Lesser on subjects in natural history such as plants, flies and conchae. There are several essays on plants by the botanist Tobias Conrad Hoppe. In issues three, five and seven there is an essay on chemistry in which the work of Paracelsus, Stahl, Becher, Glauber, Pott and the Phlogiston theory are discussed.

Of several essays by Mylius, his "Nachricht und Gedanken von der Elektricität des Donners" is of interest. He describes the experiments of Benjamin Franklin whom he credits with having discovered the resemblances between electricity, thunder and lightning. He also reports the reception of Franklin's experiments in Paris, London, Petersburg and Bologna. In Germany, the experiments were reproduced by Winkler in Leipzig, Bose in Wittenberg and Ludolff in Berlin.[25] In the twenty-fourth issue appeared the posthumous Mylius essay "Beschreibung einer neuen Thierpflanze, in einem Schreiben an den Herrn Haller", which he sent from London in 1753. The essay dealt with the popular subject of transitional creatures between the plant and animal kingdoms, which demonstrate that there are no sharp divisions between the kingdoms of nature.

In the last volume edited by Kästner, there are several interesting essays by him. In the twenty-third issue there is his "Dem Andenken seines Freundes Christlob Mylius gewidmet", in which he reviews the latter's life and comments on his achievements and bright prospects. He concludes with a poem which pictures Mylius after death traveling to the planets in our solar system:

> Er sieht des Monds uns nie gesehnen Rücken,
> Und nah am Mars, noch einmal umgekehrt,
> Fühlt er für uns: "Wie? jenes Punctes Stücken
> "Sind Menschenblut, sind ewge Seelen werth!"
>
> .....
>
> Drauf hat sein Flug den Ring Saturn gefunden,
> Und weil er bald sich senkt, bald wieder steigt,
> Wird das für ihn ein Schauspiel von Secunden,
> Was spät sich uns in fünfzehn Jahren zeigt. (932)

He rises to higher regions beyond the world of matter where he will find fulfillment of his earthly aspirations.

---

[25] See Fritz Fraunberger's *Elektrizität im Barock* (Köln, 1964) for the early history of the explorations of electrical phenomena between 1600 and 1800.

Kästner was a strong defender of the Linnaean system of classification, as we find in several of his contributions to the last issues of the periodical. In "Ob der Mensch in die erste Ordnung der vierfüssigen Thiere gehöre", he defends the Linnaean system against the criticism that he has placed man in a class with the animals due to superficial resemblances. In the last issue there is another defense of Linnaeus entitled, "Über die systematische Eintheilung der Mineralien, Pflanzen und Thiere in Classen und Ordnungen". In the same issue, is his even more interesting essay "Von dem Stufenmässigen Steigen in der Vollkommenheit des Naturreichs". Here he speaks of the manifoldness of nature which exists in harmony and symmetry. He characterizes the order in nature's variety with images such as "die Stufenleiter der Natur" and "die Ketter der Wesen". He pays tribute to Linnaeus as one who has found this order: "Es ist schade, dass man bisher die Ordnungen in den Geschöpfen, in Absicht der Geschlechter und Arten noch nicht vollkommen berechnet und in Klassen gebracht hat. Der unsterbliche Linnäus hat hierinn sehr glückliche Versuche geleistet. Ihn hat die Natur bis in ihre Schlafkammer gelassen, und ihnen die Entkleidung ihrer Kinder, der Pflanzen und Thiere zu bemerken erlaubet, und seine närrischen Neider haben aus Verdruss sich ausgeschlossen zu sehen, ihn wenigsten in derselben keine Ruhe lassen wollen" (1480).

With these selections from the periodical, it can be seen that the didactic intent of Der Naturforscher is continued here with the emphasis, however, not on conveying the fundamentals of science or what has become accepted and established, but on informing the interested public, with readable essays and translations, of some of the events taking place at the frontiers of science.

Similar to the periodicals of the Gottsched school, in their efforts to teach science to the layman and to assimilate the sciences into liberal learning, were the periodicals of the Hamburg physician, Johann August Unzer (1727–1799). His periodicals were not as well known, but followed the same purpose. In his Gesellschaftliche Erzählungen für die Liebhaber der Naturlehre (Hamburg, 1753), there are some fine essays on the subject of natural history. "Garten-Betrachtung", in the third number, has detailed descriptions of plants and insects. In "Physicotheologische Betrachtungen einiger Vögel" in number twenty-seven, he refers to Malpighi's studies of chick embryos and praises him for his boldness "in die Werkstatt der Natur zu blicken" (356). He also quotes some physicotheological verses on birds by the "erhabene Brockes" (356). In the preface to his Der Arzt. Eine medicinsche Wochenschrift (Hamburg, 1759–1764), Unzer says that with this periodical he wishes to follow the example of Addison's Spectator and write of medicine in a manner both instructive and amusing. Even though many of the articles on medicine are quite technical, he succeeds in the purpose.

Another periodical by Unzer is Der physikalische und oekonomische Patriot (Hamburg, 1756–1758). In the preface, he explains that the general nature of his periodical was changed by the occurrence of the earthquake at Lisbon on November 1, 1755. In the first year of the periodical, more than half of the articles are concerned with this earthquake in particular and with earthquakes and other subterranean circumstances in general. The interest in earthquakes continues also during the second and third years of the periodical, though there are more popular essays on medical subjects.

Another group of scientific periodicals with a didactic intent were those of Johann Daniel Denso (1708–1795), a professor of rhethoric and poetry at the Gymnasium in Stettin and later rector of the Gymnasium in Wismar. He encouraged the study of the natural sciences in the schools and contributed to the popularization of science with his three periodicals, *Physikalische Briefe* (1752), *Monatliche Beyträge zur Naturkunde* (1752) and *Physikalische Bibliothek* (1754–1756). He was also the author of a long physicotheological poem, "Beweis der Gottheit aus dem Gras."

Finally, I should like to call attention to the significant number of essays about scientific subjects in several well-known literary journals published around the middle of the century: *Der Mensch,*[26] *Der Glückselige,*[27] *Bibliothek der schönen Wissenschaften und der freyen Künste,*[28] *Der Nordische Aufseher*[29] and *Briefe, die neueste Literatur betreffend.*[30] There is a satire on the inhabitation of the moon and a report on comets; there are many essays about natural history subjects such as collections of natural curiosities, the Ledermüller-Buffon controversy over Leeuwenhoek's spermatozoa observations, Reimarus' ideas on animal instincts; there are other essays about scientific method, the use of German in scientific writings, the social value of science, its contribution to human happiness and support of religion.

These essays with their affirmation of the sciences, were not written with any distinct didactic intent, but apparently with the understanding that scientific subjects would be of interest to an educated man. As such they are evidence that science had found a place in the community of letters.

---

[26] (Halle, 1751–1756), edited by S.G. Lange and G.F. Meier. See nos. 56, 78, 316, 463, 481.

[27] (Halle, 1763–1768), edited by S.G. Lange and G.F. Meier. See nos. 7, 8, 68, 69, 76, 91, 93.

[28] (Leipzig, 1757–1767), edited by Nicolai and Mendelssohn. See volume 10, no. 1.

[29] (Leipzig, 1758–1761), edited by Johann Andreas Cramer. See nos. 2, 70, 82, 94, 116, 117, 161, 162.

[30] (Berlin, 1759–1765), edited by Lessing, Mendelssohn, Nicolai. See letters 26, 27, 120, 130, 242.

E. OTHER GERMAN SOURCES FOR THE DIFFUSION OF THE SCIENCES

In the preceding discussion of popular literature on science I have tried to show what the main foreign and native sources for the dissemination of scientific material were. The compendiums of science, the physicotheologies and the periodicals were spreading interest and instruction about the sciences to various levels of the population in all parts of Germany. However, these were by no means the only native German sources to stir and fulfill the growing interest in science. In this last section I shall indicate what other works by German authors were available to contribute to the diffusion of the sciences.

Encyclopedias and histories of learning which were being written in German in the first half of the eighteenth century all took the new sciences into account to varying degrees. The encyclopedias in question are Jablonski's *Allgemeines Lexicon der Künste und Wissenschaften*[1] (Leipzig, 1721), Walch's *Philosophisches Lexicon*[2] (Leipzig, 1733) and Zedler's *Universal Lexicon*[3] (Halle, 1732–1750). Even though none of these authors are scientists themselves, the sciences are well represented. They are aware that the scientific method used by the moderns is different from that of their predecessors. Walch in the preface to the first edition of his encyclopedia, speaks of three sects, the Aristotelian, the Cartesian and the Epicurean, by which he understands the followers of Gassendi. From these he distinguishes the eclectics who belong to no sect and practice the method of experimentation. As examples he cites Newton, Hartsoeker, J.C. Sturm, J.J. Scheuchzer, Wolff, Boyle and Leeuwenhoek.

The treatment of science in these encyclopedias is on the same level as that found in the compendiums of science, though much briefer. It is doubtful, however, that the encyclopedias themselves contributed much to the diffusion of science. Rather the inclusion of science is an indication of the extent to which the sciences had already been assimilated.

---

[1] Johann Theodor Jablonski, *Allgemeines Lexicon der Künste und Wissenschaften; oder kurtze Beschreibung des Reichs der Natur, der Himmel und himmlischen Cörper, der Lufft, der Erden, samt denen bekannten Gewächsen, der Thiere, Steine und Ertze, des Meeres und der darinn lebenden Geschöpffe; ingleichen aller Menschlichen Handlungen, Staats-Rechts-Kriegs-Policey-Hausshaltungs-und Gelehrten Geschäffte. . . .* (Leipzig, 1721); other editions appeared in 1748 and 1768.

[2] Johann Georg Walch, *Philosophisches Lexicon, darinnen die in allen Theilen der Philosophie, als Logic, Metaphysic, Physic, Pneumatic, Ethic, natürlichen Theologie und Rechts-Gelehrsamkeit, wie auch Politic fürkommenden Materien und Kunst-Wörter erkläret, und aus der Historie erläutert; . . .* Leipzig, 1726); a second edition appeared in 1733 and a fourth in 1775.

[3] Johann Heinrich Zedler, *Grosses vollständiges Universal Lexicon aller Wissenschaften und Künste* (Halle, 1732–1754). Philip Shorr's *Science and Superstition in the 18th Century* (New York, 1932) treats science in this encyclopedia but, unfortunately, his historical perspective leaves much to be desired. Science in the German encyclopedias of the first half of the eighteenth century is a study that has yet to be undertaken.

Science and its history are also well represented in the histories of learning of which we can cite the following: Jacob Friedrich Reimmann's *Versuch einer Einleitung in die Historiam Literariam derer Teutschen* (Halle, 1708–1713), Gottlieb Stolle's *Anleitung zur Historie der Gelahrtheit* (Jena, 1736),[4] Nikolas Hieron. Gundling's *Historie der Gelahrtheit* (Frankfurt, 1734–1746) and Johann Andreas Fabricius' *Abriss einer allgemeinen Historie der Gelehrsamkeit* (Leipzig, 1752–1754). Of special interest is Reimmann's history of learning, because its third part focuses on science in Germany from the Renaissance to the beginning of the eighteenth century. As in the case of the encyclopedias, the presence of science in these reference works, written by non-scientists, is evidence of the spread of science that had already taken place.

More significant for the spread of scientific thought were popular scientific works on astronomy and natural history by German scientists and amateurs of science. We shall begin with the works of ten astronomers and amateurs, all of which taught the facts and figures of the new astronomy, as well as some of the popular speculations that this new astronomy invited.

Ausführliche Erklärung über zwey neue Homännische Charten, als über das Systema Solare et Planetarium Copernico-Hugenianum (Nürnberg, 1707) by Johann Gabriel Doppelmayr (1671–1750) is a practical work on astronomy to aid in forming a conception of the new world system and in working out specific problems in astronomy. Doppelmayr also wrote a Latin astronomy, *Atlas novus coelestis* (Nürnberg, 1742) and translated John Wilkins' *The Discovery of a New World*.

Another practical work on astronomy is Johann Georg Hagelganss' *Machina Mundi Sphaerica cum Planisphaerio,* oder *Vollständige Beschreibung einer . . . zweyfachen Welt-Kugel* (Frankfurt, 1738). He concludes the work with a praise of German contributions to the discovery and development of the Copernican system of the world.

Johann Christian Müldener's *Astronomischer und geographischer Begriff, von dem natürlichen Zustande unserer Welt und Erdkugel, in 17 Schreiben, einer auf dem Lande wohnenden Frau von Stande eröffnet* (Dresden, 1729) is as the title indicates in the manner of Fontenelle's *La pluralité des mondes*. The first six letters present the teachings of modern astronomy with an emphatic defense of the Copernican system of the world. The remaining letters deal with physical phenomena on earth. The author clearly aspires to teach science to the laity and succeeds in presenting his material in an instructive and entertaining way.

Einleitung zu denen Mathematischen Wissenschaften (Jena, 1726) by Johann Bernhard Wiedeburg (1687–1766) includes a long section on astronomy in which the Copernican system of the world and numerous problems of

---

[4] The first edition appeared in 1718 and the second, third and fourth in 1724, 1727 and 1736 respectively.

astronomy are explained. In his discussion of the planets and their satellites, he contends that they are all inhabited by rational creatures. Wiedeburg's *Astronomisches Bedenken* . . . (Jena, 1744) is an examination of the systems of Thomas Burnet, William Whiston and Johann Heyn. He rejects their arguments based on principles of astronomy and scientific law and contends that the creation, flood and final conflagration can only be understood as miracles. Opposite the title page stands a quotation from Derham's *Astro-Theology* in which the beauty, harmony and perfection of God's creation are asserted with the implication that man's reason is inadequate to reconstruct the creation, as the cosmogonies tried to do.

Johann Leonhard Rost (1688—1727), an astronomer in Nürnberg who was also a popular novelist, wrote three German works on astronomy: *Astronomisches Handbuch* (Nürnberg, 1726) — first edition, 1718 — *Der Aufrichtige Astronomus* (Nürnberg, 1727) and *Compendiöse Vorstellung des gantzen Welt-Gebäudes* (Nürnberg, 1743). The first and the third present the Copernican system of the world in great detail. He fully accepts the doctrine of the plurality of inhabited worlds according to which every star is a sun and center of a planetary system. The second work is devoted primarily to solving practical problems of astronomy such as the prediction of lunar and solar eclipses. The first work is preceded by a translation of Domenico Cassini's history of astronomy, *Vom Ursprung, Fortgang und Aufnehmen der Astronomie,* translated by Johann Philipp von Wurtzelbau, the translator of Christian Huygens' *Cosmotheoros.*

Christian Gottlieb Semler's (1715—1782) *Astrognosia Nova oder Ausführliche Beschreibung des gantzen Fixstern und Planeten Himmels* (Halle, 1742) again presents the fundamentals of the new astronomy. He explains the advantages of the Copernican system, refutes the Tychonian system and then goes beyond Copernicus by maintaining that there are an infinite number of stars, each the center of a planetary system. Within our solar system he explains what is known about the planets and then develops for each planet the astronomy that its inhabitants would have. He proves *a priori* and *a posteriori* that the planets are inhabited. In the text he demonstrates solutions to numerous practical problems in astronomy.

Two amateur astronomers, Eberhard Christian Kindermann and Johann Heyn (1709—1746), a clergyman, stirred up much controversy in Germany in the 1740's with their works about astronomy. Though their theories strike us as fanciful today, as they did many of their contemporaries, through them astronomy became a popular issue and thus contributed to the spread of interest in it.

Kindermann's most important publication was *Reise in Gedancken durch die eröffneten allgemeinen Himmels-Kugeln* . . . (Rudolstadt, 1739) which he signed with his initials, "von Einem Christlichen Künstler". A few years later the work was edited again under the title *Vollständige Astronomie oder Sonderbare Betrachtungen derer vornehmsten an dem Firmament befindlichen Planeten und Sternen* (Rudolstadt, 1744), this time with the addition of his full name. In the presentation of its material it is a textbook on astronomy. He proceeds, as most of these texts do, by stating the facts and figures about the sun, the planets, their satellites, the comets and the stars. He follows the examples of Fontenelle and Huygens in assuming that the planets are inhabited and in trying to describe the astronomy which the inhabitants would have. However, what are conjectures for his predecessors are presented as facts by him. His detailed knowledge of the planetary inhabitants was an imaginative fiction rather than a conjecture. Moreover, he claims Biblical verification for the belief in planetary inhabitation by a fanciful interpretation of several verses from the Psalms.

As one reads through the text one comes across further examples of an indiscriminate mixture of fact, conjecture and fiction. He maintains the earth is only fourteen times larger than the moon, that Sirius is closer to the earth than Saturn and that Saturn's ring is composed of numerous moons. He claims to have invented an optical instrument with which he can see the opposite side of the earth. His knowledge of the stars is startling. In each stellar constellation only the largest star is supposed to be a sun, the remaining being its planets. He also claims to have measured the distance between the stars. The work resembles Johann Gottlob Krüger's imaginative *Träume* in which the author dreams of planetary voyages. However, Kindermann presents his work as a serious astronomy which led to an almost unanimous condemnation in the review journals. The reviewer in the *Göttingische Gelehrte Anzeigen* of 1744 describes the book as follows: "Diese Astronomie ist von gantz besonderer Art, wegen der seltenen Sachen, so man darin nicht suchen sollte, und die einem Paracelso oder Böhm ähnlich sehen" (894). The review in Mylius' *Philosophische Untersuchungen* (1744) begins as follows: "Der weltberühmte Herr Kindermann, dieser neue Ricciolus, thut wohl, dass er die in diesem Buche enthaltenen astronomischen Betrachtungen sonderbare Betrachtungen nennet. Denn er hat in der That in der Astronomie etwas sonderbares gethan . . .".

More in keeping with his interests is his piece of science fiction, *Die Geschwinde Reise auf dem Lufft-Schiff nach der obern Welt* (1744). It is a tale of a space voyage to a satellite of Mars which Kindermann claimed to have discovered on July 10, 1744. The space ship was built according to the instructions which had been given in his *Vollständige Astronomie*. The earth's gravity was to be overcome by attaching to their sail boat six metal balls in which a vacuum had been created to make them, and thereby the ship, lighter than air. To descend they would gradually permit air to enter the metal balls. The voyage of discovery is a mixture of astronomic lore and moral reflections. The inhabitants they encounter on this satellite of Mars have not experienced a Fall and, therefore, are more perfect than man. The space voyagers are told that every star is the center of inhabited planets and that this was one of the mysteries that was lost to man with Adam's Fall. Like good natural historians they request some natural curiosities to take back to earth with them.

In 1747 Kindermann returned once more to the task of writing an astronomy text with his *Collegium Astronomicum* (Dresden und Leipzig, 1747) which he intended as the second part of his *Vollständige Astronomie*. A different Kindermann seems to be writing here. It is a practical astronomy in which astronomical instruments, measurements and terms are explained and specific problems of astronomy solved. It is all very legitimate, though at times his presumption is apparent. For example, in discussing the atmosphere of the moon he promises the following: "Ich werde mir Mühe geben, so ich lebe und gesund bleibe, in einer allgemeinen Physic, wohin folgendes sonderlich gehöret zu erweisen, dass nicht allein ein jeder Cörper des Himmels eine würckliche Atmosphaeram sondern auch eine jede Creatur, von Menschen bis auf das Insect, eine nach ihrem Cörper proportionirliche Atmosphaeram gewiss habe." (180). Here as elsewhere his ambition and claims for knowledge exceed his or anybody's capacities. This fantastic element in a man who clearly has some foundation in astronomy made him the center of controversy in the 1740's.

No less controversial a figure was Johann Heyn. Like Kindermann he took the conjectures of others and raised them to articles of faith. In his case it was primarily Whiston's cometary theory which explained the creation, the flood, the final conflagration according to natural laws.

Heyn's first and most significant publication was *Versuch einer Betrachtung über die Cometen, die Sündflut und das Vorspiel des jüngsten Gerichts, nach astronomischen Gründen und der heiligen Schrift angestellet* (Berlin und Leipzig, 1742). There is a preface by Johann Christoph Gottsched in which he briefly discusses the history of cometary theory and defends the Whistonian theory. Gottsched had given a favorable account of Whiston's views in his *Erste Gründe der gesammten Weltweisheit* and in this preface again defends primarily Whiston's rationalism rather than Heyn's phantasy.

The work itself is divided into five chapters. The first one is entitled "Von astronomischen Gründen" and presents the basic teachings of the new astronomy. The second chapter, "Von der Vernunft, der heiligen Schrift und den Wunderwerken," tries to prove that reason and Revelation do not contradict one another. He states this principle as follows: "Weil die Vernunft eben sowohl ein Geschenke Gottes ist als die Schrift, Gott aber sich, wegen seiner höchsten Vollkommenheit, nicht widersprechen kann, so können diese beyden Offenbarungen einander nicht zu wieder seyn. So bald sich daher ein Widerspruch zeigt: so hat man entweder seine verdorbene Phantasey mit der Vernunft verwechselt; oder man hat die Erklärung eines guten einfältigen Mannes für den wahren Sinn des heiligen Geistes gehalten" (141). This contention prepares the way for the next two chapters, "Von der Sündflut" and "Von dem Vorspiel des jüngsten Gerichts," in which he teaches the Whistonian theory and proves that there is Biblical evidence in its support. With regard to the flood he refers to a Talmudic tale which narrates that God in order to punish men threw upon the earth stars called "Kima" which in turn caused the flood. His analysis of this Hebrew word proved to his satisfaction that it means what the word comet means to us. Furthermore, he found the word "Kima" three times in the Bible, Job 9,9, Daniel 39,31, and Amos 5,8 which led him to the proud conclusion, "Ich habe also die Whistonische Lehre von der Sündflut durch die älteste Tradition bestätiget, welches Whiston für eine unmögliche Sache gehalten hat". In the fourth chapter he proves not only that there is Biblical support for the cometary cause of the final conflagration but that this cataclysm would occur in the very near future. In the last chapter he preaches repentance.

Heyn's attempts to find Biblical verification for Whiston's theory and his insistence that the end was near aroused much opposition from his fellow clergymen. His second major work, *Gesamlete Briefe von den Cometen, der Sündflut und dem Vorspiel des jüngsten Gerichts* (Berlin und Leipzig, 1745), was written in defense against his critics. Of special interest is the twenty-seventh letter which consists of a 240 line didactic poem on Heyn's teachings by Christlob Mylius, Lessing's cousin.

The controversy that arose because of his theories and his stubborn defense of them brought the subject of astronomy and especially Whiston's theory to the attention of many. The controversy itself, though it is a historical phenomena of some interest, has been neglected by historians. Ferdinand Josef Schneider's article "Kometenwunder und Seelenschlaf"[5] is the only extensive treatment of Heyn's theories. Schneider found mention of Heyn only in Hagenbach's *Lehrbuch der Dogmengeschichte* (Leipzig, 1888) and in Erwin Thyssen's dissertation, *Christlob Mylius* (Marburg, 1912). I can add the reference in Otto Zöckler's *Geschichte der Beziehung zwischen Theologie und Naturwissenschaft* (Gütersloh, 1877–1879), pp. 160–161.

From the controversial figures Kindermann and Heyn, I turn to two scientist-philosophers who acquired reputations for rigorous thought, namely Immanuel Kant (1724–1804) and Johann Heinrich Lambert (1728–1777). Both of these thinkers extended Newtonian principles of gravity to all heavenly bodies in their search for order in the entire universe. The works to be considered were not particularly well known, and it cannot be claimed that they contributed much to the dissemination of astronomy themes. However, both of the reputable thinkers entertained themes and speculations that recur repeatedly in our period.

---

[5] *Deutsche Vierteljahrsschrift für Literaturwissenschaft und Geistesgeschichte,* 1940 (201–231).

The work in question by Immanuel Kant is *Allgemeine Naturgeschichte und Theorie des Himmels* (1755).[6] Like so many of his contemporaries, Kant speculated about the origin of creation. In his cosmogony there is an original chaos of particles which in accordance with the laws of gravity are mutually attracted. They are drawn to points of greater density and thereby form many isolated masses which are the beginnings of future stars. With the gravitational principles of attraction and repulsion, he builds up his cosmology in which every star is the center of a solar system and in which the stars themselves are not scattered at random but are grouped in stellar systems that resemble planetary systems in many ways.

The third part of this work deals with the very popular theme of the inhabitation of planets which Kant takes very seriously though, of course, only as a speculation. His arguments in favor of this belief are essentially nature's plenitude and the universality of nature's laws. Like so many others he finds it inconceivable that only this small planet is inhabited. At the same time he grants that it would not be incompatible with nature's plenitude to have some uninhabited planets just as there are some uninhabitable regions on the earth. Other popular speculations found here are the ladder of creation, including species from the lowest to the highest; man as merely a species on the middle rungs of the ladder; and the soul's further unfolding after death by higher experiences on other planets.

Johann Heinrich Lambert had the same intention as Kant in his *Cosmologische Briefe über die Einrichtung des Weltbaues* (Augsburg, 1761) in extending Newtonian principles beyond our solar system to the universe, to establish a rational, lawful order for the infinite universe. Unlike Kant, he did not attempt a cosmogony but confined himself to cosmological principles. He realizes that what he was attempting was barely a beginning and that the discovery of the true order of the entire universe is left to future generations: "Wir erwarten noch die Copernicus, Keplers und Newtons für den ganzen Weltbau . . ." (Vorrede, XXIV).

Lambert viewed his work as a continuation of Fontenelle's *La pluralité des mondes,* though he granted that his own literary skill was far inferior to that of Fontenelle. Instead of the animated conversations of the French work, we find here a continuous narration in the form of twenty letters. They are written in conversational tone but lack the sense of awe, wonder and inspiration in regard to the vast universe that is conveyed to the reader in Kant's work as well as in Fontenelle's. The same popular themes are there; however, he is more emphatic than Kant about the presence of various forms of rational life on other planets in all solar systems. He uses teleological arguments throughout the text and considers that form of reasoning as a valid supplement to the scientific method

6 *Sämtliche Werke* (Leipzig, 1867), Volume 1.

of seeking empirically verifiable natural laws. He rejects the cosmogonies of Burnet and Whiston but accepts as a likelihood that the comets are inhabited. He also speculates seriously about the nature of the inhabitants of planets and comets with relation to their physical circumstances.

Now let us turn to the broad field of natural history whose popularity was enormous in Germany, as has already been observed in the preceding sections. Probably the best bibliographical source for the literature on this subject is Julius Bernhard von Rohr's *Physikalische Bibliothek,* brought up to date in its second edition, (Leipzig, 1754) by Abraham Gotthelf Kästner. It lists scientific works in all languages and especially Latin and German books published in Germany between 1650 and 1750. As was seen in the case of the physico-theologies, natural history attracted many amateurs of science who produced some of the most interesting and popular books on subjects from natural history. I shall confine the discussion to several of these which have been available in first or early editions.

First let us take up the *Geschichte der Erde in den allerältesten Zeiten* (Halle, 1746) by Johann Gottlob Krüger (1715–1759). We have already met Krüger as author of a compendium of science and shall encounter his imaginative work, *Träume,* in the second part. He wrote numerous works on earthquakes, electricity, mathematics, the education of children and psychology. Although as a physician and experimentalist he ranks as a professional scientist, the above work on cosmogony, geology and paleontology does belong more to the amateur category. More than half of the book is devoted to an examination of cosmogonies whose authors have tried to explain scientifically the changes that have taken place on earth and at the same time remain within the framework of Genesis. The result of this has been, "... dass eine Menge süsser Träume, seltsamer Phantasien und wunderbare Erdichtungen in die Naturlehre gekommen sind, ..." (12). He examines the systems of Descartes, Burnet and Whiston and exposes their insufficiencies. He accepts fossils as evidence of a flood or floods but denies that any of these were identical with the Biblical flood. As a Newtonian he is somewhat partial to Whiston's speculation and admits, "Dass wir aber in der That keine wahrscheinlichere Erklärung der Sündfluth haben, als die Whistonische ist ..." (86). He explores numerous other matters pertaining to the structure of the earth such as the different strata of earth, floods, earthquakes, volcanoes — always searching for the causes. Krüger's good literary style makes this one of the most readable popular scientific works of the time.

One of the best known natural historians in Germany was Johann Leonhard Frisch (1666–1743). He was a clergyman, a rector of a Gymnasium, author of a German-Latin dictionary and a member of several scientific academies. His popular *Beschreibung von allerley Insecten in Teutsch-Land* (Leipzig und Berlin, 1720–1738) appeared in thirteen parts, with 273 engravings by his son, J. Leopold Frisch. There was a second edition of this work, (Berlin,

1766–1779). In the preface to the first volume he explains that he has used German for those many people who enjoy natural history but are not fluent in Latin. Furthermore, he has confined himself to insects in Germany, since there are enough there to occupy him for a lifetime. Finally, he believes that microscopic studies of insects reveal the greatness of God as much as the astronomers' study of the heavens. In the text he names and describes the parts of the insect body, he examines insects' eating, drinking and habitation, their contact with other insects, their mating habits, their growth and the process of metamorphosis. Less emphasis is placed on anatomy and much more on the insect's way of living within the context of nature: "Es ist am angenehmsten wann man es lässt wie es Gott in der Natur selbst geschaffen hat, da alles durch einander kriecht oder fliegt" (III, 36). Altogether the thirteen parts of the work cover the circumstances and habits of three hundred insects found in Germany.

He also began *Vorstellung der Vögel in Deutschland* (Berlin, 1763) which was based on his collection of stuffed birds. Of the twelve classes of birds included, the first four were described by him, the rest by his son, who also provided the illustrations.

An interesting amateur scientist was Georg Wolfgang Knorr (1705–1761), an engraver by profession and natural historian by inclination. He collaborated with Martin Tyroff, another engraver, in the edition of the elaborately illustrated *Physica Sacra* by Johann Jakob Scheuchzer. He became an enthusiastic collector and illustrator of fossils and decided to prepare a complete treatise on the subject. He lived only long enough to complete the first volume of *Sammlung von Merckwürdigkeiten der Natur und Alterthümern des Erdbodens welche petrificierte Cörper enthält* (Nürnberg, 1755–1773), completed by Johann Ernst Immanuel Walch, a geologist. He also began a botanical work, *Allgemeines Blumen-Kräuter-Frucht- und Gartenbuch in welchem ganz neue und nach der Natur selbst abgemahlte Figuren von Blumen, Kräutern, Bäumen, Stauden, Früchten und andern Gewächsen vorgestellet werden* ... (Nürnberg, 1750–1768). Incomplete was also left his best known work, *Auserlesenes Naturaliencabinet, welches aus den drey Reichen der Natur zeiget, was von curiösen Liebhabern aufbehalten und gesammlet zu werden verdienet,* (Nürnberg, 1754). The second edition, (Nürnberg, 1766–1767), completed by his associates, is provided with both a French and a German text. The two large folio volumes, notwithstanding the title, are devoted primarily to marine life, insects, birds, reptiles and quadrupeds. In the preface to the second volume, the author suggests how a cabinet of natural curiosities should be arranged. The work is richly illustrated, which was the rule rather than the exception in these labors of love by amateurs of science.

August Johann Roesel von Rosenhof's *Insectenbelustigung* (Nürnberg, 1746–1761) is an excellent example of art and science meeting in the work of an amateur natural historian.[7] Von Rosenhof (1705—1759), the son of an engraver, was a miniature painter whose profession led him to natural history, as he explains in the preface to his first volume: "Um aber nun in selbiger so vollkommen zu werden als es nur immer meine Kräfften zulassen wollen, habe ich die genaue Betrachtung derer Wercke der Natur, derer Geschöpfe und ihrer Affecten niemalen aus der Acht gelassen, weil doch nur derjenige der beste Mahler ist, der die Natur am vollkommensten nachzuahmen weis" (leaf A2v). He was also inspired by the poetry of Brockes and Derham's *Physikotheologie* as well as the insect studies of his predecessors, Lesser and Frisch (leaf A3r-v). In the preface he also quotes long passages from Réaumur's *Mémoires pour servir à l'histoire des insectes* on the uses of insect studies and from Charles Bonnet's *Idée d'une Echelle des Etres naturels* about the ladder of nature. Bonnet maintained that the polyps discovered by Abraham Trembley were a species that indicated the transition from the plant to the animal kingdoms. In a diagram von Rosenhof characterizes the arrangement of the classes from the elements to man in Bonnet's ladder of creation. He concludes his preface with dedicatory poems and reflections sent to him by Barthold Heinrich Brockes, Friedrich Christian Lesser, Johann Gottlob Krüger and several others.

Von Rosenhof's illustrations of insects, painted and engraved by himself, form the most outstanding quality of the work. In the text he proves himself to be an accurate observer of the habits and circumstances of hundreds of insects. He follows the systems of classification of other natural historians but relies on his own observations in describing the processes of birth, growth and metamorphoses. The four volumes contain descriptions of over three hundred insects and over two hundred fifty plates of illustrations.

In the preface to the concluding volume, edited posthumously by his son-in-law, Christian Friedrich Carl Kleemann, also a miniature painter, we get some idea of the high esteem Rösel von Rosenhof enjoyed among his contemporaries. Among the poems and reflections in praise of the deceased author cited by Kleemann, there are passages from the correspondence between the French entomologist Réaumur and Georg Matthias Bose,[8] a professor of physics at the University of Wittenberg, in which we see the high value Réaumur placed on the work and the efforts he made to have it translated into French. Of the poems in praise of Rösel, we shall quote only one by Peter Heinrich Tesdorpf:[9]

---

[7] *Insectenbelustigung* was published in four parts: I, 1746, II, 1749, III, 1755, IV, 1761. One of the few histories of science to discuss this work is Friedrich Simon Bodenheimer's *Geschichte der Entomologie bis Linné* (Berlin, 1928).

[8] Bose (1710—1761) wrote several Latin works on electricity and one didactic poem in German: *Die Elektricität nach ihrer Entdeckung und Fortgang* (Wittenberg, 1744).

[9] Tesdorpf (1712—1778) is also author of the following poem: *Versuch einer Beschreybung vom allerschönsten und beynahe allerkleinsten Vogel, der unter dem Namen Colibrit bekannt ist* (Lübeck, 1753).

Ihr Völker, die ihr sonst die schönsten Bücher schreibt
Und den Verstand und Fleis bis zur Bewundrung treibt.
Hier seht ihr die Natur mit solcher Kunst vereint,
Dass es zu Rösels Ehr die zweyte Schöpfung scheint.
Ein Werk, drinn jedes Thier gleichsam lebendig liegt
Und nach Apollos Kunst die Menschen selbst betriegt.
Mit einem Wort ein Werk, davon ihr müst gestehn:
Es habe noch die Welt desgleichen nicht gesehn.
O Nachwelt! nur umsonst wirst du dich einst bemühn,
Von neuen einen Mann, wie Rösel ist, zu ziehn.
Der Kenner sieht es schon mit Janus Augen ein,
Ihm werde niemand gleich zu allen Zeiten seyn.
Sieg prange, Deutschland, dann mit diesem grossen Ruhm,
Doch ehre Röseln auch, dein theures Eigenthum.
Und ihr, die ihr Gefühl von Rösels Werken habt,
Dankt Gott, der euch zur Lust den Mann so hoch begabt. (IV, 27)

Rösel completed one work in natural history, namely, *Die natürliche Historie der Frösche hiesigen Landes* (Nürnberg, 1751–1758). The work contains a German and Latin text, twenty-four plates of his own illustrations and a preface by Albrecht von Haller.

Science and art were again united in *Mikroskopische Gemüths- und Augenergötzungen* (Nürnberg, 1760–1765), the work of the amateur scientist Martin Frobenius Ledermüller (1719–1769), a lawyer by profession and microscopist by avocation. The work includes specimens from mineral, plant and animal life, but observations of insects and marine life predominate. It is distinguished from Rösel's work primarily in that Ledermüller presents only microscopic observations and not descriptions of insect life. For example, he describes the circulatory system of the frog or the wing of a butterfly or the pollen of a flower. He made his own drawings of his observations; the plates were provided by the engraver Paul Nussbiegel. The work was thoroughly reviewed in Gottsched's *Das Neueste aus der anmuthigen Gelehrsamkeit.*[10]

Prior to the above work Ledermüller published two studies of his microscopic observations in defense of Leeuwenhoek's discovery of the existence of seminal animalculi: *Physicalische Beobachtungen derer Saamenthiergen . . .* (Nürnberg, 1756) and *Versuch zu einer gründlichen Vertheidigung derer Saamenthiergen . . .* (Nürnberg, 1758). These were written against the French naturalist Buffon who had attempted to refute Leeuwenhoek's findings. Equipped with his own observations and extensive knowledge of the microscope, Ledermüller was able to show that Buffon's opinions were based on an improper use of the

[10] 1759 (154–158, 472–474); 1760 (85–91, 334–341, 654–662, 915–920); 1761 (574–582), 1762 (742–751).

microscope. The works are provided with illustrations of the spermatozoa and microscopes he used. Both essays were reviewed in *Briefe, die neueste Literatur betreffend,* the twenty-sixth and twenty-seventh letters of March 15, 1759.

The numerous studies of minute life by natural historians gave scientists and philosophers ammunition to combat the Cartesian mechanistic conception of animal behavior, according to which animals were soulless machines. The nature of the animal soul became an issue that stirred both laymen and scientists in the first half of the eighteenth century. The followers and students of the Leibniz-Wolffian school opposed the Cartesian view of animals. From the Leibnizian point of view, the principle of continuity forbade the sharp distinction between animal life and man. Wolff stressed the similarity between the organs and functions of animals and humans; he maintained that animals share with man sense perception, imagination and memory. The animal soul as a simple substance was also immortal and differed from the human soul in its lack of the higher rational faculties. The Wolffian point of view on the animal soul predominated in Johann Heinrich Winkler's "Gesellschaft guter Freunde" which he organized at the University of Leipzig for the study of animal psychology. The society was composed of Winkler's students who wrote essays on the subject sometimes going beyond Wolff by attributing even reason to the animals. These essays were published under the title, *Philosophische Untersuchungen vom Seyn und Wesen der Seelen der Thiere* (Leipzig, 1741–1745).[11]

A most significant work on the subject of animal souls is *Versuch eines neuen Lehrgebäudes von den Seelen der Thiere* (Halle, 1750) by Georg Friedrich Meier (1718–1777). In the histories of literature Meier is mentioned as a disciple of the Wolffian aesthetician, Alexander Gottlieb Baumgarten, as a supporter of the Swiss in their controversy with Gottsched and as a member of Samuel Gotthold Lange's Halle circle. Together with Lange, Meier was also the editor of three moral weeklies: *Der Gesellige* (1748–1750), *Der Mensch* (1751–1756) and *Der Glückselige* (1763–1768). In addition to his literary and aesthetic interests, as a professor of philosophy at the University of Halle, he also published numerous works on philosophic problems, to which his work on animal souls belongs.

The book begins with an imaginative episode. He scoffs at the notion that man is the center of the universe, and to gain a better perspective he undertakes an imaginative journey to other planets. He reflects about the unlimited number of solar systems in infinite space and that the same kind of manifoldness of living forms that is found on earth can be expected on other heavenly bodies. From the vast world he then turns to the minute and ponders on the world found in a drop of water, in a grain of sand. The theme of the manifoldness and variety of life returns him to his subject with the reflection that the souls of

11 For a discussion of this society and their publications see Lois Westen's *'Melitto-Logia' The Mythology of the Bee in Eighteenth-Century German Literature* (University of Illinois, 1952), pp. 69–78.

animals surpass those of man in variety and diversity. He continues with Wolffian arguments to demonstrate that animals have souls, that these souls are immortal and that they possess the capacities of sensation, imagination, memory and also simple rational functions such as identifying and having clear concepts of individual objects. More Leibnizian is the contention that God wishes the world to be thought, but since there is too much in nature for man alone, the animals are needed to think the numerous objects of nature. Different gradations of animal souls are needed so that the world can be perceived from many different points of view. In the concluding pages of the book, he suggests a hypothesis which went far beyond the claims of the Wolffians, namely, that even though the animals do not now have the higher rational capacities, they may acquire them in the course of time:

> Ich behaupte: dass die Seelen der Thiere dieses Erdbodens, ausser den Menschen, in diesem Leben, keine allgemeine deutliche Erkenntniss haben; . . . . Dass es aber verschiedene Classen der unvernünftigen Thiere, in Absicht auf die Grade des Verstandes gebe; und dass sie endlich nach vielen Verwandlungen durch den Tod in einem Zustand kommen werden, in welchem sie den Gebrauch aller Grade des Verstandes und der Vernunft erlangen, und folglich zu der Staffel der Geister werden erhoben werden. (107)

This gradual ascension of the animal soul to human spirit is not to be understood in any modern evolutionary sense. Rather it is what Arthur O. Lovejoy means by the "temporalizing of the Chain of Being". Meier's hypothesis indicates a shift from a static to a dynamic concept of nature in which "becoming" has been substituted for "being". From this point of view, animals with their potential for eventual development have acquired a status of being almost human: "Nimmt man meine Meinung von den Seelen der Thiere an, so kann man alle Thiere in diesem Leben by nahe als Kinder betrachten, die vor dem Gebrauch ihrer Vernunft sterben" (117). As I shall indicate in the second part, Meier's influence on Wieland is apparent in the poet's Natur der Dinge. How Meier's hypothesis fared in the age of idealism should prove to be a fruitful study.

More conservative but highly significant was the thought of Hermann Samuel Reimarus (1694—1768) on the subject of the animal soul. Reimarus had studied theology, philosophy and philology at the University of Jena and was professor of oriental languages at the Gymnasium in Hamburg. With his observations and reflections about animal life he ranks as an amateur scientist for whom these studies were an integral part of his philosophic and religious point of view.

In the histories of literature Reimarus is mentioned only as the author of the Fragmente eines Ungenannten, published by Lessing in the years of 1773 to 1781, in which Reimarus exposes the Bible, Revelation and the church to the criticism of an uncompromising and consistent rationalism. However, in his own lifetime he suppressed this radical tendency and was known primarily for two works that were constructive rather than critical. In the first of these, *Die vornehmsten Wahrheiten der natürlichen Religion,* he defends the principles of natural religion, that reason is in harmony with faith, that God is the creator of the world and of living beings, that the soul is immortal and that purpose can be found in all natural phenomena.[12] He polemicizes against Buffon and Maupertuis who opposed teleology and praises the works of physicotheologically oriented writers like Derham and Nieuwentyt. Of interest to our discussion is the fifth chapter which is devoted to the question of purpose in the animal kingdom. To prove his point, he examines animal instincts, especially those he calls "Kunsttriebe", namely, the natural skills that contribute to the preservation of the individual animal and the species.

Animal instincts are the main subject of the second book well known in his life time, *Allgemeine Betrachtung über die Triebe der Natur.*[13] Like Wolff he attributes to animals a soul with sense perception, imagination and memory but without the capacity to form clear concepts. The instinctual life of animals, therefore, plays the most important role in providing for their preservation. He distinguishes various instincts, those that are purely mechanical, those that require conceptualization, however vague and indistinct, and those by which the animals seem to choose what is pleasurable and avoid what is threatening. Man's reason surpasses these instinctual capacities, for with it he can form clear concepts, distinguish the present from the past, choose and judge. Animals in turn surpass man in that they possess significant, highly specialized and complex skills, purely spontaneously, by nature. These Reimarus calls "Kunsttriebe". No man is a born weaver, hunter or blacksmith. However, the spider, the moth, the bee, the beaver, all have skills that contribute decisively to their preservation without any training, practice or experience. No animal lacks the "Kunsttriebe" necessary for its well-being; no animal has unnecessary or superfluous "Kunsttriebe"; these instincts are the same in different geographical areas; in the offspring they are always the same, neither better nor worse; animals do not acquire new "Kunsttriebe", nor do they lose any; every animal exercises its "Kunsttriebe" without any previous practice, with a complete and consistent skillfullness.

Reimarus considers these "Kunsttriebe" as God's gift to the animals just as He has granted man the gift of reason. This analysis of these instincts is to inspire in men greater appreciation of their capacity to reason and at the same time demonstrate that God has provided for the animals as well. Though

---

12 (Hamburg, 1766). The first edition appeared in 1754 and a fifth edition in 1782.
13 *Allgemeine Betrachtungen über die Triebe der Natur, hauptsächlich über die Kunsttriebe, zum Erkenntnisse des Zusammenhanges der Welt, des Schöpfers und unsrer selbst* (Hamburg, 1760). A second edition appeared in 1762.

Reimarus as a rationalist valued man's rational faculty by which he surpasses the
animals, he nevertheless, as so many of his time, insisted on recognizing the
proximity of animals to man on the ladder of nature, on a humane attitude
toward animals, on reverence for that which is below man, as well as for that
which is above him.

The last amateur natural historian we shall consider is Johann Georg Sulzer
(1720—1779) who is primarily known for his work on aesthetics, *Allgemeine
Theorie der schönen Künste und Wissenschaften* (1771—1774). In his youth,
however, he was an eager student of natural history. In 1741 he published *Kurze
Anleitung zu nützlicher Betrachtung der schweizerischen Naturgeschichte*
(Zürich, 1741). A few years later he edited Scheuchzer's *Naturgeschichte des
Schweizerlands* (1746). Until 1760 he made several contributions on scientific
subjects to the *Jahrbücher der Berlinischen Akademie*.[14] Most popular were two
works of his youth containing philosophic, moral and aesthetic reflections about
the works of nature as seen from the point of view of modern natural history. In
well-written essays, the young Sulzer reflects the spirit of the times by treating
certain themes that had almost become conventional by the middle of the
century.

The two works in question are *Versuch einiger moralischen Betrachtungen
über die Werke der Natur* (Berlin, 1740—1745) and *Unterredungen über die
Schönheit der Natur* (Berlin, 1750).[15] The former is divided into six essays or
contemplations, each taking some scientific theme as its point of departure.
Microscopic observations of minute living beings led him to reflect about the
manifoldness of nature, the thousands of known species on this planet, the many
more that are being discovered every day, the many more that can be expected
on other planets. After picturing this vastness, he notes that all these species can
be arranged in an orderly progression from the lowest to the highest with only
minute differences between them. He has no doubt that the ladder of nature
extends beyond man to God and that these higher species will be found on other
planets. He entertains similar reflections in connection with observations he
made through a telescope. He ranges over the vast distances, the unlimited
number of stars, each the center of a planetary system and tries to conceive of
the enormous number of living beings in the universe in view of the great
quantity found on earth. Purpose in nature is another theme to which he returns
frequently. Even the apparent disorders in nature are demonstrated to have
purpose. He chides Thomas Burnet for contending that mountains are an
imperfection and shows instead the purposefulness of mountains.

---

14 For a chronological list of Sulzer's works see the appendix to his *Vermischte
Philosophische Schriften* (Leipzig, 1773).
15 Both works were reissued in 1770 and 1774; the latter edition was available for this
study.

The second work is in the form of five dialogues on subjects related to nature. In the first he describes the beauties of nature in the plant and animal kingdoms. He refers to the harmonious formation of living beings and their orderly arrangement in a chain of beings. He also elaborates on the beauty of a cabinet of natural curiosities. In the second dialogue he compares nature's art with man's art and finds the former decidedly superior. The subject of the third dialogue is again the orderliness of nature and presence of purpose in natural phenomena. In the fourth he examines several curiosities in the kingdom of nature: electricity, the magnet, quicksilver, fossils, chemical experiments, reproduction in plants and animals, the polyps, metamorphosis in insects and the skills of animals such as the bee, the spider, the beaver. The last conversation stresses that a contemplation of nature leads man to God.

These two works of Sulzer probably do not contain a single original thought. That in itself makes them significant to this study. Young Sulzer's interest in natural history and his philosophic reflections about nature came to him so spontaneously simply because they had become so widespread by the middle of the century.

Other sources that contributed to and nourished the growing interest in the sciences were travel journals and private collections of natural curiosities. A bibliography of the former can be found in the fifteenth chapter of von Rohr's *Physikalische Bibliothek:* "Von den zur Naturhistorie ganzer Länder und Gegenden gehörigen Schriften".[16] The most famous of the scientifically oriented travel reports were, of course, those by Scheuchzer and Haller who described their travels over the Alps. Another well-known travel account was Zacharias Conrad von Uffenbach's *Merkwürdige Reisen durch Niedersachsen, Holland und Engelland* (Ulm, 1753–1754). The author, one of the most learned men of his time, records his encounters with scientists in other lands, their collections of natural curiosities, their physical instruments and his own observations of natural phenomena. The *Physikalische Bibliothek* also indicates which travel accounts were translated into German. The subject index of Price's *Humaniora in Germany in the eighteenth Century* lists numerous German translations of English travel accounts. As far as the private collections of natural curiosities are concerned I have already noted in the discussion of Lesser's *Testaceo-Theologia,* his list of eighty private collections of which sixty-five were owned by Germans. In the periodicals there are frequent references to collections of natural curiosities. That the collectors were mostly amateurs of science is further evidence of the popularity of the sciences by the middle of the eighteenth century.

---

[16] Julius Bernhard von Rohr, *Physikalische Bibliothek* (Leipzig, 1724); the second edition of 1754 edited and brought up to date by A.G. Kästner is the more valuable one and the one I have used for this study.

Part II:
THE POETRY

As I have already noted in the introduction, the subject of science in the poetry of the German Enlightenment has not received much attention from scholars. Christof Junker's *Das Weltraumbild in der deutschen Lyrik von Opitz bis Klopstock* (Berlin, 1932) studies one astronomy theme; Karl Richter's "Die kopernikanische Wende in der Lyrik von Brockes bis Klopstock" (*Schiller-Jahrbuch*, 1968, 132–169) is for the most part inadequate as a study of the new astronomy in the German literature of the Enlightenment; and Lois Westen's *"Melitto-Logia" the Mythology of the Bee in Eighteenth-Century German Literature* (Diss., University of Illinois, 1952) focuses on one natural history theme.

In view of the material presented in the first part of this study, concerning the diffusion of science through popular literature, it is clear that men of letters had ample opportunity to become familiar with the new sciences. The task of the second part is to demonstrate that this did indeed happen and that the interest in the sciences is reflected in the poetry.

I shall discuss scientific themes in the poetry of about fifty poets, whose works, with a few exceptions, were published between 1720 and 1760. The poets will be presented in chronological order, since I believe, that is the most consistent and appropriate procedure in a study of this kind. The usual divisions and classifications of poets, as found in the literary histories, are not useful here.

Some poets will be treated briefly, others more extensively, depending on the quantity and variety of the scientific material. Thus this part consists of a discussion of science in the poetry of twenty-one poets, from Brockes to Wieland, followed by a brief survey of scientific themes in the works of an additional thirty-one poets, again arranged chronologically.

As was the case in the first part, here too several authors and their works are rescued from oblivion. Some of these poets are relatively or entirely unknown to literary historians. Most of the poetry I examine here is rarely considered and then only cursorily. Yet, when seen from the perspective of our study, that is, science in poetry, these forgotten works acquire significance. There are the compendiums of science in verse, "Die drei Reiche der Natur", "Der Fromme Naturkundige", "Die Gottheit" and "Die Körperwelt und ihr Einwohner der Mensch", by Brockes, Sendel, Behr and Leinker, respectively. These are long didactic scientific poems that follow the structure of the compendiums of science. There are also shorter didactic poems that focus on single scientific themes; for example, the poems about cometary theory by Kästner and Mylius: "Philosophisches Gedicht von den Kometen" and "Lehrgedicht von den Bewohnern der Kometen". There are long philosophic poems with much scientific material: Brockes' New Year's reflections, Zernitz' "Gedanken von den

Entzwecken der Welt", Creuz' "Lucrezische Gedanken", Dusch's "Die Wissenschaften" and Wieland's "Die Natur der Dinge". I also consider several well-
known literary figures like Gottsched and Bodmer. Their controversy over poetic
theory receives ample treatment in every history of German literature. But, who
knows that Bodmer made interesting literary use of popular themes from
astronomy and natural history in his epic poem, *Der Noah,* and who knows that
Gottsched's occasional poetry, dismissed even by his biographers, contain many
of the scientific themes of his time? Also considered are several prose works
with significant scientific material: Drollinger's letter, "Über die Aurikeln",
Gellert's lectures, "Moralische Vorlesungen", Krüger's imaginative essays,
"Träume", Mylius' satire, "Anfangsgründe der Physikopetitmaitrick", Dusch's
poetic prose essays, "Schilderungen aus dem Reiche der Natur und Sittenlehre"
and Weisse's comedy, "Der Naturaliensammler".

In these and many shorter works — as unknown as those cited above — an
enormous quantity and variety of scientific themes were found. This will
become even clearer in part three, where I summarize and survey the main
themes. It will also become clear that the scientific material in the poetry, in
many respects, parallels the scientific material in the popular literature.

1. Barthold Heinrich Brockes (1680–1740)

One of the most striking occurrences in the period of German literature with which we are dealing is the extraordinary popularity of Barthold Heinrich Brockes from the 1720's to the middle of the eighteenth century. He was quoted, praised and revered not only by fellow poets but also by scholars, theologians and scientists. By the middle of the century his popularity had begun to wane and before long was eclipsed altogether. For the last two centuries, his nine volume *Irdisches Vergnügen in Gott*[1] has been known only to the specialists who granted the work historical significance but denied it aesthetic value. Recently, however, scholars have read Brockes again and have come to different judgments. Von Faber du Faur has referred to him as "the first great impressionist"[2] and Harold Jantz has indicated that Brockes sustained aesthetic excellence throughout his nine volumes.[3] Indeed, a thorough study of Brockes' artistic craftsmanship is needed and would return to him some of the esteem he enjoyed in his own time.

The concern here is with the scientific themes in the *Irdisches Vergnügen in Gott* which are usually ignored by the commentators. The only exception is Christof Junker's study of the concept of space in lyric poetry, in which he ably discusses Brockes' modern cosmology.[4] Manikowsky in his dissertation on Brockes' "Weltanschauung" could have considered the scientific material, but his primary concern is with the subjects of God and man.[5] Another work in which a treatment of the scientific themes could have been expected is Willy Vontobel's study of German didactic poetry in the eighteenth century.[6] Unfortunately, he judges didactic poetry by standards extraneous to it and thus has little praise for any of the thirty didactic poets he examines. Of Brockes he says, "Seine Gedichte sind alle ohne innere Nötigung geschrieben. Sie sind nicht erlitten und nicht errungen" (48). In regard to another poet he passes a similar judgment: "Er ahnt nicht einmal, dass Poesie notwendiger Ausdruck ist inneren Erlebens und Strebens" (141). Such a philosophy of art simply excludes didactic poetry, and we can only wonder why the author undertook his study at all.

Another work that touches on scientific themes in Brockes' poetry is *Natural Science in German Romanticism* by Gode-Von Aesch.[7] In his chapter "The New

---

[1] *Irdisches Vergnügen in Gott, bestehend in Physikalisch-und Moralischen Gedichten* (Hamburg, 1721–1748). The following editions were available for this study: I, 1737; II, 1734; III, 1736; IV, 1736; V, 1735; VI, 1740; VII, 1746; VIII, 1746, IX, 1748.

[2] Curt von Faber du Faur, *German Baroque Literature* (New Haven, 1958), p. 357.

[3] Harold Jantz, "Brockes' Poetic Apprenticeship", MLN, Vol. 57, No. 4 (October, 1962), 439–442.

[4] *Das Weltraumbild in der deutschen Lyrik von Opitz bis Klopstock* (Berlin, 1932).

[5] Fritz von Manikowsky, *Die Welt- und Lebensanschauung in dem "Irdischen Vergnügen in Gott" von Barthold Heinrich Brockes* (Greifswald, 1914).

[6] *Von Brockes bis Herder* (Bern, 1942).

[7] (Columbia University Press, 1941).

Lucretius", he rejects Brockes as a candidate for the new Lucretius because his work does not have a "structure, system or totality" (39). I shall take this judgment as the point of departure for the examination of scientific themes in Brockes' poetry.

The subject of Lucretius in German culture of the eighteenth century requires treatment of its own. Brockes is one of the many anti-Lucretian poets of the first half of the century in that he intends to prove the existence of God and His qualities out of the works of nature. His belief is as authentic and personal as Lucretius' belief that nature is autonomous and that the gods are a fiction and need not be feared. Brockes, however, does follow in Lucretius' footsteps by giving an account of the works of nature from the scientific point of view of the time. There is no plan or design to the *Irdisches Vergnügen in Gott* that could be identified by a perusal of the table of contents of the nine volumes. Indeed, from the multitude of titles one finds there, one concludes that they were composed entirely at random. The randomness of the composition does not preclude, however, that a coherent structure may be present.

I shall begin by examining several of his long didactic poems with scientific subject matter: "Das Wasser" (I, 290–316), "Das Feuer" (I, 338–384), "Die Erde" (II, 227–251), "Die Luft" (II, 272–298), "Die fünf Sinne" (II, 328–380) and "Die drei Reiche der Natur" (IX, 5–310). The first four of these poems consider natural phenomena on our planet, divided according to the four elements. The approach is similar to that in the compendiums of science. The material is treated in the spirit of science-for-the-layman as we have it in the physicotheologies. The nature of the elements is examined, then specific phenomena and their use to man. In "Das Wasser" he studies the tides, floods, different bodies of water like oceans and rivers, lists several specific rivers and describes sea animals and sea vegetation. "Das Feuer" considers various theories about fire, circumstances under which fire arises, volcanic eruptions, subterranean fires and the effect and power of fire. In "Die Erde" he examines the size of the earth, the nature of gravity, the interior of the earth, metals, minerals, stones, diamonds and subterranean fires and waterways. In "Die Luft" he stresses the importance of that element to all life, he discusses the experiments with the air pump, describes the expansion and contraction of the air under different circumstances, resulting in phenomena like clouds, snow, hail, dew, fog and wind.

In "Die fünf Sinne" he describes the physical organs involved in sensation, the subjective aspect of sensation and the joy and importance of sensation to man. As he does frequently, he questions whether intelligent beings are limited to five senses. If we had only four senses, he reasons, we could not conceive the nature of the fifth. Similarly, there may be a sixth sense unknown to us but possessed by inhabitants of other planets or by our spirits after death. The senses that we do have, he grants, are appropriately balanced. If our eyes, for example, had microscopic or telescopic capacities we would see either too much or too little.

"Die drei Reiche der Natur" presents the main facts about metals, plants and animals in the manner of the compendiums of science. He divides the metal kingdom into five classifications: metals, half metals, earth, salts and stones. He enumerates many individuals in each classification giving the salient characteristics of each. We are informed about gold, silver, copper, iron, tin, lead, mercury, antimony, bismuth, sulfur, arsenic, salt, saltpeter, borax, alum, vitrol, naphtha, amber. Among the stones, the magnet is given special consideration. Many precious stones are described individually. All this is typical of compendiums of science in prose and verse.

In the next section on the plant kingdom, he praises the work of Grew and Malpighi on plant anatomy and proceeds to describe the parts of plants and their functions. He praises modern scientists for having learned so much about plants that they can now be classified better. He enumerates twenty-two species of plants with many more sub-species. He describes many individual plants, especially flowers and fruits.

In the final section on the animal kingdom, he discusses bodily functions such as the circulation of the blood, nourishment, digestion, reproduction and the parts of the body that are involved. He gives a classification of animals and enumerates and describes dozens of individual animals.

The structure so far considered is that of the compendiums of science which divide natural phenomena according to those that occur in the heavens, in, on and about the earth and forms of life on earth. Astronomy is not dealt with in any of these long didactic poems. However, there is astronomy lore in dozens of long and short poems in all the nine volumes. We shall select a few passages from these poems as examples of didactic verse on the subject of astronomy.

An exercise of the imagination in which Brockes and many of his contemporaries like to engage is to survey the heavenly bodies by stages, from the earth, to the moon, to the planets and beyond our solar system to the stars. A typical example of that is found in "Das Grosse und das Kleine":

Er schwang hierauf durchs Auge seinen Sinn,
Jedoch nur Staffelweise,
Zuerst von seinem Stand bis an die Wolcken hin.
Von da schwang sich des Geists und Blickes schneller Lauf
Bis an des Mondes Kreis hinauf.
Nicht gnug, er eilte weiter fort,
Und stieg nach dem verklärten Ort,
Wo er der Venus Glantz, und nahe
Bey ihrem Schein, Mercur, ersahe.
Von da stieg er bis an das Licht,
Und dacht' an uns'rer Sonne Gläntzen.
Er flog noch die entleg'nen drey,

Mars, Jupiter, Saturn, vorbey,
Ja leg't in einem Augenblick
Viel tausend Millionen Meilen
Bis an das Fix-Gestirn zurück,
Noch nicht genug. Er wollte weiter eilen;
Er that's; sah' von der Sternen-Sonnen Scharen
Die, so am tiefsten noch entfernet waren.
Er sah' der Milch-Weg's-Sterne Schein
Die sichtbar und zugleich unsichtbar seyn. (I, 144—145)

Another favorite astronomy theme is to cite sizes of heavenly bodies as determined by modern astronomers. In "Die himmlische Schrift" he compares the sizes of the largest planet Jupiter and the sun with that of the earth:

Indem ja Jupiter allein,
Nach aller Stern-Verständigen Beweis,
Mehr als acht tausend mal soll grösser seyn,
Wie unser gantzer Erden-Kreis.
Ob gleich Huygenius, Cassin,
Horoccius und Wendelin,
La Hire, nebst Flamstedius,
Auch Newton und Ricciolus,
Von unsrer Sonnen Grösse schreiben,
Sie sey entsetzlich, und die Zahl,
Wodurch diess helle Licht-Gefässe
An Grösse dieser Erden Grösse
Noch überträf', auf viel viel hundert tausend treiben;
So wollen wir jedoch das allerkleinste setzen,
Und sie auf hundert tausend mahl
Nur grösser, als die Erde, schätzen. (II, 216)

The enormous distances between heavenly bodies are used frequently by Brockes to convey the vastness of space. In "Gottes Tempel" he illustrates the enormity of the distances between the earth and the sun and beyond to other stars by stating the time it would take a cannon ball to make the journey:

Wär ein' abgeschossne Kugel mehr als 24 Jahren,
Ungehemmt und unverändert, in geradem Strich, gefahren:
Wäre sie doch an den Ort, wo der Sonnen Feuer prangt,
Von dem Kreise dieser Erde, lange noch nicht hingelangt.
Welch ein Abstand! welch ein Raum! zu dem nähesten Altare!
Aber lasst uns in dem Tempel noch im Geiste weiter gehn,
Und den ungemessnen Abstand zu der andern Sonne sehn!
Wär es möglich, dass die Kugel sechsmal hundert tausend Jahre,

In beständger Schnelligkeit, stets gerade vor sich flöge;
Würde sie (o! aller Grösse übergehnder Wunderraum)
Dennoch zu dem ersten Fixstern, als der andern Sonne, kaum,
Hin- und angelanget seyn . . . (VI, 4)

Another method he uses to construct in the imagination an image of the
infinity of space is to count the visible stars of various magnitudes until the
countlessness of stars is experienced:

Man stelle sich den Raum, in welchem sich die Kreise
Der Irrstern um die Sonne drehn,
Als eine Kugel vor, von welchen wir dergleichen Sonnen Welt,
In Fixstern erster Gröss, (wie es sich denn verhält)
Nicht mehr, als dreyzehn sehn.
Wenn wir nun weiter gehn:
So werden sich, in den noch tiefern Gründen,
An solchen Sonnen-Welt- und Planetarschen Ründen,
Die sich um ihre Sonn, als wie die unsre, drehn,
Schon mehr, als hundert, finden,
Die wir denn wirklich sehen können,
Und Stern' der andern Grösse nennen. (VI, 113).
. . . .

Sizes, distances and numbers of heavenly bodies are recurrent themes in
Brockes' poems. They are the steps on which he leads the imagination from the
visible to the spiritual. Our purpose here is to stress that throughout his nine
volumes, Brockes teaches modern astronomy. The structures of the long didactic
poems considered above are similar to those of the compendiums of science with
their arrangement of natural phenomena according to divisions which we can
describe as macrocosm, geocosm and microcosm. It is not simply a random
encyclopedic compilation but involves an intelligible order of phenomena which
gives a comprehensive view of the totality of the kingdom of nature.

Let us continue in the search for a structure, an order underlying the poetry
of Brockes. In addition to the many poems dealing with astronomy, there are
many that have natural history as their subject, as the table of contents of any of
the nine volumes can tell us. The study of astronomy and natural history became
popular pastimes after the invention of the telescope and the microscope when
these became accessible to the layman. Brockes frequently refers to observations
with the telescope and the microscope:

Ich nam ein Perspectiv zur Hand,
Da ich denn, an der Sonnen Körper, ein nie gesehnes Wunder fand. (VI, 108)

Ich richtete mein Perspectiv nachher auf einen Fixstern hin,
Den Unterscheid des Lichts zu sehn, der zwischen ihnen und Planeten, . . . (VI, 441)

Er setzte sich darauf ins Gras,
Die grosse Kleinheit zu betrachten,
Nahm sein Vergröss'rungs-Glas,
Das unserm Augen-Strahl
Jedweden Vorwurf fünfzig mal
Vergrössert zeiget, . . . (I, 146)

Als iemand dich beschäfftigt fand,
Durch ein Vergrössrungs-Glas ein Würmchen anzusehen, (IV, 145)

Was haben wir von dem, was in dem Samen stecket,
Durch Microscopia nicht allererst entdecket! (IV, 270)

Von unsers Schöpfers Gröss' und Wunder mehr zu fassen,
Und Seiner Wercke Meng' noch tieffer einzusehn,
Als von der Menschheit sonst geschehn,
Hat Er die Menschheit wehrt geachtet,
Und, vor nicht gar zu langer Zeit,
Ein Fern- und Grösserungs-Glas erfinden lassen. (IV, 328)

In many poems, as for example in "Das Grosse und Kleine" (I, 143—148), he
shifts from the telescope to the microscope, from astronomy to natural history.
This transition from the vast to the minute is carried out extensively in the long
new year's reflection for 1730 (IV, 458—491). He surveys the planets of our
solar system and the stars beyond in a way already familiar to us. Then he turns
to the world of minute phenomena:

Ein iedes Blat, ein iedes Tröpfchen Nass,
So in der Thiere Cörpern stecket,
Wenn man dieselbige mit Fleiss und Ernst bemerckt,
Zeigt uns viel lebende Geschöpfe. Man entdecket
Sie Schaaren-weis', und fast bey Millionen. (476)

This leads him to reflect on the gradual differences between the species in the
vegetable and animal kingdoms. The image of the ladder of creation extended
beneath and beyond man is then used by Brockes to unite both realms:

Indem ich nun des Schöpfers Lieb' und Macht,
In dieser Wunder-Leiter Länge,
Und ihrer Sprossen grosse Menge,
Die von uns abwärts führt, betracht;
Werd' ich aufs neu (o Wunder) sehr gerühret
Durch eine Leiter, die ich seh,
Dass sie mich noch weit höher in die Höh,
Als jene niederwärts mich führte, führet. (479)

This image, not unique to Brockes, of course, but shared by most of his contemporaries, represents one of the ordering principles of Brockes' poetry.

The ladder of creation beyond man offered Brockes subject matter for speculation. His attempts to extend the world of nature from the perceived to the possible is an integral part of his vision of nature. His speculations frequently take the form of trying to conceive the nature of the intelligent beings inhabiting other planets. In the new year's reflection for the year 1722 (I, 423–457), which takes the form of a dialogue on the question of a plurality of inhabited worlds, the speaker who represents the poet's viewpoint speculates about the creatures who might inhabit those other worlds:

> Zudem so steh' ich ja nicht zu,
> Dass es dort Menschen sind, wie ich und du.
> Es können Engel, Thiere, Geister
> Theils nicht so gut, theils herrlicher, als wir
> Bewohner, Bürger oder Meister
> Von andern Erden seyn. Mir kommt es glaublich für
> Dass, da schon hier die Wunder-Eigenschaft
> Der wirckenden Natur und der Verändrungs-Kraft
> Die Unerschöpflichkeit in allen Dingen weiset,
> Man dort, durch unleugbare Schlüsse,
> Von Gottes Macht ein gleiches glauben müsse. (436)

This is an example of going from the real to the possible. Since nature on our planet is observed to be inexhaustible and versatile, one can expect nature to be just as inventive there and provide those many planets with a variety of creatures. In the poem "Vier Welte" (VI, 281–282) he observes four planets and muses over the richness of nature which has provided such a variety of worlds and creatures:

> Ich stelle mir
> So vieler tausendfach-geformter Creaturen,
> Uns unbegreiflichen Figuren,
> Veränderung, Beschaffenheit und Zier,
> Den tausendfach-verschiednen Grad,
> Von Schatten und von Licht, von Farben und von Kräften,
> Von tausenfach von uns verschiedenen Geschäfften,
> Die jede Creatur vermuthlich dorten hat,
> In einer dunklen Klarheit für. (282)

Of the many poems that deal with this theme there are several in which our poet undertakes dream journeys to other planets and communicates with the inhabitants there. In "Traum-Gesicht" (IV, 192–199) he travels to worlds where the inhabitants have only one of the five senses. The moral that the poet wants to teach is that they with only one sense are more pious than earthlings with five. His experience, however, brings the dreamer to the reflection that in the kingdom of nature other worlds might exist whose inhabitants have more than five senses:

> Noch fiel bey meinem Traum mir bey,
> Ob es nicht möglich, ja sogar auch glaubhaft sey.
> Dass, da des Schöpfers Macht nicht zu erschöpfen ist,
> Nicht noch verschiedne Erden
> Im Reiche der Natur vielleicht gefunden werden,
> In welchen den Bewohnern nicht allein
> Fünf Sinnen, noch vielmehr, vielleicht geschencket seyn. (198—199)

In a continuation of this dream "Zum Traum-Gesicht" (VI, 291—295), the poet dreams of a space journey he undertakes with an inhabitant of the planet Jupiter. This creature with whom he communicates telepathically had been studying the ways of the earthlings and had come to the conclusion that they were "Mitteldinge" between the animals and the more advanced inhabitants of Jupiter. In "Inseln" (V, 162—164) he undertakes a dream journey to the moon where a moon inhabitant explains to him the origin of the satellite out of the earth's substance.

One more example of how Brockes transcends the visible world of the scientists to what may lie beyond it occurs in one of his philosophic poems, namely, his New Year's reflection for 1718 entitled "Die Zeit" (I, 389—392). He claims there that our conception of time as something absolute and real is an illusion, a subjective factor. The source of our sense of time, he maintains, is the daily and annual motions of our planet which give us the awareness of change:

> Wann unser irdischer Planet
> Im Schatten bald, und bald im Sonnen-Strahl,
> Drey hundert fünf und sechzig mal
> Sich um sich selbst herum gedreht,
> Und so zugleich den grossen Kreis vollendet,
> In welchem ihn der Sonnen Lebens-Brand,
> Durch Gottes mächtge Wunder-Hand,
> Beständig um sich dreht und wendet;
> So haben wir hiedurch in Jahre, Tag' und Stunden
> Uns, was nicht theilbar ist, zu theilen unterwunden,
> Und gleichsam einem Theil der dunckeln Ewigkeit,
> Die unzertrennlich währt, worin wir alle schweben,
> Den Namen Zeit,
> Die zu vergehen scheint, da wir vergehn, gegeben. (389)

It is primarily these regular revolutions of our planet that cause us to divide the indivisible; hours, days, years are the divisions we have imposed on eternity. To escape the inevitability of the consciousness of time which obscures the awareness of eternity, our poet raises his spirit beyond revolving, moving heavenly bodies where, since there is no motion, there is no time:

Wann nemlich, durchs Gesicht, mein Geist sich aufwärts lenckt,
Sich in den tieffen Raum des Firmamentes senckt,
Und durch den Zwischen-Stand der stet-und-regen Sterne,
An einen Ort gedenckt,
Der von dem Erden-Kreis so ferne,
Dass ihn ihr Schatten nicht, im Drehen, treffen kann;
So deucht mich, treff ich da was ewig-ruhigs an. (391)

This conception of space untouched by either motion or time, Brockes views as a visible image of eternity:

Dort ist kein Sturm, kein Wind, kein Morgen, keine Nacht,
Kein Wetter, keine Luft; nichts, das Bewegung macht;
Kein Nebel, kein Geräusch, kein Jahr und keine Zeit.
Scheint also diess ein Raum, der, von der Ewigkeit,
Uns fast was sichtbares und wesentliches zeiget. (391)

The goal toward which this reflection moves is, of course, the recognition of God. We have here the physicotheological pattern of going from the creation to the Creator. But his analysis of motion, time, space and eternity shows us a much more sophisticated physicotheologian than we are accustomed to from the commentators on Brockes' poetry.

The examination of scientific material in the *Irdisches Vergnügen in Gott* has not revealed a single uniform structure. Nevertheless, the judgment that the nine volumes of verse are a random compilation of poems without any "structure, system or totality" is misleading. Brockes is the poet of the real and of the possible. As a didactic poet of science, he surveys the discernible realms of nature. His vision of nature, however, leads him beyond what is to what may be. Nature does not stop with the perceived world. Nature extended beyond the physical touches the spiritual and requires both the man of science and the man of faith.

2. Carl Friedrich Drollinger (1688—1742)

In the second edition of Drollinger's works of 1745,[1] several eulogies are included which give us a very clear idea of Drollinger's interest in science, specifically, natural history. There is an introduction to his life and works in the form of an address held in 1743 in memory of the deceased poet by Johann Jakob Spreng, professor of rhetoric and poetry in Basel. Referring to Drollinger's contributions to the Deutsche Gesellschaft in Leipzig, Spreng speaks of him as "ein gründlicher Natur- und Gottesgelehrter" (xxx). He also speaks of Drollinger's work in natural history with his teacher, Benedict Stähelin, first as a student and then as an independent researcher:

> Eine edle Ergetzung fand er ebenfalls in der Betrachtung der Naturschätze, und vornemlich der Kräuter und Blumen. Er untersuchte teils allein, teils mit Herrn Professor Stähelin einem der erfahrensten Kräuterkündiger unserer Zeit, ihre Arten, ihre Teile, ihre Gebäude, ihre Kräfte, ihre Schönheiten, ihre Entwickelung und Fortpflanzung, samt ihren übrigen Eigenschaften so genau und so lang, dass Er nicht nur, was Andere davon schreiben, als ein sichtlicher Zeuge und Selbstforscher, entweder wiederlegen, oder erweisen, sondern auch zuweilen die Lehrbegihrde seiner Freunde und Bekannten mit gantz neuen Entdeckungen aus dem Reiche der Blumen vergnügen konnte. Indem Er allso den Schöpfer, allenthalben fand, teilte Er schon im Vorschmacke die Freude mit jenen Geistern, die immer um die Gottheit schweben. (xxv)

Drollinger, in the Brockes tradition, praised God in the firmament as well as in minute life on earth, as Spreng points out in his commemorative ode:

> Du schwungest Dich der höchsten Sphäre
> Mit deines Geistes Flügeln vor,
> Und drangst durch jene Feuermeere
> Zur unerschaffnen Sonn empor.
> Wie die dem Schöpfer nächsten Geister,
> So machtest Du Dich nicht nur Meister
> Vom kleinen Punkt der nidern Welt.
> Du hieltst den Himmeln selbst Gerichte
> Mit Neuton, der das Gleichgewichte
> Der Sternenreiche hergestellt. (L)

Drollinger as an astronomer as well as a botanist raised himself to the station of those angelic spirits who behold perpetually and fully what the pious scientist perceives only in fragments. We see that Spreng reflects the opinion of many of

---

[1] Carl Friedrich Drollinger, *Gedichte* (Frankfurt, 1745), hrsg. von Johann Jakob Spreng.

his contemporaries that Newton was the great synthesizer of the new system of the heavens. The verse about the uncreated suns is most interesting, since it is an allusion to the speculation about a continuous creation and destruction of solar systems.

Spreng continues in his ode with a reminder that Drollinger, even though a scientist, never lost sight of himself as a creature of God:

Doch eitel ungeheuers Wissen
War Deiner Seelen viel zu klein;
Drum war Dein Herz und Geist beflissen,
In Gott und sich gelehrt zu seyn.
Wenn Andre sich in Sterne wagen,
Und nach unzählbarn Welten fragen,
Sich aber selbst vergesslich fliehn,
So wolltest Du Dich erst erfinden,
Und Deines Wesens Zweck ergründen,
Weil sonst Dir alles übrig schien. (L)

This edition of Drollinger's works concludes with a collection of eulogies dedicated to the poet. The most interesting one is by Barthold Heinrich Brockes whom Drollinger admired so much. According to him, Drollinger is not one of those rigid souls who fails to see God in the starry firmament or in terrestrial vegetation. On the contrary he is one of the great souls who can lead others to God through contemplation of his works:

Nun finden sich zwar hier und dar erhabne Geister, grosse Seelen,
Die ihres wahren Endzwecks hier nicht nur, wie Andre, nicht verfehlen,
Da sie den Schöpfer sehn und schmecken; nein, die den Irrenden zu Gut
Die Gottheit in den Creaturen, in Himmel, Erde, Luft, und Flut,
Allgegenwärtig darzustellen, und aus der Blindheit uns zu ziehen,
Um Gott in unsrer Lust zu ehren, in reinen Liedern sich bemühen:
So wie vom grossen Drollinger bewundernswürdig ist geschehn,
Wie wir in seinen herrlichen, nie gnug gepriesnen Schriften sehn. (377)

In Drollinger's works themselves, a most explicit statement of his interest in natural history is found in his letter of 1739 to the above mentioned Stähelin, entitled "Über die Aurikeln." He begins his letter by speaking of his interest in plant life which was due primarily to the professor's instruction: "Durch Ihren Unterricht sind mir die Schätze der angenemen Flora hauptsächlich bekannt worden. Und nun bin ich dergestalten davon eingenommen, dass ich mich täglich mit Euerer Hohedelgebohrnen über ihre Schönheiten unterhalten möchte." (330)

He then turns to his own observations of the late blossoms of his auriculas: "Ich habe mich seit einigen Wochen mit Betrachtung der Spätlingsblühte von meinen Aurikeln belustiget. Sie ist nur ein Schatten von der wunderwürdigen Haubtblühte, die uns der Frühling gewähret. Und doch finden wir noch Tausend Annemlichkeiten dabey. Man weiss nicht, was man an diesen holden Pflanzen zuerst bewundern solle: das zierliche Laub, den prächtigen Stengel, die Schönheit der Blumenblätter, und den unendlichen Unterschied in ihrer Bildung." (330–331)

Drollinger, the poet, then weaves a charming Ovidian tale about the metamorphosis of this plant from a simple, non-descript healing herb to its present beauty: "Ehedessen zwar waren die Aurikeln gar schlecht geschmücket, wie viele andere heilsame Kräuter; bis sie endlich durch einen merkwürdigen Zufall zu der gegenwärtigen Schönheit gelangten. Vielleicht ist diese Begebenheit Euerer Hohedelgebohrnen noch nicht bekannt. Der Vater Ovidius hat vergessen, uns solche zu erzählen. Ich will sie aber Denselben getreulich mitteilen." (331–332)

The tale which Ovid never told is as follows: Hygiea, the goddess of health, once left her beloved Epidauris and accompanied by her attendant, little Telesphorous, ventured forth into new areas to look for plants with healing powers. They finally came to the Swiss Alps where they met the goddess Flora, herself. As the goddesses discussed the plants of the area, Hygiea raised the paradox that Flora had endowed the most useless plants with the greatest beauty but left the most beneficent unadorned. Flora was amused by the criticism but never having experienced illness, had no sympathy for the matter. Shortly thereafter, however, the goddess injured her arm on a rock while examining some flowers and for the first time experienced pain. Hygiea came to the rescue with a few leaves from the humble auriculas whose curative powers healed the wound in only a few hours. Out of gratitude Flora bestowed on this plant its present beauty. Thus the metamorphosis.

Then the poet leaves mythology and turns to serious questions of natural history, specifically the problem of preformation and encapsulation, namely, the theory that the whole plant is concealed in the seed and, moreover, that all future plants till the end of time are actually encapsulated in the first seed: "Wie gehet es mit dieser Vermehrung zu, und was für unbegreifflicher Wege bedienet sich die Natur in diesem grossen Werke? Ist es möglich, dass in dem ersten Sämlein alle diejenigen Pflanzen verborgen gelegen, die davon hergestammet, und noch bis ans Ende der Welt herstammen werden? Dass eine ganze Pflanze schon wirklich darinn gesteckt, mit allen ihren Teilen, mit Hundert, mit Tausend, mit etlich Tausend Samenkörnlein? Dass ein Jedes derselben wieder ein Gewächse mit eben so vielen Samen, und abermal andere Pflanzen, in sich beschlossen? und so fort bis ins unendliche." (338–339).

This theory was widely discussed and accepted at the time. Yet Drollinger, as many natural historians, raised questions about its validity:

Wenn dieser Grundsatz richtig ist, woher kommt denn die viele Verschiedenheit der Farben? Wie geht es, dass aus dem Samen einer Grasblume so viel
rohte oder gesprengte entstehen? Doch dieses ist ein geringes. Vielleicht
wirken die verschiedenen Nahrungssäfte den Unterschied. Vielleicht ist die
weisse Blume von dem männlichen Samen einer Rohten befruchtet worden,
dass sie weisse Kinder bringt. Aber wohher entstehet denn die so sehr
veränderliche Form der Blumenblätter? .... Der unendliche Unterschied in
der Anzahl der Blätter erweckt eine weit grössere Schwürigkeit wider obige
Lehre. Eine einfache Grasblume hat insgemein vier Blätter. Wenn ich aber
ihren Samen in gutes Erdreich säe, wenn ich die jungen Pflanzen oft versetze
und sorgfältig behandle, so bekomme ich gefüllte Blumen, deren Eine wol
fünfzig Blätter hat. Sind diese gleich Anfangs im Samen verborgen gewesen?
Es ist keines Wegs gläublich. Denn ohne den guten Grund, die Wartung, die
Versetzung, und dergleichen Umstände wären die Blumen wol immerhin
einfach und vierblättericht geblieben." (339—340)

It is interesting to note that the editor of this edition, Spreng, has no
reservations about the preformation theory. In his footnote to the above, he
maintains that the fifty leaves are contained in every seed but develop only in
the proper environment.

Drollinger continues his speculations by suggesting a remarkable theory to
account for these variations in plant life: "Sollte es dannenhero so lächerlich
seyn, wenn wir diese Wunderwerke einem höhern Ursprunge, einem wirkenden
Wesen zuschreiben, das der Schöpfer zu dem Ende verordnet, und dem er
hierinnen einige Freyheit gegeben, aber solche doch mit gewissen Grenzen
umschränket hat: Einem Wesen, das, je nachdem ihm die Natur oder Kunst zu
Hülfe kommen, die Blätter der Blumen vermehren, ihre Farben und Gestalt
einiger Massen verändern, doch aber niemals ihr Geschlecht völlig verwandeln,
noch aus einer Aurikel eine Tulpe machen kan." (340—341)

It is not clear how seriously he took this idea of a being, neither God nor
nature, whose main characteristic is that of a formative power. It is to his credit,
however, that he recognized that the preformation theory was insufficient to
account for the enormous variety apparent in nature and that another factor
must be present. The editor, however, refers to this thought as only "ein
poetischer Einfall" and sees no need to deviate from the theory of preformation:

Leuwenhoek, und andere, die unter diesem Vorgänger in die geheime
Werkstätte der Natur eingedrungen, geben uns so deutliche und gewisse
Nachricht von der Zeugungsart der Pflanzen, dass ich nicht sehe, warum man
von ihrer Meynung abgehen solle. Sie versichern uns, dass man vermittelst der
Vergrösserungsgläser in gewissen Samenkörner die darinnen verschlossen
gewesenen Bäume mit Blättern, Stamm und Wurzeln nach ihrer Art ganz
eigentlich unterscheiden können. Nun aber ist die Wirkung und Entwickelung

der Natur einerley zu allen Zeiten und in allen Pflanzen. Demnach ist ein Samenkorn anders nichts, als eine eingewickelte und eingekürzte Pflanze; und alle die unzählbaren Gräsgen, Kräuter, Blumen, und Bäume, die sich jährlich hervorthun, sind so alt, als die Welt selbsten. Ich melde solches nur für diejenigen Leser, deren Umstände eben nicht erlauben, sich in den Schriften und Schulen der Naturkündiger viel umzusehen. (341)

There is a poetic treatment of the subject of plant life in a poem entitled "Auf eine Hyacinte", which he addressed to his friend, Eichrodt, a physician. The same fascination with plant life, its exterior forms and inner spirit, permeates this poem which is one of his most beautiful. The subject of preformation and encapsulation theories again arises in the very middle of the poem, but the primary theme is the drama of the growth of a plant.

The poem begins with a lament over the passing of summer and the disappearance of vegetation:

Bis Flora, voller Gram bey ihrer Kinder Leichen,
Uns endlich gar verliess, und zu den schönen Reichen,
Zu jener Gegend floh, da Phöbus rege Kraft
Ein immerwährend Grün und stete Blühte schafft. (66)

Anthosander, a devotee of Flora, refuses to accept this fate and conspires to outwit Winter:

Er hielt ein manches Glas bis oben angefüllet
Mit jener Segensflut, die aus den Wolken quillet,
Die die Natur gekocht, und aus der Lüfte Schooss,
An Wuchs und Kräften reich, auf unsern Boden goss. (66)

Into these glasses he places bulbs, and then the drama of growth begins. Time is compressed and we see the plant unfold before our eyes:

Doch schied vor allen sich von der gemeinen Mänge
Ein Hyacintenkiel mit zierlichem Gepränge.
Des Frühlings schönstes Kind hielt seine Kluft versteckt,
Bis Florens eigne Hand es nach und nach entdeckt.
Drey Tage stund er kaum auf dem crystallnen Trohne,
Als schon der Wurzeln Heer gleich einer runden Krone
Aus seinem Kerker brach, von dem erregten Duft
Gereizet und gelockt. Des Zimmers warme Luft
Befördert ihren Trieb sich weiters auszudehnen.
Wie eine holde Reih von Perlenweissen Zähnen,
Wenn sie der erste Druck aus ihren Höhlen stösst,
Bey einem zarten Kind sich allgemach entblösst:
Nicht anders drangen sich der Zasern erste Spitzen

Durch den geschwellten Kiel aus Hundert kleinen Ritzen;
Und füllten nach und nach, gleich einem dichten Strauss
Verwirrt, doch angenem, den Raum des Glases aus.
Bald zeigte sich ihr Tuhn. Es schwand des Wassers Mänge;
Die Wurzeln zogen es durch ihre kleinen Gänge,
Gehöhlten Teicheln gleich, und sogen seine Kraft,
Sein fünfftes Wesen, aus zu ihrem Nahrungssaft.
Das Wachstum folgte drauf. Der Kiel war nunmehr offen.
Aus dessen Spitze bald, nach Anthosanders Hoffen,
Ein gelblich-grüner Berg geschlossner Blätter stiess,
Und uns ein Vorgebirg der frohen Hoffnung wies.
Doch fehlt die Blume noch. Du Muter aller Dinge,
Vergönne, dass ich jetzt in dein Geheimniss dringe,
Dass ich ein Zeuge hier von deinen Wundern sey;
Und lass mir einen Blick in deine Werkstatt frey!
Zwelf Wälle stunden da, Zwelf runde Festungswerker
Gewölbten Mauern gleich, ein angenemer Kerker,
Mit Nahrungssaft gefüllt, in dessen engem Zwang
Der Blätter dichter Busch sich in einander drang.
Ihr Innerstes beschloss der Schönheit Meisterstücke.
Zwelf Knöpfgen hatten sich mit künstlichem Geschicke
In einen Knopf gedrängt, dcr fern von Licht und Tag,
Wie eine Fichtenfrucht, in seiner Muter lag. (67–68)

Here he interrupts the drama with a speculation about causes. He has
described this plant from the outside, its exterior parts, now he wishes to
penetrate to that which is within, the unknown mysterious force that makes the
plant what it is. He addresses his questions to his friend, Eichrodt:

Belehre deinen Freund, der von Begihrde brennet,
Wie man den dunkeln Weg verborgner Weysheit kennet,
Woher das erste Seyn so vieler Wunder fleusst,
Und was für Ordnung sich in ihrer Zeugung weist!
Ists ein besondrer Geist, der alle diese Schätze
Nach unsers Schöpfers Schluss, dem ewigen Gesätze,
In jeder Pflanze wirkt, und die, die ihm vertraut,
In vorgeschriebner Art zu seiner Wohnung baut?
Wie? oder sind es wol verborgne kleine Gänge
Unzählbarer Figur, unendlich-grosser Mänge,
Worinn der waiche Saft, allmählich eingedrängt,
Nach seiner Formen Art die Bildungen empfängt?
Vielleicht auch lehrst du mich, dass Tausend Millionen,
Dass Pflänzgen sonder Zahl in einem Sämgen wohnen,

Da stets ein Inneres im Äuseren versteckt
Sich bis zur Ewigkeit entwickelt und entdeckt. (68–69)

The first suggestion that a formative spirit is responsible for all the complexities of plant growth we have already met in his letter to Stähelin, as well as the third suggestion that innumerable plants are encapsulated in a seed. The second suggestion is interesting, for here he considers the possibility that the causes of plant formation must be sought in the anatomy and physiology of plants.

However, he despairs of knowing the hidden causes of growth and prefers to return to the exterior form of the plant:

Vergebens, werter Freund! Ich kenne meine Schwäche.
Mein Blick erforschet kaum der Körper äusre Fläche.
Der Ursprung ihrer Pracht, der Bildung dunkles Spiel,
Ist meinem blöden Licht ein Abgrund ohne Ziel.
Die Allmacht hat sie selbst mit einer Nacht umringet,
In deren Tiefe nicht der Allerklügste dringet.
Mich schreckt die Finsterniss, und weiset meine Blick
Ermüdet und beschämt zum Äuseren zurück. (69)

His description of the gradual unfolding of the stem is another fine example of his delight in visual forms and compensates for his ignorance of hidden causes:

Er kam, als wie ein Turm aus seinen tiefen Gründen;
Sein Kommen fiel ihm schwär. Nach langem Unterwinden
Durchdrang sein rundes Haubt des Kieles enge Kluft,
Und drückte mühsamlich sich in die freye Luft.
Bald sah man seine Pracht in neuem Schimmer blühen;
So wie vor Sonn und Licht die bleichen Schatten fliehen,
So wich die grüne Nacht, die auf den Knöpfen lag,
Der Farben erstem Spiel, dem Einbruch von dem Tag.
Dann folgt der volle Glanz in ungesäumter Eile.
Der kleine Stengel stieg, wie eine kleine Säule
Von Iaspis ausgedreht, mit schneller Macht empor;
Um sein erhabnes Haubt erschien der volle Flor: (70)

His delight in natural history is expressed once more in his poem, "An sein Vaterland" (81–90), which begins with a reminiscence of his friendship with Stähelin and their explorations of "die Werkstatt der Natur".

In the introduction by Spreng it was seen that astronomy was also one of Drollinger's interests. In the poem "Lob der Gottheit", astronomy appears in the familiar theme, praise of God in nature. The poet wishes to comprehend the great Being and turns his eyes to the unexplored abyss above him. The immensity of the heavens, however, prompts him to return to earth to find Him in more immediate natural phenomena:

In deinen unumschränkten Gränzen,
Da so viel Tausend Sonnen glänzen,
Vergehet aller Sinnen Kraft.
Es eilt mein Geist bestürzt zur Erden,
Um neuer Wunder voll zu werden,
Die Gott so nahe vor uns schafft. (6)

After surveying God's beneficence in earth, water and air phenomena, he turns to another familiar theme, namely, the renunciation of scientific knowledge for self-knowledge:

Genug, mein Geist, von fremden Werken!
Auf, schaue, was du selbsten bist!
Du wirst in dir ein Etwas merken,
Das mehr, als Stern und Sonnen, ist.
Du zählst belebt die todten Sterne;
Du missest ihre Gröss und Ferne:
Sie sind an Witz und Athem leer.
Du übersteigst der Sonnen Helle,
Und, wenn ihr Lauff unendlich schnelle,
So ists dein Denken noch vielmehr. (11)

The scientist, especially the astronomer, so proud of his exact measurements and calculations, does not thereby come any closer to understanding the life and soul of man.

Yet a few stanzas later, to convey the vastness and incomprehensibility of God, he turns again to the starry heavens:

Ihr, die ihr messet und ergründet,
Was Erd und Himmel in sich hält:
Auf! dass ihr eine Grösse findet,
Die grösser sey, als alle Welt.
Vermehret sie mit neuen Zahlen
Zu hundert-tausend-tausendmalen!
Erschöpfet eurer Geister Macht;
Und denket dann, dass eure Lehre
Von euers Schöpfers Allmachtsmeere
Noch keinen Tropfen ausgedacht!. (13)

The same ambivalence toward man's scientific knowledge, especially astronomy, appears in his poem "Über die Unsterblichkeit der Seele". On the one hand, to prove the grandeur of the human spirit, he points to its achievement in astronomy:

> Wer zählt das Heer der Lichten Sterne?
> Wer misst der Sonne schnellen Lauff?
> Wer dringt in ungemessne Ferne,
> Und deckt des Himmels Ordnung auf?
> Ists nicht des Geistes Wunderstärcke? (21)

Yet three stanzas later he returns to the inability of this knowledge to contribute anything to man's destiny:

> Es bringt doch unsrer Gaben Mänge
> Uns oft im Leben nur Verdruss.
> Wie mancher kürzt nicht seine Länge
> Durch vieles Wissens Überfluss?
> Gebricht mirs hier an Ruh und Glücke,
> Obgleich kein Fernglas meine Blicke
> Des Mondes Flecken je gelehrt:
> Ob Huygens Fleiss in jenen Fernen
> Mit keinen neuen Folgesternen
> Die Herrschaft der Planeten mehrt? (22)

The astronomer's knowledge of far away worlds is here taken as representative of human knowledge and its irrelevance to man's life.

In his essay "Von den Eigenschaften eines Kunstrichters", we find a completely secular statement about nature: "Zuvorderst folget der Natur, und messet eure Urteil nach ihrem gerechten und unänderlichen Probmasse. Sie irret niemals. Sie ist ein klares, ein unwandelbares, ein göttliches Licht. Sie gibt allem Kraft, Leben und Schönheit. Sie ist zugleich die Quelle, der Endzweck und die Probregel der Kunst. Aus ihrem Vorraht nimmt die Kunst alles, was sie mit rechte braucht." (194—195)

In view of what precedes, it is clear that the nature he speaks of here is the nature of natural history, immediate, plentiful, beautiful. Although he will readily admit that God is present in every blade of grass, it has become clear that plant life does not inspire in Drollinger primarily pious sentiments but rather aesthetic ones.

In the letter to Stähelin, Drollinger exhibited his scientific curiosity and in the Ovidian tale also his poetic imagination. Similarly in the poem "Auf eine Hyacinte" Drollinger was the natural historian approaching nature with careful, minute observations as well as the poet with his imaginative dramatic description of growth, the enthusiasm over visual form and the appreciation of the beauty, variety, and plentitude of the works of the great creative artist, nature. Though he also praises the achievements of the astronomers, he expresses doubts more often in this connection about the relevance of scientific knowledge to the life of man.

3. Daniel Wilhelm Triller (1695–1787)

The physician Daniel Wilhelm Triller was one of Brockes' better known followers, though he owed his fame as much to his medical work as to his poetry. His six volumes of *Politische Betrachtungen* span a period of three decades from 1725 to 1755 and even longer, considering the fact that the second edition of the fourth volume, including his elaborate attack on modern science and philosophy, was published in 1766.[1]

The poems which include scientific themes are physicotheologically oriented though the didactic element is predominant. His knowledge of science and of the achievements of individual scientists is more extensive than that of Brockes. This appears not only in the text of the poems, but especially in the copious footnotes, which make of some of the longer poems treatises of "science for the laymen".

The scientific subjects treated in the poems are similar to those in the *Irdisches Vergnügen:* astronomy, earth phenomena, natural history and medicine; the latter, of course, are more widely represented in Triller's poems. One striking difference between the two poets is that in Triller's later years and later volumes there is increasing opposition to modernity, including modern science, and a greater insistence on orthodoxy.

In "Das gestirnte Firmament" (I, 1–3) there is the cosmic view, so familiar from Brockes, of thousands of suns and infinite space. In "Die Sonnenfinsterniss" (I, 353–356) there is a description of a solar eclipse. In "Zufällige Gedanken bey Erblickung eines grossen Cometen" (IV, 378–388), he challenges the view of most of his enlightened contemporaries that comets have no meaning. He grants that they have natural causes, but insists that God can use a purely natural phenomenon like a comet or the rainbow as a warning or sign to man. Written in 1744, the poem expresses the above mentioned turn to orthodoxy.

"Die Luft" (I, 35–45) is a didactic poem in which he describes the properties of air and many of its functions. He reviews several of the significant experiments with air:

> Wohin Guericke gehöret,
> Der zuerst die Kunst gelehret,
> Wie man mit gar leichter Müh
> Einem Raum die Luft entzieh;
> Welches Boyle vergrössert,
> Aber Hauksbee mehr verbessert.

---

[1] *Poetische Betrachtungen über verschiedene aus der Natur- und Sittenlehre hergenommene Materien,* 6 Bände (Hamburg, 1750, 1746, 1750, 1766, 1751, 1755). The first editions were: 1725, 1737, 1742, 1747, 1751, 1755.

Sonderlich zeigt von der Schwehre
Die aus Glas geblasne Röhre,
Die dem Torricellius,
Als Erfinder, bleiben muss:
Wo man am Mercur erblicket,
Wie die Luft nach Graden drücket. (I, 37)

"Der Ursprung des Blitzes und Donners" (I, 364—384) is another didactic
poem in which he explains the natural causes of thunder and lightning:

Salpeter nun und Schwefel sind
Hier für die Aeltern zu erklären,
Als die das fürchterliche Kind,
Den Donner, zeugen und gebähren,
Der sich durch schnellen Blitz entzündt;
Denn durch Salpeter kömmt der Schlag,
Der Blitz durch Schwefel, an den Tag: (I, 367)

On the subject of natural history there are many didactic poems, of which
two of the longer ones are on bees (I, 22—34) and frogs (I, 148—159). They are
natural histories in which the behavior of these creatures is described. In the
latter poem he gives a detailed account of the mating habits of frogs.

Some of the didactic poems on medical subjects are "Der Schlaf" (I,
122—126) and "Das Fieber" (I, 127—132) where these conditions of the human
body are described from a physician's point of view. "Die Erzeugung und Geburt
eines Menschen nebst denen Haupttheilen des menschlichen Körpers" (I,
160—212) is an anatomy of the human body and some of its functions. With the
footnotes it is a medical text for the layman in verse. Of interest is also his
"Trauer- und Lobgedicht über . . . Hermann Boerhaave" (III, 70—91) in which
he reviews Boerhaave's achievements in natural history, chemistry, anatomy and
the practice of medicine. He pictures the spirit of the dead scientist in his new
environment where he sees fully what can only be surmised in life:

Ihm schliessen sich die Elementen auf;
Er kennt genau der weitsten Sterne Lauf,
    Und kann nun nah des Milchwegs Lichter zählen.
Er wundert sich, und stutzt, wenn er erblickt,
    Dass Newton hier fast wirklich wahr geträumet,
    Und sein Begriff sich mit den Sachen reimet,
Die doch so fern von ihm hinweg gerückt,
    Er misst und prüft die schweifenden Planeten
Nach ihrem Lauf, Trieb, Abhang und Gewicht;
Er weis genau die Farben von dem Licht,
    Und kennt gewiss den Ursprung der Cometen. (III, 86—87)

This is a recurrent theme in the eighteenth century, and usually Newton is cited as that mortal who came closest to the mysteries of nature. It is noteworthy here because it shows Triller still committed to the value of modern science.

His long poem "Sichre Anweisung zur wahren Weltweisheit" (IV, 1–80) is unique because of its elaborate criticism of modern science and philosophy.[2] His dislike of modernity was already apparent in his preface of 1751 to volume five, where he mocked the new expressions "Schöpferisch schreiben, schöpferisch dichten, einen Schöpfergeist haben" (V, preface 4). In this poem which was one of his last compositions, he challenges the faith of modern scientists that they have banished Aristotle's occult qualities and have substituted for it certain and demonstrable knowledge:

> Wir haben der Natur den Vorhang weggeschoben,
> Und uns mit keckem Schritt in ihr Gemach erhoben,
> Was Feuer, und was Luft, was Erd und Wasser sey,
> Davon fällt weiter nun kein Zweifel jemand bey.
> Wie fest sich unsre Seel an ihrem Körper binde,
> So, dass er, wenn sie denkt, den Eindruck gleich empfinde,
> Der Pflanzen Trieb und Wuchs, der Menschen Zeugungskraft,
> Hievon hat man ja nun vollkommen Wissenschaft. (IV, 3)

He reminds the moderns of their theodicies, pre-established harmonies and monads and asks whether these are not as obscure as occult qualities. They are deluded about their knowledge and cover their ignorance with words. What do they know about fundamental natural phenomena, he asks. If one asks them what fire is, they answer:

> Dass es ein Körper sey, der leichte, hell und lichte,
> Durchdringend, geistig, schnell, der brennet und verbrennt,
> Bald was vereiniget, bald etwas wieder trennt,
> Und was dergleichen mehr: doch diess sind Eigenschaften,
> Die äusserlich allein am Feuer sichtbar haften.
> Doch alles dieses bringt uns den Begriff nicht bey,
> Was eigentlich an sich des Feuers Wesen sey. (IV, 13)

The scientist can do no more than describe the surface; the essence is not accessible to him:

> Was euch bekannt, ist mehr ein seicht historisch Wissen;
> Als eine Folgerung von unfehlbaren Schlüssen,
> Ihr seht nur äusserlich der Sachen Zifferblat;
> Nicht, wie das Räderwerk den Trieb von innen hat. (IV, 14)

[2] In the text of the poem there are references to the Lisbon earthquake of 1755; the footnotes refer to publications as late as 1764. Therefore, it is likely that the poem was written in the early 1760's.

He then surveys the fields of science with his questions about fundamentals and taunts the moderns for their evasive answers:

Ich wende mich zu euch, ihr Weisen dieser Zeit,
Ihr die ihr der Natur geheime Räthe seyd,
Euch muthig in die Höh und in die Tiefe schwinget,
Und immer auf Beweiss und feste Gründe dringet;
Erbarmt euch über mich, nehmt euch doch meiner an,
Und lösst die Zweifel auf, die ich nicht heben kan. (IV, 53)

Even Newton is not excluded from his criticism:

Wie hoch ist Newton nicht, der grosse Geist, gestiegen,
Dass ihm nicht viele nach, geschweige nahe, fliegen,
Der mit erstaunlichem noch nie erhörtem Fleiss,
Selbst einen Sonnenstrahl so zu zergliedern weiss,
Dass er sich wiederum in sieben kleine trennet,
An deren jedem man die eigene Farb' erkennet;
Der Himmel und Natur zum schärfsten durchgespührt,
So weit der höchste Witz die Menschen möglich führt,
Der die Planeten misst, und schreckender Cometen
Verworrnen Gang erklärt; läst dunkle Qualitäten
Doch endlich gerne zu, und saget redlich frey,
Dass menschliche Vernunft sehr eng umgränzet sey. (IV, 64—66)

He does not question Newton's achievements in optics and astronomy; he simply points out that with his gravity Newton also confessed ignorance and took refuge in occult qualities.

The true task of philosophy, he concludes, should be to teach man self-knowledge, that is, awareness of his limitations and to support and defend the faith against its adversaries, of which modern philosophy has produced so many.

Triller's rejection of the optimism and faith of the Enlightenment may simply be the voice of his old age. Yet these sentiments were not at all uncommon at the time. In Triller's case it is significant that his poetry spans the period from the 1720's when he shared the optimism of the moderns to the 1760's when faith in the philosophy of the Enlightenment began to waver.

4. Gottfried Ephraim Scheibel (1696—1759)

Gottfried Ephraim Scheibel's poem *Die Witterungen. Ein Historisch- und Physicalisches Gedicht* is a 228 page discussion in verse of weather phenomena, agriculture and related themes.[1] Vontobel refers to the poem as "ein ungeheuerliches Lehrgedicht".[2] The poem is monstrous only if judged by extraneous standards, if one expects of it what it was not intended to be. Let us hear from the preface what Scheibel himself intended with the poem:

> ... so wollte ich meinen Landesleuten, besonders denen, so der Landwirthschaft ergeben sind, ein Vergnügen machen und ihnen meine Untersuchung und Beschreibung von Witterungen in einer ihnen deutlichen und verständlichen Schreibart liefern. Ich habe mir also den Vergil, Lucrez und den Opitz zum Muster erwählet. ... (Preface 4)

He has studied weather phenomena and their influence on agriculture and wishes to entertain and instruct his countrymen, especially those engaged in agriculture, with what he has found. This is certainly a most legitimate goal of a didactic poem. Anything but monstrous are his models, Virgil, Lucretius and Opitz, who also wrote didactic poetry on scientific and practical matters. The latter's "Vesuvius" is especially pertinent to Scheibel's work. In that poem Opitz described and tried to explain disruptive natural phenomena like volcanic erruptions and earthquakes. This is similar to Scheibel's purpose. He is convinced of the orderliness and lawfulness of nature, yet appalled at the devastation that unbridled phenomena like floods, storms and droughts can cause in the life of man. This paradox is the motivation that led to the present work.

The poem is divided into three parts; historical, didactic and moral. In the first part he describes calamities that have occurred in his native Silesia during the past fourteen years. He writes of heavy rains, storms, floods, famine, pestilence, drought and an invasion of grasshoppers from the east. There were, of course, intermittent periods of peace when agriculture flourished and harvests were rich. He stresses the contrast between the tranquility and wholesomeness that could be man's lot and the misery caused by these disruptive factors, and conveys, thereby, if not a sense of tragedy, a sense of pathos.

The second part presents his reflections on the causes of weather pheonomena. He divides weather phenomena into regular, orderly, predictable phenomena and those that are extraordinary and unpredictable. The former are such that accompany seasonal changes which are caused by the motions of the earth around the sun; the latter are the ones he wants to explain.

In discussing the earth he refers to the French expedition of Maupertuis and

---

1 (Breslau, 1752).
2 *Von Brockes bis Herder*, p. 65.

Clairaut to Lapland in 1736 which provided evidence that the earth was not entirely round but flat at the poles:

> Die Welt, so wie sie itzt von uns bewohnet ist,
> Schwebt nicht ganz kugelrund, wie man beyn Alten liest,
> Vielmehr beym Pol gepresst und seitwärts nur erhoben,
> Diess hat gelehrter Fleiss, der nicht genug zu loben,
> Auf Reisen angemerkt. Woher? ist noch nicht klar;
> Genug sie nahmen diess bey Untersuchung wahr,
> Als sie des Polus Höh in Norden abgemessen,
> Wo Härte, Kält und Frost die armen Lappen pressen. . . . (60)

These results were hailed at the time as a verification of Newton's theory of gravity and contributed to the decline of Cartesianism. Scheibel, however, asks, "Woher? ist noch nicht klar". Presumably he rejected the theory of gravity because he needed the aether of the Cartesians to explain unusual weather pheonomena:

> Wenn ich oft bey mir selbst recht diesem nachgedacht,
> So hab ich überzeugt den Schluss daraus gemacht:
> Dass alle Witterung, von der ich itzo singe,
> Bloss durch des Äthers Kraft zuförderst hier entspringe. (67)

His main contention is that since the causes of unusual, extraordinary weather phenomena have not been found in our atmosphere, they must lie beyond it. He maintains that the weight and motions of the moon and the planets cause reverberations which are transmitted into our atmosphere through the aether. In a footnote he explains his view as follows: "Ich stelle mir die Theilchen des Äthers wie Kugeln vor, die an einander stossen. Wird durch eine starke Bewegung eines Planeten ein Theil derselben heftig gerühret: so wird desselben Druck fortgepflanzet, und berühret den Körper eines andern. Dieses deucht mich eine wahrscheinliche Ursache ausserordentlicher Witterung zu seyn, wenn man keinen Einfluss oder Ausdunst der Planeten zugeben will" (119). He believes that the study of planetary influences would be much more worthwhile than the frivolous fictions about journeys to the planets. He even prefers the cometary theories of Johann Heyn in so far as he maintains that comets can influence weather phenomena on earth.

He is fully aware that he is advocating an unpopular thesis by insisting on planetary influences. These were rejected as part of the superstitious past. Yet he maintains the existence of planetary influences could be proven if they were given proper attention. He suggests that learned men in all parts of the world collaborate to make weather observations and at the same time take note of the positions and movements of the planets. Thus, he certainly does not suggest magical or supernatural explanations of weather phenomena. Nor is he satisfied with the explanation that they are acts of God. Though completely orthodox in his religious views, he insists that the extraordinary weather phenomena that create such havoc on earth have natural causes which can be discovered if they are sought in nature.

Though the main intent of the second part of the poem is to explain his reflections on the causes of extraordinary weather phenomena, there are frequent digressions on the beauties of nature. He is especially effective in describing the regular, orderly transitions of weather phenomena corresponding to the change of seasons and the peaceful agricultural pursuits of man.

The third part of the poem is devoted to a defense of the Christian faith against atheists and naturalists. Though in the previous section he subscribed fully to the scientific enterprise, here he voices doubts:

> Man misst die Höhen aus, die wir doch nicht besteigen;
> Ein langes Sehrohr muss uns neue Sterne zeigen,
> Die nie das Aug erblickt; man kennt die Mondenwelt,
> Und was der Sonnen Gluth für Wirbel in sich hält;
> Wie ein Trabantenheer den Jupiter begleitet,
> Und der Saturnus bald mit Henkeln ausgebreitet,
> Bald wieder enger glänzt. Was wagt nicht Menschenfleiss?
> Er sparet keine Zeit, scheut nicht Gefahr noch Schweiss,
> Das Wesen aller Ding und Körper zu ergründen,
> Ja, eine neue Welt, wärs möglich, zu erfinden.
> Was von Prometheus das Heidenthum geglaubt,
> Dass er dem Jupiter ehdem das Feur geraubt,
> Zeigt deren Forschern an, die itzt in unsern Zeiten,
> Um neu Erfindungen recht um die Wette streiten. (164)

The image of the modern scientist cast in the role of Prometheus, impiously trying to transcend the limitations of human nature, was not uncommon in the eighteenth century.

The poem concludes with a tribute to Brockes who inspired Scheibel to seek knowledge of God, the world and himself.

5. Albrecht Jacob Zell (1700–1754)

Albrecht Jacob Zell's *Erweckte Nachfolge zum Irdischen Vergnügen in Gott* (Hamburg, 1735) is a 700 page collection of poems written proudly in imitation of the master's poetry. As is to be expected, the disciple's imitation frequently falls short of his model.

As far as scientific themes are concerned, he shares many of Brockes' interests. In several poems he travels the familiar journey from the planets to the stars to a realization that space is infinite. In "Die unendliche Grösse des Schöpfers aus Betrachtungen der Sternen" (575–587), he distinguishes between the stars that are apparent to the naked eye and those revealed only by the telescope:

> Ein Fern-Glas schärft dir auch die Augen,
> Dass sie unsichtbares zu sehen taugen.
> Fleug dahin erst. Wie steigen nun die Höhen
> Von Sonnen, die wir sehn, zu den, die nicht zu sehen,
> Itzt aber langt kein Fern-Glas weiter zu . . . . (583)

In "Das Nichts der Menschen in Ansehung der Welt, des Himmels, und des Schöpfers" (588–605), he lists facts and figures about planets and stars until immeasurable space transcends his reason and reveals the nothingness of man. "Die nohtwendigen Drehungen der Erd Kugel" (653–697) is didactic verse which gives a detailed description of the diurnal and annual orbits of the earth and describes the calamities that would follow if these orbits were not exactly as they are.

The world of natural history is also represented. In an oratorio "Die Erschaffung der Welt" (85–159) which follows the Genesis account from the Creation to the Fall, he describes Adam's gradual awareness of his environment, his amazement and fascination with the world of nature around him. Adam notes the animals on land and in the sea, birds, plants and flowers, until he is finally led to recognize God the Creator. Adam, in other words, is a pious eighteenth century natural historian. In another oratorio, "Vergnügung des Gesichtes und Gehöres im Frühling" (190–219), he describes the transition from winter to spring, the growth and unfolding of the beauties of nature.

Zell, as Brockes before him, is aware of the world of the microscope as well as that of the telescope. In "Der Saamen der Pflantzen" (179–189) he describes the wonders in a seed as revealed by the divine gift of the magnifying glass:

> Es ist bekannt,
> Der Saame schliesse Wunder-klein
> Die Pflantze gantz und gar mit allen Blättern ein;
> Allein dis Wunder recht zu fassen,
> Hat Gott uns die Vergrösserungs-Gläser

Erfinden lassen.
In einer Bohnen-Saamen Pflantze
Kann man durch solches Glass den Stengel deutlich sehn,
Voll enger Blässgen holtz'ger Fäser,
Man sieht, da Blätterchen aus ihrem Stengel gehn,
Schon Knosp' und Knoten dran . . . (179)

Another interesting scientific theme is found in his "Gottes Grösse in den Wassern" (313–320), in his description and explanation of ocean tides:

Des Mondes reger Creis dehnt, presst und drengt die Luft,
Die Luft treibt, stösst die Fluht, die Fluht entweicht dem Duft,
Dann schwellen die Wasser und steigen hinauf
Doch wenn der Mond entweicht, die Luft nicht mehr gespannt,
So kehret mit der Luft die Fluht zum vorgen Stand,
Dann sincken die Wasser mit fallendem Lauf. (315)

This Cartesian explanation of the tides is another scientific theme he shares with Brockes.

Finally, his poem "Der Natur-Geist" deserves to be mentioned for its description of nature:

Es zeiget die Natur
In jeder wachsenden, beselten Creatur
Ihr' beygelegte Kraft und unsichtbare Macht,
Durch welche sie im Wachsen fortgebracht,
Nach ihrer Art formiret,
Mehr oder minder ausgezieret; (366)

Nature is here described as a mysterious invisible power, the source of life and growth, suggesting an autonomy that anticipates a later conception of nature.

6. Johann Jakob Bodmer (1698—1783)

Johann Jakob Bodmer's *Der Noah* was one of several Biblical epics written in Germany around the middle of the eighteenth century.[1] The model and inspiration for all of them was Milton's *Paradise Lost*. This was especially true in Bodmer's case, since he translated the Milton poem in 1732. Although Klopstock's *Der Messias* was the more popular of the Biblical epics, *Der Noah* is the more interesting for this study. With its many reflections on religion and nature, it expresses the spirit of the Enlightenment. The characters of the poem are the two patriarchs, Noah and Sipha, the former's three sons and the latter's three daughters. Noah's sphere is primarily the moral; he communicates with the angels, receives instructions and teaches them to his family. Sipha and Japhet are the scientists who study nature enthusiastically and praise God in His works. Fortunately, we have an excellent commentator on the poem in the person of the young Wieland, who wrote his *Abhandlung von den Schönheiten des epischen Gedichts 'Der Noah'* while he was Bodmer's house guest in Zürich.[2] As a contemporary and close associate of the author his comments on the scientific material in the poems are of special interest.

Of the poem's twelve cantos, the first six deal with the period immediately preceding the flood and the last six with the flood and various circumstances pertaining to it. The most striking scientific theme in the poem is Bodmer's use of a comet to explain the natural causes of the flood, wherein he followed William Whiston's theory very closely.[3] Wieland justifies this use of a scientific hypothesis in the poem:

> Erstlich hat er die Whistonische Hypothese von den physicalischen Ursachen der Sündflut, nach den Rechten der Poesie, für wahr angenommen, und dadurch nicht nur die Maschinen, durch welche so wichtige Veränderungen auf unserm Planeten gemacht werden, entdeckt, sondern sich auch ein weites Feld zu den grössesten Beschreibungen eröfnet, welche unsere ganze Seele ergreiffen und in Erstaunung setzen.[4]

The use of a comet as the cause of the flood provides a dramatic quality to the poem which it would not have had if the flood were treated simply as a supernatural, miraculous occurrence. Toward the end of the sixth canto, the sons of Noah begin to wonder from where the enormous quantities of water required for a universal flood would come:

---

[1] (Zürich, 1752). Revised editions appeared in 1765, 1772 and 1781.
[2] (Zürich, 1753).
[3] C.H. Ibershoff in his "Whiston as a source of Bodmer's *Noah*", SP, XXII (1925), 522—528, quotes parallel passages from Whiston's *New Theory of the Earth* and Bodmer's *Noah* to prove the obvious, that Whiston's work is a source for the poem.
[4] Wieland, *Abhandlung von den Schönheiten des epischen Gedichts 'Der Noah'*, p. 233.

Und für unsern Verstand ists wol ein schweres Geheimniss
Wo so viel Wasser vereinigter Meer' herkommen soll; können
Unter dem Boden so unermessliche Beken mit Flut seyn?
Doch sind solche darinn verborgen, so sind sie da ruhig;
Was für ein Hebezeug soll die Wasser von da heraufholen?
Dieses kann nur die Macht, die im Anfang den Erdball erschaffen;
Doch wir zweifeln, dass sie die Schöpfungsgesetze verändert. (198)

The mechanistic scheme of Descartes and the gravitational theory of Newton
received their earliest popular treatment by Burnet and Whiston, respectively, to
answer this very question that puzzles the sons of Noah.

In the seventh canto the drama begins to unfold with Sipha's telescopic
observation of a new star which was to be the comet of destruction:

Sipha schickte die Zeit her sein scharfbewaffnetes Auge
Oft nach dem nächtlichen Himmel, wo er vom äussersten Norden
Über den Inseln ein neues Gestirn aufgehend erblickte; (209)

Sipha identifies the newly sighted heavenly body as a comet and an
experienced astronomer explains to the Noachides the nature of comets:

Alle die hat am Tag der ersten Erschaffung die Allmacht
In die Wüste des Aethers mit andern Planeten geworfen,
Wo sie in ihrem excentrischen Weg unendlich umschweifend
Sich um unzälige Welten von Himmel zu Himmel umwinden;
Kreislängen, die das Auge nicht misst, die Zahl nicht berechnet. (210)

In continuing his explanation of comets, he considers the destruction that
such a comet could cause on earth by approaching too closely. It could consume
the planet entirely or cause a shift in the position of poles, or the vapors of the
comet's tail could descend upon the earth and increase the waters to cause a
universal flood. Thus, Sipha by natural reason surmises what is revealed to Noah
by Raphael in the eigth canto, namely, that this comet will indeed carry out
God's design. Very soon thereafter the feared moment arrives:

Als der Komet den Gränzen der Erde so nahe gekommen,
Dass er kaum seinen Durchschnitt von ihrer Kugel entfernt flog;
Sah man des Oceans Flut das Ufer furchtsam verlassen,
Rückwärts über sich steigen, die Breiten des Rückens erheben,
Und mit sichtbarem Schwellen dem Stern entgegen aufthürmen. (249)

The use of the Whistonian theory is especially successful in describing the
chaos of the inundation resulting from the gravitational struggle between comet
and earth: "So stark zog der Komet, so stark zog wieder die Erde; / Aber die
Erde zog stärker, wiewol zu ihrem Verderben" (251).

In the ninth canto the comet is observed in the orbit of Mercury, having left behind it a devastated earth. Bodmer, following Whiston's theory closely, brings the comet back a second time in its ascent from perihelion:

> Denn der geschwänzte Komet, der mit einer schnellern Bewegung
> Als des Mondes ist nach dem Reiche der Sonne geeilt war,
> Und den Himmel in kurzer Zeit zu verlassen bedacht schien;
> Blieb mit geändertem Schluss im Widder stillstehn, und wandt sich
> Plötzlich, und eilte zurück in die Örter disseits der Sonne. (302)

This time, however, the comet did not pass as closely and the conflict of gravitational forces was not as severe. The earth did pass through the comet's tail and thereby received ninety more days of heavy rain before the comet continued on its eccentric orbit:

> Neunzigmal stieg der Tag vom Himmel, und neunzigmal bracht er
> Neue Wolken herab, und neue Krüge mit Wassern
> In den Wolken, die Beute der zweiten kometischen Ankunft.
> Aber der Stern, der sie misste, floh nach dem Bären im Norden,
> Eben den Weg, den er kam, Jahrhunderte jenseits zu laufen,
> Wo sich sein Pfad um unzählige fremde Sternen herumdreht,
> Durch eccentrische Längen und Krümmen, durch die ihm zu folgen,
> Unsern Weisen es noch an tüchtigen Augen gefehlt hat. (326)

This second passing of the comet is strictly according to Whiston's theory who thereby wanted to account for the Biblical story that the waters continued to mount after the forty days rain and his own computations of the comet's orbit. He also follows Whiston in explaining how the waters subsided. Because of the pressure of the flood waters, the earth expanded causing new fissures in the surface through which the waters began to fill the vast subterranean caverns. In the concluding canto God shows the Noachides, as a sign of reconciliation, the rainbow which is described according to Newton's color theory:

> Vielmals brach sich das Licht im Schoss der treufelnden Urnen,
> Schlug sich vielmals daran, und prellte zurück, bis die Stralen
> Alle Farben in ihrer verschiedenen Ordnung durchliefen.
> Neuton hat erst des Lichts verschiedene Faden getrennet,
> Als er ihm in den lichten Meander der Mischung gefolget. (410)

The last two lines with the specific reference to Newton are omitted in the 1765 edition.

The Whistonian theory is by no means the only scientific theme in the poem. Sipha and Japhet are both natural historians and there are frequent occasions before the arrival of the comet when they discourse about nature's works.

Wieland again defends the poet's characterization of these early men as serious students of nature:

> Was ist wahrscheinlicher, als dass so aufmerksame Naturforscher, wie die ältesten Menschen, theils aus Nohtwendigkeit, theils um den Pflichten der vernünftigen Geschöpfe Gottes genug zu thun, seyn musten; Naturforscher, welche, ganze Jahrhunderte durch, ihre Beobachtungen fortsetzen konnten, und von den verdriesslichen Zerstreuungen frey waren, von denen nach der Einrichtung der spätern Welt sich so wenige entledigen können; nicht nur auf die meisten Entdeckungen gekommen, die man vornemlich seit den glück-lichen Zeiten gemacht hat, da Bacon angefangen, den Philosophen die Versuche und die Induction, als eine reiche Mine der nützlichsten Wahrheiten, anzubefehlen; sondern dass ihnen auch tausend Kräfte und Beschaffenheiten natürlicher Dinge bekannt gewesen, von denen wir nichts wissen, und deren Kentniss vielleicht unsern Enkeln aufbehalten ist.[5]

Thus young Wieland believes that the modern inductive scientific method is a rediscovery of an ancient practice and suggests that these early men, unencumbered by vain distractions and with their longer life span had even been more advanced in their scientific knowledge. He repeats this point of view later to justify Sem's knowledge of plants:

> Es wird sich, wie ich hoffe, niemand befremden lassen, dass Sipha und Noahs Söhne in der Geschichte der Pflanzen nicht weniger erfahren gewesen als Malpighi oder Ray, es müsten denn diejenige seyn, welche sich mit dem Lucretius und einigen neuern einbilden, die Bewohner der ersten Welt seyen mit Thierfellen angethan, in Wäldern herumgekrochen, haben Eicheln gefressen, und so wenig von Gott, Natur, oder Tugend gewusst, als diese Herren von der Bibel wissen.[6]

The contrast that Wieland makes here between Bodmer's as well as his own view of the civilization of early man and that of Lucretius shows us two distinctly different views of primitivism.

In the fourth canto Deborah, one of the daughters of Sipha, narrates what her father had once taught their mother about his scientific studies. She describes, for example, his enthusiasm over the new worlds he had discovered through his lenses:

> O was ward für ein Buch vor seinen Augen eröfnet,
> Als ihm gegeben ward, Krystall in Linsen zu schleifen!
> Er sah in der Schöpfung die neue Schöpfung entstehen,
> Die kein Weiser zuvor vermuthet hatte; Geschöpfe

---

[5] Wieland, *Abhandlung von den Schönheiten des epischen Gedichts 'Der Noah'*, p. 77.
[6] Ibid., p. 246.

Wohnten in solchen Dingen, die niemand für wohnbar gehalten;
Sah den Monden vertieft und erhöht, wie Thäler und Berge.
Was er auf Erd und am Himmel von Gottes Handschrift enthüllte,
Schwieg er nicht seiner Vermählten, für sie die süsseste Speise. (114)

Sipha's joy over the worlds of the microscope and telescope were certainly understood by Bodmer's contemporaries, who experienced the same delight. Furthermore, Sipha like any eighteenth century natural historian, was led from these worlds to speculate about the continuity between the small and the large:

O ein unendlicher Raum vom Menschen zum obersten Engel,
Mit unendlichen Graden erfüllt, olympischen Wesen!
Unter der Geisterwelt verschwindet die irdische Kette.
Eh die Natur sich gesetzt den irdischen Menschen zu bilden,
Hat sie vorher unzählige Male versucht, was sie könnte;
Aber sie hat nicht bey dem Menschen die Arbeit vollendet,
Sondern sie führt die bildende Hand von Arbeit zu Arbeit,
Jede verschieden; sie lässt nicht einen Grad unerfüllet. (114)

The image of a chain of beings, a continuous gradation of species, seemed as appropriate to Bodmer's contemporaries as it does here to Sipha. It is significant that Bodmer shows us nature experimenting before the creation of man; this suggests a time interval between the lower forms and man and might be an example of what Professor Lovejoy calls the temporalizing of the chain of being.

In the sixth canto, as the Noachides are preparing the ark, Sipha explains to them his mechanical and scientific inventions, among them the technique of preparing lenses for microscopic and telescopic observations. With these lenses they then observe phenomena which had hitherto been either too small or too large:

Damals sahen sie nie vermuthete Thierchen im Leben,
Die sich in Dingen enthielten, die man unwohnbar gehalten.
Weiter erblickten sie neue Planeten; um einige, Ringe,
Thäler und Berg in dem Monde, der unsern Erdball begleitet,
Flecken im Feurigen Meere der Sonn; im Hesperus sahn sie
Abnahm und Wuchs, und vollen und Mittelschein, alle Gestalten,
Welche den Mond verwandeln; sie sahn der Planeten Umwenden
Um sich selber, den Tag, die Nacht, und die Monden derselben, ... (196)

Here there is a list of some of the most significant astronomical discoveries of the seventeenth century that contributed to the new cosmology: mountains and valleys on the moon, sun spots, the phases of Venus, the rotation of planets on their axes and the planets' own satellites. The realization that the planets resembled the earth led them, further, to the belief that these heavenly bodies must also be inhabited, a conclusion which Wieland supports emphatically in his commentary.

In the eighth canto the entry of the animals into the ark takes place: "Sie giengen in harmonischer Ordnung hinein, von Gott unterrichtet" (242). Wieland points out that they enter the ark according to the system of Linnaeus: "Der Poet beschreibt sie . . . nach der Anordnung, die Hr. Linneus in seinem System der Natur gemacht" (268). The animals appear by classes, first mammals, then birds followed by amphibians, worms and insects. Fish are omitted, of course, but Noah indicates later that God would provide for their survival as a class. Within each class several species are described according to distinguishing characteristics. Birds, for example, enter in the following order:

> . . . Zuerst das Geflügel
> Mit krummhackigten Schnäbeln, gefrässige, beissende Vögel:
> Dann die Arten des Spechts mit convexen, klemmenden Schnäbeln:
> Dann die, so schwimmen, mit Schnäbeln wie sägende Zähn' eingeschnitten. . . .
> (243)

Insects also belong to this orderly array of living beings. To justify their place in the ark, the poet refers to the work of the entomologist Réaumur who revealed a complexity and harmony in these tiny creatures comparable to that found in the heavens:

> Alles dies Volk von Gewürm beschleusst ein Schwarm Ungeziefer,
> Die Verachtung der Menschen, eh ihr vertrauter Raumüre
> Ihre kleinen Maschinen hoch zu den Sternen erhoben;
> Als in den Muscheln und Säften und kleinsten Theilchen der Thierchen
> Er verdecktere Spiel' und krümmre Meander entdeckt hat,
> Denn in dem Wurf und der gleichen Bewegung der Sphären erscheinen. (244)

When the creatures are all in the ark, Japhet expresses his amazement over what he sees with familiar images: "Eine vollkommene Kette zusammenschliessender Glieder!" and "Eine schön abgezirkelte Leiter verschiedenster Wesen" (246). As an enthusiastic natural historian he looks forward to the prospect of studying the ladder of creation during the time of the deluge. The ark for him is nothing less than "der Natur Kunstkammer" (247). This scene suggests indeed that the God who instructed the animals to enter the ark so systematically is himself nothing less than a natural historian.

The action narrated in the poem is seen at times from a cosmic perspective. In Bodmer's universe every star is a sun and thus the center of a solar system with inhabited planets and satellites. This perspective is especially apparent in the discourses between Noah and the angel Raphael, who moves swiftly among the solar systems. In the third canto before the fate of the earth has been revealed, Raphael tells Noah of an inhabited planet belonging to the star Arcturus. A comet entered this solar system, turned the planet into a burning mass and dragged it along its own eccentric path. We have here a final conflagration, at which time, according to the Whistonian theory, a planet becomes a comet.

In the tenth canto the reader learns what happens to the souls of the sinners who were drowned in the deluge. They are brought to a solar system at the outer reaches of the universe. The seventh and most distant moon of a planet, so distant from its sun that it is hardly illuminated by its rays, there on that lonely uninhabitable satellite of an uninhabitable planet of a star at the very edge of aether, the souls of damned find their final abode (300–301).

In the same canto there is a description of a happier community, the inhabitants of our own sun. Lamech, the father of Noah, concerned about the fate of his son, left the realm of the blessed and with the speed of lightning passed by countless solar systems until he came to the star that is our sun. There he learns of the earth's circumstances from the inhabitants of the sun who are:

Nicht von menschlicher Bildung, und nicht vom irdischen Staube;
Aber mit eigner Schönheit geschmückt vom Stofe des Lichtes,
Würdig der unerschöpflichen Kunst, mit feinern Gliedmassen,
Ihrem Platze gemäss, die Glut der Sonne zu leiden . . . . (311)

Their description of the devastation caused on earth by the comet is a review of the events already narrated, but this time as witnessed from a vantage point far from the earth. The sun inhabitants inform Lamech that they are most interested in the future of the planet, since the sun receives those souls who are separated from their bodies before reason has attained maturity.

In the concluding canto Raphael departs from Noah with the explanation that he must journey to a planet in a solar system of the Milky Way whose inhabitants are free of original sin and are, therefore, immortal in body and soul. His task is to bring the oldest of these immortals beyond the aether to the throne of God.

News of these communities of rational beings beyond the earth adds to building a cosmic perspective of God's creation and also gives a view of the ladder of creation beyond man thereby complementing the ladder of creation beneath as we have it in the ark. With these themes from astronomy and natural history, Bodmer's Noah is one of the most characteristic examples of science in the poetry of the Enlightenment.

7. Johann Christoph Gottsched (1700–1766)

Johann Christoph Gottsched's efforts to popularize the sciences as a
translator, author of a compendium of science and editor of periodicals have
already been discussed. Literary histories, primarily concerned with his work in
the drama and his controversy with Bodmer and Breitinger, do not comment on
his poetry. His considerable production of occasional and didactic poems are
written in the spirit and style of his times.[1] As is to be expected, his scientific
interests are reflected in his poetry.

In his "Ode. Über den Tod Herrn Christian Ludewigs . . . .", (1732) he exalts
the new age in which the sciences have made so much progress. He asserts that if
men continue to follow reason, the golden age would surely come. In a few
stanzas he summarizes some of the significant discoveries of the new sciences:

Des Erdballs Umkreis ist erkannt,
Sein Inhalt durch und durch gemessen;
Die lange Ruh ist ganz verbannt,
Darinn er vor der Zeit gesessen.
Er muss, nach der Planeten Art,
Um seinen Mittelpunkt, den Sonnenkörper rollen:
Da dieser seinen Lauf erspart,
Und alle Sterne sonst geruhig stehen sollen.

Man schreibt dem Laufe der Natur
Die ordentlichsten Grundgesetze;
Man kömmt auf ihrer Kräfte Spur,
Und findet der Bewegung Schätze.
Man weis, was in den Lüften kracht,
Und was den Ocean zur Fluth und Ebbe zwinget?
Was Schlossen, Sturm und Regen macht?
Warum die Erde bebt, warum ihr Abgrund springet?

Man hat den Menschen selbst erforscht,
Und seiner Glieder Bau zerleget;
Man weis, was unsern Leib zermorscht,
Und wie das Herz im Busen schläget.
Man hat den Gliedern nachgespürt,
Die manchen Nervengang in das Gehirne schicken,
Von dem, was sie von aussen rührt,
Dem Geiste, der da wohnt, die Bilder einzudrücken.

Man hat so gar des Geistes Kraft,
Der uns zu Menschen macht, ergründet;

---

1   *Gedichte,* ed. Johann Joachim Schwabe, 2 vols. (Leipzig, 1751).

Und kennt mit guter Wissenschaft
Was in uns denket und empfindet.
Man thut sein einfach Wesen dar,
Das keine Fäulniss trennt, kein Moder kann verderben;
Und macht es durch Beweise klar,
Das unsre Seelen nicht, wie diese Körper, sterben. (I, 168–169)

The first stanza refers to the Copernican revolution which put an end to "die lange Ruh" of the earth and placed it in a planetary orbit about the sun. Not only is the earth's orbit known, but also its circumference and content have been measured, so that for the first time man has attained thorough knowledge of his habitat. In the second stanza he states the new belief in the lawfulness of nature and describes some of the natural phenomena on earth whose laws are now understood: motion, thunder and lightning, tides, storms and earthquakes. In the third and fourth stanzas he comments on the discoveries the new sciences have made about man; the anatomy of the human body has been studied and the human mind and soul have been explored. The progression is from the heavens to the earth to man. Such surveys of natural phenomena were quite customary in didactic poems and essays.

The sciences are also celebrated in a didactic poem, "Lehrgedicht; Wodurch die Medicin beschimpft werde . . ." (1732), in which he contrasts the guesswork of the physicians with the reliable knowledge the scientist attains in such disciplines as anatomy and astronomy. His opinion of medicine is expressed as follows:

. . . Allein, wenn die Chymisten
Sich stets mit Salz, Mercur und lauter Schwefel brüsten;
Daraus, nach ihrem Wahn, ein jedes Ding besteht:
Wenn Stahls berühmte Zunft sich offenbar vergeht,
Der Körper Wirkungen den Körper abzustreiten.
Und der Arzneyen Kraft von Geistern herzuleiten;
Gesundheit, Krankheit, Tod, ja Beine, Fleisch und Blut,
Sammt allem, was der Bau des blossen Leibes thut,
Der denkenden Vernunft des Menschen zuzuschreiben;
Wie kann denn eure Kunst in wahrem Ansehn bleiben? (I, 566)

In view of the fact that the Paracelsians' three elements and Georg Ernst Stahl's animism, alluded to above, were dominant in medicine at the time, one can understand Gottsched's preference of the study of the sciences to the practice of medicine.

The sciences are again dealt with in "Ode. Dass die Poesie am geschicktesten sey, die Weisheit . . . fortzupflanzen . . ." (1733). The Goddess Minerva appears to the poet and exhorts the poets of the time to use their art in the service of wisdom. Man will attain wisdom, the Goddess teaches, if he recognizes the rational order which God has implanted in nature. To impart this insight she leads the poet through the realms of nature, beginning with the human body, then the cosmos as a whole and finally the earth. This time the progression is from microcosm to macrocosm to geocosm (II, 167—171).

The new age of enlightenment is again the subject of his "Ode. Auf . . . Herrn Christophs, des . . . Grafen von Manteufel Hohes Geburtsfest" (1741):

Gesegnet sey die neue Zeit!
Da sich die Finsterniss zerstreut,
Die den verhüllten Weltkreis deckte;
Da Deutschland und der Britten Reich,
Der Franz und Wälsche fast zugleich,
Den muntern Kopf zur Arbeit streckte.
So ward nun, nach verstrichner Nacht,
Der Wahrheit Licht hervor gebracht.

In Deutschland hub die Klarheit an;
Copernik war der grosse Mann,
Dem Keplers Fleiss bald nachgekommen:
Bis Gerke, Scheiner, Marius,
Und Tschirnhaus, und Hevelius,
Thomas' und Leibnitz Platz genommen:
Daraus das heitre Licht entspringt,
Das itzt in aller Augen dringt. (II, 107)

The first stanza depicts the new learning as a European phenomena, as a result of collaboration among various nations. In the second stanza Gottsched, never modest about Germany's contributions to science, lists German scientists of the seventeenth century.

Themes taken from astronomy appear frequently in Gottsched's occasional poetry. Of all the sciences, he was undoubtedly most familiar with astronomy as a student and as an amateur observer. In an ode to a friend whom he had known for five years, "Ode. An Hrn. Prof. Joh. Friedrich Mayen" (1729) he describes the duration of the time of their friendship in terms of sixty revolutions of the moon about the earth and five revolutions of the earth about the sun:

Sechzigmal hat ihren Bogen,
Mit veränderlicher Pracht,
Phöbe, das Gestirn der Nacht,
In gewölkter Luft durchzogen.
Fünfmal hat diess Norderland,
Auf der Tellus krummen Reise,
In dem länglichrunden Kreise,
Sich der Sonnen zugewandt. (I, 204)

In his "Jubelrede auf die Erfindung der Buchdruckerkunst" in 1740, he indicates the passage of time from 1440 to 1740 by referring to the earth's three hundred annual revolutions about the sun: "Dreyhundertmal hat sich der Tellus Ball / Den Thierkreis wirbelnd durchgeschwungen . . ." (II, 313). In an ode on the death of a princess of Anhalt-Köthen, he compares the disappearance of this light on Köthen's firmament with the moon's loss of light in a lunar eclipse:

Wie, wenn bey hellgestirnter Nacht
Diana ihren Glanz verlieret,
So oft ihn ihres Wirbels Macht
In unsers Erdballs Schatten führet; (I, 84)

In an Ode "An Herrn Hof- und Justizrath Benemannen . . ." (1773), he consoles a father over the death of his son, by reminding him of the destruction that takes place among heavenly bodies and that, therefore, man should accept his mortality as inevitable:

Erhebe Sinnen und Gemüth,
Bis in des Himmels blaue Ferne;
Wo, wie du weist, in jedem Sterne,
Ein ganzer Sonnenkörper glüht.
Dreht jeder nicht um seine Glut
Ein Heer von Welten in die Runde?
Belebt sie nicht zu jeder Stunde
Der warmen Stralen Silberfluth?
Und gleichwohl hat man wahrgenommen,
Dass mancher Lichtquell schon verglommen.

Des Pöbels Schrecken, ein Komet,
Mit seinem ungeheuren Schwanze,
Was ist er, in dem trüben Glanze?
Ein Erdball, der zu Grunde geht!
O! gehn hier ganze Welten ein,
Wenn Frost und Hitze sie verheeret;
Und werden Sonnen auch verzehret:
Wie kann ihr Bürger ewig seyn?
Wie kann der Mensch, der Wurm auf Erden,
Dem Untergang entrissen werden? (I, 117–118)

In the first stanza he refers to the new cosmology in which every star is a sun and, therefore, a center of a planetary system. Suns perish, he continues, and thus many worlds dependent on them perish with them. In the second stanza he again pictures the destruction of worlds by reference to Whiston's cometary theory in which comets are planets that are in the process of perishing. These reflections are part of the new cosmology in which the belief in the immutability of the heavens has been supplanted by an awareness that in the entire universe creation and destruction continue.

The new cosmology is again the subject of at least one half of his "Ode. Als der Verfasser sein Fünfzigstes Jahr zurücklegte" (1750). The purpose of the poem is to give thanks to God for all the benefits he has enjoyed during his life, and to express his gratitude to the Divinity who is not only the creator and sustainer of the vast cosmos, but also provides for insignificant man. Of interest to us is the first section of the poem where he describes the wise design of the cosmos. He begins with the motions of the planets:

Wer hing der Wandelsterne Lauf
In ungleich grossen Höhen auf,
Und hiess sie um die Sonne fliessen?
Wer wies doch jedem seinen Kreis,
So kräftig, dass sie Bahn und Gleis
Im Schwunge nicht verlassen müssen?
Da sonst, was sich mit Schleudern regt,
Den Mittelpunct zu fliehen pflegt.

Wer wies doch allen Achsen an,
Um die ihr Körper wirbeln kann,
Wie sich der Erdball selbst beweget?
Wer zeichnete den Angelstern
Dem einen nah, dem andern fern,
Von dem, der unsern Erdpol träget?
Der uns die Zeit von Tag und Nacht,
Zwar ungleich, doch beständig macht.

O Schöpfer! Deine Weisheit bloss
Gab dort und hier den ersten Stoss,
Davon die Kugeln seitwärts rollten;
Das machts, wenn sich der Erdball dreht,
Dass Lenz und Sommer erst entsteht,
Dann Herbst und Winter folgen sollten;
Indem die Nord- und Süderwelt,
Sich wechselnd nach der Sonne stellt.

Der heisse Weltstrich nicht allein,
Sollt reich an Thier und Pflanzen seyn,
Und stets von heissen Stralen schmelzen.
Nein! auch das Nord- und Süderland
War eignen Bürgern zuerkannt:
Drum muss die Erde so sich wälzen;
Dass jeder Theil zu seiner Zeit,
Durch grössrer Wärme Kraft gedeiht. (II, 231—232)

In the first stanza he depicts our solar system with the planets revolving about the sun in orbits that retain their order by a proper balance of centripetal and centrifugal forces. The succeeding stanzas declare that the earth's daily rotation about its inclined axis and its annual orbit about the sun provide it with day and night and the seasons. In the last stanza he stresses the importance of the obliqueness of the earth's axis by virtue of which every part of the globe receives a stronger portion of the sun's warmth.

The poet continues by arguing that these same circumstances described above apply also to the remaining planets of our solar system, and that they too must be inhabited:

Nicht kleiner ist der Kugeln Werth,
Die unsre Sonne noch verklärt,
So nah und weit sie immer schweben!
Sie wärmen sich an ihrem Licht,
Dem auch der Wechsel nicht gebricht;
Wie sollte kein Geschöpf da leben?
Wie sollte nur die Erd allein,
An Thier und Menschen fruchtbar seyn?

Nein Nein! umsonst liess Gott gewiss
Fünf Kugeln, Licht und Finsterniss,
In festgesetzter Zeit nicht fühlen:
Umsonst schuff Er nicht Wärm und Frost,
Für Länder wo Er keine Kost,
Für Thier und Menschen, wollt erzielen!
Wo Winter, Lenz, und Sommer ist,
Wird was beseeltes nicht vermisst.

O! Jupitern muss offenbar,
Der schönsten Monden doppelt Paar,
Nicht ganz umsonst die Nacht erfreuen!
Wo zündet wohl ein kluger Mann
In wüsten Feldern Fackeln an,
Die Finsternisse zu zerstreuen?
O Schöpfer! Deiner Weisheit Pflicht,
Thut wahrlich was vergeblichs nicht.

Der Erdkreis ist so reich bewohnt,
Doch glänzt ihm nur ein kleiner Mond:
Dort hast Du viere dran gewendet.
Saturn hat kaum an fünfen gnug,
Davon der ungleich schnelle Flug
Sich in sehr kurzer Zeit vollendet;

Wer glaubt nun, dass ihr Silberlicht
Umsonst der Nächte Schatten bricht? (II, 232—233)

The argument for the inhabitation of the planets is teleological. Since the other planets share with the earth those motions that create conditions for life, then there must be life there, for God would not have created them so without a purpose. In the last two stanzas he maintains that the earth so richly inhabited has one moon, which also was not created without any purpose. All the more reason then to believe that Jupiter and Saturn with four and five moons are also inhabited.

He continues with the reflection that the moon has an atmosphere with moisture and since it receives light and heat from the sun, it must also have inhabitants. Following the speculations of Johann Heyn, he does not hesitate to populate even the comets:

Genug! die Weisheit schuff die Welt,
Die doch viel mehr noch in sich hält,
Als lauter Sonnen und Planeten.
Wo bleibt die ungemeine Zahl
Der durch den blassen Dunst und Strahl,
Geschwänzt und bärtigen Kometen?
Darauf, o Gott! Dein Allmachtruff,
Nicht minder Creaturen schuff.

Ihr seltner Lauf entrückt sie nur,
Auf einer langgestreckten Spur,
Viel Jahre durch, dem Blick der Erden.
Doch können sie, bald kalt, bald warm,
Durch Deiner Güte Vaterarm,
Wohl an Geschöpfen fruchtbar werden:
Wenn selbst der Dampf, der uns erschreckt,
Sie vor der Sonnenhitze deckt.

Schon mehr als dreyssig sind gezählt,
Wo unsrer Sonne Licht nicht fehlt.
Wer weis? ob wir die Hälfte kennen?
Wir wissen ja das Zehntheil kaum,
Von dem, was in des Himmels Raum,
Für flammenreiche Kugeln brennen:
Die doch der Ausspruch kluger Welt
Schon längst für lauter Sonnen hält. (II, 235)

Comets like planets have a calculable and, therefore, orderly orbit. Their orbits differ from those of planets in that comets are brought closer to and farther from the sun. However, he suggests that God's beneficence could have

provided vapors to protect the comet's inhabitants from the sun. In the last
stanza he comments that there may be more comets and even more stars,
"flammenreiche Kugeln", each of which are suns. He concludes this section of
the poem with another popular conception, namely, that there exist higher
creatures in other heavenly bodies more capable than man of revering God:

Der trefflichsten Geschöpfe Zier,
Viel tausend Geister dienen Dir,
Die dort in höhern Sphären wohnen.
Erhabne Seelen bessrer Kraft,
Von ungleich grössrer Eigenschaft,
Verehren Dich zu Millionen.
Wie können wir uns unterstehn,
Unendlicher! Dich zu erhöhn? (II, 236)

In this connection another popular theme can be mentioned, namely, the
transition of the human spirit after death to a more enlightened condition where
the questions asked on earth are swiftly answered. In "Lobgedicht. Auf des
Reichsgrafen von Manteufel Absterben" (1749), the count's spirit is met by
other spirits who inform him of the enlightenment that awaits him:

Komm, mehre Du die Zahl, die hier in süssen Stunden,
Mehr Wahrheit eingesehn, als noch die Welt erfunden;
Die von des Schöpfers Macht und Weisheit mehr erblickt,
Als dort, euch Sterbliche nur wie im Traum entzückt.
Hier wirst Du im Revier von Millionen Sternen,
Des höchsten Wesens Rath und Vorsicht preisen lernen;
Die nichts vergeblichs schuff, nichts ordnet, nichts erlaubt,
Als was das Ganze ziert, ihm keine Schönheit raubt,
Hier sieht man, dass was dort der Weisen Witz verstricket
Auch Engel lüstern macht, die Seeligen entzücket. (II, 411)

The same theme appears in "Lobgedicht. Auf die Durchlauchtigste Louise".
The God Apollo appears to the poet in a dream and describes how Princess
Louise, who throughout her life had applied herself industriously to the sciences
will be delighted with a fulfillment of her quest:

Da wird sie deutlich sehn in was für weiten Kreisen,
Die Welten ohne Zahl um ihre Sonnen reisen.
Was hier Copernicus, und Kepler und Hugen,
Nur halb und halb errieth, das wird Sie ganz verstehn;
Was Fontenelle schreibt von Bürgern der Planeten,
Was Whiston glaublich macht; vom Wesen der Kometen,
Was von der Wirbel Art Des Cartes uns gelehrt,
Durch was für Gründe man ihm diesen Bau gestört;

Wie Neuton Licht und Stral in sieben Farben spaltet;
Wie die Magnetenkraft im ganzen Himmel waltet,
Wenn jeder Hauptplanet die nahen Kugeln zeucht,
So dass ihm kein Trabant aus seinem Gleise weicht;
Wie Leibnitz Seel und Leib nach neuer Art verbunden,
Und was die Weisen sonst mit vieler Müh erfunden:
Das alles wird sie sehn, das wird ihr grosser Geist,
Aufs gründlichste verstehn. (II, 395)

These few lines allude to some of the major discoveries and speculations of
the new learning: the heliocentric system of the world as developed by
Copernicus, Kepler and Huygens, Fontenelle's inhabited worlds, Whiston's
cometary theory, Descartes' vortices, Newton's color theory and his theory of
gravitation and Leibniz' pre-established harmony between body and soul. It is
interesting to note here that Gottsched, as well as many of his contemporaries,
places the pseudo-scientific conjectures of a Whiston and a Fontenelle in the
same list of scientific achievements with the theories of Copernicus, Kepler,
Huygens and Newton.

Finally, there is his "Ode. Auf das berühmte Kaiser-Karls-Bad". (1749). The
mineral springs in question are surrounded by such towering mountains that
they obstruct his view of the heavens and, consequently, interfere with his
astronomical work:

Berühmte Thäler, deren Seiten,
Schon seit der grossen Sündfluth Zeiten,
Der steilsten Berge Wand umgab!
Von Süd und Ost, und Nord und Westen
Blickt, zwischen dünnbelaubten Ästen,
Ein nackter Fels auf mich herab.

Der Himmel ist mir halb verstecket,
Ein dicht umzogner Vorhang decket
Mir fast der Sterne grösste Zahl.
Bey Nacht, wenn ich mit Neutons Röhren
Den Ring Saturns, den Mars will ehren,
Verbergen sie sich auf einmal. (II, 74)

In the first stanza it is interesting to note that he speaks of the mountains as
having existed since the time of Noah's flood, since it may be an allusion to
Burnet's theory of the origin of mountains during the flood. In the second
stanza it is amusing to see that the telescope has become "Neutons Röhren".
What interests him about these springs is the origin of the warm curative waters.
He reasons that they must have their origin in subterranean recesses of the earth

in whose abysses there must be a source of heat. He puzzles over the origin of this central heat.

> Ists wahr? was nährt denn solche Flammen?
> Was führt den Zunder hier zusammen,
> Der so viel tausend Jahre brennt?
> Ists nicht? Was kann den Quell erhitzen,
> Den man bey ungeschwächtem Spritzen,
> Drey hundert Jahre siedend kennt? (II, 78)

He answers these questions with the following conjecture:

> Glimmt noch ein Funken von dem Brande,
> Der in des Erdballs erstem Stande,
> Diess ganze Rund in Glut gesetzt? (II, 78)

He suggests that the internal heat in question is residual heat from the earth's first state. He may have in mind Whiston's cometary theory according to which planets were once comets, or Buffon's theory that the planets were originally fragments of the sun broken off by the impact of a comet. Four important themes are under discussion in the poem: the origin of mountains, the origin of the warm mineral waters, the origin of the internal source of heat and the origin of the earth itself.

The presence of this variety of scientific themes in Gottsched's poetry is no surprise. His activity as a popularizer of science demonstrated that he was a man of letters who had thoroughly assimilated the new sciences. The appearance of his scientific interests in the poetry confirms this and emphasizes even more how much the sciences were a part of his world view. It is also important to note that his main interests are in astronomy and physics, fields in which natural laws can be verified by experiment and mathematical calculations. Natural history does not seem to have been as interesting to him.

8. Friedrich von Hagedorn (1708—1754)

Born in the same year as Albrecht von Haller, Hagedorn also published his first poems, *Versuch einiger Gedichte* (1729), in the year of origin of Haller's "Die Alpen". Like Haller he was one of the beloved poets of the 1730's and 1740's. Unlike Haller, he had no scientific training and is known solely for his literary work. It is, therefore, noteworthy that in his poems there are indications that he was interested in the sciences and kept informed by reading scientific works.

In a poem appearing in the first edition of his poems in 1729,[1] he praises the gift of wisdom which raises men above the controversies and passions of daily life. The wise man attains his peace by contemplation, by searching for the causes of things:

> Wie glücklich ist nicht der, so dieses Firmament,
> Der Sonnen Lauff und Bahn, der Sterne Grösse kennt,
> Dem auch die Schöpfungs-Art des Allmacht-Spruchs: Es werde!
> Der Wesen Zeugungs-Krafft, der Lauff, der Punct der Erde,
> Des Meeres Ebb' und Fluht, die Himmels-Lufft, der Wind,
> Der Zeiten Witterung nichts unerforschtes sind!
> Des Welt-Bau's weiter Raum, Blitz, Donner, Sturm und Keile,
> Der Cörper Krafft, Figur, Bewegung, Lage, Theile,
> Gesetze, Schwere, Druck, Verändrung, Widerstand,
> Schall, Wärme, Licht und Stral, nichts ist ihm unbekannt. (51)

The natural phenomena enumerated here are encompassed by astronomy, biology, meteorology and physics. The wise man who understands these phenomena, he continues, is raised above selfish interests and attains happiness. Here he asserts the moral as well as the intellectual value of scientific studies.

In one of his later poems "Die Glückseligkeit" (1743),[2] there is a similar affirmation of scientific learning. He has a learned man say the following:

> Ich forsche, was sich stets in jenen Welten dreht,
> Was Orpheus, Epicur und Brunus ausgespäht,
> Wie jenes Firmament ein Heer von Sonnen zieret,
> Ein neuer Stern erscheint, ein alter sich verlieret,
> Was Flamsteed glücklicher, als Liebknecht, uns entdeckt,

---

[1] Friedrich von Hagedorn, *Versuch einiger Gedichte. Deutsche Litteraturdenkmale des 18. Jahrhunderts,* Nr. 10, Hrsg. von Bernhard Seuffert (Heilbronn, 1883), p. 51.
[2] *Poetische Werke* (Hamburg, 1769), 3 vols. The remaining references to Hagedorn's poetry are all from this edition. First editions of his works are as follows: *Versuch einiger Gedichte* (1729), *Versuch in poetischen Fabeln und Erzählungen* (1738), *Sammlung neuer Oden und Lieder* (1742—1752), *Oden und Lieder in 5 Büchern* (1747), *Moralische Gedichte* (1750).

Wie weit sich ihre Zahl und ihre Gröss erstreckt.
Was auch der Pöbel weiss, kann mich nicht lüstern machen.
Ein philosophisch Aug ergetzen hohe Sachen:
Wie jeder Hauptplanet, im Bau der besten Welt,
Durch Wirbel reger Luft die Laufbahn richtig hält,
Stets um der Sonne Gluht elliptisch sich beweget,
In dem sonst dunklen Kreis Land, Berge, Wasser heget,
Und, unsrer Erde gleich, vielleicht mit Menschen prangt,
Die auch Systemata, so gut als wir, erlangt,
Und unter denen itzt, zum Nutzen ihrer Sphären,
Vielleicht ein andrer Wolf, ein andrer Newton lehren.
Sieht mich die Mitternacht bey meinem Sehror wach;
So ahm ich höchstvergnügt berühmten Männern nach:
Und so entdeck ich selbst, was, auch bey wachen Stunden,
Ein Deutscher, ja so gar ein Domherr ausgefunden. (I, 22—23)

This statement includes many astronomy themes of the time: The plurality of worlds, the continued creation and destruction of stars, the sizes and numbers of stars, the elliptical orbits of planets, the inhabitation of planets, praise of Newton and Copernicus. It also suggests a statement of faith that the structure of the cosmos has been thoroughly investigated and that what the great astronomers have discovered can be verified by an amateur with his telescope.

Hagedorn provides in his footnotes the sources with which the reader can assure himself of the truth of the statements about science. He refers to a bibliography of ancient and modern writers on the tradition of a plurality of inhabited worlds in Fabricius' *Bibliotheca Graeca,* also to Thümmigs *Versuch einer gründlichen Erläuterung der merkwürdigsten Begebenheiten in der Natur* and to Wolf's *Elementis Astronomiae.*

It is quite appropriate that he uses astronomy as representative of the new learning. In the year 1743, two hundred years after the death of Copernicus, the new system of the cosmos had been firmly established by over a century of measurements and calculations. This confidence in the astronomer's knowledge is so great that it is extended to the speculation about the inhabitation of other worlds in this solar system as well as other solar systems, a speculation which is given almost as much credence as the regularity of the planets' orbits.

However, Hagedorn doubts that the new learning about distant heavenly bodies, no matter how verifiable, can give man real happiness. He recommends the example of Socrates who stressed self-knowledge and human values:

Nutzt nicht der grobe Pflug, die Egge mehr dem Staat,
Als ihm ein Fernglas nutzt, das dir entdecket hat,
Wie von Cassini Schnee, von Huygens weisser Erde
Im fernen Jupiter ein Land gefärbet werde?

Sah nicht ein Socrates aufs menschliche Geschlecht,
Und hatt er etwa nicht bey seiner Strenge Recht,
Die von der Wissenschaft der Sterne nichts behielte,
Als was dem Feldbau half, und auf die Schiffahrt zielte?
Mich däucht, er gründte sich auf die Erfahrenheit:
Das, was uns glücklich macht, sey nicht Gelehrsamkeit. (I, 23—24)

The sciences are depicted as extraneous to the daily life of man and instead,
the practical arts like agriculture are extolled. In a footnote he recalls a passage
from the voyage to the Houyhnhnms in Swift's *Gulliver's Travels* where one of
the Houyhnhnms ridicules modern science which produces either mere conjectures or a knowledge, even though it be certain, that is of no use. His
conclusion, here as elsewhere, is that learning by itself does not bring happiness.

Another example of Hagedorn's doubts about the value of learning to man
occurs in the edifying poem "Die Freundschaft" (1748):

Ja, stieg ein Sterblicher in die entferntsten Sphären,
Und sähe Welten selbst, wovon die Räthsel lehren,
Und säh, im öden Raum, von Menschen abgewandt,
Die Werkstatt der Natur, der Sonnen Vaterland;
So würde doch zu bald der Kenntniss Freude fehlen,
Träff er nicht jemand an, ihm dieses zu erzehlen. (I, 77)

Even if he were given a glimpse into nature's own laboratory in the vast spaces of
the cosmos, there would be no joy in such learning if there were no friend with
whom to share the vision. The human experience of friendship, of human
community, he maintains here, has more pertinence to man's life than answers
to riddles.

In his poem "Der Gelehrte" (1740), he does voice respect for the man of
learning and his new discoveries in science:

Der Körper Stoff, was ihre Kraft erhält,
Wie jede wirkt, sieht Er von allen Seiten.
Sein Witz durchstreift so gar die Geisterwelt,
Das dunkle Land entlegner Möglichkeiten,
Und spähet dort mehr Dinge seltner Art,
Als ein Ulyss bey seiner Höllenfahrt. (I, 87)

However, in the same poem he makes it clear that he values the life of
learning not so much for its own sake, but because it is more likely to lead to
virtuous, non-frivolous conduct.

Another area of Hagedorn's scientific interest lies in natural history. This is
not so apparent in the poems themselves as in the copious footnotes where he
cites as his sources the most recent works on natural history. In regard to these

footnotes, he says in the introduction of 1750: "Ihre Absicht ist, ungegründeten Deutungen möglichst zuvorzukommen, zu beweisen, ein weiteres Nachdenken zu veranlassen, und zu unterhalten: denn auch dieser Endzweck ist mir nicht überflüssig. Gelehrten mögen also einige nur ergetzend, andere Unwissendern nur gelehrt scheinen." (p. XII)

In his poem "Die Freundschaft", he maintains that virtue is achieved only by hard work and active participation. The lazy man he compares to a fly that does not use the wings nature gave it:

Der Unbehülfliche hat angebohrne Gaben,
Wie Geizige den Schatz, wie Feige Waffen haben,
Und ist der Fliege gleich, die nicht zum Flug sich regt,
Obgleich ihr die Natur die Flügel beygelegt. (I, 63)

This is accompanied by a long footnote with references to the *Abhandlungen der Königlich-Schwedischen Academie der Wissenschaften* (1748), Réaumur's *Memoires pour servir à l'Histoire des Insectes* (1740) and Gould's *Account of English Ants* (1747) with which he documents that there are such flies who do not use their wings at all and the consequences that follow.

References to insects and animals with explanatory footnotes occur frequently in his *Fabeln und Erzählungen*. In the fable "Der Löwe und die Mücke" he describes the gnat as follows:

Sie putzt ihr Panzerhemd, die Schuppen um den Leib,
Und ihren Federbusch, lässt beyde Flügel klingen,
Zieht alle Schwerter ein, die aus dem Rüssel dringen,
Und hält sich für kein schlechtes Weib. (II, 41)

This is explained in a footnote with a quotation from Pluche's *Spectacle de la Nature* in which the behavior of these insects is discussed. He also refers to the *Histoire des Abeilles* in the *Bibliothèque Raisonnée*, 1745.

In the fable "Die Ameise und die Grille", he describes contrasting qualities of the ant and the cricket:

Es sang die heischre Grille
Die ganze Sommerzeit,
Da sich in aller Stille
Die Ameis auch erfreut.
Sie häuft der Zellen Fülle
Mit kluger Emisgkeit.

Die Grille singt voll Freude
Um Feld und Busch und Hain,
Und sammlet kein Getreide
Zum nächsten Winter ein ... (II, 206)

In the footnote he grants the poet the freedom to attribute the quality of
cleverness to the ant according to tradition; however, he points out that on the
basis of careful observations by natural historians that "... die englischen und
folglich auch andere europäische Ameisen weder Korn essen, noch Vorraths-
kammern für den Winter haben". (206)

In his poem "Die Thiere" he takes up the problem whether animals have the
capacity to think and judge or are mere machines as Descartes says. He cites
examples of the behavior of rats and beavers, again documented in the
footnotes with quotations from current works of natural historians such as
Guer's *Histoire critique de l'ame des bêtes* (1749) and de Blainville's *Travels
through Holland, Germany* . . . .(1743). His conclusion is that animals do share
with humans some capacity to reason:

> Wer lehret aus gewissen Gründen,
> Dass Thiere blosserdings empfinden?
> Hat hier die Ratze nicht gedacht?
> Verrieth die Rettungsart, die sie so wohl erlesen,
> So schön vollführt, sein geistiges Wesen,
> Das zweifelt, forscht, und Schlüsse macht? (II, 28)

Concerning the industry and achievements of the beavers, he says:

> Wer war der Plato dieser Thiere?
> Wer lehrte sie, was ich hier spüre:
> Kunst, Ordnung, Witz, Bedachtsamkeit?
> Soll man die Fähigkeit, wodurch sie dieses können,
> Gefügter Theile Wirkung nennen?
> Wo ist ein Uhrwerk so gescheidt? (II, 31)

He concludes with a rejection of Descartes' contention that the behavior of
animals can be explained as the motions of a machine:

> Entdeckt man weiter nichts an ihnen,
> Als die Bewegung der Maschinen,
> Der Urtheil und Bewusstseyn fehlt?
> Cartesius bejahts; doch ist ihm Recht zu geben? (II, 31)

In view of Hagedorn's tendency to find human qualities in animals, it is of no
surprise to find him amused by Ludwig Holberg's tale of Nicolaus Klimm's
journey to the empire Mezendore, populated only by plants and animals who
not only have the capacity to reason but use it better than any society of men.
In his poem "Mezendore" Hagedorn describes the citizens of this realm:

> Herr Nicolaus Klimm erfand
> Mehr Länder, als ich Reime,

So gar ein unterirdisch Land
Vernünftiger Thier' und Bäume.
....
Des Landes Name klinget fein,
Und schmeichelt recht dem Ohre.
Es heisset, (was kann schöner seyn?)
Es heisset Mezendore.
Hier hat das thierische Geschlecht
Und jeder Baum das Bürgerrecht . . . (III, 54)

The scientific themes found in Hagedorn's poetry and the supporting footnotes reveal a literary man who had assimilated some of the significant aspects of the new learning in astronomy and natural history. We can also note that in both these areas he looks for human values and qualities. Though he respects the discoveries and exact measurements of the astronomers, he insists on the priority of human values in the life of man. Similarly, in his consideration of animal life, he stresses the human qualities which he maintains animals share with man and rejects the mechanistic view of Descartes.

9. Albrecht von Haller (1708–1777)

Albrecht von Haller achieved distinction as a man of science and as a man of letters. His scientific work included botany, natural history and especially anatomy and physiology. His influence on the progress of the natural sciences in Germany was enormous: as a medical researcher, as a professor of medicine at the University of Göttingen, as a medical bibliographer,[1] as founder of the scientific society at Göttingen and as editor of and contributor to the *Göttingische Gelehrte Anzeigen.*

As a man of letters he is primarily known for his collection of poems, *Versuch Schweizerischer Gedichte,* which was edited eleven times between 1732 and 1777. Not as well known were his political novels written in his later years. Only recently Haller was evaluated as a literary critic on the basis of his reviews in the *Göttingische Gelehrte Anzeigen.*[2] Examples of his wide range of interests, which included also social, philosophical and religious problems, can be found in the *Tagebuch seiner Beobachtungen . . . .*[3]

Of the extensive secondary literature on the life and works of Haller, the biography of Johann Georg Zimmermann is especially valuable.[4] As a student and associate of Haller he was well acquainted with his scientific and literary work. Of interest is his statement that Haller's observations on his botanical trips through the Alps are the basis for the nature descriptions in "Die Alpen".[5] For example, he quotes four lines describing a crystal mine which Haller had visited and studied:

Im nie erhellten Grund von unterirdschen Grüften
Wölbt sich der feuchte Thon mit funkelndem Krystall,
Der schimmernde Krystall sprosst aus der Felsen Klüften,
Blitzt durch die düstre Luft und strahlet überall. (II, 405–408)

The succeeding lines describe hot mineral springs in a valley so cold its inhabitants must leave it in the winter; this was also visited and observed by Haller:

Im Mittel eines Thals von Himmel-hohem Eise,
Wohin der wilde Nord den kalten Thron gesetzt,

---

[1] See John F. Fulton, *The Great Medical Bibliographers. A study in humanism* (Philadelphia, 1951).

[2] Karl S. Guthke, *Haller und die Literatur* (Göttingen, 1962). After a careful examination of the Haller manuscripts, Guthke established that Haller had contributed about 9,000 reviews.

[3] Albrecht von Haller, *Tagebuch seiner Beobachtungen über Schriftsteller und über sich selbst* (Bern, 1787), edited by Johann Georg Heinzmann.

[4] Johann Georg Zimmermann, *Das Leben des Herrn von Haller* (Zürich, 1755).

[5] Ibid., pp. 69–76.

Entspriesst ein reicher Brunn mit siedendem Gebräuse,
Raucht durch das welke Gras und senget, was er netzt.
Sein lauter Wasser rinnt mit flüssigen Metallen,
Ein heilsam Eisensalz vergüldet seinen Lauf;
Ihn wärmt der Erde Gruft und seine Fluten wallen
Vom innerlichen Streit vermischter Salze auf:
Umsonst schlägt Wind und Schnee um seine Flut zusammen,
Sein Wesen selbst ist Feur und seine Wellen Flammen. (II, 411–420)

There are numerous scientific themes in Haller's poems collected under the title *Versuch Schweizerischer Gedichte.*[6] These poems, written in the brief period between 1729 and 1736, were quoted frequently; his reputation as a poet during the eighteenth century rested on them.

By far the best known poem in this collection is "Die Alpen" (1729), in which he extols the virtues of the unsophisticated, idyllic way of life of the mountain villagers in the Alps. The only science they know is what they have learned through practical experience and what is useful to them in their way of life. The villagers spend the leisure hours of the long winter evenings in song or serious discussion. Those who are familiar with nature's ways instruct their neighbor:

Der eine lehrt die Kunst, was uns die Wolken tragen,
Im Spiegel der Natur vernünftig vorzusehn,
Er kann der Winde Strich, den Lauf der Wetter sagen,
Und sieht in heller Luft den Sturm von weitem wehn:
Er kennt die Kraft des Monds, die Würkung seiner Farben,
Er weiss, was am Gebürg ein früher Nebel will: (40–41)

This man has not theorized about nature, but he understands the variety of weather phenomena and can predict on the basis of his experience. Another villager is a student of natural history:

Bald aber schliesst ein Kreis um einen muntern Alten,
Der die Natur erforscht, und ihre Schönheit kennt;
Der Kräuter Wunder-Kraft und ändernde Gestalten
Hat längst sein Witz durchsucht, und jedes Moos benennt; (43)

This amateur natural historian appreciates the beauties of nature, classifies plants and knows their medicinal virtues. The science that these villagers practice is as natural and uncontrived as their way of life in general. They do not indulge in theorizing and system building to explain what man need not and cannot know.

6 (Bern, 1777), eleventh edition.

In his "Gedanken über Vernunft, Aberglauben und Unglauben" (1729), Haller lists some of the extraordinary achievements of modern science. With his reason he seems to have achieved the impossible:

> Was nimmer möglich schien, hat doch sein Witz vollbracht,
> Und durch die Sternen-Welt sich einen Weg erdacht.
> Dem majestät'schen Gang von tausend neuen Sonnen,
> Ist lange vom Hugen die Renn-Bahn ausgesonnen,
> Er hat ihr Maass bestimmt, den Körper umgespannt,
> Die Fernen abgezählt, und ihren Kreiss umrannt. (61)

Nature has revealed her mysteries to man the measurer:

> Was die Natur verdeckt, kan Menschen Witz entblössen,
> Er misst das weite Meer unendlich grosser Grössen,
> Was vormals unbekannt und unermessen war,
> Wird durch ein Ziffern-Blatt umschränkt und offenbar.
> Ein Newton übersteigt das Ziel erschaffner Geister,
> Find die Natur im Werk, und scheint des Weltbaus Meister;
> Er wiegt die inn're Kraft die sich im Körper regt,
> Den einen sinken macht, und den im Kreiss bewegt,
> Und schlägt die Tafeln auf der ewigen Gesätze,
> Die Gott einmal gemacht, dass er sie nie verletze. (62–63)

Here he refers to the progress of science through measurement and mathematics best exemplified by the work of Newton, the new Moses who has given man the tablets on which God's eternal laws are written. This is one of the earliest examples of Newton, pictured as the priest of nature. Yet the poet takes no pride in these achievements, in fact, he comments, "Euch selbst misskennt ihr, sonst alles wisst ihr eh" (63). The warning, that the success of scientific knowledge of nature may distract man from self-knowledge which is more pertinent, is a recurrent theme in Haller's poetry and in that of many of his contemporaries.

Yet Haller is certainly not against science, but only against the impious pride in man's own achievements which it may engender. Toward the end of the same poem he surveys the works of nature in the heavens and on earth to show that the more we know of them, the more they lead us to the Creator. Thus science can also lead to piety. Above all, man must realize that knowledge has its limits: "... auch Weisheit hält ein Maass, / Das Thoren niedrig dünkt, und Newton nicht vergass (84). Thus, Newton is not only the model scientist, but also the model pious scientist.

The question of the extent and limitation of scientific knowledge is again raised in "Die Falschheit menschlicher Tugenden" (1730). Newton's achievements are once again cited as the highest attainment of human science:

Wie durch unendlicher vorborgner Zahlen Reyh,
Ein krumm-geflochtner Zug gerecht zu messen sey;
Warum die Sterne sich an eigne Gleise halten;
Wie bunte Farben sich aus lichten Strahlen spalten;
Was für ein inn'rer Trieb der Welten Wirbel dreht;
Was für ein Zug das Meer zu gleichen Stunden bläht;
Das alles weiss er schon: . . . (105)

It is a succinct statement of Newton's major accomplishment: the new mathematical method with which the curved planetary orbits can be calculated, the color theory, the theory of gravitational force which explains diverse phenomena like planetary orbits and the tides. Yet all this is only the outer shell of nature: "Ins innre der Natur dringt kein erschaffner Geist . . ." (106). And once again he asserts that Newton was fully aware of this limitation of scientific knowledge.

In the poem "An Herrn D. Gessner" (1734), he lists the scientific interests of his friend Johannes Gessner with whom he botanized and traveled across the Alps. First he praises his work in mathematical physics where he followed Newton's path:

Bald steigest du auf Newtons Pfad,
In der Natur geheimen Raht,
Wohin dich deine Mess-Kunst leitet:
O Mess-Kunst, Zaum der Phantasie!
Wer dir will folgen, irret nie;
Wer ohne dich will gehn, der gleitet. (157)

He also praises his work in medicine,

Du siehst des Herzens Unruh gehn,
Du kennst ihr Eilen und ihr Stehn,
Und die Vernutzung an den Rädern. (157)

as well as his love for botany:

Bald lockt dich Flora nach der Au,
Wo tausend Blumen stehn im Thau,
Die auf dein Auge buhlend warten; (158)

In Haller's poetry there are also several other themes related to science and popular among his contemporaries. In "Über den Ursprung des Übels" (1734), he speculates about the human condition and tries to conceive of other perspectives. For example, he considers the possibility that there could be more than five senses, that the reality which we perceive is limited by a narrow view; the angels, he suggests, might have a thousand senses and see in full clarity, directly and immediately what we perceive only through the limited mediation of our five senses (176). Or, he considers the possibility that evil is a circumstance that exists only on this planet and that in the multitude of other planets varying degrees of virtue prevail; perhaps, he suggests, our world, plagued by evil, contributes to the perfection of the whole, in that it fulfills one of the possibilities (196–197).

The scientific themes in Haller's poetry can be found in the poetry of many of his contemporaries. There is a respect for the achievements of modern science, with Newton represented as the outstanding example of what man can accomplish with scientific method. There are warnings against transcending the limits of reason and science and suspicions of systems that explain everything. Science is considered a threat to man if it leads to pride, but a boon if it leads to piety.

As far as these poems are concerned, there is no indication that the religious and scientific views of Haller are in conflict, as Margarete Hochdoerfer maintains.[7] The conflicts he felt over religious matters were of a religious nature and not precipitated by his commitment to science. Nor is Stephen d'Irsay convincing in his comparison of Voltaire and Haller.[8] He argues that Voltaire found a philosophic point of view compatible with science, but that Haller, as a traditionalist, could not do so and remained throughout his life torn between divergent points of view. There were inner conflicts in Haller's life, but it is also doubtful that Voltaire's deism and cynicism are more compatible with science than Haller's orthodoxy and piety.

    7 Margarete Hochdoerfer, *The Conflict Between the Religious and Scientific Views of Albrecht von Haller* (Lincoln, Nebraska, 1932).
    8 Stephen d'Irsay, *Albrecht von Haller, eine Studie zur Geistesgeschichte der Aufklärung* (Leipzig, 1930).

10. Christian Sendel (1719–1789)

Little is known about Christian Sendel, and his compendium of science in verse, *Der Fromme Naturkundige*,[1] is relatively unknown. Poggendorff[2] lists him in his handbook, but with the sole comment that he was a physician in Danzig. Meusel[3] provides the information that he was born in Colbing in 1719 and that he was a physician and a professor of natural history at the Gymnasium in Danzig. He also lists several Latin works published after 1743 but no mention of *Der Fromme Naturkundige*. Zöckler[4] cites the work as an example of physicotheological poetry. Kirchner[5] describes it as a periodical of forty installments, published in 1740.

Der Fromme Naturkundige is divided into forty parts of installments appearing in Danzig between June 28, 1738, and November 7, 1739. In 1738 they appeared weekly, but in 1739 only bi-monthly; the entire collection was published in book form in 1740. The justification for considering this work as a book rather than a periodical is that there was one author and a single plan underlies the whole work.

To refer to this work as a physicotheology in verse, as Zöckler does, might obscure the true nature of the work, if it leads one to expect a predominantly theological orientation. As the title indicates, there surely is a theological orientation, yet as a careful reading of the text shows, the substance of the work is science. There are long theological passages demonstrating the purpose of this or that natural phenomenon, and every section concludes with a praise of God in nature; nevertheless, the work as a whole is primarily scientific in point of view. The verse form indicates, of course, that the work is in the tradition of didactic poetry and is intended as a popular presentation of the new learning for the layman. In the early sections, the dialogue form, the imaginative space flights, and an encounter with an inhabitant from the moon indeed attest to the popular nature of the work. It must not be forgotten, however, that the work does convey a considerable amount of straightforward scientific material.

Before proceeding to a detailed discussion of the work, a short survey of the poems's structure should be helpful. In the first section the author discusses God's creation of the world out of nothing; henceforth, he maintains, God can be recognized in his creation. Sendel grants the importance of revelation, yet

---

[1] (Danzig, 1740).

[2] Johann Christian Poggendorff, *Biographisch-Literarisches Handwörterbuch zur Geschichte der exacten Wissenschaften*, II, (Leipzig, 1863), p. 903.

[3] Johann Georg Meusel, *Das gelehrte Teutschland oder Lexikon der jetzt lebenden Teutschen Schriftsteller*, third edition (Lemgo, 1776), p. 1121.

[4] Otto Zöckler, *Geschichte der Beziehungen zwischen Theologie und Naturwissenschaft* (Gütersloh, 1877–1879), II, p. 112.

[5] Joachim Kirchner, *Die Grundlagen des deutschen Zeitschriftenwesens*, II (Leipzig, 1931).

maintains that to be most fully inspired by faith in God, one must seek him in nature. This is his justification for the survey of the realms of nature in the next thirty-nine sections. Sections two to twelve are the liveliest of the work. From this discussion of far away planets and suns, he turns to phenomena belonging entirely to our planet. Sections thirteen to twenty-four offer compact discussions of specific physical phenomena, mostly in the realm of optics and meteorology or, at any rate, natural phenomena occuring in the earth's atmosphere, above the earth's surface. Then he descends to the surface of the earth itself with an account of mountains in the twenty-fifth section. In sections twenty-six to twenty-nine he enters the interior of the earth and reveals man's knowledge of metals and minerals. In the thirtieth section a variety of water phenomena are presented. In the next four sections he moves on to the plant and animal kingdoms which then lead naturally to man. In the remaining sections Sendel, the physician, gives quite a detailed account of the human body. Thus, we have the following divisions according to subjects: astronomy, sections two to twelve: physics, sections thirteen to twenty-four; natural history, sections twenty-five to thirty-four; anatomy and medicine, sections thirty-five to forty. From this brief survey it can be seen that the author has attempted to give the layman a compendium of the scientific knowledge of his day.

The sections on astronomy are of special interest because the didactic presentation of material is enlivened by imaginative episodes. Sections two to four present knowledge about the moon in the form of dialogues between Sternlieb, an amateur astronomer, and an inhabitant of the moon whom the former meets during his dream voyage to the satellite. Sternlieb had, of course, anticipated the moon's inhabitation, for through his telescope he had noted the remarkable similarity between earth and moon:

> Sein grosses Ferneglass entdeckte deutlich gnug,
> Wie viel er Ähnlichkeit mit unsrer Erden trug.
> Er folgerte hieraus in ungefälschten Schlüssen,
> Dass auch auf seinem Rund Geschöpfe wohnen müssen,
> Die mit Vernunfft begabt, mit Geist und Feur belebt,
> Die Seligkeit, worinn der grosse Schöpfer schwebt,
> Und das was ihnen mehr Desselben Hände gönnen,
> Zu seinem Lob und Preiss geschickt geniessen können. (9)

Sternlieb takes issue with a book which contends that only the planets but not the moon are inhabited. The book in question is, of course, Huygens' *Cosmotheoros,* as Sendel points out in a footnote. Sternlieb's conviction is finally confirmed when, while dreaming, he is transported to the moon. The author advises the reader in another footnote not to take this episode lightly, for he has based his material on the best observations of the most famous astronomers. Indeed, frequent footnotes supply astronomical facts and sources.

For his description of the moon, for example, Sendel relies for his terminology and figures on the work of Johann Hevel.

Before Sternlieb meets his counterpart on the moon, he marvels at the many vegetable and animal species he finds there; they lead him to a praise of God in nature as found on the moon. Finally, he meets a moon inhabitant who, fortunately, also turns out to be an amateur astronomer. As the "Mond-Bürger" tells him at the very beginning:

Ich war, noch eh du kamst, nur eben ausgegangen
Umb die Betrachtungen von neuem anzufangen
Die ich so lange Zeit, so offt von deiner Welt
Von ihrem Lauff und Schein mit Mühe angestellt. (15)

What follows is a fascinating discourse between the two about moon and earth astronomy. The central subject is astronomical data as a moon astronomer would perceive it. The fifth section, a continuation of this dialogue, opens with considerations on the reciprocal value of earth and moon toward one another. As we would expect, this leads him to comment on the orderliness of the cosmos and the divine will responsible for it:

Und sieht aus diesem klar, dass Gott die Ordnung liebt,
Und als der Ordnung Gott uns diese Mittel giebt,
Umb uns, wie er befiehlt, nur eifrig zu bestreben,
Im Lassen und im Thun fein ordentlich zu leben. (27)

The dream concludes with Sternlieb's view of the cosmos through a moon telescope. Sternlieb is struck by the fact that the cosmos as a whole looks the same from the moon as it does from the earth. The moon inhabitant, however, bids him to look at his earth to demonstrate that his moon perspective can show him something new. And indeed, the sight evokes Sternlieb's amazement, for now he witnesses with his own eyes a confirmation of the Copernican theory:

Zuvor war nechst dem Rand ein grosser heller Flecken,
Und diesen kan ich nun nicht mehr daselbst entdecken,
Dieweil er sich versteckt; er hiess America,
Jetzt stehet Engelland an dessen Stelle da.
Sonst hab ichs nicht geglaubt, und endlich nur gemeinet,
Da mir der Wahrheit Glantz itzt in die Augen scheinet,
Jetzt bin ich überführt, jetzt seh ich alles klar,
Was mir vorhero nur ein Schein der Wahrheit war. (28)

He continues to elaborate on the virtues of the Copernican theory and its superiority over that of Ptolemy.

Before the conclusion of the dream, the "Mond-Bürger" hands Sternlieb a work on astronomy he has written, with the assurance that the language used therein will not be strange to him since it is a universal one, namely, the language of astronomy. This suggests Sendel's belief in the attainability of reliable knowledge about nature, and that nature itself is reliable in its orderliness.

Sections five to eight discuss the remaining planets of our solar system. Sternlieb is still the narrator except that in section seven a new episode is introduced. In response to Sternlieb's fervent prayer for enlightenment in matters of astronomy, Urania, "Die Forscherin der Sterne", appears and instructs her disciple Himmelhold concerning Jupiter and Saturn. The dialogue between the two, as overheard by Sternlieb, constitutes sections seven and eight.

Though a considerable amount of astronomical facts and figures are supplied by the footnotes, the text itself is quite informative and compact as a few samples will show. The following passage about Mars tells some of our knowledge about the planet through our telescopic observations:

> Mars borget seinen Schein, wie uns ein Fern-Glas zeiget,
> So nur das eine Theil, das sich zur Sonnen neiget,
> Erhellt, erleuchtet sieht, Mars, sag ich borgt den Schein,
> Vom Urquell unsers Lichts, dem Sonnen Feur allein.
> Und dies entlehnte Licht giebt uns dann zu erkennen,
> Er sey nur an sich selbst ein dunckler Ball zu nennen.
> Ein Ball, der täglich sich umb seinen Angel kehrt,
> Wie dieses ebenfals ein Ferne-Glas erfährt,
> Wenn es die Flecken sieht, die Zeichen grosser Seen,
> Zuweilen hie, dann da, und dann nach hinten gehen.
> Ein Ball, den eine Last gedrückter Lüffte trägt,
> So wie man, wenn er sich in seinem Lauff bewegt,
> Und seine Dichtigkeit der Sternen Glantz verstecket,
> Der Dünste dicken Kreys umb ihn genau entdecket. (42)

Or, in the case of Mercury, in a few lines he states the length of that planet's orbit in comparison to ours, the nature of the seasons there, and by means of an example indicates what temperatures are found there:

> Den Creys-Lauff weiss man wohl den dies Gestirn durchrennt,
> Sein Jahr, als welches man drey unsre Monath nennt.
> Man weiss dass dieses Jahr kein Winter frostig machet
> Man weiss es dass allhier ein steter Sommer lachet;
> Ein Sommer, da vom Feur der Sonnen alles schwitzt,
> Wenn diese den Mercur auf solche Art erhitzt,
> Dass könt einmahl das Zinn der mässig warmen Erden
> In jenes heisse Land herauf versetzet werden:
> Würd es den Augenblick zu einen weissen Fluss,
> Der eben so zerlieff als hier Mercurius. (47)

Of all the elaborate astronomical facts, figures and explanations which are found in these sections, of special interest is his conviction that all the planets are inhabited by rational creatures. In connection with the moon it was seen that he rejected Huygen's doubts about the inhabitability of that satellite. As far as the planets are concerned, his belief in their inhabitability is even stronger, and the subject recurs at considerable length in every section pertaining to the planets.

The main argument that underlies this conviction is the analogy between the planets and the earth. The first step is always to prove that the heavenly body in question is indeed a planet, that is, that it has no light of its own but simply reflects that of the sun, that it revolves on its axis and about the sun, as does the earth, and finally, that there is evidence from telescopic observation that an atmosphere and water prevail. From this it is then concluded, that the conditions making life possible do exist and, therefore, must exist according to God's wisdom and power. A good example of this reasoning appears when he discusses the likelihood of Mars' inhabitability:

> Cassini, hat ihn schon vor langer Zeit bemerckt,
> Und Römers Fern-Glas es zu gleicher Zeit bestärckt.
> Sie sahen zwar wie Mars den Stern nicht mehr verdeckte
> Doch darum dieser nicht die Strahlen weiter streckte;
> Biss endlich ziemlich weit der Mars gewichen war,
> So stellten sich darauf die Strahlen wieder dar.
> Was, frug man hier, hat uns das Licht des Sterns geraubet,
> Nachdem der dichte Mars den Durchgang ihm erlaubet.
> Die Dünste brechen sonst den aufgefangnen Schein:
> Drumb muss auch umb den Mars ein nasser Dunst-Kreys seyn. (43)

Cassini and Römer had observed that when Mars traverses a star, the latter's rays are blacked out not only then, as one would expect, but also for some time after Mars no longer covers the star. Sendel concludes that Mars must be surrounded by an atmosphere containing moisture, to cause a refraction of the sun's rays. With this given, our author then draws the inevitable conclusion:

> Man schloss noch mehr hieraus: Lufft, Winde, Wolcken, Regen
> Sind also gleichfals ihm deswegen beyzulegen,
> Und sein versorgtes Rund ist also so gebaut,
> Dass fast die Wahrheit selbst sich darzuthun getraut
> (Denn Gott und die Natur pflegt nichts umsonst zu weben,)
> Es müssen so wie hier im Mars Geschöpffe leben.
> Geschöpffe, deren Geist den Höchsten Geist erkennt,
> Den Schöpffer gross und starck und weis' und gnädig nennt.
> Noch andre, welche zwar kein Geist, kein Sinn belebet,
> Und deren stummer Mund doch Gottes Ruhm erhebet. (43)

Another interesting example occurs in his discussion of Jupiter's inhabitants. Himmelhold had raised the difficulty involved in Jupiter's vast distance from the sun whose rays would be so weak upon their arrival that they might not even register in the eyes of Jupiter's inhabitants. Urania, however, sees no problem in this for God has the power, she maintains, to fashion the eyes of the inhabitants in such a way that the sun's rays, though weak on earth, would suffice there:

Der Stern im Auge nimmt wie uns die Sehe-Kunst
Aus der Erfahrung lehrt in dunckler Finsterniss
Verwundernswürdig zu, und wird hingegen kleiner,
Fällt ein geschwindes Licht uns plötzlich in die Augen.
Was wärs? wenn man daher aus dem geschwächten Licht
Das Jupiter geniesst, und aus bemeldtem Satz
Der klugen Sehe-Kunst vielmehr vermuthen wolte,
Dass da der Augenstern den Jupiters Bewohnern
Leicht mercklich grösser ist, auch Auge Kopf und Glied
Nach der Proportion des grossen Augen-Sterns
Weit ausgespanter seyn. (55–56)

According to the science of optics, she reasons, that larger pupils would enable Jupiter's inhabitants to see well enough. Such an argument is pregnant with implications. It suggests relativity, flexibility and variety in nature and when extended to other solar systems, inexhaustible possibilities in God's creation.

A further example of this apporach is Urania's contention that not only Saturn but also its moons and even the ring about Saturn are inhabited. To convince an incredulous Himmelhold who is concerned about the absence of the sun's warmth at such a distance, she replies:

Warum das? sind die Cörper
Im hitzigen Mercur von solcher Dichtigkeit,
Dass ein geschwüles Licht sie desto mehr beseelt:
So sind auch im Saturn die Wesen seiner Dinge
Von so beweglichen und Wärme vollen Theilen,
Dass der schon matte Strahl zu ihrer Förderung
Ja gar Vollkommenheit gerade tauglich ist. (63)

Once again the point is made that life forms are not fixed and limited to those on earth, that under different circumstances, different forms are possible. It is a recognition of the malleability of nature and the relativity of perspective in nature.

After Saturn he considers the nature of comets in section nine. He inveighs against superstitious beliefs associated with comets, gives a short history of cometary theory and states his preference for the contemporary theory, that they are heavenly bodies with measurable orbits.

The next section is an interlude in the form of an oratorio, devoted to a praise of the sun and its many life giving qualities. The author abandons his Alexandrine verses here and exhibits his poetic virtuosity with considerable enthusiasm. At the same time, the didactic purpose is not forgotten, since facts and figures about this center of the universe are dutifully given. In the next section, in which he returns to his customary verse pattern, he continues with the sun, giving special attention to the light giving rays. He gives a detailed explanation of color phenomena which follows the Newtonian theory as the following indicates:

> So bald sich nun das Licht mit einem Cörper paart,
> So gleich erblickt man ihn gefärbt und angemahlet
> Nach dem gebrochnen Licht, das von ihm rückwerts strahlet. (86)

In one respect it was quite appropriate that, having gone to the farthest reaches of the solar system, Saturn and the comets, he should then return to the sun, the center. For whether the author was aware of it or not, a system having a center and a circumference suggests compactness and unity, and it was fitting to assert this prior to his journey beyond our solar system in the next section.

In the twelfth section he takes another imaginative journey. While he is marveling at the multitude of stars, he is lifted into outer space:

> Wie wird mir, da die starren Blicke
> Auf diese ferne Wunder sehn?
> Mich dünckt die Erde weicht zurücke,
> Nechst mir seh ich den Mond sich drehn,
> Mars, Jupiter, Saturnus eilen,
> Ich mit und ohne viel Verweilen,
> Bin ich im äussern Sonnen-Reich; (93)

His realization that every star is a sun with its own planets, and that these solar systems are unlimited in number, overwhelms him and leads him to God, the source of this multitude of systems.

This then concludes his discussion of astronomy. In the remaining sections there are no flights of the imagination, no grand visions as in the foregoing. For the most part he gives a sober account of a variety of natural phenomena with some space devoted to pious and teleological reflections.

It has already been indicated that the next twelve sections belong to the realm of physics. More specifically, those natural phenomena are taken up that occur in the atmosphere of our planet; they can be further subdivided into optical and meteorological phenomena. He discusses the nature of air, winds, snow, rain, fog and hail. Specific weather changes are described and their causes delineated. The sun's rays are carefully analyzed with special attention to color phenomena in general, as well as specific phenomena like the rainbow, the sun's halo, aurora borealis, and zodiacal light.

His procedure is to take a specific phenomena like the air or light rays and then enumerate the various significant qualities of the subject. At times he is purely descriptive, but frequently he discusses in detail the cause of certain observed phenomena. In these sections considerable space is also devoted to a demonstration of usefulness of these phenomena to man and of the presence of purpose in nature. Since it would be unwieldy to discuss each section in greater detail than I have already done, I shall select certain highlights, either to illustrate his method or because they are valuable examples of science in verse.

He begins section thirteen by invoking the experiment of von Guericke with the air pump to elucidate the qualities of air, which is the main theme of the section:

> . . . Dem nun besser nachzudencken,
> Geht er zu der klugen Pumpen, welche Guericke erdacht,
> Die der Lüffte Eigenschafften ihm umb desto klärer macht.
> Muntre Vögel werden kranck, dehnen die gezuckten Glieder,
> Wenn die Lufft in etwas weicht, ja sie sincken gäntzlich nieder,
> Wenn ihr Leben nebst dem Athem und der Lufft zugleich entgeht,
> So dann lehret dass kein Leben ohne Geist und Lufft besteht,
> Wenn dieselbe sonsten nur in der rechten Maasse bleibet,
> Weil, so bald er sie hierauf dichter in einander treibet,
> Der darein gesetzte Vogel mercklich schwerer Athem zieht,
> So, dass er ihn eben endlich wie die andern sterben sieht. (98)

The experiment proves that life is dependent on just the right measure of air. He continues with descriptions of various other qualities of air, such as the following:

> Öffters eilt der junge Tag aus der frühen Morgen-Wiegen,
> Eh wir noch die Sonne selbst in die wachen Augen kriegen,
> Wenn dieselbe erst allmählig unsre muntern Grentzen grüsst,
> Ob der Tag gleich eine Weile schon bey uns gewesen ist.
> Wie geschieht dis? weil die Lufft, so die obre Gegend füllet,
> Und auf die bereits der Strahl der nicht fernen Sonnen quillet,
> Mit geschickter Hand ihn beuget, bricht und denn der Erden beut,
> Wenn sie ihn auch selbst durchs Brechen erstlich mehr und mehr verstreut.
> So wie es sich nun verhält, wenn der Tag uns aufgewecket,
> So geschieht es eben auch, wenn die Sonne sich verstecket. (100)

Thus, the air's capacity to refract sunlight explains the appearance of daylight prior to the rising of the sun.

Of his long discussion of weather changes and causes of those changes, the following is an interesting example:

Als erst die Allmacht diese Welt
Mit starcker Hand ans Licht gestellt,
Und schon der Sonnen-Feuer brannte,
Umb welches aber noch zur Zeit
Der Erden Unvermögenheit
Bey ihrem ersten Nun nicht rannte;
Befahl der ewgen Weisheit Mund,
Weil sie es so am besten fund,
Umb ihren Endzweck zu ergreiffen,
Der Erden jetzt vollführte Bau
Der solt ins künfftige genau
Im Thier-Creiss umb die Sonne schweiffen.
Und hieraus ist der Unterscheid
Der Wetter in den Lauff der Zeit,
Gleich als die Reise fürgenommen,
Zum Wohl der gantzen Welt gekommen. (129–130)

The earth's annual orbit about the sun is the basic cause of the change in seasons, and Sendel here attributes their arrangement to God who designed it for the good of man. He treats many other specific weather phenomena, frequently showing how they are really a chain of phenomena all interrelated with one another.

Of the numerous optical phenomena discussed in these sections, the one explaining the rainbow and color phenomena in general is of interest, because here there is a good statement of Newton's color theory in verse. I shall quote the passage at length:

Ein jeder Sonnen-Strahl theilt, wenn er sich hinab
Und in den Tropffen senckt, in bunte Zweige ab.
Und ob viel Strahlen gleich in einen Tropfen fallen,
Und auf die Art getheilt zurück herunter prallen,
So trifft doch einer nur dem Grad nach unsern Blick,
Der andern Strahlen Schein fält anderwerts zurück.
Der Äste sind nur fünf die an des Tropfens Flächen,
Wenn ihn der Strahl durchbohrt, sich abgesondert brechen
Wir wissen es vorher, dass in dem Sonnen-Schein
Fünf Farben, roht und gelb, grün, blau und purpur seyn
Ein jeder Ast des Strahls hat eine dieser Farben,
Weil einge Äste nun des dichten Wesens darben,
Das andrer Fasern steift, so beugt der dünne Ast

Sich nicht so tief herab, als wie des andern Last.
Daher dann wie man sieht, der Purpur unten stehet,
Die blaue Farbe folgt, und nach der grünen gehet
In dem gefassten Rang die dünnre Gelbe fort,
Die dünneste ist roht, und nimmt den höchsten Ort.
Der Winckel Unterscheid, worinn die Strahlen reisen,
Kan also nur allein verschiedne Farben weisen. (140—141)

The references to the refraction of the light in a raindrop are, of course, in regard to his discussion of the formation of the rainbow. The explanation of the appearance of color in the. above passage is quite complete. The composite nature of light, the different angles of refrangibility corresponding to the different colors and the arrangement of the rays from purple below to red above — all this is in accord with what had already become the prevailing, the Newtonian, theory of color. At the conclusion of this section he raises the question whether the rainbow was created by God after the flood as some maintained. Since he had just given explanation of the rainbow according to natural causes, he must grant that since the existence of water and sunshine, rainbows also existed. He compromises by suggesting that though the rainbow existed before the flood, it became a sign for man only after the flood. Another example of compromise between science and religion, with religion having to accomodate itself to the claims of science.

As a final illustration of his treatment of atmospheric phenomena, his introduction to his discussion of fog can be cited:

Des Nebels dichter Dufft
Besteht aus nassem Dunst, der in der untern Lufft
Wenn ihn die Kälte drückt, sich so zusammen ziehet,
Dass der verwehrte Blick nichts, was er decket, siehet.
Weil, wenn der Sommer wärmt, der Dunst hinaufwerts steigt,
So wird kein Nebel nicht zu seiner Zeit gezeugt;
Wenn aber Herbst und Frost die Dünste niedertreiben,
So muss er freylich wohl bey uns hier unten bleiben;
Und wenn die Kälte noch die Unter-Lufft beschwert,
So wird von ihr der Fall ihm ebenfals verwehrt;
Auch muss noch, soll er nun an unserm Ort entstehen,
Kein Wind, der ihn zerstreut, durch unsre Gegend gehen. (154)

It is a good example of his matter of fact, common-sense approach to natural phenomena. The explanation, furthermore, is a fine example of the clear-cut mechanistic, cause and effect approach to nature, characteristic of the scientific method of the time.

In section twenty-five the author finally comes down to earth in his survey of natural phenomena. He begins with mountains, then goes into the interior of the earth to discuss metals and minerals, then comes the domain of water and finally the plant and animal kingdoms. We have called these sections natural history, since descriptions of mineral, vegetable and animal kingdoms were usually considered as belonging to that discipline.

The four sections on metals and minerals are quite thorough in their elaboration of details. Of metals he considers six: gold, silver, tin, copper, lead and iron. He analyzes the physical and chemical properties of each metal and then proceeds to a lengthy discussion of the uses of metals to man, as for example:

> Lasst uns mit kurtzem auch den Vortheil überdencken,
> Den die Metalle noch den Wissenschaften schencken.
> Der Sternkunst geben sie so manches Instrument,
> Wodurch man des Gestirns Schein, Lauf und Art erkennt.
> Und den gepriesenen GOTT aus Dingen, die entfernet,
> Ja wohl so gut und schön als aus den nächsten, lernet.
> Die Kentniss der Natur ist ziemlich hochgebracht
> Nachdem die Pumpe da, so Guericke erdacht,
> Die aus Metall besteht. Und die Zergliederungen
> Des allen was nur lebt, die wären nie gelungen,
> Wenn Ertz und Werckzeug nicht die Spuren und die Bahn
> Zu dem was uns verdeckt, geschicklich aufgethan. (208)

Thus, astronomy, physics and anatomy are indebted to metals. This, of course, is only one justification for the existence of metals, since he tries to be almost exhaustive in his search for purpose.

In his discussion of minerals he is again very thorough in classification and in description of their properties. As an example let us take the section on salts. First, he gives us a definition of a salt:

> Man nennet dies ein Saltz, was zwar zusammen hält,
> Doch welches auch, wenn es ins Feur geschüttet wird,
> Und wenns ins Wasser kommt, zerflüsset und zerschmeltzt.
> Das also einfach ist, dass jedes Theil davon,
> An Wesen und Natur, dem Gantzen ähnlich bleibt,
> Und auch auf eine Art in unsre Zungen würckt. (211)

Here there are the physical and chemical properties, the latter being simply the reaction of the substance to fire. Next follows an enumeration of various salts such as saltpetre, borax, salammoniac and alum. He gives the outstanding properties of each salt and sometimes the likeliest location. There are similar instructive passages about naphtha, lime, pitch, vitriol, bismuth, zinc, hematite and others.

Section twenty-nine is devoted entirely to stones. He divides them into

precious and base stones according to how they reflect light; the precious stones
reflect it, the base absorb it, and there is a middle class that does so only
partially. He analyzes the composition of stones as follows:

> Wir sehen Saltz und Erd und Schwefel in den Steinen
> Durch Wärm und zähes Nass sich dergestalt vereinen,
> Dass den entstandnen Stein kein starcker Hammer-Schlag
> Gedehnet, sondern eh zermalmet liefern mag,
> Dass ihn kein Küchen-Feur, so starck es ist, verzehret,
> Dass er im Wasser nicht in kleine Theilgen fähret. (226)

Then he goes on to his classification of stones into three categories, naming
some thirty stones, with the magnet getting special attention. He concludes with
a praise of God in stones.

The next section considers water and the various forms in which it is found
on earth. At the beginning he again describes some of the properties of water:

> Des Wassers Cörper flüsst,
> Weil zwischen ihm viel Wärme ist,
> Die seine Theilgen sich nicht fest
> Verbinden lässt.
> Wiewol es auch im Winter frieret,
> So bald die Wärme sich verlieret.
> Das Wasser ist wol tausend mahl so schwer
> Als eine reine Luft;
> Dagegen der Mercur es ohngefehr
> Biss vierzehn mahl noch überwieget. (234)

Water, then, has a certain quantity of heat without which it freezes, and it is
heavier than air but lighter than mercury. These, in short, are its chemical and
physical properties. He continues with a description of springs, rivers, seas,
oceans, snow, rain and other manifestations of water. Again, as is to be
expected, he takes up the uses of water. He also raises the subject of water's
destructive power in floods and storms but assures the reader that these are
simply instruments of God. Here, as well as throughout the work, the goodness
of nature is defended.

Sections thirty-one and thirty-two include the plant kingdom. The first
section offers a very detailed description of the parts of plants and the structures
and functions of those parts. He furthermore explains the processes by which
plants receive nourishment and grow. He does raise the question of manifoldness
in the plant kingdom but gives no classification of species. In other words, he is
interested in what plants have in common, not in the multiple differences that
create different species. In this respect, he does not approach his subject as a

natural historian who would be more interested in variety and in classifying variety.

In section thirty-two he raises the subject of the birth of plants and considers several theories to account for the phenomena. He rejects all theories except the one which by the middle of the century had received wide recognition, namely, preformationism which considered the whole plant to exist already within the seed. An extension of the preformation theory was encapsulation which claimed that within the first of every species, at the beginning of creation, were contained the seeds of all subsequent offspring. As the following passage shows, Sendel was an adherent of this theory:

> Da beyde Meynungen nicht Stich und Probe halten,
> So lässt man füglicher die letzte Meynung walten,
> Die Malebransch ersann, dass nemlich allbereit
> Der Schöpfer aller Welt gleich in der ersten Zeit,
> Da Erd und Acker ward und Gras und Pflanzen brachte,
> Was je geblüht, und blüht, und einst noch blühn wird, machte;
> Dass schon der erste Kern die Kernchen all enthielt,
> Die GOTT biss an die Zeit der letzten Welt erzielt;
> Dass eins im andern steckt und auf verborgne Weise,
> Dann, wenn es wachsen soll, das finstere Gehäuse
> Verlässt und sich hieraus entwickelt und verliert,
> Und gross und zeitig wird, und alles bey sich führt,
> Was noch aufs künftige der Höchsten Weisheit Seegen
> In seines Saamens Schooss beliebet hat zu legen,
> Will dies der Phantasey gleich etwas schwerlich ein,
> So wird doch die Vernunft hiemit zufrieden seyn. (251—252)

The next two sections on the animal kingdom resemble the foregoing in that the author again does not enumerate a variety of species with appropriate classification, but is interested only in what they have in common. He discusses in detail the structures and functions of the parts of animals such as fibres, bones, nerves and so on. In the thirty-fourth, he gives a clear description of the circulation of the blood, which begins as follows:

> Die Blut-Gefässe sind also mit Blut erfüllt,
> Das aus dem Herzen so, als einem Brunnen, quillt,
> Und durch der Adern Weg in alle Theile fliehet,
> Und sich dann wiederum zurück zum Herzen ziehet.
> Der ersten Adern Art, die es vom Herzen führt,
> Heisst man Arterien, wo man den Puls verspürt.
> Die andern gegentheils, wodurch es rückwerts rennet,
> Sind Venen, die man deutsch nur von dem Blut benennet. (268—269)

The remaining sections of the work are devoted to the human body. The descriptions are so detailed that these sections could be called a medical text in verse. Sections thirty-five and thirty-six deal with the digestive and circulatory systems, the following two sections cover sensation, and in section thirty-nine the brain is examined. In the final section he surveys the entire animal kingdom and describes the similarities and differences between man and the species beneath him.

It has been difficult to do justice to this 320 page verse compendium of early eighteenth century science. From the selections given, it can be seen that the value of the work doesn't primarily lie in its aesthetic virtues, though the verses show the author to be quite capable in his handling of verse patterns. It does deserve notice in other respects: It is valuable as a source book of scientific learning of the early eighteenth century; its scientific material is comparable to what one would find in science textbooks and compendiums of the time, and it is significant as an attempt to popularize scientific learning, to enlighten the layman concerning man's knowledge about nature.

11. Georg Heinrich Behr (1708—1761)

Georg Heinrich Behr was one of several physicians in the eighteenth century who achieved distinction in both medicine and literature. The son of a physician, he was born in Strassburg where he began his medical studies. He continued at Leiden where his teachers were Boerhaave and Albin, and after attending several other German universities where he also studied mathematics, philosophy and literature, he returned to Strassburg and began his career as phyiscian and author. He was president of the "Teutsche Gesellschaft zu Strassburg" and a member of the "Kaiserliche Akademie der Naturforscher". Although most of his many medical works were in Latin, he recognized the desirability of German for medical writings and wrote several in his native language.[1] His two poetic works of interest to us are *Die Gottheit oder Lob und Erkänntniss des Schöpfers aus seinen Geschöpfen,*[2] a 147 page poem in Alexandrine verse containing much scientific material and *Die schwache Wissenschaft der heutigen Ärzte,*[3] a satire on contemporary medicine also in Alexandrine verse.

Die Gottheit . . . is very pertinent to this investigation, for it is a survey of the domains of nature for the layman. It is clearly a didactic work which intends to enlighten the average reader about the works of nature, but solely within the deistic framework. The inculcation of piety is the primary aim of the poem, yet the text and the supporting footnotes also impart much useful information about natural phenomena, as discovered by scientists both ancient and modern. In the footnotes, the ancient sources most often quoted are Pliny and Cicero with occasional references to Lucretius, Virgil and Galen; the modern sources most often cited are Brockes, Triller, Derham and Scheuchzer. There are also generous excerpts from the poems of Brockes and Triller in the footnotes. From the selection of modern authors we can certainly see that Behr is not writing to professional scientists but to laymen who are more likely to know these popular authors than scientific texts.

In the very beginning of the poem he states the purpose of his work:

Mein Geist ist viel zu schwach, nach Würden
    Dich zu achten;
Desswegen will ich Dich, nur im Geschöpf be-
    trachten;
Da find ich stets von Dir die allerreinste
    Spur. (8)

---

[1] *Physiologia medica, oder richtige und umständliche Beschreibung des menschlichen Leibes* ·(Strassburg, 1736). *Die Nothwendigkeit und Nutzbarkeit der Deutsch geschriebenen Arzneybücher* (Strassburg, 1739), *Zwey Bücher von der Materia Medica oder vollständige Beschreibung aller und jeder Arzneymittel* (Strassburg, 1748).
[2] (Frankfurt und Leipzig, 1752).
[3] (Strassburg, 1753).

In the footnote corresponding to this passage he names predecessors who have followed a similar course: Ray, Nieuwentyt, Brockes, Triller, J.A. Fabricius and Derham. Like these authors Behr writes a popular natural history for the layman to enlighten and exhort to piety. All these authors make atheists and naturalists their opponents and exclude them from the community of scientists. Behr, then, belongs to this tradition of praising God in nature. The great fear of these pious scientists, somewhat justified to be sure, was that the scientific discoveries of causal connections within nature might lead some to conclude that nature is autonomous and self-sufficient. Therefore, the constant refrain in the poem is that no matter how much we know, the phenomenon in question is still so complex and mysterious, that only God could be the creator. Nature, as a living organism with a life of its own, is constantly denied, for behind every natural phenomenon stands God, and without Him the phenomenon would be impossible.

With this theme as the refrain throughout the entire poem, Behr moves through the book of nature systematically and thus gives his poem a precise structure. He begins with man, more specifically man's five senses, then comes vegetation, to be followed by living creatures "In Wassern, in der Luft, in Wäldern und in Fluren". (48) Correspondingly he takes up fish, then birds and insects, and finally mammals. The last section of the poem is an extension of vision beyond this planet to other solar systems. It is a cosmic view so popular with the poets of the Brockes school in their praise of God in nature.

It is noteworthy that Behr does not follow the usual order of surveys of the domains of nature. The customary procedure at this time was to follow the biblical account of creation by beginning with the heavenly bodies and then proceeding from the lower forms of life to man. Behr, however, begins with man, especially his senses, and then moves up the ladder of creation and concludes with the cosmos.

Let us now return to the beginning of the poem and examine his treatment of the various themes. After announcing that the object of his poem is the praise of God in nature in the tradition of Brockes, Derham, Triller and others, he turns to man and discusses the intricacies of his physical nature with which, as a physician, he was thoroughly acquainted. He quickly qualifies these considerations with an emphatic denial that nature alone is responsible for the miracle which is the human body:

Was ist denn die Natur? Woher ist sie entsprossen?
Sie ist ja nichts für sich! Aus Gott ist sie geflossen! (16)

This is part of his refrain, that only God is revealed in the works of nature and not some autonomous force independent of God. This is stated most emphatically here at the beginning, and it is a theme to which he returns with insistence.

He then takes up man's senses one by one, with the lengthiest discussion devoted to the sense of sight. His approach is mostly descriptive with an absence of detail which, as a physician, he could have supplied. The information he does supply is sufficient, however, for his main purpose, which is to demonstrate that neither man nor nature but only God could have been the cause:

Gewisslich! wer hiebey den Schöpfer nicht erkennt,
Und nur in der Natur diss Meisterstück will suchen,
Ist ausgelassen toll, und billig zu verfluchen, ... (37)

Next he turns to life below man, the vegetable and animal kingdoms:

Ich finde meinen Gott in Wiesen, Wald und Fluren,
In Wasser, Erd und Luft, bey allen Creaturen:
Kurtz: aller Orten sind von Ihm die schönsten Spuren. (38)

In this section as well as throughout the poem, he tries to show that individual plants and animals thrive so wonderfully, because they are so appropriately placed in their respective environments. This then leads to his major theme that only God could have had the omniscience for such a design. From such discussions we are forced to conclude that Behr sees nature as essentially good and positive, while denying its autonomy. Since God stands behind every phenomena, any negative quality about it would unavoidably be God's responsibility and this is impossible. We have here, then, a statement of the "Aufklärers" conviction in the goodness of the world about him with sin and evil entirely removed from the sphere of nature.

His discussion of animal species begins with sea life and continues with life in the air, that is, birds and insects, followed by the creatures on earth, the mammals. His procedure is to enumerate individual fish or birds and describe what is unique about their physical structures, habits, and environment. It is noteworthy that in so doing he is frequently struck by the variety he finds in nature:

Betrachte fernerfort bald den, bald jenen Fisch;
Er sey, gross oder klein, in Flüssen, See und Teichen!
Wird einer je davon dem andern völlig gleichen?
Sind sie, in ihrem Strohm, gleich schwimmend, flinck und frisch?
Wer machet diesen hoch, und jenen tiefer schwimmen?
Woher pflegt dieser sich zu schlängeln und zu krümmen?
Wer mag die Ursach wohl hievon genau bestimmen? (51)

Variety in nature, nature's plentitude in bringing forth living beings was, of course, one of the very popular themes in the eighteenth century. Since this quality was usually stressed by poets and philosophers who subscribed to a more secular view of nature as an independent organism, it is significant that Behr, who denies this, nevertheless shares this awareness of nature's richness.

The insect world fascinates him especially, as it did many of his contemporaries. It provided such an apt contrast to the grand and immense works of nature and permitted the pious poet to demonstrate that God encompasses all dimensions. Behr also stresses that the insect world, in its minuteness, is so well designed that it exceeds the capacities of the best artist or technician and that therefore only God could be the designer.

He proceeds to the next rung of the ladder of creation, which is the world of mammals, divided by him into domesticated and wild ones. He takes up some fifteen animals, one by one, and each time drives home his main argument. Though the descriptions, again, are not precisely scientific, they are appropriate for this natural history for the layman. The footnotes continue to refer the reader to more scientific accounts of each subject.

The final section is devoted to God's vast creation in unlimited space beyond our tiny planet. This was a subject that especially inspired the poets and thinkers of the Brockes school. Behr also takes delight in lifting his imagination to the boundlessness about him:

> O ungemessene und Gräntzen-lose Gruft! . .
> Ist's möglich, dass mein Geist dich sattsam kan ergründen?
> Kan man von deinem Raum auch je ein Ende finden?
> Du gantz unendliche und unumschränckte Luft!
> Wie gross, wie tief, wie breit, bist du mir nicht zu nennen?
> Wer mag die Weite wohl von deiner Höh' erkennen,
> Worinn, Millionen weis, die schönsten Lichter brennen. (126–127)

In this section the reader is overwhelmed in the text, and especially in the footnotes, by the latest facts and figures about sizes and distances of heavenly bodies. We find also the familiar argument of concluding by analogy from our solar system to those millions of others whose suns we barely see as tiny lights at night. The millions of stars he assumes without question are suns like ours:

> Sie sind, wie jeder sieht, der hellen Sonne gleich.
> Da diese nun dis Rund durch ihren Schein erquicket,
> Die Erde wärmt und nährt, mit Gras und Bäumen schmücket,
> Kurtz: alles hier belebt, vollkommen macht und reich!
> So scheinen sie mir auch fürwahr dazu zu dienen,
> Dass mancher Erdenball durch solche möge grünen,
> Und darum stehen sie auch an jenen Himmels-Bühnen. (130–132)

The orderliness of this infinitude of heavenly bodies brings him back to his refrain:

Denn dieser Lichter Meng und unzählbares Heer,
In ihrem Lauf betracht, da keins das andre hemmet,
Nie an einander stosst, sich niemahls häuft noch stemmet;
Obgleich derselben sind, so viel, als Sand am Meer.
Muss dich vom grossen Gott aufs neue überführen . . . (136—137)

Here we see once again that the lawfulness of the heavenly bodies in their orbits had become fully accepted and is here cited as evidence of God's work.

Toward the end of his poem he turns to the sun and praises its majesty as a sign of God's even greater majesty:

O Wundervolles Licht! Monarch und Fürst der Zeit!
Du feurigs Freuden-Meer! der Creaturen Wonne!
Du reicher Wunder-Brand! du stets beflammte Sonne!
Du hellster Freuden-Strahl! du Feind der Dunckelheit!
Du Brunnquell der Natur und ihrer Zeugungs Säfte!
Du Ursprung alles Triebs und der Belebungs Kräfte!
Du, von des Schöpfers Macht mir zeugendes Geschäfte! (140—141)

It is an interesting passage, for Behr throughout had been very careful to place God behind every natural phenomena. This deistic piety limited the scope of his imagination acutely. The above passage seems to be the only one in which his imagination takes flight and slightly transcends its deistic bounds. The sun, as the life giving source of nature, as the vivifying origin of all natural drives and instincts, does suggest a vision of nature which, though a creature of God, has an autonomy of its own and is a living organism. The latter certainly was becoming the dominant view of nature by the middle of the eighteenth century.

From this discussion it is clear that this poem belongs to a cultural approach toward the sciences typical of the first half of the century, in that the new sciences, with rare exceptions, are assimilated into a pious deistic framework in which the imagination is strictly held in check. Nature, on the whole, is granted little existence of its own; it is a static structure whose dynamism belongs entirely to God. And yet this approach did contribute to the future dynamic, organismic concept of nature, for as the traditional God receded into the background, those grand qualities always attributed to him, mystery, wisdom, grandeur, complexity, now were imputed to nature. Thus the divinization of nature was prepared by these homely and naive speculations. As the traditional God became less credible, a divine nature became more plausible, since it was less dependent on religious tradition and faith, above religious sects and disputations, and especially since it was immediate and accessible to the senses.

Thus, though the poem belongs to the earlier didactic tradition, it plays its part in preparing future, more sophisticated developments. It is one of the many Christian Lucretius poems of the eighteenth century, in that it tried to assimilate the new sciences, the new knowledge about nature into a Christian framework.

Behr's satire on medicine is also interesting for this study, though the treatment of medicine in poetry and popular literature is a topic by itself. *Die schwache Wissenschaft der heutigen Ärzte* is a didactic poem in which the poet seeks to expose the shortcomings of medicine, past and present. The text is again supported by copious footnotes which provide a good selection of the medical literature of the time and should be of interest to the medical historian.

In the very beginning he raises the question why medicine is in such a low state in such an enlightened period. He grants that mathematics, anatomy and chemistry have contributed much to medicine, as for example:

Denn die Zergliedrungs-Kunst hat vieles aufgedecket,
Was, bey den Alten noch, im Finsteren gestecket.
Den Blut-Kreis, viel Gefäss', den Milch- und Nahrungs-Saft,
Die Dauung, das Gesicht, Gehör, und Zeugungs-Kraft,
Und was dergleichen mehr, hat man, durch dieses Wissen,
Nun klar und kund gemacht, und schönstens abgerissen. (13)

Though he cites many examples of the value of mathematics and chemistry in the improvement of medicine, he concludes that, on the whole, the value of these subjects has been exaggerated to the point that the practice of medicine had been undermined. In the following passage he mocks mathematics, anatomy and chemistry as they are used in medicine:

Ob dieses Zäsergen klein oder gross aussiehet;
Ob es sich Senkel-recht, nauf-oder nab-wärts ziehet;
Ob solches Schnecken-weis, halb-rund gewunden, geht;
Ob's aber völlig sich zu einem Zirkel dreht:
Ob's drey vier Linien breit sich von dem Knorspel endet;
Ob's aber sich zum Bein zuletzt noch selbsten wendet;
Ob's roth, ob's weiss erscheint; mit einem Nerv'gen prangt;
Ob noch ein Ädergen zu solchem hingelangt.
Ob Würmgen in dem Blut; ob Würmgen in dem Saamen,
Durch was für eine Kraft sie in das Eylein kamen.
Ob eine Spinnweb-Haut die Frucht zugleich umschliesst;
Und wie der Nerven-Saft, hin zu den Theilen, fliesst.
Diss und dergleichen Tand, samt andern Hudeleyen,
Bringt mir, in meiner Noth, sehr weniges Gedeyen. (22—25)

The next section is a survey of medical theory and practice, from the earliest times to the present, most of which is also given satiric treatment. In the earliest times physicians relied entirely on experience in their practice:

Empirisch hat man zwar, in erster Welt, curiret;
Da die Erfahrung nur die ältsten Ärzt' regieret.

Allein, weil diese Cur nicht völlig gut gethan,
Fieng man auf andre Art zu practiciren an. (30)

The shortcomings of this purely empirical approach were soon apparent and to experience was added reasonable reflection. The result was the dogmatic approach of Hippocrates:

Erfahrung, mit Vernunft, und reifem Überlegen,
Schlug meistens trefflich an, und bracht erwünschten Seegen.
Drum lehrte Hippocrat, dogmatisch, drauf zu sehn;
Wo man den Kranken wollt', nach Wunsch, zu Handen gehn. (31)

According to Behr's description of this dogmatic method, it consisted of recording observations of the symptoms of diseases and the results of treatments attempted, thereby providing guidelines for other physicians. Contrasted to this dogmatic approach was the practice of each physician following only his own experience, which frequently was no more than whim.

Behr approves of the method of Hippocrates and regrets that it was soon abandoned by those who wished to be cleverer. He pays tribute to Galen's diligence and thoroughness yet suggests he was too speculative. Then in quick succession he takes up the theories of Paracelsus, Helmont, Sennert and Sylvius. He has praise only for Sennert, whom he describes as having selected, in his medical practice, the best from the past and the present.

Next comes a long discussion of the mechanism versus organism controversy between the followers of Descartes and those of Stahl. He gives the Cartesian mechanists credit for their contributions to medicine:

Das Triebwerk der Natur sah' man sehr deutlich ein,
Man sah', dass alles hier nur müss mechanisch seyn.
Drum suchte man, mit Müh, diss mehr noch zu erklären,
Damit doch künftighin die Ärzte klüger wären. (52)

Nevertheless, he believes that the mechanical approach has been so exaggerated that it has led to many "Narrenspossen".

Stahl, with his organism theory that places only the soul as the source of all illness, is ridiculed and refuted. The soul, Behr maintains, does not cause the physical operations of our bodies:

Denn, wie mag selbe wohl das Herz zum Schlagen bringen?
Wie macht sie doch das Blut zu allen Adern dringen?
Wie sondert sie die Gall doch in der Leber ab?
Wie schützt sie denn den Leib, für Seuchen, Tod und Grab?
Steht's denn derselben frey hier etwas zu verrichten?
Kan sie, das mind'ste nur, bey diesen Sachen schlichten?
Sie wolle, oder nicht, so geht's doch immer fort:

Der Mechanismus nur verricht diss hier und dort!
Denn der ist die Natur dess Hippocrat gedenket:
Der bleibt es nur allein, der hier die Sachen lenket. (61)

The physician, he continues, can intervene only in the workings of the body's
mechanism to cure an illness, whereas the soul is beyond his reach.

The second half of the satire is devoted to the foibles of physicians of his own
time. The tendency of his contemporaries toward eclecticism, he believes, is
merely an excuse for ignorance and leads only to mixed and confused teachings.
He ridicules the fad of experimenting with electricity in the curing of illnesses.
Electricity may have some use, he grants, but not in such universal application as
the faddists would have it. He is merciless with those Germans who take their
medical training in France and learn everything but medicine. His impatience
knows no end with the pomposity of physicians who are greedy for titles,
honors and high fees, but who have neither capacity nor desire to practice their
profession honestly. Finally he exhorts his colleagues to continue learning
throughout their careers from both their own experience and the experience of
others as that has been recorded in medical literature.

Since the poem is really more satiric than didactic, we do not really get a
direct statement of the author's own medical theories. From his abhorrence of
fads, however, we do get some impression of his perspective. He seems to have
good common sense when he recognizes the folly of practicing medicine only
from one point of view, whether it be mathematics, chemistry, mechanism,
electricity or any other system based on one approach alone. His criticism of
both the followers of Descartes and those of Stahl shows again that he has a
sense of proportion, that he doesn't sacrifice good sense for the sake of
consistency as the devotees of systems do. Finally, his espousal of the method of
Hippocrates in the beginning and his emphasis at the end on the need of the
physician to supplement his own experience with that of others, as written down
in the best medical books, suggests that he was aware of the need to establish
general standards for medicine and that those standards must be based on the
experience and reflection of the best.

12. Samuel Gotthold Lange (1711—1781)

Samuel Gotthold Lange, the son of the famous Halle theologian, Joachim Lange, followed in his father's profession. At the University of Halle, however, he studied physics, mathematics and medicine in addition to theology. He was a member of the literary societies at Greifswald and Jena and in 1741 was elected to the Kaiserliche Akademie der Naturforscher zu Wien. In German literary history he is known for his translation of Horace's odes and his own *Horatzische Oden* (1747) as well as his literary collaboration with Jakob Immanuel Pyra.

In the *Horatzische Oden*[1] there are a few items worthy of mention. "Die Schöpfung der Freude" is a short survey of creation from the cosmos, through the animal species, to man, according to the stages of the biblical account, with the creation of joy as the ultimate goal of the Creator. His description of the creation of worlds is noteworthy for the reference to Newton:

Nun wird der öde weite Raum besetzt
Mit rohen Welten, tüchtig zur Verzierung,
Mit wässrigen noch ungeschiednen Lasten,
Kein Neuton misst den weiten Abstand aus,
Den sie, der Freuden künftge Sammelplätze,
Schnell fülleten. So ward die grosse Weite. (83)

Apparently the poet found no better way to describe the vast distances involved than to say that not even Newton could measure them. It is another example of Newton as the representative of mortal man's attempt to grasp the universe with his reason and science. Also of significance is that the first act of creation placed innumerable worlds into orbit but left them in a rough primitive condition. This then permits the Biblical story of creation to account for the subsequent development but only as far as our planet is concerned. Before he turns to this local creation he looks once more into outer space to behold the order that has been established there:

Am Firmamente glüht der Sternen Heer
Im festerm Sitz, und rund um sie bewegen
Sich im gemessnem Lauf die Erdenbälle. (84)

In "Die rechte Grösse, oder das Lob der Schweizer", he praises the courageous Swiss who surmount the vicissitudes of life and cultivate the arts and sciences. In addition to the achievements of Bodmer, Breitinger and Haller, the scientific work of Bernoulli and Euler is mentioned:

---

[1] Samuel Gotthold Lange, *Horatzische Oden* (Halle, 1747).

Er dringt ins Reich des ungemessnen Raums,
Bestimt Bernoullen gleich der Dinge Maass,
Durchdringt den Raum der Welten gleich dem Euler . . . (92)

In "Einladung an Hr. Germershausen" he reminds his old friend Germershausen of their long standing friendship. He recounts how the Goddess Minerva introduced him to the sciences:

Sie lehrte Dich den grossen Neuton kennen,
Und zeigte Dir die nackende Natur,
Und Zahl, Gewicht und Maass, damit der Schöpfer
          Den Weltbau versehn. (112)

Newton once again is cited as the pinnacle of human scientific achievement. The reference to bare nature endowed with number, weight and dimension is a description of the new scientific attitude toward nature which converts nature to measurable quantities.

In "Die Freunde" he pays tribute to his many friends, such as Pyra, Gleim, Meier, Germershausen and Sulzer. Of the latter he says:

Sein forschend Auge misst die Gestirne,
Ihm zieret sich mit Blumen das Jahr,
Ihm öfnet sich der Schatz der Natur. (146)

It is simply a metaphorical statement of Sulzer's interests in astronomy and natural history.

In an appendix of poems by his wife, Anna Dorothea Lange, the poem, "An Hr. I.C. Hessen", is of interest because the subject of Noah's flood appears in it. Here as so often elsewhere a fusion of the Biblical account with scientific explanation is involved in the treatment of the theme:

Der zornige Gott liess Fluthen und Wellen herbrausen,
Es öfneten sich die weiten Fenster des Himmels;
Der Erdball erschrack, und gab aus Tiefen das Wasser,
          Die Wuth versank im trüben Schlamm. (168)

God's anger precipitated the catastrophe, of course, and in accordance with the speculations of Burnet and Whiston, the interior of the earth had to supply the huge quantities of water necessary to cover the entire globe. That the flood was a universal one had been accepted throughout the eighteenth century because of the interest in fossils which were being found in all parts of the world. In the very next stanza the subject of fossils comes up:

Es änderte sich die sumpfige Fläche des Erdballs,
Ein finsterer Wald ward nun in Grüfte verschüttet,

Bewohner der See, die Fische, Muscheln und Schnecken,
    Versenkten sich und wurden Stein. (168)

A third theme closely related to the subject of Noah's flood was the origin of mountains. According to the speculations of Burnet, mountains were created at the very time of the deluge and indeed our poetess indicates that she shares this belief:

Dort welzete sich durch Schwemmung gewaltiger Fluthen
Ein mächtig Gebürg, und wuchs, die Wolken durchborend,
Ein finsteres Thal schien in den Abgrund zu stürzen.
    So ward die Alpenreiche Schweiz. (168)

Finally, there is a comic poem by Lange written more than twenty years after the collection of poems considered above. In 1769 he published *Der Komet, mein letztes Gedicht* which appeared the following year, somewhat shortened in the *Almanach der deutschen Musen auf das Jahr 1770*.[2] It is a comic tale in rhymed verse, about a comet as a person who is exorcised and forced to reveal the story of his origin. He turns out to have been a poet who ruined his fame by writing too much especially after his limited talent was exhausted. He then ceased to be a star generating its own light and became a mere comet with a diluted light trailing behind it:

Da ward ich, statt ein Stern zu bleiben
Glanzlos, und zieh zu meiner Schmach,
Ein wässrich Schwanzlicht hinten nach! (216)

Of interest are the author's references to the theories of Whiston and Newton about the origin and function of comets, before he gives his poetic vision of the exorcised comet's own account.

To begin with he considers the theory of those who contend that comets are mere vapors. From this he turns to a consideration of the Whistonian theory:

Ein andrer kam mit stolzen Sitten,
Whistonisch warnend hergeschritten,
Den Finger an die Stirn gedrückt. (209)

"Whistonisch warnend" may refer to Johann Heyn who had aroused new interest in Whiston's theories for which he claimed to have found scriptural support. What follows is a brief and correct account of some Whistonian ideas:

Er sprach: "Freund, glaube, was ich sage:
"So reist, an seinem jüngsten Tage,
"Ein Erdball, aus dem Punkt verrückt.

---

2 *Almanach der deutschen Musen* (Leipzig, 1770), pp. 209–216.

"So reist auch eine künftge Erde
"Als Chaos, dass sie Ordnung werde.
"Auch unser Ball war ein Comet:
"Eccentrisch lief er durch die Ferne,
"Besuchte fremder Pole Sterne;
"So ordentlich er nunmehr geht!
"Einst bringt, an seinem jüngsten Tage,
"Er fernen Welten ihre Plage,
"Und wird ein drohender Comet. (209—210)

This is a statement of the Whistonian viewpoint. All planets were once comets and shall again return to that condition between chaos and order. Creation and Final Judgment are the transitional stages from comet to planet and from planet to comet. It is the proper balance of gravitational forces that is the source of a planet's orderly existence. Without this balance the orbit becomes eccentric with a corresponding loss of natural order as we know it.

Lange continues this theme with a digression on Bodmer's *Der Noah,* which uses the Whistonian cometary theory as an explanation for Noah's Flood:

Mich zupfte, in der Schweitz gebohren,
Freund Bodmer, sacht an meine Ohren,
Und wiess mir seine Noachid. (210)

Tongue-in-cheek he imitates Bodmer's style in recounting the fierce gravitational struggle between the earth and the approaching comet whose proximity caused the deluge.

A calmer tone is finally taken when the Newtonian explanation of comets is given:

Dort spricht am englischen Gestade,
Ein Newton von des Irrsterns Pfade,
Und rechnet seinen Umlauf aus.
Er hat ihm Zeiten, Tag und Stunden
Recht parabolisch ausgefunden,
Und zeigt, dass ohne Furcht und Grauss
Er sich allein nur schaden könne,
Nah an dem Sonnenlicht entbrenne,
Im Anfang fliessend wie ein Brey,
Dann tausend Jahre glühend sey. (211—212)

According to the calculations of Newton a comet's orbit is subject to the same laws as any other heavenly body. Though its orbit is parabolic rather than elliptical as that of a planet, it is nevertheless just as predictable and thus as orderly and, consequently, need not be feared. As we have noted above, however, the poet prefers his own imaginative explanation of the origin of a comet to those of Whiston and Newton.

The scientific themes that were found in Lange's poems are all related to astronomy which he views as that human discipline that has discovered certain and reliable knowledge about the world. He celebrates Newton as the astronomer who has brought this science to its present successful state. Whiston, a Newtonian, appealed more to Lange's imagination and sense of humor than to his intellect.

13. Christian Friedrich Zernitz (1717—1744)

Christian Friedrich Zernitz studied philosophy and mathematics, as well as poetry at the University of Leipzig where he also came under the influence of the Gottsched school. The model for his didactic poetry, however, was Albrecht von Haller. Christian Heinrich Schmid in his *Anthologie der Deutschen* comments as follows about Zernitz' poetry: "Apollo hatte ihm keine sehr feurige Einbildungskraft verliehn, und so erwählte er sich das Lukretzische Lehrgedicht. Er stellte sich den Hr. v. Haller zum Muster vor, und er erreicht ihn zuweilen . . . .".[1] Indeed, his best works are his long philosophical poems in the Lucretian tradition of didactic poetry with scientific and philosophic themes.

Zernitz' poetry enjoyed some popularity in his lifetime, because about a dozen of his poems appeared in the *Belustigungen des Verstandes und des Witzes* of 1742 and 1743. He was soon forgotten, however, and only Johann Jakob Dusch in his *Briefe zur Bildung de Geschmacks* comments on his poetry with interest and approval.[2] I shall discuss three of Zernitz' longer philosophical poems which contain a veriety of scientific themes: "Der Mensch, in Absicht auf die Selbsterkenntnis", "Philosophische Gedanken über die göttliche Weisheit bey dem Sterben der Menschen", and "Gedanken von den Entzwecken der Welt".[3] The first and second of these had previously appeared in *Die Belustigungen* . . . of 1743.

"Der Mensch, in Absicht auf die Selbsterkenntnis" develops one of the recurring themes of the poetry of the Enlightenment, namely, the priority of self-knowledge over all other knowledge. In the very beginning of the poem he contrasts the knowledge man has acquired of the outside world by use of his senses and reason with his ignorance of his own heart:

> Wie glücklich hat der Mensch nicht Sinnen und Verstand
> Bey Dingen ausser ihm, im Forschen, angewandt.
> Jedoch sein eignes Herz, der Grund zum ächten Heile,
> Bleibt nur der Gegenstand gewohnter Vorurtheile. (72)

The preconceptions that blind the heart to its own well-being are the main subject of the poem. First, however, he describes the successes man has had in seeking knowledge about the world of nature:

> Wohin ist der Verstand des Menschen nicht gedrungen?
> Der fernen Welten Bau ist seiner Hand gelungen.
> Von der Planeten Lauf bestimmt er jeden Grad,

---

1 (Frankfurt and Leipzig, 1770), p. 18.
2 (Leipzig and Breslau, 1764—1773), Part I, letters 26, 27; Part III, letters 6, 7.
3 *Versuch in Moralischen und Schäfergedichten* (Hamburg and Leipzig, 1748), pp. 72—94, 95—100, 142—173.

Und beugt mit weiser Müh die Himmelssphär ans Drat.
Er ahmt dem Schöpfer nach des Bogens bunten Schimmer,
Den, der in Wolken zeugt, macht er im dunkeln Zimmer:
Und wie des Körpers Last nach Regeln sich bewegt,
Hat sein Versuch vorlängst ihm gründlich dargelegt.
Sein Witz und Zirkel misst Zeit, Grössen, Raum und Flächen.
Ihm stärkt ein Glas den Stral, den Luft und Ferne schwächen.
Er untersucht voll Fleis der Wesen innre Kraft,
Und bringt, was er entdeckt, in Lehr und Wissenschaft.
Luft, Feuer, Erde und Meer, Metall und Thier und Pflanze,
Und wo es möglich wär, durchforscht er gar das Ganze. (72—73)

In this brief survey of the sciences of the time, he takes note of the new astronomy which has calculated the orbits of distant planets. The line "Und beugt . . . die Himmelssphär ans Drat" suggests an attempt to illustrate the effect of gravity in linking the heavenly spheres to one another. He refers to Newton's color experiments by which he reproduced the rainbow's colors in his darkened room. He refers to the laws of moving bodies discovered long ago by Galileo and to man's successes in measuring and exploring the realms of nature.

He does not disapprove of these scientific pursuits but regrets that the successes in discovering the laws of nature leave untouched the chaos that exists within, in the moral sphere of human life.

However, a contemplation of nature could serve as a guide for man in his own life:

Doch, weil man sich zu oft im Wahr- und Falschen täuscht,
Und unser sinnlich Herz, statt Guten, Böses heischt:
So merk durch Zeit und Raum die Ordnung in den Dingen
Den Zweck, der Gott bewog, sie einst hervor zu bringen.
Sieh, wie der Wesen Zahl so wohl und weislich stimmt,
Das Itzige den Grund von dem Vergangnen nimmt.
Die Grösse des Verstands wirst du darinnen finden,
Sähst du nur alles ein, und könntest es verbinden.
Betrachte keinen Theil vom Ganzen abgetrennt,
Obleich dein kleiner Geist allein nur Theile kennt.
In dem Zusammenhang lässt sich nur Gutes richten;
Diess gilt in der Natur, diess gilt auch in den Pflichten. (86—87)

As the study of final causes complemented the study of efficient causes in the Wolffian system, so does Zernitz here recommend that a realization that nature is permeated with purpose imparted to it by God can give man a natural religion which could bring order to his moral life. Experimental science by itself satisfies only his desire to know. The teleological approach to nature shows man his place within the context of nature.

Another aspect of the teleological approach to nature is physicotheology whereby nature is considered holy, as a creation of God:

> Die grosse Welt ist ihm der Tempel seiner Ehre;
> So viel Planeten sind, so viel sind auch Altäre,
> Wenn du, o Heiliger! den Himmel prächtig wölbst,
> Die Erde weislich zierst, schmückst du dein Wohnhaus selbst. (88)

Nature, viewed as the temple of God, reminds man of his Creator. In this respect nature is a reliable and consistent source of God's revelation to all men at all times:

> Kein falsch Erklären tilgt der Wahrheit tiefe Spur,
> Kein unterschobner Satz verdrehet die Natur.
> Gott gab sie uns zum Buch, vor Völkern aller Welten,
> Vor Menschen aller Zeit. (88—89)

In the second poem under consideration, "Philosophische Gedanken über die göttliche Weisheit bey dem Sterben der Menschen", the poet's conception of nature is again the central theme. Before explaining the significance of man's mortality, he describes the role of death and destruction in nature as a whole. In nature there is no permanence, but constant change. Nevertheless, there is no real destruction either; substances simply undergo a transformation of form. He states this principle of conservation as follows:

> Gott, der nach seinem Rath der Dinge Daur erhält,
> Baut aus dem alten Stoff stets eine neue Welt.
> Denn aller Dinge Zeug, der einst vom Nichts entstanden,
> Und aller Wesen Kraft ist noch bis itzt vorhanden.
> Kein Staub verfällt in Nichts; kein Theil wird ganz verbraucht;
> Er dient zu fernerm Zweck. Was von dem Meer verraucht,
> Erhält das trockne Land, zur Fruchtbarkeit, durch Regen;
> Was aus der Sonnen stralt, dient, Lüfte zu bewegen; (95)

There is a constant formation and transformation in nature. Nor is this activity arbitrary or chaotic: "Ihr Bilden ist an sich der Wechsel in den Schranken" (95). Thus both change and permanence characterize nature.

Once he has established these general principles about nature, he turns to man, whose mortality is the subject of the poem. Man's fear of death is due to a misconception about nature's processes. If the human body were not subject to destruction, but were granted the same immortality as the spirit, an imbalance in nature would be the result:

> Bedenke! wenn dein Leib, der hier in manchem Bild,
> Bey Dingen neben ihm den Weltraum mit erfüllt,

Sich ausser der Natur zu Gottes Thron erhübe,
Dass dann ein leerer Raum allhier zurücke bliebe,
Und dass der schwere Druck von mancher obern Welt,
Die fernes Gleichgewicht in ihren Sphären hält,
Die endlich leichte Erd, der täglich Schweer entgienge,
Ohn allen Widerstand aus ihrer Laufbahn drünge. (97)

His argument here is that if human bodies were not subject to the same principle of conservation as all other material objects, then there would result a diminution in the total substance of our planet and thus the delicate balance of gravitational forces which keep the planet in its orbit would be jeopardized. This is a unique application of the theory of gravity. Yet it emphasizes the poet's view that man as a mortal creature is an integral part of ever changing, but indestructible nature.

Zernitz' best and longest philosophical poem, "Gedanken von den Entzwecken der Welt", contains a variety of scientific themes. The central thesis of the poem, as the title indicates, is the operation of purpose in nature. His teleology, however, is not an anthropocentric one; he makes it quite clear that his goal is not to show that man is the main recipient of God's design in the creation. It is the design itself which he displays with example after example. His goal is to demonstrate the wisdom of God in His creation. The scientific material appears whenever he wishes to focus on the design, its intricacies, rationality, harmony and wisdom. He introduces the problem by exhorting man to examine his dwelling place, the world:

Geh, weisestes Geschöpf der Erden, brauch Verstand,
Dein Wohnhaus ist die Welt, miss hier das feste Land,
Senk dort ein Bley ins Meer. Prüf Flammen, Erde, Lüfte,
Sieh hier ein flaches Feld, dort ungeheure Grüfte,
Erforsch des Körpers Last, der ohne Geist sich regt,
Den innern Widerstand, der Theile um sich trägt. (144)

The natural phenomena he mentions here are those that can be divided according to the four elements, water, fire, earth and air. About all these phenomena man must ask why and, thus, he will finally be led to God according to whose purpose nature functions. Because of this purpose, the multiplicity of natural phenomena is sustained by lawfulness:

Darum bleibt ungeschwächt das Maas gesamter Kräfte,
Des Körpers innrer Druck, sein ewiges Geschäfte,
Die stille Ähnlichkeit in Arten und Geschlecht,
Verhältnis jedes Theils zur grossen Welt gerecht. (145)

There is variety in nature but also perpetual recurrence: the forces of the physical world are conserved according to appropriate proportion and each species reproduces according to its kind. This is a law of nature on which order depends, without which chaos would result. We shall see further that our author believes chaos is the only conceivable alternative to the order of the world as it is.

A scientific event of great importance for demonstrating order in nature and science's capacity to understand that order was the success scientists had in proving that the earth was flattened at the poles, as Huygens and Newton had maintained on the basis of the theory of gravity. In 1735 the Académie des Sciences sent expeditions to Peru and Lapland to measure meridian arcs in different latitudes. The measurements made at Torneå in Lapland in 1736 under the direction of Maupertuis verified that the earth was flattened at the poles. The following passage refers to the expedition, its dangers, its sponsorship by the king, the primitive Lapps and the expedition's success in verifying Newton's and Huygen's calculations:

> Ihr Himmelskundige durch Müh nie abgeschreckt,
> Ermuntert durch den Lohn, wenn Wahrheit ihr entdeckt,
> Verlasst die sanfte Ruh für die Gefahr der Reise,
> Und theilet unterm Nord die holen Himmelskrayse,
> Bestimmt im Siebeneck und nach der Berge Höh,
> Die gleichsam Punkte sind die Mittagslinie,
> Messt von Torneå an bis Kittis zu dem Zeichen,
> Zum Wohl des Staats den Zweck des Königs zu erreichen,
> Verführt der Lappen Wahn der euer Instrument
> Bey dem ihr Vorsicht braucht, für euren Gott erkennt;
> Und zeiget was vom Pol bewehrt geschlossen werde,
> Wie Neuton und Hugen an der Figur der Erde. (146)

This combination of a conclusion arrived at mathematically on the basis of theory and verified experimentally by an elaborate expedition strengthened the popular faith in scientific method.

Zernitz carefully distinguishes between man's knowledge of God and his knowledge of nature. The latter is the domain of the scientist and it is limited:

> Nicht dass der Mensch versteht das Wesen in den Dingen,
> Wornach sie ehedem vom Nichts zum Daseyn giengen;
> Nein zeige nur allein dem forschenden Bemühn,
> Wie Ding und Kräfte sich auf andere beziehn.
> Wie alles wechselnd wirkt, wie aus den ersten Quellen
> Die ferne Ordnung fleusst, zu tausend späten Fällen, . . . (147)

Man's knowledge is partial, imperfect as regards ultimate, first causes; he can, however, show the connections and interrelations. Man can know efficient and final causes within nature, though he cannot penetrate to the essence of the world, nor can he know how the Divine act of creation was fulfilled. Man can, however, conclude from his knowledge of nature that the order he finds there is a necessary one. For, if the organization of nature were different, chaos must necessarily result:

Wilst du im Schattenriss des Himmels Ordnung sehn,
So setz das Gegentheil von Dingen die geschehn,
Rück in Gedanken einst die Erd aus ihrem Gleise?
Der Sonnen näher zu durch engre Umlaufskrayse,
Und sieh des prächtgen Baus veränderte Gestalt,
Die Luft vermehrete dem Feuer die Gewalt,
Es müst in heissen Fluss Stein und Metall zergehen,
Kaum liessen noch zurück das trockne Salz die Seen,
Nachdem der grösste Fisch von naher Glut erhitzt,
Im Eysmeer kurz zuvor das dicke Fett verschwitzt,
In Dünste stiegen auf der Erden innre Säfte,
Und wirksam blieben nur allein die Feuerkräfte.
Die Alpen senkten sich von dem erhabnen Stand,
Und der Natur zerriss das allgemeine Band,
Die gleiche Schweere wich' im Schmelzen und Verbrennen,
Die Körper würden sich fast bis zum Urstaub trennen,
Dir wär alsdann, o Mensch, die erste Welt ein Traum,
Sie und du wärst verstäubt im tiefen Himmelsraum. (148)

This remarkable passage demonstrates Zernitz' thought on the interrelatedness of natural phenomena. If the earth's orbit were shifted slightly, its harmonies and proportions and balances would be suspended, and the planet would be reduced to chaos and the world we know would remain as a mere dream. The purpose of this exercise of thought or rather exercise of the imagination is to prove that this is the best of all possible worlds. Thus man should revere the wisdom of God who has created a lawful nature not subject to the ravages of chaos:

So lern, o Erdensohn, die ewge Weisheit ehren,
Die solche Welten wählt, geschickt zu ihren Sphären,
Die aller Sternen Reih und Maas und Stand durchdenkt,
Bevor sie einen Staub mit Wirklichkeit beschenkt,
Die, so die Himmelsluft gepresset und verbreitet,
Dass sie fast sonder Zeit den Lichtstrahl zu uns leitet,
Die die Materie die Dingen Schweere bringt,
Um jeden Wanderstern in schnelle Zirkel schwingt, . . . (148—149)

The scientific material of the last four lines is of interest because it presents the Cartesian view of light as something that is conveyed instantaneously by an aether-like substance which also serves the function in Descartes' vortices of keeping the planets in their orbits.

So far in this poem as well as in the others under discussion, the author has reflected on general principles and qualities of nature which permeate and sustain it and which point to the wisdom of the creator. We can say that nature as a whole has been under consideration. Now, however, in the middle of the poem, a new theme is introduced revolving around one of the very crucial scientific controversies of the time, namely, the nature of the animal soul and the difference between man and the animals. Descartes, a century before, had characterized animals as mere machines without mind, without soul. For Descartes the difference between man and the animals is as sharp as between mind and matter. Zernitz, like many of his contemporaries, took issue with the Cartesians on this matter. Zernitz begins his attack with the question:

Von wannen ist der Wahn bey Weisen doch entstanden,
Es wär in Thieren nicht ein Geist der denkt vorhanden? (150)

He wishes to show that the difference between man and the animals is only one of degree and that man, notwithstanding his superior powers, is an integral member of the domain of living beings:

Aus ihren Handlungen, aus ihrer Bauart Werken,
Kann man Vergleichung dort, hier stille Triebe merken,
Das Thier wirkt gleich so gut, nach seiner Kraft als wir,
Und was ist sonst der Mensch, als nur das klügste Thier. (150)

He offers numerous examples from the animal kingdom, descriptions of the behavior of various animals, their responses to various situations to force recognition of the presence of feelings and thoughts in animals: the blackbird that flees the hawk experiences fear just as the warrior in the presence of a superior enemy; people migrate to better lands as do birds when the seasons change; the faithful dog surely experiences more than instinct in his expression of friendship for his master.

Man's intellect, too, lacks the capacity to fathom certain things:

O Weiser lehre mich, da Schweere dich hier hält,
Die Wirkung der Natur in der Saturnus Welt
Wie oder lass allein nur von Neapel hören,
Durch welchen Zufluss sich Vesuvens Flammen nähren, . . . (152—153)

Yet, he continues, that does not deprive him of reasoning capacity altogether, and thus the same can be concluded about the animals.

His next step in raising the stature of animals and saving them from the machinations of the Cartesians is to maintain that in their own sphere they are able to provide for their needs as adequately as man in his sphere:

> Kann auch die Schwalbe nicht ihr Nest corinthisch schmücken,
> Sie kennet keine Pracht und hebt nicht Quaderstücken,
> Inzwischen wird ihr Koth zum Bau so tüchtig seyn,
> Als dir weit klügrer Mensch, Holz, Kalk, Metall und Stein. (153)

Animals have their own uniqueness and excellence which are different from those of man but to which they have as much right as man to his:

> Es herrscht ein Gleichheitsrecht bey aller Creatur.
> Von Mensch und Thieren ist die Mutter die Natur.
> Das Leben hauchet sie in aller Blutgefässen,
> Von ihr sind jeder Geist und Glieder zugemessen,
> Umsonst wirkt Weisheit nie. . . . (154)

The chasm introduced between man and the animals by the Cartesians is here bridged by the conception that mother nature is the source and life giver of both. A further conclusion from this equality of right in the kingdom of living beings is that it would be foolish for man to believe that the animals exist solely for his sake.

> Die Triebe der Natur sucht jeder Geist zu stillen,
> So weit lebt Vieh und Wurm nicht um des Menschen willen. (158)

Just as all living beings are equal in the eyes of nature, so also does heaven bestow justice and mercy equally:

> Der Himmel achtet nicht den Abstand tiefster Grade,
> Gerechten Theil nimmt Mensch und Wurm an seiner Gnade. (161)

It is clear that Zernitz decidedly rejects any anthropocentric teleology that sees all living creatures designed for the good of man. It seems that the conception underlying Zernitz' declaration of rights for all living beings is the principle of continuity of all species from the lowest to the highest. Thus there is a hierarchy in the animal world, but not one in which the function of the lower is solely to serve the higher, but one in which each species serves the whole realm of living beings by fulfilling its own uniqueness.

After leaving the problem of the animal soul, he returns to general considerations about the workings of nature, this time as a model for man in the moral sphere. He notes once again that if one examines natural phenomena closely, one detects a fine balance and proportion underlying all life:

> Forscht man in der Natur mit aufmerksamer Pflicht,
> Zuviel Beschwertes sinkt, zu stark Gebognes bricht,

Die Pflanze einst gezeugt in hitzig feuchtem Sande,
Verdirbt itzt schattenreich im unbestrahlten Lande;
Man seh, wie mit dem Nass die leichte Flamme ringt,
Die Änderung des Orts Bewegung, Ruh verdringt,
Die erste Wirklichkeit sich in den Dingen schwinden,
Wenn starkes Gegentheil mit Macht wird überwinden. (164)

In this respect man should imitate nature in his own moral life. The wisdom
and rationality that pervade nature can serve as a guideline for man in the
organization of his own life. The balance that he finds in nature is, of course,
present in his own body since it belongs to the domain of nature:

Ein Kunstwerk ist der Leib, wo schon gespannte Sehnen,
Im mässig klugen Brauch sich ohne Schmerzen dehnen,
Wo solche Nerven sind in jedem Punkt zerstreut,
Die starker Stoss verletzt, gelinder Druck erfreut,
Wo flüssiges Geblüt im Herzen nimmer säumet,
Das die Bewegung schützt, der Müssiggang verschleimet . . . (165)

Our bodies retain health by the avoidance of excess. Pleasure and pain
consistently guide our actions to preserve that delicate physiological balance
which constitutes health. Zernitz then concludes that in the moral sphere a
parallel situation exists, in that conscience provides the pain of guilt when we
leave the path of moderation and the pleasure of inner peace when we follow the
golden mean. Thus, man has the potentiality to attain what nature already has,
namely, rationality, proportion, harmony, balance.

He concludes the poem with consideration about death and the eventual
destruction of the universe and the question of God's justice in regard to these
fearful matters. He introduces the problem by noting that stars are destroyed,
and since as suns they sustain life on many planets, the destruction of such a star
involves the destruction of many worlds like ours:

Wie aber, wenn man nun im Raum des Himmels spührt,
Dass sich von seinem Stand ein Stern in Nichts verliehrt,
Der auch Planeten dort durch Wärm und Licht beglückte,
Ein gross System erhielt, mit Farben Wesen schmückte,
Wenn die verloschne Sonn kein Leben weiter haucht,
Wenn unermessnes Licht in ihr ist ausgebraucht,
Wie kann, o Ewiger, wenn Erden untergehen,
Mit ihrem Untergang doch deine Huld bestehen? (166—167)

Zernitz explains that the destruction of worlds is a part of God's design, as
well as in accord with natural laws. Of interest is also a related theme about the
age of the earth and the enormous changes that have taken place on earth in the
course of time:

Der Anfang einer Welt ist Gott nur offenbahr,
Und Usser bleibt vielleicht noch weit vom Schöpfungs Jahr,
So viel erkennen wir, wenn tief in Erden-Gründen,
Wir noch das Bett des Meers bedeckt mit Muscheln finden,
Wenn auf gebliebnem Sand der weggewichnen Fluth,
Itzt Bette, Erde, Thon, in festen Lagen ruht,
Und die Natur nie springt zu Zwecken zu gelangen,
Dass ihr zu diesem Bau geraume Zeit vergangen. (169)

Change is a law of nature and, therefore, the poet is pleased to refer to evidence that indicates that the earth has experienced change. The presence of sea beds covered with sea shells deep beneath the ground and the presence of strata of earth and clay near the shore indicate that a recession of the sea must have taken place. Since he believes that nature does not act abruptly, he realizes that a long period of time must have elapsed for such changes to have occurred. Zernitz, therefore, reflects here the tendency by the middle of the century to question the traditional account of the age of the earth.

He concludes the poem with images of the transfiguration of man and the world after the destruction of their present state of existence. For the transfiguration of the human soul he uses a botanical image:

Der Tod der unsern Leib mit Fäulnis einst durchdringt,
Macht dass der edle Theil der Geist sich höher schwingt;
So wie vom Saamenkorn die Staude sich erhebet,
Wird auch zuerst der Mensch im dunklen Stand belebet,
Er keimt in der Geburth, wächst durch die Lebenszeit,
Und seiner Blüthe Frucht ist die Unsterblichkeit. (172)

Human life is a process of growth which resembles that of a plant. In the case of human being, the culmination of life, his fruition, is immortality which is attained after death. The world, too, in analogy with the human soul undergoes a transfiguration upon the destruction of its present form:

Ja, wenn denn endlich auch nach Gottes weisen Schluss,
Das prächtge Weltgebäud in Nichts sich stürzen muss,
Wenn nicht zum Mittelpunct die Schweere mehr wird dringen,
Wenn Sonnen nicht mehr sind, sich Erden nicht mehr schwingen,
O: so verklährt doch dann des alten Raumes Nacht,
Gott, deiner Weisheit Glanz mit neuer Lieb und Macht.
Vielleicht wird in dem Raum, wo Welten gehn verlohren,
Den Geistern eine Welt, ein Himmel auserkohren. (173)

When the laws of nature which sustain our universe cease to function, then God may create a new world to house the immortal spirits. This image, as the previous one, suggests that the transfigured product bears some resemblance to the original. For, when the suns no longer shine, God's light must again triumph over darkness as was the case in the creation of this world according to the Biblical account. Furthermore, as the last lines indicate, this transfigured world will also be in space where the present worlds exist. It may be possible to conclude, then, that Zernitz considers the transfigured state of both man and the world as an extension or heightening of nature as we know it now, rather than as something fundamentally different.

14. Johann Peter Uz (1720—1796)

Johann Peter Uz is well known from the histories of German literature as one of the Anacreontic poets around the middle of the century. For the study of scientific themes in his poetry the critical edition of August Sauer was used, which contains all variant texts, as well as a documentation of the chronology of the poems.[1]

In "Tempe" (1755) the cosmic perspective is well represented in the flight through space of Urania, the muse of astronomy. She leaves our rougher atmosphere, "die Werkstatt rother Blitze", and moves on to other solar systems never viewed by astronomers, from which the earth is reduced to insignificance. Our poet, however, prefers not to follow the muse's flight:

O göttlich hoher Flug!
Mein Flügel ist nicht stark genug,
Sich dir auf Neutons Pfad, o Muse! nachzuschwingen. (86)

"Neutons Pfad" stands for the orbits of heavenly bodies or for the system by which the order in the heavens is plotted. Newton's name had become representative of man's knowledge of the heavens.

In "Gott der Weltschöpfer" (1768) there is a similar imaginative journey to other solar systems, peaceful in their orderly orbits, yet awe inspiring to our poet who rushes for safety to the narrow boundaries of our earth:

Ihr Himmel, öffnet euch, dass ich bewundernd preise,
Wie Sonn an Sonne friedlich gränzt,
Und, ewig unverwirrt im angewiesnen Kreise,
Doch weit gebiethend, jede glänzt!
Umsonst! die schwindelnden Gedanken,
Verlohren in dem grossen Blick,
Entfliehen in die Schranken
Der niedern Welt zurück. (210)

In "Die Glückseligkeit" human happiness is understood to be dependent on the order which God has imparted to the entire cosmos.

Es flammt ein Welten-Heer in angewiesnen Gränzen:
Es ist im lichten Raum, wo in bestimmter Bahn
Die ungezählten Sonnen glänzen,
Der Ordnung alles unterthan. (111)

---

[1] Johann Peter Uz, *Sämtliche Poetische Werke,* Hrsg. von August Sauer, in *Deutsche Litteraturdenkmale des 18. und 19. Jahrhunderts,* XXXIII—XXXVIII (Stuttgart, 1890). All quotations cited in the text come from this edition.

Cosmic order prevails not only in our solar system, but beyond that the innumerable suns are also subject to precise limits. Order also prevails among creatures from the lowest to the highest:

Ihr [Die Ordnung] Band verknüpfet alle Wesen,
Vom Staube bis zu Cherubim. (112)

Just as the macrocosm and the geocosm are obedient to the laws of order, so man, the microcosm, attains happiness when he puts his own life in order.

In his "Theodicee" (1755) the poet again elevates himself to a cosmic view, from which our planet appears diminished in size and significance:

Ich habe mich empor geschwungen!
Wie gross wird mir die Welt! die Erde flieht verschlungen:
Sie macht nicht mehr allein die ganze Schöpfung aus!
Welch kleines Theil der Welt ist Rheens finstres Haus!
Und, Menschen! welche kleine Heerde
Seyd ihr nur erst auf dieser kleinen Erde! (137)

Compared to the resplendent heavenly bodies in space, our earth is "Rheens finstres Haus", merely a heavenly body without its own light. Beyond our narrow sphere there is a host of inhabited stars in immeasureable space:

Seht, wie in ungemessner Ferne
Orion und sein Heer, ein Heer bewohnter Sterne,
Vor seinem Schöpfer sich in lichter Ordnung drängt." (138)

Possibly, because our own planet has become so insignificant from this cosmic perspective, does he make a plea for tolerance of all creatures on our earth no matter how small:

Gönnt gleiches Recht auf unserm Balle
Geschöpfe andrer Art! Ihr Schöpfer liebt sie alle:
Die Weisheit selbst entwarf der kleinsten Fliege Glück (137)

All creatures have their proper place in an orderly nature:

Die niemals flüchtig springt, und stuffenweise nur
Auf ihrer güldnen Leiter steiget,
Wo sich der Mensch auf mittlern Sprossen zeiget. (139)

Nature's orderly procedure, her golden ladder, assures man a significant role, though the planet he inhabits is insignificant in boundless space.

Finally, there is his longest, and next to his "Theodicee" his best known work, the didactic poem "Die Kunst stets fröhlich zu seyn" (1760). Uz asserts here that the art of attaining happiness presupposes the acquisition of wisdom which includes a study of the sciences:

Lauf einmal, edler Freund, mit eilenden Gedanken,
Die Wissenschaften durch; miss ihre weiten Schranken:
Sieh, wo der grösste Witz nur zweifelt, oder schweigt,
Und wo die Menschheit sich in ihrer Grösse zeigt." (238)

The wise man also studies the kingdom of nature:

Durchforscht ihr weites Reich, wo jene Sonnen glänzen,
Die uns die Nacht verräth, und findet keine Gränzen,
Und stets von Welt auf Welt geflügelt hingerückt,
Erblickt er immer Gott, bewundernd und entzückt.
Ermüdet senkt er sich, mit irrenden Cometen,
Nach unserm Aufenthalt, dem schattichten Planeten, (237)

Here once again there is a statement of the cosmic perspective. The poet
revels in the splendor of distant suns; yet, exhausted, he must seek refuge on our
"schattichten Planeten" by which he implies that man is earth-born, unac-
customed to too much light, in need of the earth's semi-darkness. Here on earth
the enlightened man will survey the order of nature and find God in all things:

Er freut sich überall, zur Schande stolzer Blinden,
Die Ordnung der Natur und Gott in ihr zu finden,
Gott auf dem Ocean und im bestaubten Wurm,
Im sanftbewegten Gras und im erzürnten Sturm; (238)

Once again a journey in the vastness of space has brought the poet back to
earth, apparently with a strengthened desire to find the order of nature and God
on mother earth, so insignificant from the cosmic perspective.

Throughout the poem the orderliness of nature is asserted. The following
statement of the rule of eternal laws is typical:

Die Schöpfung wird regiert nach ewigen Gesetzen!
Wir sehn der Sterne Lauf mit schauderndem Ergötzen:
Sie wandeln heut, wie stets: der allgemeine Plan
Weist Sonnen ihr Geschäft und ihre Herrschaft an.
Der Schnee hält seine Zeit und seine Zeit der Regen:
Des Windes Flügel muss nach Regeln sich bewegen:
Ein mächtiges Gesetz hält in der Wolke Schooss
Des Donners Grimm zurück, und lässt den Donner los.
Die junge Flora lässt sich von Gesetzen leiten:
Des Tejers Rose glich den Rosen unsrer Zeiten:
Das Kraut pflanzt sein Geschlecht, wie seit der Schöpfung, fort: (260)

The eternal laws referred to here are the laws discovered by the scientist: the
astronomer who studies the orbits of heavenly bodies, the physicist who is
concerned with the physical phenomena on earth, and the natural historian who

studies the growth of plants. It is implied that the same kind of lawfulness prevails on earth and in the heavens, the lawfulness of nature. It is furthermore implied throughout the whole poem that man must achieve the same lawfulness in his own life that he finds in nature.

Summing up, it is clear that Uz' view of the large cosmos and our earth has been influenced to a considerable degree by the natural sciences of his time. His cosmic perspective is a vision provided by the astronomers, and his belief in all-pervading lawfulness, which includes our insignificant earth, "Rheens finstres Haus", our "schattichten Planeten", has been given substance by the physicist and the natural historian. His piety, too, has been given support by the sciences, for through them God's design in nature can be grasped by man. Finally, a recurring theme which seems to be the goal of much of his reflection is that the natural lawfulness apparent everywhere in the creation can also be realized in man.

15. Christlob Mylius (1722–1754)

Mylius has already been encountered in this study as editor of the two popular scientific periodicals, *Der Naturforscher* and *Physikalische Belustigungen*. He was a student of Gottsched, a friend and associate of Kästner and esteemed by his cousin Gotthold Ephraim Lessing.

It was Lessing who edited his writings in 1754 after his untimely death.[1] His evaluation of Mylius' work takes the form of six letters which he had written to a friend about Mylius and which he offers as a preface to his edition. His criticism of Mylius' literary work is at times severe, as is to be expected from Lessing. However, he expresses faith in his cousin's talent which he is sure would have developed in time.

He fully respects Mylius' love for natural science and his desire to achieve distinction as a scientist as well as a poet. At the end of his first introductory letter, he speculates that the same enthusiasm for learning which led him to leave his homeland for his projected trip to America is now undoubtedly urging on his liberated soul from planet to planet to seek out the truth that scientists such as Newton have only surmised here.

Mylius' prose works in Lessing's edition have considerable literary merit and contain some interesting scientific themes. His long essay, "Betrachtung über die Majestät Gottes", had first appeared in the *Belustigungen* . . . of November and December, 1743. It conveyed the enthusiasm of young Mylius for the works of nature as revelations of God's majesty. Unlike many edifying tracts with the same theme, in this one there is a strong emphasis on the conviction that only the scientist with his exact knowledge and close acquaintance with nature is in a position to recognize and appreciate the divinity that must stand behind all natural phenomena.

The non-scientist in his approach to nature is necessarily superficial: "Wer kein Liebhaber natürlicher Dinge und Begebenheiten, wer kein Naturforscher ist, der wird die bewundernswürdigen Werke der Natur und die Veränderungen, welche darinnen vorgehen, ohne Neugier, ohne Nachforschung, ohne Aufmerksamkeit, ohne Bewunderung und ohne Erkenntniss der Majestät Gottes anschauen". (11).

He continues with numerous examples to show how much better the scientist, as a trained observer and experimenter, can penetrate to a true understanding of nature. He ranges from the microscopic to the telescopic world, giving facts, figures and dimensions to picture the extent of nature's ways. He presents a panorama of natural phenomena, beginning with the treasures of the earth's interior and the treasures of the seas and oceans. From there he returns to the surface of the earth and to a consideration of plants and

---

[1] Christlob Mylius, *Vermischte Schriften* (Berlin, 1754), edited by G.E. Lessing.

animals and humans, stressing with each the various structures and their functions. The panorama is completed again with the assertion of the scientist's superior knowledge of God's nature. The non-scientist, he says, has no more conception of his globe than the frog does of the ocean. The scientist, however: "... erhebt sich mit einer ruhmwürdigen Kühnheit; er schwingt sich durch Luft und Wolken, und schauet mit seinen geschäfftigen Gedanken von einer unermesslichen Höhe herab, auf die Halbfläche der Erdkugel" (24).

In the second half of the essay, he returns to his panorama, but this time extends his view to the universe beyond this planet, not only in our solar system, but in the millions of systems beyond this one. He speaks of thousands of millions of stars and attempts to give the reader some idea of the numbers and dimensions and distances involved. He considers not only stars, but also the innumerable planets revolving about these suns: "Bisher habe ich mit dem Naturforscher nur die unbegreifliche Anzahl, Grösse und Entfernung der Fixsterne erwogen und bewundert. Nun will ich mit demselben die noch weit grössere Anzahl der dunkeln Weltkörper, der Wohnungen aller beseelten Geschöpfe, der Planeten, betrachten." (36)

This thought enthralls him, for he now conceives of these planets in analogy to our planet, each with dual motions giving it the seasons, day and night, and each inhabited by living creatures. Finally, he returns to the comets with allusions to the theories of Whiston and Heyn, and stresses their significance in the revelation of God's majesty. The essay concludes with thanks to scientists who have devoted themselves to the study of the cosmos: "Habet Dank, ihr, die ihr eure Bemühungen, eure Kräfte, euer Leben auf die Erforschung der Natur gewandt habet, und noch wendet! habet Dank, ihr, die ihr insonderheit die Grösse und Pracht des Weltgebäudes, durch unermüdete Beobachtungen, in ein so helles Licht gesetzt habet! Copernicus, Hevel, Hugen, Newton, Whiston werden, um ihrer Verdienste willen, unsterblich seyn; und dein Ruhm, grosser Wolf! wird sich zu keiner Zeit in einige Grenzen einschlissen lassen." (42).

The essay is very much in the spirit of the times. Like so many other essays singing the praise of God in nature, it emphasizes the value and the necessity of natural science for an authentic appreciation of nature and thus of God in nature.

His essay, "Untersuchung, ob die Thiere um der Menschen willen geschaffen sind", which appeared in the October, 1744 issue of the *Belustigungen...*, answers the question stated in the title affirmatively. He tries to prove with numerous examples that, directly and indirectly, the main purpose of animals is to serve the good of men. Though the answer is not very distinguished, considering the tendency by the middle of the century to grant animals an existence for their own sake, the essay does show the author's awareness of the richness and manifoldness of the animal kingdom. In the related essay, "Untersuchung ob man die Thiere, um physiologischer Versuche willen, lebendig eröffnen dürfe", the answer is also affirmative and in the same vein as the previous one. The essay is interesting because Mylius uses his medical training to show the value for man of dissections of animals.

In the essay, "Drey Gespräche über wichtige Wahrheiten", the first conversation, "Von der Unendlichkeit der Welt", is pertinent, for here the author exercises his imagination by a contemplation of the heavens. On an evening that is so bright that stars of the sixth magnitude are visible, Sternhold and Grundman converse about the universe. Sternhold explains the fantastic facts and figures about the heavens beyond our own solar system until he is led to the possibility of the endlessness of the world:

> Wenn sie auch die äussersten wären: so würden sie doch unwidersprechliche Zeugen von der Grösse des Schöpfers seyn. Aber man hat keinen Grund zu glauben, dass sie die Grenzen der Welt sind. Sie kommen uns, nur unsers Standes wegen gegen sie, so klein und entfernt vor, dass nicht noch entferntere seyn könnten. Es können ihrer aber gar wohl noch viel tausend Millionen über ihnen seyn, von welchen wir, wegen ihrer noch weit grössern Entfernung, gar keine Spuren sehen können. Es kann seyn, dass die Geschöpfe auf den Planeten, um die Sterne der sechsten Grösse die Sterne in der Milchstrasse so deutlich sehen, als wir die Sterne der andren Grösse. Und da sich ohne allen Zweifel auch um die Sonnen in der Milchstrasse Planeten schwingen, und diese auch bewohnet sind: so können ja wohl die Einwohner derselben die uns ganz unsichtbaren Sterne mit der grössten Deutlichkeit sehen, von den Geschöpfen in diesen Sonnenwirbeln aber kann man ein gleiches sagen, und —. Doch ich gehe zu weit, und komme endlich gar auf die Gedanken, dass die Welt unendlich ist. (93—94)

This is an excellent example of our author's imagination being led by astronomical considerations to the conception of the infinity of the universe. Of course, Sternhold, in the above passage, shirks from the final conclusion, but is then forced by his interlocutor's logic, to accept the boundlessness of the universe.

Related to this essay is his "Gedanken von dem Zustande der abgeschiedenen Seelen," in which Mylius reflects on the likelihood that souls liberated from their bodies upon death will ascend to the other heavenly bodies in the boundless universe. The essay is a dialogue between Phaon, an orthodox theologian, who sticks to tradition, Kleon, a jurist, who remains uncommitted and Damon, a progressive theologian versed also in the arts and the sciences, who eagerly follows the flights of his imagination. The latter, of course, speaks for Mylius. Unswayed by the objections of his friends, Damon clings to his beliefs, enchanted by the prospect of joining the souls of the greatest astronomers of the past, especially Newton, in a perfect contemplation of the universe: "Denn ich werde alsdann nicht nur überhaupt in die beglückte Gesellschaft der tugend-haften Geister kommen, sondern auch mich an dem vollkommensten Umgange mit den zur Anschauung der himmlischen Körper erhabenen Sternkündigern, und besonders meines Newtons, dieses grossen Geistes, und dieses allervortrefflichsten unter den Sternkündigern, ergötzen, und in seiner Gesellschaft dem majestätischen Schöpfer an seinen Werken ewig bewundern und ihn loben und anbethen" (147).

The last two prose works of interest are humorous and good examples of Mylius' wit. The essay "Sendschreiben von dem Aufnehmen der Naturlehre" contains several tongue-in-cheek proposals to enlist the foibles and vices of men in the service of science by having men do simply what is most natural for them. Thus the avaricious would be asked to work out the as yet incomplete logarithmic system, which would appeal to them due to their love of counting. The stingy who are so used to a careful scrutinizing of coins would be called upon to examine and count the stamens, pistils and flowers of plants, thereby putting Mr. Linnaeus in their debt. The ambitious who are so concerned with their honor and the perpetuation of their names should be persuaded to build astronomical observatories and botanical gardens, for this would surely bring them more honor than their precious palaces. The spendthrifts should sponsor scientific voyages to all parts of the world as well as unusual enterprises like building space ships which would be manned by the quixotic and by dare-devils. As far as the bureaucrats are concerned who have so much time on their hands, they could be urged to make collections of natural curiosities, to supplement and complete natural history collections. With these and other witty suggestions Mylius offers amusing social satire as well as a vision of how much still needs to be done and could be done for the furthering of the sciences.

Finally his "Anfangsgründe der Physikopetitmaitrick", which had appeared in 1747 in *"Der Naturforscher"*, is a parody of the practice of his time to construct systems pretending to scientific and mathematical accuracy. He develops his new science, complete with axioms, postulates, theorems, observations and experiments, which he defines as "eine Wissenschaft von der physikalischen Einsicht der jungen Herren." The name of his science is derived from the French term for a young gentleman, namely, "petit maître". A typical example of his wit is the third theorem that young gentlemen are scientists. His proof is as follows: "Die jungen Herren können küssen, (16.#) und küssen auch wirklich (17.#) Küsse sind physikalische Versuche. (20.21.#.) Wer also küsset, der macht physikalische Versuche. Wer aber physikalische Versuche macht, der ist ein Naturkundiger (19.#) Dannenhero sind die jungen Herren Naturkundige." (272—273).

In his poetry, as is to be expected, there is a variety of scientific themes. Some of his poems such as "Der Morgen", "Der Frühling", "Die Sommernacht" are primarily nature descriptions which, though they contain no science as such, reveal the careful observer of natural phenomena. His ode "Auf die Gegend bey Gera", which first appeared in Der Naturforscher in 1748, is especially rich with descriptions of the natural historian. As occurs so often in poetry inspired by such considerations, we find here the conception of nature as an artist greater than any human artist. In comparing Leipzig's artistically designed gardens with Gera's unadorned natural beauty, he says:

> Wo sich Natur und Kunst verbinden
> Behält stets die Natur den Preiss
> Sie braucht nie schwacher Menschen Hülfe;
> Am stärksten reizt sie ohne Kleid. (571)

He does not oppose nature to art but maintains that nature is the greater artist, that its works are unparalleled: "Sie zeigt sich allzeit schön und prächtig, / In stets veränderter Gestalt. (571)

This is an example of the aesthetic approach to nature which appears frequently by the middle of the eighteenth century.

There are quite a few poems, however, that contain specific scientific themes. His "Gedanken bey einer Mondfinsterniss" is a dramatic description of the lunar eclipse of August 30, 1746. The poem begins with the plea that the clouds will be scattered in time so that the astronomers, equipped with "Hevels Sehror", will be able to observe every detail:

> Ihr Wolken! weicht den Mittagswinden,
> Verlasst und reinigt unsre Luft!
> Lasst uns die seltne Lust empfinden,
> Zu welcher uns die Sternkunst rufft!
> Zeigt, wie vom Schatten unsrer Erde
> Der volle Mond verfinstert werde! (418)

The clouds subside temporarily and permit the poet-astronomer to describe the stages of the eclipse: "Seht, wie am ostlich obern Rande / Der Mond sein fremdes Licht verliert!" (421)

Mylius conveys a sense of suspense and movement, on the one hand, by calling attention to the clouds that occasionally obstruct the view and on the other, by naming the lunar craters as they are gradually darkened by the earth's shadow:

> Ein neuer Auftritt! zum Gewehre!
> Der Schatten dringt schon tief hinein.
> Er rückt bereits zum kalten Meere!
> Bald wird Eudox verschwunden seyn.
> Der Pfuhl des Tods, die See der Regen
> Erblassen seines Anblicks wegen. (421)

This enumeration of the moon's landmarks contribute to the picture of the astronomer at his telescope, eagerly noting every significant detail perceived. The poem concludes with a praise of astronomers who prefer observation to sleep and the hope that the moon will soon grant the pleasure of a similar spectacle.

"An den Aeolus", which first appeared in 1747 in *Der Naturforscher,* is a similar poem celebrating a solar eclipse in July, 1748. The poem is addressed to Aeolus, the God of Winds, who is asked to keep the sky clear of wind so that Urania, the Muse of astronomy, may reveal to her priests a rare phenomena. Urania appears to her son Euler and gives him a preview of this spectacle:

> Dort in des Löwens dunklem Zeichen
> Wird Lunens Lauf die Sonn erreichen,
> Und deinen Welttheil wird ihr Schein
> Durch sie fast ganz entzogen seyn. (576)

She promises him further that in his honor the city of Berlin will be favored by seeing the eclipse under rare circumstances:

> Dir aber, liebster Sohn! zu Ehren
> Sieht dein Berlin den Mond bekränzt.
> Der wird die Dunkelheit vermehren,
> Bis ihn der Sonne Licht umglänzt. (576)

Indeed, the poet continues, Euler saw this unusual sight, where the sun stands directly behind the moon entirely darkened except at the circumference, so that the sun's light is visible only as a shining wreath about the moon. Euler is duly thankful for a vision that neither Newton nor Cassini had seen.

Astronomy is again the main theme in his long poem, "Lehrgedicht von den Bewohnern der Kometen", which he wrote to dispel Kästner's doubt about the inhabitability of comets. The main theme, thus, of the poem at hand is the inhabitability of comets which Mylius affirms most emphatically. In the first hundred lines of the poem, Mylius makes a survey of our knowledge of astronomy. Like Ikarus, but without the drastic consequences, he wishes to soar through the heavens to inspect the many orbiting bodies. He expresses his faith in man's capacity to provide the means some day for space flight:

> Ist es der klugen Welt bis itzt noch nicht gelungen,
> Dass ein erfundner Flug sie in den Mond geschwungen,
> Ja in dem weiten Raum des Sonnenheers gebracht:
> So ist diess Glück vielleicht der Nachwelt zugedacht. (350—351)

Until that becomes possible, however, he must content himself with an imaginary flight which he then undertakes.

He expresses the hope that his intuition about the inhabitation of comets will one day be verified just as Newton's reasoned conclusion that the earth is flat at the poles was demonstrated by the Maupertuis expedition to Lapland:

Dort, wo das rohe Volk der feigen Lappen friert,
Vom Kittis, nah am Pol, wo man kein Feuer spürt
Das aus der Sonne fleusst, hat er den weiten Bogen,
Der Tag und Nächte theilt, bis Tornea gezogen.
Dort hat im Messen ihm der Augenschein gezeigt,
Dass unterm Pole sich der Erden Fläche neigt,
Doch Newton wusste längst, was Maupertuis gesehen,
So gut, als wär von ihm selbst der Versuch geschehen.
O könnt ich so, wie er, auf sichre Gründe baun,
Und, was kein Auge sieht, mit meinem Geiste schaun! (352–353)

This was an example to Mylius and his contemporaries of scientific achievement. A theory arrived at by mathematical reasoning was verified by experiment. Of course it was also another example of Newton worship. Newton again represents the heights which human reason can attain. Mylius thus wishes that this example of intellect and enterprise by Newton and Maupertuis may also be true in the case of his own speculations. His main argument for the inhabitation of comets is the inhabitation of planets which he accepts fully:

Warum entvölkert man nicht der Planeten Rund?
Sie machen Gottes Macht und Weisheit klärer kund,
Wenn sie bevölkert sind. Das thun auch die Kometen;
Ja, wegen ihrer Zahl, noch mehr, als die Planeten.
Ohn Absicht, handelt ja ein kluger Bauherr nicht. (355)

Since God's wisdom and might demand the inhabitation of the planets, the same should hold true of comets which are even more numerous. Essential to this argument is the resemblance between comets and planets. That the comets are heavenly bodies with measurable orbits is again cited as an achievement of "Newton's Kunst":

Entwerft mit Newtons Kunst des Schwanzsterns weiten Lauf.
Durch des Saturnus Kreis führt ihn bis da hinauf,
Wo Sirius sein Licht durch tausend Wirbel streuet . . . . (356)

He is, of course, aware that the orbit of a comet would create unusual conditions such as extreme cold and heat. He agrees that human life exactly as we know it would not be possible under such conditions, but maintains that relativity is a rule in nature and that even within the limited perspective on our planet we can perceive nature's capacity for variety:

Die Mannichfaltigkeit der prächtigen Natur
Zeigt uns im Kleinen auch verschiedner Wesen Spur,
Die, wenn sie Hitz und Frost in gleicher Stärke rühren,
In ihrer Körper Bau nicht gleiche Wirkung spüren. (357)

As one of his examples, he cites the existence of amphibious creatures on earth. Just as they can live in two elements, water and air, so perhaps comets are inhabited by creatures who can live in fire as well as in air:

> Vielleicht vermag das Volk auf brennenden Kometen,
> Das in der Luft sonst lebt, auch Feuer nicht zu tödten,
> Wie jene Thiere nicht das Wasser tödten kann;
> Trifft man sie lebend auch gleich in der Luft sonst an. (358)

Another possibility, he maintains, is that the vapors surrounding the comet are so thick that the sun's rays are sufficiently impeded. As far as extreme cold is concerned, possibly comets contain an inner heat which suffices when its orbit removes it far from the sun; as another possibility, he suggests, that the life span of comet inhabitants is so short that the change from extreme heat to extreme cold is not noticed.

His conviction about the variety of which nature is capable, the many possibilities of nature, is most impressive. He is very much aware that the reality which we know on our tiny planet does not begin to exhaust nature's ways. Thus by using his imagination, his understanding of natural law, and his conviction in God's purpose, he feels justified in populating the comets as well as the planets.

He concluded his poem by rejecting the view of those who populate the comets, but only with the evil, thus making comets into orbiting hells. This he feels is a "falscher Wahn". Finally he names Whiston and Heyn as the sources of the views to which he subscribes:

> Was Whistons Witz erfand, was Heyn noch mehr bestärkte,
> Als er selbst in der Schrift des Grundes Spuren merkte,
> Kann meiner Meynung nicht des Beyfalls Hindrung seyn. (326)

In the poem, "Auf den Tod weyland Herrn Johann Heyns", he once again defends Heyn and his cometary theories. What was Heyn's crime in his "Kometenbuch", for which he is being so maligned, he asks. Did he deny the creator, did he preach revolution, or had he been infected by Spinoza's poison? Not in the least, he simply taught and confirmed what Whiston long before had taught. Is his teaching false simply because it can't be found in the catechism or because there is no clear statement of it in the Bible? It is true, he continues, that the orbits of heavenly bodies do not interfere with one another. Nevertheless, God's design may include an occasional cometary collision, as Heyn and Whiston indicated. So, Mylius argues, at the very least Heyn's theory is not impossible. Finally, though Heyn cannot prove his theory to everyone's satisfaction, he, Mylius, is convinced that Heyn was motivated by honesty and love of truth, and thus his name deserves better treatment.

In connection with Mylius' interest in this cometary theory, mention should be made of his didactic poem, "Vom Vorspiel des jüngsten Gerichts", which he sent to Heyn and which the latter published in his *Gesamlete Briefe von den Cometen* . . .[2] Heyn himself considered this 240 verse poem to be an excellent exposition of his theory: "Denn das Lehrgedicht vom Vorspiel des jüngsten Gerichts stellet den Inhalt meines Buches so vollständig vor, dass ich zweifeln muss, ob mir selbst alles so beygefallen seyn würde: wenn ich eine Geschicklichkeit in der Poesie besässe, und solche Sachen in Versen hätte vortragen sollen." (791).

In the poem Mylius insists that the cometary theory he is expounding is based on reason and scripture. The order of nature, he contends, was not disturbed when Noah's flood was caused by a comet and will again not be disturbed at the Last Judgment, which will also be caused by a comet obedient to natural law. His description of the paradisical state on earth that will follow the Last Judgment is interesting:

Die Erde wird alsdenn von bösen Dünsten rein,
Das schöne Paradies, und so vollkommen seyn,
Als sie vor Zeiten war, eh Regen, Flut und Giessen
Pracht, Anmuth, Fruchtbarkeit mit sich dahin gerissen.
Wie jährlich sich der Mond zwölf mal um sie bewegt,
Bevor die Sündflut kam, die sie so stark erregt;
Wie sie, eh ein Comet der Ordnung Lauf geendet,
Sich um die Sonne nur, nicht um sich selbst, gewendet. (785)

In other words, the comet causing the Last Judgment will eliminate the diurnel motion of the earth, which had been imparted to it by the comet causing Noah's flood. Thus, there will then exist the paradisical state of perpetual light.

The central portion of the poem presents the body of Heyn's cometary theory and argues for the plausibility of the whole idea. As is to be expected, Mylius draws on Newton's theory of gravity to support his defense:

. . . Nun zeigt ein grosser Geist,
Den die gelehrte Welt in Newtons Schriften preist,
Dass jedes Rund der Welt das andrer zu sich ziehet,
Dergleichen Wirkung man an den Magneten siehet. (786)

The last portion of the poem is a call for repentance in anticipation of the Last Judgment, which is more in accordance with the interests of the theologian Heyn than those of the poet-scientist Mylius.

Of other poems containing some scientific themes, there is his "Beweis eines neuen Lehrsatzes in der Mechanik", in which he warns against man's all too great

---

2 Johann Heyn, *Gesamlete Briefe von den Cometen, der Sündflut und dem Vorspiel des jüngsten Gerichts* (Berlin and Leipzig, 1745).

pride in machines. In "Der beschämte Gottesleugner" he uses familiar arguments to demonstrate to an atheist that the existence of the cosmos requires a creator.

Finally, it is relevant to refer to Mylius' poem "Abschied aus Europa" which Lessing praised highly. Although the poem does not contain any scientific themes as such, it refers to the scientific journey to America which Mylius had planned. The story of the project, the sponsors, the fund-raising problems, and the precise purpose of the trip are all amply discussed in the dissertations[3] on Mylius. A brief reference can be made to Mylius' diary of his trips through Germany to Holland and then to England, where he met an untimely death before he could depart for America. His diary, available in an abridged form in *Bernoulli's Archiv*[4] ... gives some idea of how carefully Mylius prepared for his trip to America for the purpose of observing and collecting natural curiosities and contacting men of science there. The diary is full of descriptions of large and small natural history collections, astronomical observatories, technical instruments and the like. Furthermore, he tells of his visits to famous scientists and natural historians like Lesser in Nordhausen, Musschenbroeck and Lyonnet in Holland and Bradley in London. Along with the scientific observations, Mylius records his observations of customs and habits of the communities he visits. Judging from this, the journey to America would have been most enlightening for his contemporaries, and we can only conjecture that the resulting account would have been another fine example of our author's literary and scientific talents joining and complementing one another.

[3] The two dissertations on Mylius are Erwin Thyssen's *Christlob Mylius* (Marburg, 1912) and Rudolf Trillmich's *Christlob Mylius* (Halle, 1914).

[4] Christlob Mylius, *"Tagebuch seiner Reise von Berlin nach England, 1753"* in Johann Bernouilli's *Archiv zur neuern Geschichte, Geographie, Natur und Menschenkenntniss,* V—VII (Leipzig, 1786—1787).

16. Nikolas Dietrich Giseke (1724—1765)

Nikolas Dietrich Giseke was the son of a Lutheran clergyman who rose to high position in the church. In Hamburg with the support of Brockes and Hagedorn, he received an excellent education. From 1745 to 1748 he studied theology and literature at the University of Leipzig. His friendship with Cramer, Ebert, Klopstock, Gärtner and others led to his participation in the *Bremer Beiträge*. Several poems in imitation of Thomson and his long eulogy on Brockes show that he shared their perspective on the fundamental issues concerning God, nature, and man. An examination of scientific themes in his poems[1] will show also that he belongs to the Brockes and Thomson tradition.

Let us turn to one of his earliest poems, the "Gedanken von der göttlichen Regierung" of 1745. Here he asserts that nature demonstrates the justice and reliability of God's rule so that man can take joy in the creation even though it includes death and destruction:

Und hier, wo sonder Ruh in stetem Unbestand,
Diess aufwächst, jenes fällt, er mit seiner Hand
Die grosse Kette fest, die alles so verbindet,
Dass man Gott allemal voll Huld und Weisheit findet. (5)

The image of the chain is intended to represent the interrelatedness of all natural phenomena. Thus if man does not see the justice of a specific event which causes him pain, he must take a wider perspective and recognize that the good of the whole is involved.

The dominant thought of the poem is that nature and its laws are wise solely because of God, according to whose design all was made. Any alternative, such as for example, that nature be subject to the will and whims of man is shown by Giseke to result in anarchy:

Ja, sollte die Natur dir unterwürfig stehn,
Unwillig müsste sie in andre Gleise gehn.
Schnell hiessest du den Nord in seine Klüfte fliehen,
Und Wolken dürften nie die neue Sonn' umziehen.
Ihr Strahl fiel' ungeschwächt auf das erfreute Feld,
Schüf' einen längern Tag, und eine reichre Welt,
Die bald, wenn lange Glut sie ausdörrt' und verzehrte,
Nach Schatten ächzete, und gern der Sonn' entbehrte. (6—7)

Nature is wiser than man simply because it is not subject to whim and fancy, but because it is governed by laws which are not of man's design. The lawfulness

---

1 *Poetische Werke* (Braunschweig, 1767), edited by Carl Christian Gärtner.

of nature as revealed by the scientists is here used as evidence of nature's wisdom and divine origin.

In "Schreiben über die Zärtlichkeit in der Freundschaft . . ." of 1746, he criticizes various types of people who because of one flaw or the other are incapable of true friendship. The philosopher, for example, has penetrated the deepest secrets of creation, he knows the orbits of heavenly bodies and the rules according to which physical bodies behave. However, his learning has made him too pretentious for ordinary human feeling and thus he is incapable of true friendship. This is an example of the view that though science, the knowledge of nature, is a valuable achievement, it does not lead to self-knowledge or human fulfillment. Knowledge of nature here has become something cerebral, abstract, detached from the personal life of the subject, the knower.

His "Schreiben an einen Freund, von dem Werthe der Wissenschaft" seems at first to extol the devotion to reason and science, for in the beginning he maintains that they lift man above the empty distractions of society. Yet he quickly adds that learning alone can also be very shallow:

Sein Blatt von Ziffern voll, sein Zirkel in den Händen,
Sein Geist, der ietzt vielleicht in andern Welten irrt,
Und dort bekannt zu seyn, der Erde fremde wird,
Kann ihm des Pöbels Lob, nicht wahren Vorzug geben.
Die Weisheit kennt ihn nicht, und wird ihn nicht erheben. (73)

Learning can deceive if it is not complemented by virtue, which consists first of a recognition of God as creator. Only with this orientation can the study of nature serve man's humanity rather than detract from it:

Wenn denn sein kühner Geist in Schlund und Abgrund steiget,
Wo wieder Meer und Fluth ihm neue Wunder zeiget,
Wenn er aus Wissbegier mit edlem Flug sich hebt,
Dahin, wo in der Luft der Vögel König schwebt,
Wo Welten stets im Lauf nie ihre Bahn verkennen,
Und höher noch gesetzt, unzähl'ge Sonnen brennen:
Dann lernt er höchst entzückt, was unser Vorzug ist,
Und wie kein Sterblicher des Schöpfers Grösse misst. (73—74)

A proper study of nature's wonders, above as well as below, must always lead to a recognition of God. This is self-knowledge, and knowledge of nature rightly understood will lead to it.

His didactic poem, "Versuch vom Gebete" of 1757, is a refutation of the freethinkers who maintain that chance and accident rather than a creator are responsible for the cosmos. His main argument against them is the all-pervading lawfulness of nature, which he finds in the tiniest as well as in the grandest

natural phenomena. Man's knowledge of astronomy, however, provides him with
his most effective ammunition:

> Siehe, da schwimmen, (unzählbare Heere!) die Sonnen
>   und Erden
> In den uferlosen Tiefen des Weltraums; und friedlich
> Schwimmen sie neben einander. Sie halten immer die
>   Bahnen,
> Die sie einmal giengen. Nicht Eine verirret; nicht Eine
> Stösst und verdrängt den Nachbar. (40—41)

In the immense space of the universe, countless heavenly bodies obediently
adhere to their regular orbits, never infringing on those of their neighbors. The
precise lawfulness of these heavenly bodies is demonstrated by man's success in
measuring and predicting their paths:

> Der Mensch weiss
> Jedes Gestirnes Stelle. Nicht Eines sucht er vergebens.
> Ihm ist der Gang der Planeten und ihrer Trabanten nicht
>   fremde.
> Er bestimmt ihn voraus, und irrt nicht. Auch den Kometen
> Merkt er ihre Bewegungen ab. Bald wirds ihm gelingen,
> Sie untrüglich vorher zu verkündigen. (41)

This is an expression of the poet's faith in human knowledge as represented
by astronomy. The order found in the heavens by the astronomer offered visible
evidence of a creator and testimony that man had the capacity with his reason
and sense to understand the divinely created nature in which he had his home.
Astronomy was that human discipline which best revealed God to man and
which granted him the assurance that God's design in nature was comprehensible
to him. The next step was to expect that God's purpose for man was as lawful
and as comprehensible as nature itself:

> Der Gott, der den Sternen
> Ihre Bahnen zeichnet, und um die leuchtenden Sonnen
> Die erleuchteten Erden herumwälzt, bestimmt auch das
>   Schicksal
> Aller Geschöpfe, die er in so viel Welten gesetzt hat. (42)

From astronomy, then, Giseke, as many of his contemporaries, derived the
gratifying conviction that God, nature and man's function were meaningful and
comprehensible.

In Giseke's poetry there is a whole-hearted acceptance of science, but only in
so far as it can be assimilated within a pious, deistic philosophy of life. The work
of the scientists has revealed Got in nature and the lawfulness of the universe, all

of which provides ammunition against the freethinkers, who substitute chance for a divine Creator. At the same time, scientific work, done for its own sake, for the purpose of accumulating knowledge outside of a deistic religious framework, is viewed with great suspicion. Scientific knowledge is legitimate only when it contributes to self-knowledge and knowledge of God. Knowledge of nature is held in the highest esteem by our poet when he views it as the means to attain knowledge of self and of God.

17. Johann Siegmund Leinker (1724—1788)

Johann Siegmund Leinker was born in Nürnberg and studied at Regensburg, Nürnberg, Altdorf and Helmstädt, where he earned his medical degree. After extensive travels he returned to Nürnberg in 1748, where he became a member of the "Collegium Physicum". He also became a member of the "Teutsche Gesellschaft" in Altdorf in 1759, and in 1767 he was accepted into the "Gesellschaft zum Nutzen der Wissenschaft und Künste" at Frankfurt. He complemented his medical and scientific work by translating medical works into German and by writing poetry. In addition to the two odes under discussion here, he also wrote a Latin poem on electricity.[1]

Let us now turn to his two odes entitled *Die Körperwelt und ihr Einwohner der Mensch.*[2] The title suggests that the two poets form a unity, and such is the case as we shall see. We shall begin with the preface and then take up the odes individually.

In the preface to the reader, Leinker states his purpose of writing poetry about scientific subject matter. It is interesting that he speaks of the collaboration of science and poetry as if it had become an established procedure: "Seitdem die Dichtkunst in dem Klange der Reime ihren Vorzug nicht alleine mehr wehlen darf; so sucht sich dieselbe mit den Gedanken eines Weltweisen immermehr und mehr zu verbinden. Sie macht daher selbst auf die Wissenschafften Ansprüche." (2)

He continues to explain the respective functions of poetic form and and scientific content. Whereas poetic devices amuse the senses, scientific truths impart to the work a quality of depth which it would not otherwise have: "Ihre Fabel belustiget die Sinne, fordert aber ihren Schmuck von Wahrheiten und belebet mit jener Geiste ihre Bilder. Je erhabener der Gegenstand, je würdiger werden die Züge angebracht. Und was ist erhabener als die Natur in ihrer Ordnung, Wirkungen und Geschöpfen? " (Preface 2). His conclusion that nature and our scientific knowledge of nature's ways is a most fitting subject matter for poetry is very relevant to this study. In his two odes he diligently carries out his conception of poetry.

His first ode, as the title indicates, is devoted to the world of natural phenomena exclusive of man. The sequence in which he takes up natural phenomena is conventional for the first part of the century. He begins with the vast phenomena of the starry heavens and works his way down to earthly phenomena, which he categorizes according to the four elements.

In the beginning of the poem he refers to the Biblical story of creation. Thereafter, however, his only source is the scientific study of nature. The first

---

1 Johann Siegmund Leinker, *Electricitas. Carmen Latinum elegiacum* (Nürnberg, 1758).
2 (Frankfurt und Leipzig, 1759).

scientific discipline he takes up is astronomy, for he maintains it is appropriate
that man, the masterpiece of creation, should contemplate the cosmos.

In a brief history of astronomy he alludes to Ptolemy's and Brahe's
achievements and to the ancient heliocentrists such as Philolaus and Aristarchus.
It is, however, the system of Copernicus that he celebrates and explicates:

> Es kommt Copernicus aus Preussen,
> Und setzt die Sonne mitten hin,
> Um diesen Körper die Planeten,
> Wozu sich Mond und Erde zehlt.
> Merkt wird dies Lehrgebäud erwählt
> So ist kein Umschweif mehr vonnöthen,
> Die Sonne steht, die kleinre Erd
> Lauft, und der Mond ist ihr Gefährd. (16)

In this first mention of the Copernican system he emphasizes its simplicity as
compared to the systems it replaces. In the next few pages he tells the story of
our solar system with relatively few and compact verses. The planets are
enumerated in the proper order, distances are alluded to and the duration of
their orbits compared to the earth's. Very briefly he refers to the probability of
the inhabitation of the planets:

> Wer sagt mir, wer dort oben sitzt.
> Wo Wesen göttlich wohnen müssen?
> Denn jene Körper (giebt man acht)
> Sind nicht sogar umsonst gemacht. (18)

In one very compact stanza he speaks of Kepler's contribution to the
Copernican system:

> Was eines Keplers Fleis gewonne,
> Das thut sich in Planeten kund,
> Als der sie ihrem Thron zur Sonne,
> Der Ordnung gleichsam nach verbund.
> Wenn er durch länglicht weite Creise
> Den Abweg von der Sonnen schlos,
> So war die Richtigkeit sehr gros,
> Bey aller Prüfung der Beweise,
> So dass auch der Copernicus
> Von neuem Recht erhalten mus. (19)

In these lines he states the significant results of Kepler's astronomical labors,
namely, that the planets' orbit is elliptical with the sun at one of the foci and
that this contributed to the substantiation of the Copernican system.

In another stanza he states succinctly how astronomers draw conclusions
from their observations:

Wie? Flecken haben die Planeten?
Und zwar Mars, Venus, Jupiter,
Was kan uns dieses überreden?
So leuchten ihre Berge her,
An diese müssen Thäler gränzen,
An diese Seen, und wer wer weis
Was mehr? Sie deckt ein Wolkencreis,
Gnug wenn die Flecken wechslend glänzen,
So schliesst man aus der Wendung gar,
Derselben Tag und Nacht und Jahr. (19)

The observed phenomena are spots on the planets. These spots suggest
reflected light from mountains which in turn imply valleys and seas, and where
there is water there must be an atmosphere. Moreover, the alternate glow of the
spots indicates the movement of the planets, enabling astronomers to ascertain
the length of day and year.

Another stanza is devoted to the question of satellites that famous
astronomers like Galileo, Cassini, Huygens and the German Marius have
discovered. Like many of his contemporaries, he raised the question of a possible
satellite of Mars which reasoning by analogy called for.

A considerable section is devoted to comets; this gives occasion for a tirade
against superstition and an exhortation to accept the judgment of astronomers:

Dort leuchten düstere Cometen,
Und der gemeine Mann erschrickt,
Krieg, Pest und Hunger will ihn tödten,
Sobald er dies Gestirn erblickt,
Um Fixstern, um der Sonnen Gränzen,
In langer, engenrunden Bahn,
Gehn sie erhitzt und brennen an,
Daher die langen Schweife glänzen,
Die also unser Auge find,
Sind die so unsre Sonn entzünd. (20)

The first four lines refer to superstition, with the remaining lines offering the
scientific account that comets are heavenly bodies, moving about the sun in
elliptical orbits. He points out that the correct view of comets eliminates
Descartes' vortices and the belief of Kepler and Hevel that comets are mere
vapors. He reiterates that they are part of the original creation of the cosmos.

He also introduces Whiston's cometary theorizing to which he gives sympathetic treatment though not credence:

Indem ich einen Whiston höre,
Wie gerne folgt der Beyfall ihn,
Wahrscheinlich lässet seine Lehre,
Ein Chaos in Cometen glühn,
Des Falles Straf war ein Comete,
Die Eden aus der Lage sties,
Den Lauf der Achse werden lies,
Und macht die Sündflut alles öde,
So wird das Wasser so ersäuft,
Von einem solchen Druck gehäuft. (21)

Although he takes no position himself in this passage, he describes some of Whiston's speculations, namely, that a comet is a heavenly body in a state of chaos, that a comet caused the earth to acquire a diurnal rotation at the time of Adam's fall — originally, due to the absence of diurnal rotation, the length of a day and a year were the same — and that a comet was also the cause of Noah's flood.

Again he exhorts the reader to take advantage of the night's silence to contemplate the heavens with his telescope. As night subsides, however, so does the possibility of astronomical observation. He thus turns his attention to the most striking phenomena of the day, namely, light and its source, the sun. The interest in light indicates that his attention is now turned to earthly phenomena, and that is the case, after he enumerates the most significant facts about the sun, such as its distance from the earth, the sun spots, and the sun's revolution about its own axis.

Next follows a lengthy discussion of the nature of our planet earth. Again the stanzas are very compact and convey much information in a few lines, as for example:

Hier unter dieses Strahls Vermögen
Welzt sich die Erde stet und sacht.
Durch ihr gedoppeltes Bewegen
Entsteht ein Jahr, ein Tag und Nacht.
Von ihrer völligen Figure
Sprach Piccard und Casini frey,
Sie wäre rund so wie ein Ey,
Biss man die Pole platt erfuhre,
Bis ein sehr forschendes Paris,
Maupertuis nach Lappland hies. (27)

In the first four lines, the earth's diurnal and annual revolutions are referred to as causes of changes in day and year. In the last six lines, recent theories about the figure of the earth are alluded to. Picard and Cassini had denied the circular roundness of the earth, and finally the expedition of Maupertuis to Lapland demonstrated that the earth was flat at its poles. He raises the possibility of a theory that would encompass both the roundness and flatness of the earth, namely, the pulsation of the earth, whereby its shape would fluctuate according to the direction of its axis.

Other theories of the earth are mentioned. According to some, the earth is a huge magnet. Halley, he maintains, had considered the middle of the earth to be a magnet. Burnet's theory is also referred to in a few lines:

Wenn Burnet seine Schichten legt,
Aus welchen Wasser ausgedrungen,
Bis zur Befruchtung auf dem Schlamm,
Der Sonn erzeugend Feuer kam. (28)

Here we have some of the essential points of Burnet's theory. The crust of the earth is composed of several layers through which water burst to cause the great flood. The last two lines refer to the sun's function in Burnet's theory of creating life out of the slime through its warmth.

Lucretius is also praised as one who sang of the earth: "Lucrezens feurige Gedichte / Besängen kühn hier die Natur." (28) It is significant here that our author was able to refer to Lucretius without commenting on his impiety. Apparently the latter's attempt to give a scientific explanation of natural phenomena is what Leinker associates with the name of Lucretius.

Johann Gottlob Krüger's history of the earth receives special praise:

Doch in der ältsten Zeit Geschichte
Giebt Krüger uns die beste Spur.
Wie sehr von Rissen durchgebrochen
Zerlechzt der Berge steiler Lauf.
Man hebt versteinte Merkmal auf,
In Fischen, Muscheln, Blättern, Knochen,
Zum Zeichen dass die erste Fluth
Gewaltig auf dem Land geruht. (28)

The last four lines refer to Krüger's attempt in his *Geschichte der Erde*[3] to ascertain the age of the earth. The use of fossils as evidence of the universality of the flood was by this time quite a commonplace.

Having examined theories concerning the earth's origin and form, he now turns to an exploration of the wealth of phenomena found on this earth, to which he refers as "Die Mutter unsrer aller". He introduces the subject matter of the next few pages as follows:

[3] Johann Gottlob Krüger, *Geschichte der Erde in den allerältesten Zeiten* (Halle, 1746).

Das Reich der Thiere und der Pflanzen,
Das Reich der Steine und Metall,
Der Vorsicht Reichthum überall,
Dient einzeln wundersam dem Ganzen, (29)

He surveys these kingdoms of nature in the manner of a natural historian by
enumerating individual species. He breaks the monotony of these enumerations
by assuming the role of a traveler who swings around the globe to various distant
lands, taking note of the many phenomena before him. For example, in the
Americas many precious stones are found and he takes this occasion to mention
some of them:

Dort in Americaner Lande
Entdeckt man das was kostbar ist.
Der Königliche Diamante,
Saphir, Schmaragd und Amethist,
Granate mit dem Hyacinthe,
Der Chrysolite, Chrysopras,
Opal, Berille, der Topas
Und der Rubin sind wie ich finde,
Die Gattungen vom Edelstein,
So hell und ganzdurchsichtig seyn. (36)

This is only his point of departure, for now he continues with other stones,
classifying them, as was the custom, according to their ability to reflect or
transmit light. From these he goes to other treasures found in the earth, namely,
the metals and half metals which he enumerates dutifully.

In the next few pages he offers an interesting contrast between occasional
cataclysmic natural events such as earthquakes, volcanoes, and storms, on the
one hand, and the wholesome consistency and regularity which characterize
nature most of the time. He alludes to Vesuvius and Lisbon as evidence of
nature's awesome destructiveness and, as evidence of nature's beneficence, he
presents four short vignettes of the seasons, depicting nature's changes as
orderly, predictable, and as a boon to man.

As in the previous pages he had confined himself to phenomena associated
with the earth, in the subsequent pages he describes natural phenomena
associated with water, followed by air phenomena and finally those connected
with fire. This categorization of phenomena according to the four elements was
still quite acceptable at the middle of the century.

He begins his compendium of water phenomena with a discussion of
cataclysmic events such as the sudden appearance of islands or the disappearance
of lands in floods like Atlantis. He also suggests that islands like Sicily or Great
Britain originally were attached to the mainland but were separated through

some violence caused by the waters. After these phenomena are narrated, he turns to the positive features of water. He lists some of the animals found in the sea, as well as other treasures such as corals and shells. He also enumerates the many forms in which water appears such as oceans, rivers, wells and along with each mentions the benefits that man derives from them.

The next category of phenomena are those associated with air. He explains the necessity of air to life and concludes that "Sie muss der Erden Seele seyn". He mentions certain specific atmospheric phenomena like rain, hail, snow, northern lights, halos and rainbows and speaks of the many useful phenomena associated with air. Finally, the crucial scientific experiments performed by Guericke, which dramatized its essential qualities, receives attention:

Und was man vorhin nicht geglaubet,
Hat Otto Gericke erreicht,
Da er die Luft in Pumpen schraubet,
Wird sie elastisch, schwer und leicht.
Kein Schlag wird unter Glocken klingen,
Der Flammen helle Glut erlischt,
Es drückt die Luft, die Wasser springen,
Sie dehnt sich, da sie Blasen mischt,
Manch kleines Thier wird hier erstickt,
Indem das Blut die Adern drückt. (55)

In the remaining few pages, he briefly discusses fire, some of its qualities and uses to man. He concludes the poem with a pious exhortation to man to use his life and his rational facilites to recognize the Creator in His works. After he has thoroughly studied the works of nature about him, he should then heed the workings of his own body. This he says in the last two lines of the poem and thereby turns the reader's attention to the next ode:

Und kennt ihr alles so genau,
So merkt auf euren Cörperbau! (58)

The second ode begins with a reminder that unlike poets who sing of fables, myths, and heroes' deeds, his subject is science, specifically, the human body:

Singt Dichter, singt von Heldenthaten,
Lobt Mann und Waffen ganz genau,
Mir müsse nur mein Lied gerathen,
Ich singe von des Menschenbau. (60)

In the preface he had already justified science as a fitting subject for poetry. Here he reiterates this point of view by indicating man's yearning for knowledge of the world about him and by listing the many achievements which have expanded horizons in so many fields of learning. Thus, the poets should sing of this subject matter:

> Soll ich nun diesen Stof besingen,
> So hilfst du Muse mir nicht nur,
> Nein, sondern soll es deutlich klingen,
> Auch du, o Lehre der Natur,
> Du weist ins innerste zu gehen,
> Wenn jene nur auf Bilder dicht,
> Und wird dich mancher nicht verstehen,
> So sey auch dieses für ihm nicht. (62)

Poetry must collaborate with science to make the subject matter clear, for poetry relies too much on images, whereas science has the capacity to penetrate deeper.

He begins the story of the human body by telling of its conception and nine month sojourn in the womb. This gives him an opportunity to speak of growth from a medical point of view, without a systematic listing of the organs and parts of the body which he manages to do later. Here he gives a dynamic picture of human growth, first within the confines of the womb and then, after birth, the unfolding of the body and personality. In a few pages he tells the drama of early growth and manages to convey both excitement and medical facts, as for example:

> Im ersten Leben ruht die Lungen,
> Es schnauft kein Kind, und seht, es lebt,
> Botallens Gang ist ganz durchdrungen,
> Und der Ovale nicht verwebt.
> Doch eh das Blut hieher gelangen
> Und zu Herzkammern laufen kan,
> Hat Eustachs Valvel es empfangen,
> Durch einer eignen Vene Bahn,
> Und will es denn dem Herz entweichen,
> So mus zum Mittelpunct es schleichen. (71)

From here he follows through the growth of the infant to maturity, taking into consideration not only physical growth but the various stages of life through which a human being, as a body and as a person, passes. He speaks as an enlightened physician who is aware of growth as a composite process, involving the body, the individual person, and society. At each stage of growth there occur changes at all three levels, and Leinker manages to convey both the movement and the unity that is involved, as for example, in his account of the child's discovery of speech:

Nun merkt der Säugling Gegenstände,
Er sieht gewohnten Dingen nach.
Man fesselt ihn nicht mehr die Hände,
Es lalt, es meldet sich die Sprach.
Ein Licht das wir Begriffe nennen,
Entsteht in ihm je mehr und mehr,
Er lernet seine Freunde kennen,
Er zeigt ein achtsames Gehör,
Der Knoche wächst in Jahr und Tagen
Und lehrt sich seinen Körper tragen. (76)

The child becomes aware of his environment and of his capacity to determine
his individual existence by means of speech and action. He encounters other
children and in the meantime the body grows. Thus in a few lines the author
accounts for individual, social and physical growth at a certain stage of
development.

After bringing the human being to maturity, he turns to an account of those
life processes in the body that must be maintained to preserve physical health.
He discusses the digestive and circulatory systems with considerable medical
detail. Many organs are mentioned, but it is their functions that he emphasizes
here, so the poem retains the quality of movement with which it began.

Exactly in the middle of the poem, he stops his physiological descriptions and
asks, "Was ist die Seel? " As we saw earlier, Leinker wishes to view the human
creature as a totality and this question is quite pertinent. He briefly discusses the
religious view of the soul, but then turns to a purely secular account of the
powers of the soul:

Die Seele, schliesst, begreift und dichtet,
Sie sucht, verwirft, verknüpft und trennt,
Sie hoft und fürcht, merkt und verrichtet,
Das alles was man Leben nennt,
Sie zehlt, vergleicht und stellt in Bildern,
Sich alles recht und lebhaft vor,
Sie weis die Fabel schön zu schildern,
Sie drängt sich in des Pindus Chor, . . . (95)

In other words, the soul is the sum total of its rational, emotional and
imaginative powers. He digresses for a few pages to talk of the alterations in the
human soul caused by different environments and cultures:

Ja, welchen Einfluss in die Gaben
Soll nicht des Himmels heitres Licht
In den und jenem Grade haben?
Welch Unterscheid entsteht da nicht?

Sind hier nicht Gegenden zu nennen?
Ein jedes Volk nehrt seine Art,
Hier läst sich die Natur erkennen,
Die doppelt giebt indem sie spart. (96)

The last two lines are most interesting. It is nature's way, he says, to be lavish and thrifty at the same time. Presumably he means that nature has been thrifty in creating one human nature, every soul having the same capacities; nature's lavishness then lies in the variety of human types caused by the many different social, cultural and geographical possibilities. Indeed, his quest for a total picture of his subject, man, led him quite naturally to these anthropological considerations.

To make this point he had told some history, that is, he had exercised the soul's capacity for memory. With this comment he returns from his digression to a discussion of the soul's powers. A consideration of its rational capacity leads him back to the body, specifically the brain, and the five senses.

His next step is a quick survey of the most important organs and parts of the body. Here he is not interested in a specific system but rather in giving a picture of the body's mechanism as a whole. This leads him to the familiar thought that nature's wisdom and art as seen in the human body should be and are a model for man's art and technology:

Was Wunder, wenn der Geist im Bauen,
Pracht, Zierrat, Ordnung, Weisheit liebt,
Nachdem sein eigenes Beschauen,
Sein Leib dazu ihm Anlas giebt?
Gleichwie zu Rhodos an Colossen
Ein Wunderwerk der Welt entsprossen. (122)

Man quite naturally, he maintains here, will find in his own constructions an order and wisdom since these are so much a part of his very being.

He concludes the poem on anything but a cheerful note. Sickness, old age, and death are his final themes and they are quite appropriate to the subject of the poem, for the human body is subject to all three. After demonstrating throughout most of the poem the greatness and wisdom of the human body, he concludes with a strong reminder of man's frailty and mortality. Nevertheless, with his emphasis on the positive aspects of nature, the wisdom and self-sustaining qualities of the body, he demonstrates the new bold attitude toward nature and human nature.

Although Leinker sticks strictly to his subject matter, the work is more than a dry didactic poem. To be sure, it is didactic; it conveys much scientific material. Yet he manages to avoid a monotonous enumeration of facts. His material is presented with the enthusiasm as if he were telling a fable or singing of heroic deeds. Yet there are no dramatic episodes interspersed in his verse, no elaborate images. It has a poetic quality that is appropriate to didactic poetry. He gives us the world and man; he does not simply tell us about them, he shows them as real things as they move and grow. At the same time as a scientist he gives a deeper view and insight into the world about us and within us. Thus, he fulfills his promises to sing of the world and of man with the aid of the Muse of poetry and the spirit of science.

As an example of good didactic poetry, Leinker's work deserves mention if not in the histories of literature, then in publications devoted specifically to the eighteenth century, or to the Enlightenment like Willy Vontobel's[4] or L.L. Albertsen's[5] on didactic poetry. Yet it receives no mention at all, and of the reference works only Jöcher,[6] and Meusel[7] discuss his life and works.

---

[4] *Von Brocken bis Herder* (Bern, 1942).
[5] *Das Lehrgedicht* (Aarhus, 1961).
[6] Christian Gottlieb Jöcher, *Allgemeines Gelehrten-Lexicon* (Leipzig, 1750–1819).
[7] Johann Georg Meusel, *Lexicon der vom Jahr 1750 bis 1800 verstorbenen teutschen Schriftsteller,* Vol. 8, (Leipzig, 1802).

18. Friedrich Carl Casimir Freiherr von Creuz (1724—1770)

Friedrich Carl Casimir Freiherr von Creuz is one of the poets around the middle of the eighteenth century who was over-shadowed by the greats that followed and was soon forgotten. Undoubtedly Herder's extremely negative evaluation of Creuz' poetic talent contributed to his neglect by literary historians.[1] At the very least, his cosmological poem, "Lucrezische Gedanken," should earn him a better place in the history of German literature. One recent critic, Adalbert Elschenbroich, passes a very positive judgment on this poem when he says, "Hier führt der erlebnisechte Ausdruck vorfaustischer Elemente weit über die Aufklärung hinaus."[2] For our topic, an examination of his poetry is quite rewarding.

He was born in Homburg vor der Höhe into an old aristocratic family. In his youth he received a classical education from tutors, but in many fields he was self-taught. In 1746 the landgrave of Hessen-Homburg appointed him his Privy Councillor, and he represented the House of Homburg in many juridical matters. His love of learning won him membership in the Berlin academy as well as in the royal academies in Mannheim and Munich. His publications included philosophic and juridical works as well as poetry. His odes and poems came out in several editions in 1750, 1752, and 1753; in 1760 he published "Die Gräber", and in 1769 his collected poems appeared.[3]

I shall first examine the scientific themes in his odes and smaller poems. I have used the 1769 edition in which these poems appear unchanged from the 1753 edition, with the exception of a few explanatory comments and footnotes added in the later edition.

In "Die Gottheit" there is the familiar theme of the vastness of the universe which only God can encompass. We who are limited by our senses and narrow perspective cannot measure the number of suns which are like drops in the sea that is God. When we look at the many vast worlds about us, then we realize how incomprehensibly small our own globe is. Beyond the worlds visible to us we must also consider those millions more within the realm of possibility:

Aber, wann wir uns auch gleich
Dieses All vor Augen stellten;
Sind noch Millionen Welten
In der Möglichkeiten Reich: (I, 7)

In the same poem God's works on a small scale are also considered. When the poet looks at the variety of creatures about him, he sees at every glance in the

[1] *Sämmtliche Werke,* hrsg. von Bernhard Suphan (Berlin, 1877—1913), Vol. 5, pp. 290—303.
[2] *Neue Deutsche Biographie,* Band III (Berlin, 1956), pp. 413—414.
[3] *Oden und andere Gedichte,* 2 Bände (Frankfurt, 1769).

smallest creature a world of masterpieces. He also marvels at the images of all the many objects, infinitely small on the retina of the eyes which permit us, however, to see them according to their true sizes.

In "Philosophische Betrachtungen" the poet extols reason by whose power our spirit lifts itself above the surface of the earth and explores the heavens, traveling from world to world. In considering our world he reflects on the abundance which is prevalent everywhere and which makes it God's masterpiece. Amidst this bountifulness the arts flourish when man becomes aware of the artistic design in nature:

> Hier seh ich, wie ein Bau nach Regeln prächtig steiget,
> Wann dort mir ein Gemähld in Licht und Schatten zeiget,
> Wie glüklich die Natur den kühnen Pinsel führt. (I, 12)

In "Das Glück des Weisen" he gives us the picture of a wise man who is steadfast even when the orbit of the earth begins to grow shorter with the expectation that soon only the smoke of what once was the earth will fill empty space:

> Wann unsrer Erde Kreis einst wird der kürzste seyn,
> Wann sie der Sonn am nächsten kömmt,
> Und wann den leeren Raum, in dem der Weltbau schwimmt,
> Des Weltbaus Rauch erfüllen wird: (I, 18)

This is a reference to the final conflagration whose immediate, natural cause will be a slowing down of the earth's orbit, thereby eventually forcing it to plunge into the sun.

In "Der Tod" he speculates about the contrast between our knowledge before and after death. While we live, we see worlds rotating according to eternal laws and we see the inexpressible treasures of nature's wealth. Yet our lives are subject to accident and error. Our reason stumbles amidst error and uncertainty:

> Hier wankt, hier schwebet der Verstand
> In irrthumsreichen Labyrinthen;
> Sucht bald Begriffe zu verbinden;
> Trennt bald, die, so er kaum verband. (I, 32)

Yet once death has destroyed what life we have, then the spirit will move swiftly to inevitable conclusions, unencumbered by preconceptions:

> Doch dort, wo unter meinen Füssen
> Sich tausend Wirbel wälzend drehn:
> Dort, wird den Geist in seinen Schlüssen
> Kein Vorurtheil mehr hintergehn. (I, 32)

In "Frühlingsgedanken" Damon invites Thyrsis to contemplate nature where even a blade of grass is a mirror of the divine. Supported by science the two will pursue wisdom and will be led by the creature to the creator:

> Die Wissenschaft nährt uns mit reinster Freude;
> In unsern Zwek mengt sich kein Ehrgeiz ein.
> Hier suchen wir der Weisheit nachzuspühren,
> Und das Geschöpf soll uns zum Schöpfer führen! (I, 61)

"Die Zukunft" takes up the problem of the limitation of time to which man is subject and which thus limits his knowledge. In the flux of time all the vaunted achievements of our intellect are insignificant:

> Rühmt nicht, Verwegene! den zweiflenden Verstand,
> Der in der ungemessnen Ferne,
> Durch unzählbar bewohnte Sterne,
> Sich eine neue Bahn erfand; (I, 80)

We think that man with his soaring intellect, as exemplified by the Newtonian system, has discovered the laws of the universe. But in time this system, too, will be replaced by another better one:

> Zu thöricht stolz sind wir für unsre Schranken,
> Selbst die erhabensten Neutonischen Gedanken,
> Die übers Ziel der Menschheit gehn,
> Erzittern ist vielleicht vorm Urtheil grössrer Meister, (I, 81)

Our knowledge is confined by our condition here on earth, and we see only a small part of vast space and measure everything according to our limited perspective:

> Wir, tief-versenktes Volk, erkennen kaum
> Den kleinsten Theil vom ungeheuren Raum,
> Und unsre Wissenschaft misst sich nach unsrer Erde. (I, 81)

Thus, hardly knowing the present, we are in no position to conceive of possible creations in the future.

The poem concludes with a familiar theme:

> Du, grosser Bayle! giengst vorm grössern Leibniz her;
> Der keinem wich; Du, Newton! bist nicht mehr,
> Und um Euch werden einst noch grössre Schüler trauren;
> Ihr aber werdet dort die Ewigkeit durchdauren;
> Und seht nunmehr, da wir durch dicke Nebel sehn,
> In vollem Licht die Pracht des Unaussprechlichen,
> Und, in der Tieffe ganz verlohren,
> Den Irrstern unter Euch, der Euch gebohren. (I, 82)

The wise men of our time, who sought to penetrate the veil, now see clearly the inexpressible which we can only surmise in our present circumstances.

In the author's introduction to the poem "An die Dichtkunst", in the 1769 edition, he states his philosophy of poetry which is not unrelated to our topic. The essence of true poetry, he maintains, lies in showing us the world in such a way that great inspirations and elevated thoughts are evoked in us. We must learn our art in the school of nature where we are taught quite differently from our schools: "In der Natur selbst hängt alles ohne Sprung zusammen; aber die unterrichtende Natur überspringt in ihrem Vortrage, um mich so auszudrücken, vieles, um uns weiter fortzuhelfen. Noch ehe Städte und Schlösser waren, hatte die Natur sie schon auf Steinen gezeichnet. Wälder, Felsen und selbst Organen, als förmlich gebildete Augen, malet sie uns vor. Dichtet sie also nicht selbst? Die von der Natur selbst gemachten Auszüge ihrer Werke verdienten eine grössere Aufmerksamkeit" (I, 90). Nature herself is the artist, and by studying the design in nature's works we study nature's art.

In the poem "Die Einsamkeit" there is reference made to the current speculations concerning the changes that have taken place on the surface of the globe since earliest times. The wise man who searches for the truth in solitude concerns himself, among other things, with the presumed fiery origin of the earth and concludes from fossil remains that vast changes have taken place on our planet since the creation:

Und in die tiefste Zeit senkt er den ernsten Blik;
Dass einst die Welt gebrannt, entdekt er dort die Spuren;
Verwundernd geht er von versteinerten Figuren
Bis in dein altes Bett, verseztes Meer, zurük. (I, 139)

In another poem, "In einer stillen Nacht", he again considers the protean quality of nature on our planet as indicated by the changes of sea and earth:

Sehn wir nicht selbst des Meers Gebiete
Verrükt, und manchen Stern nicht mehr? (I, 167)

Yet not only our planet is subject to perpetual change. It is nature's way constantly to destroy and to create the new from the old.

Seht sie an neuen Welten zimmern;
Wie klug sie ihr Geschäft verkürzt,
Zum neuen Bau braucht sie die Trümmern
Der Welten, die sie niederstürzt. (I, 167)

This view was certainly supported by the scientific thought of the time, as is indicated by the above reference to stars that we no longer see. For if stars, that is, suns are created and destroyed, then that is the case with entire solar systems.

I shall now consider the scientific themes in Creuz' longer poems, "Die

Gräber", "Versuch vom Menschen" and "Lucrezische Gedanken", of which the last is especially pertinent to our study.

"Die Gräber", as the title suggests, has death as its central theme. Of the many images of death and variations on the theme we shall consider only those that contain some scientific material.

One lament which occurs frequently in poetry of this time and which we find in the poem now under consideration is the unsubstantiality of reason and scientific knowledge:

> Ja, die Vernunft hat mir zu sehr geheuchelt;
> Die Wissenschaft hat mir zu viel geschmeichelt;
> Die Wahrheit find ich nicht, die ich gesucht!
> Und grössre Zweiffel sind des Demonstrirens Frucht. (II, 109)

Death is an important factor in the unreliability of human knowledge, for the greatest minds are subject to its power:

> Vom Leibniz, welch ein Geist! ein Geist fast ohne Schranken,
> Von Newtons göttlichen Gedanken,
> Was bleibt uns? Ach, der Aschen dunkler Rest! (II, 108)

Later on in the poem there is a scene reminiscent of the appearance of the "Erdgeist" in Goethe's *Faust*. A wandering pilgrim, searching for the truth rests at a graveyard. Disturbed by the restless spirits of departed souls, he implores God to set them at rest. The "Geist der Welt" answers him:

> Ich bin der Geist der Welt, des Schöpfers Meisterstücke!
> Thier, Pflanzen, alles wird durch mich bewegt, belebt,
> Durch mich wächst euer Schaz, den ihr in Schachten hebt:
> Die Ströme theil ich aus nach Norden und nach Süden;
> Dreh eure Kugel um, und geb euch Krieg und Frieden. (II, 131)

The spirit concludes with the promise that the seeker's questions will be answered as soon as he crosses the threshold. It is interesting to note that although this spirit of the world is spoken of as God's creation, he speaks with such authority of his function as sustainer of nature and human fate that he could almost be considered a lesser deity governing the events of this globe in particular. From this, it is, of course, only a small step to a pantheistic position in which the spirit would be considered a personification of and identical with nature itself.

A theme which was already found in the shorter poems, namely, colossal changes on the surface of the earth due to natural cataclysms, occurs here also:

> Manch weites Land ist längst der Wellen Grund und Siz:
> An ehmals Thürmen und Palästen,

Versenket nun im blauen Ocean,
Hängt sich ein Muschelheer, gleich als an Felsen, an. (II, 140)

Immediately after this he reminds us that the earth has witnessed such enormous changes from its earliest times:

O reich an Scenen und Veränderungen
Warst du, o Welt, schon jung des Schiksals Trauerspiel!
Noch hattest du dem Nichts dich glücklich kaum entschwungen,
Als schon —— o welch ein kurzes Ziel!
Durch grässliche Erschütterungen
Deine stärksten Adern sprungen,
Tausend Fluten dich durchdrungen,
Und in sich selbst dein Bau, noch unvollführt, zerfiel! (II, 140—141)

This is a reference to Noah's Flood with an attempt to provide an explanation of the natural causes involved. The reference to the collapse of the yet incomplete structure of the planet and the bursting forth of subterranean waters suggests the theories of Burnet.

The theme of constant change in nature occurs again in this poem, though this time the sustaining aspect of change rather than its destructive aspect is emphasized:

So muss stets etwas untergehn,
Und so kan eines nur durchs andere bestehn.
So nähren Flüsse sich von Dünsten aus den Meeren,
Die Meere können sich nicht ohne Flüsse nähren;
Die Erde trinkt den Thau; die Sonne zieht ihn auf;
So ist der Dinge Lauf; die Welt, in der ich lebe,
Ein penelopisches Gewebe,
Ein zauberischer Zirkellauf. (II, 144)

All natural phenomena are interrelated and interdependent. The phrase, "ein penelopisches Gewebe", again reminds of Goethe's "Erdgeist" who weaves the fabric of nature.

He continues by suggesting that death itself belongs to this pattern in which there is no destruction but only metamorphosis:

Und Scenen der Verwandlungen
Sind hier natürlich und gemein:
Wie mancher Geist hat sich vielleicht dem Grab entschwungen, . . . (II, 145)

This image, so popular with poets of the 18th century, is quite appropriate at this point in the poem in that death is considered like just another natural phenomena, a part of the "zauberischer Zirkellauf". Death is not understood as a final alienation from nature, as the atheists would have it, nor as something supernatural, but as a transitional process totally within the sphere of nature. The image does not demand faith nor claim to be demonstrable truth; it requires an extension of the known processes of nature from the seen to the unseen.

Creuz' "Versuch vom Menschen" is a didactic poem in two books, the first of which appeared in 1760 with the first edition of "Die Gräber" and the second in the 1769 edition of the collected poems here used as our text. In this poem man's nature and function are considered first within the context of nature and secondly within the context of society which he creates to serve his ends. Our task again is to select and evaluate the scientific themes and reflections.

Creuz like many of his contemporaries refused to grant a fundamental difference between man and other living forms as the philosophic and religious traditions had taught for so long. There is even similarity between man and the plants:

> Ich war der Pflanze gleich; unfriedsam mit dem Raum,
> Erweitert sie ihn stets, und dähnet sich zum Baum.
> Wie wenig findet uns Malpighi unterschieden? (II, 158)

And further on he explains human sensation with an image taken from plant life:

> Ein Saft, wie Äther fein, steigt in der Nerven Röhren,
> Giebt Geist dem Aug zum Sehn, dem Ohr Gefühl zum Hören. (II, 158)

Between the animals and human bodies there are even greater similarities. When he says "Beim Menschen heissts die Hand; beim Elephant der Rüssel" (II, 162), he implies that a comparison of these two structures reveals such similarity of function that we can put them on the same plane. Or again when he says, "Dort heisst Geruch, Gehör, und hier Gefühl, Gesicht" (II, 162) he means that animals have senses which perform for them the same functions which ours do for us. In other words, physiologically we belong to the animal kingdom. He returns to this theme in the second book:

> Nun gönne, stolzer Mensch, den Thieren einen Blik!
> Ein ihnen härtres bald, bald günstiger Geschik.
> Hat sie nicht blos für dich um deinen Stamm gewunden:
> Dich, sie und Pflanzen hat hier gleicher Zwek verbunden. (II, 190)

It is a reiteration that plants, animals and man belong to the same domain of living creatures and share the same lot.

Another interesting theme in this poem is a variation on a familiar theme, namely, nature the craftsman who destroys and builds with a neutral indifference to the fate of the individual:

Es kostet die Natur des Körpers Meisterstücke
Nur eine Hand voll Erd, und wenig Augenblicke.
Was wunder, wenn sie uns, dem Wurm nicht minder hart,
In ihrem Überfluss, wie ihn, gleich wenig spart. (II, 174)

Man is a simple and fragile creation of nature, produced in such abundance, as is the worm, that we can truly say our life does not have much value. Nature herself, hidden from view, works incessantly building up and tearing down:

Sie sizt beschäftigt stets, wo sie kein Auge schauet,
In ihrer Werkstatt still, reisst nieder, fügt und bauet. (II, 174)

And yet, there is hope that nature prepares a new future for man:

Was hoff ich hier, wo ich ein Thier gleich andern bin?
Ihr Schmetterling schwebt mir stets lehrreich vor dem Sinn. (II, 174)

Here again, the image of the butterfly suggests a future for man only seemingly supernatural, but actually in accordance with the natural that is apparent to us even now.

In the second part of our poem the poet turns to the role of the sciences in the life of man. He chides man for thinking that the victory of reason over superstition has also given us certain knowledge:

Der Gottheit Grösse selbst, im kleinsten ausgezogen,
Ist längst bestimmt, gezählt, gemessen und gewogen.
Frei, nach Natur gedacht, was wurde nicht entdekt,
Als uns kein Geist mehr lehrt, und kein Gespenst mehr schrekt?
Wann Neuton die Natur vor eurem Aug entblöste;
So wisst, dass er zugleich Johannis Rähtseln löste! (II, 181)

We claim to know with our natural reason the highest things. Newtonian science, which has enlightened us about nature, claims also to reveal the true meaning of religion, undoubtedly an allusion to the many attempts to harmonize between the new science and the Bible. Yet all this is merely illusion:

Geteuschter Sterblicher! Du giebst ein ganzes Leben
Für eine Fabel hin, wann Thoren sie erheben,
Noch bist du klüger nicht, als in der ersten Zeit,
Wo ihrer Kindheit noch die Erde sich erfreut. (II, 181)

He compares our knowledge to the onions at the Nile which once were holy:

Die Zwiebel, die vordem am Nilstrom heilig war,
Stellt uns vielleicht ein Bild verhüllter Wahrheit dar.
Entwickeln lernen wir, und beim Entwickeln pralen;
Was aber lösen wir, als Schaalen nur von Schaalen?

Ins innerste Gefühl hüllt sich die Wahrheit ein.
Und ein erklärtes Wort darf noch nicht Wahrheit seyn. (II, 181—182)

All our enlightenment deals only with the exteriors which we can peel off one by one without getting to the essence. The following is another variation on the same theme:

Welch Vorzug bleibet euch, ihr Kinder hoher Sterne
Ihr Weisen, die auch ich nun näher kennen lerne!
Ihr rechnet, und ihr misst — Doch nichts zum Unterscheid!
Ihr kennet die Natur — Ihr Innres nicht; ihr Kleid. (II, 183)

The wise men, the scientists who measure and count, know only the outer garment of nature but never its true being.

This pessimism about science's capacity to bring man to the truth leads him to the position that the only justification of science is in its practical and utilitarian aspect:

Sorgt für das Wollenvieh! Gebt acht auf eure Saaten!
Seyd Weib und Kindern treu, und glaubt, auch dies sind Thaten!
Ein wenig Kunst für Noht, ein Denken ohne Zwang.
Der Erde Schichtenlag, der Wasser Fall und Gang,
Des Wetters Wechselspiel, die Würkung wenig Kräuter
Sey eure Wissenschaft, so wie der Himmel heiter.
So klar, wie euer Bach! Mit unverwirrtem Hirn,
Und nach der Nohtdurft nur betrachtet das Gestirn. (II, 194)

Such an approach to science discourages any theorizing about nature which is divorced from practical application. Investigation of natural phenomena is encouraged only if it provides the necessities of human life and promotes the welfare of human society.

Finally, there is Creuz' most interesting poem, namely, his "Lucrezische Gedanken", which is dated 1763—1764 (199) in the 1769 edition. The poem consists of five sections, the first of which is entitled "Vermischte Betrachtungen" and deals with the transitoriness of all things. The second and third sections are entitled "Ursprung der Dinge", and the fourth and fifth, "Die Seele", and have as their subject matter what those titles indicate. Roughly speaking, these sections do correspond in subject matter to those of Lucretius' poem which also deals with the transitoriness of all things, the creation of the cosmos and the qualities of the soul. However, where the latter does present a philosophic and scientific system, worked out in considerable detail, namely that of Epicurus, our poet does not, as he admits in a revealing foreword to the poem: "Die Absicht des Verfassers ist gar nicht, ein Lucrezisches Lehrgebäude zu liefern; er will nur sonst in Lucrezischem Geschmacke dichten. Was in diesem

Gedichte auch nach des Verfassers eigner Meinung philosophisch unrichtig ist, dieses kan poetisch richtig seyn, und die Freiheit, welche die alten Dichter gehabt haben, sich Götter und Göttinnen zu erdenken, und Schöne in Inseln zu verwandeln, haben wir in der Wahl falscher Hypothesen, welche die geschik-testen sind, eine poetische Tracht anzunehmen." (II, 200)

The false hypotheses of which Creuz speaks may be those he used in the sections entitled "Ursprung der Dinge" to explain the creation of the cosmos and the evolution of life; hypotheses, which, of course, are of interest to us. In the last two sections, those on the soul, he departs from Lucretius as he, himself, says, "Lucrez ich kann dein Schüler nicht mehr werden!" (II, 217), for here he considers the soul as separate and distinct from the body.

But let us return to the beginning and see what scientific material he used. Typical of the first section and pertinent to our topic are the following lines on the transitoriness of all things:

Nichts bleibt, wie's war — Hier stürzen Alpen nieder,
Und Andes stehn in einer Nacht gegründt;
Hier war einst Meer, und Sterne kommen wieder
Vom Pol herfür, wo sie verschwunden sind. (II, 202)

Here are three themes which occur repeatedly in our period: the sudden creation and destruction of mountains, the replacement of sea by land and the creation and destruction of stars. At this point, at any rate, he is sceptical of any scientific theories that have been devised to explain these phenomena:

Ach, die Natur misskennt erfundne Sätze,
Der Kunst Geburt, und falscher Weisen Traum!
Sie höret nicht der Schule stolz Geschwätze:
Sie geht vorbei, und hört den Leibniz kaum. (II, 203)

In other words, nature's purpose and design with these enormous phenomena have not yet been fathomed by the ingenuity of man.

In the second section, that is, the first part of "Ursprung der Dinge", he focuses on the primeval beginnings of the creation:

O, was geht vor? Wie plözlich? Was geschieht?
Die Stäubgen, die sich dort im Wirbel drehen,
Ziehn wild sich an — Die grösste Kugel glüht! (II, 206)

At the beginning of creation, then, there is the operation of a Newtonian attraction rather than the chance swerving of an atom as in Lucretius. Nature then begins to weave (207) her fabric, and in the whole vastness of creation the ocean is but a drop, the constellation Sirius a mere spark and entire galaxies a simple cloud (207). We, with the aid of Newton's calculations, can now see the balance in nature's works:

Nun muss man selbst dort, wo ein hohes Wesen
Dem Mond befielt: Mond sey des Wandrers Licht,
Im Himmel selbst des Neutons Ziffern lesen,
Und man spricht dort von seinem Gleichgewicht. (II, 207)

The third section, that is, the second part of "Ursprung der Dinge" is devoted to the creation and evolution of living forms. He begins with chaos:

Im Anfang war stets Chaos, immer Wüste;
Da bildet sich zulezt ein wahres Thier,
Schwebt auf dem Meer, der Monster Schaugerüste,
Stirbt, formt sich um, und kömmt ganz neu herfür.
Ihm nachgeformt sieht man sich Junge rühren,
Und aus dem Leib, indem er berstet, gehn.
In Polypen lässt von chaotschen Thieren
Noch die Natur die dunklen Spuren sehn. (II, 209)

This is undoubtedly part of the material the poet had in mind when he apologized in the foreword for opinions which are philosophically false but poetically appropriate. There is no mention here of God's act of creation. Life was created in the sea and there underwent formations and transformations which brought forth new forms. The polyps, so frequently cited by the poets, are here noted as vestiges of this early period of creation out of chaos. These living forms continued to be formed until they find their way out of the water on to the land, where they then remain fixed as species:

Doch endlich sezt ein allgemeiner Friede
Die Grenze fest, und die Natur hält Wort: (II, 209)

Now the land to which the creatures come is not yet the firm land we know; it is more plastic, more suited to complete the creation begun in the sea:

Noch weich, noch nicht befestigt mit Gefilden,
Doch reizender, als wie des Meeres Bett,
Geschikt, ein Thier vollkommner auszubilden,
Voll Lebensöhl, und fruchtbarn Leim und Fett. (II, 209)

The theory that the land itself was not yet fully formed, not yet in the final form in which we find it now is interesting. In part it suggests Burnet's theory of the earth before the deluge, when the surface of the globe was a thin crust composed of oil and dust particles. Burnet's theory differs in other respects, but they share the thought of an original earth, different from the one which we now inhabit.

Shortly afterwards the Whistonian system is also mentioned. In discussing the sperms, he insists that they did not exist from the beginning of time and that the body which produces them is prior in existence. As evidence he cites the Whistonian theory of creation and the deluge:

> Wie hätt es auch dem Schiksal trotzen können,
> Das Körpergen, das dir der Saame heisst?
> Sieht Whiston nicht den ganzen Erdball brennen,
> Und wie die Glut ihn von einander reisst?
> Hier überschwemmt, geborsten, dort gesprenget — —
> Erschreckend Bild! So war der Erde Loos!
> Dein Saamenkorn — Blieb das nur unversenget?
> Wie riss es sich verfolgt von Fluten los? (II, 210)

According to Whiston the earth was originally a comet which became a burning molten mass due to its close passage past the sun. The deluge in turn was caused by a comet, which through its proximity to the earth, by power of its gravitational pull, forced the waters within the earth to break through the firm crust and thereby flood the land.

This section on the origin of things concludes with a plea for a proper understanding of the place of animals in nature:

> Die Thiere stehn, wie wir, auf einer Leiter,
> Und, was sie sind, das waren wir vielleicht; (II, 211)

It is difficult to assess how Creuz understood this daring thought, that what the animals now are we once were. It seems to imply a transformation of the species in the course of time. At any rate, it is clear that the author does intend with this thought to remind man of the common ground he shares with the animals.

In the final two sections on the soul, there is a significant shift of emphasis. In the earlier sections the malleability of nature's creation in primeval times was in constant view. But now:

> Das Meer ist nun mit Erd und Luft im Frieden;
> Der Sonne wird ihr Kreis nicht mehr verrükt:
> Der Stoff, gezählt, gewogen, abgeschieden,
> Ist nun nicht mehr zum Schaffen gleich geschikt. (II, 212)

The earth and indeed the entire solar system have been stabilized. Matter also is no longer as subject to alteration; all is now according to measure and proportion. But even more, the species have been stabilized:

> Nur selten sehn wir neue Thiere werden,
> Wie die, die einst im Chaos sich gebildt.
> Die Arten stehn, wie Felsen, fest auf Erden,
> Ganz von der Kraft der Schöpfung angefüllt. (II, 212)

These are most significant lines. They imply that the ladder of creation was at one point in a formative state in which new species were created and previously created ones could undergo further changes. Now, however, the species are fixed and presumably will remain so until the final conflagration. This theme is repeated several times indicating the author's sense of its importance:

Das alte Meer, ganz voll von Lebenssäften,
Ist nicht das Meer, dem jezt sein Ziel gesezt. (II, 215)

Or again:

Noch stunden nicht die Oceanschen Mauren,
Die Alpen und die Pyrenäen nicht;
Noch war die Welt, Jahrtausende zu dauren,
Nicht fest genug in Angeln eingericht. (II, 215)

That these mountain ranges are a later creation again suggests Burnet's theory. That the earth in its earliest stage was not at an oblique angle to the sun, but was entirely equidistant from the sun was maintained by Burnet, Whiston as well as many others.

The final shift in emphasis is away from a scientific knowledge of nature to a knowledge of the soul of man, which is separate and distinct from the body. Scientific knowledge of nature is now disparaged:

Doch rechnet nur die Schritte der Planeten,
Des Mondes Nacht, der Sterne Finsternis!
Die Wiederkunft der streiffenden Cometen
Seht kühn voraus, und niemals ungewiss!
Dies ist nicht mehr, als wann auf seine Triften
Ein Storch voraus die Flocken fallen sieht, (II, 217)

Knowledge of self, the spiritual nature of man, now becomes the highest goal for man. Here, of course, he must part company from Lucretius, for whom the soul is no more than the functions of the body:

Lucrez, ich kan dein Schüler nicht mehr werden!
Ich find in uns zu viele Wesenheit.
Verzeiht auch mir, ihr Messer unsrer Erden,
Eucliden und Cartesen unsrer Zeit!
Bewundernd seh ich Ziffern und Figuren,
Und wie der Wiz Beweis und Lehrsaz fund;
Ich aber geh auf zugeschwemmten Spuren,
Von meinem Ich such ich den wahren Grund. (II, 217)

Also Newton, who is the main source of his perspective of nature, is pitied for his lack of self-knowledge:

Ach, dass er nicht, den wir unsterblich nennen,
Dass Neuton nicht dein grosses Wesen fand!
Ach, dass er stirbt, und ohne sich zu kennen,
Die Erde misst an ihrem lezten Rand:
Die Polen mass, und auf dem falschen Meere,
Dem Schiffer nun die Wege sichrer macht,
Und ach, sein Geist, der bis zum Sternenheere
Sich prächtig schwung, blieb von ihm unbetracht! (II, 222–223)

Although scientific knowledge is not rejected, the author certainly suggests the incongruity involved in man's extraordinary efforts to know his environment as compared to his neglect of his own self.

He concludes the poem with thoughts of the final conflagration which, consistent with his earlier approach, he explains according to natural causes; namely, the gradual approachment of the earth to the sun which, he maintains, has already been noted by the astronomers:

Es merken schon der Sterne hohe Seher
Den Untergang, zu dem der Erdball reift,
Zwar langsam, doch rükt er der Sonne näher,
Wann Kält und Eis sich unterm Nordpol häuft. (II, 224)

Now that the author's works have been surveyed individually for scientific material, let us summarize the major themes.

His attitude toward science itself is one theme that has frequently occurred. We are struck by his sceptical, even negative, evaluation of the sciences. In "Der Tod" reason is seen as subject to error. In "Die Zukunft" he cautions man from taking too much pride in the achievements of reason for even "die erhabensten Neutonischen Gedanken" are not true for all time but will soon be replaced. In the same poem man is the "tief versenktes Volk" whose narrow perspective limits his science. In "Die Gräber" reason and science are accused of deception in that they promise answers but deliver only more doubts. In "Versuch vom Menschen" scientists are chided for exceeding their limits by seeking even to explain the Bible with their fables. Science, he maintains, can never get to the essence and scientists would serve humanity best by confining themselves to practical applications. In "Lucrezische Gedanken" scientific knowledge is viewed with suspicion and disparaged for its inability to provide self-knowledge. It is only in death, as we saw in "Der Tod" and in "Die Zukunft", that the answers to the problems sought in vain by scientists here, will be revealed. By contrast, it is only in his early poem "Frühlingsgedanken" that he praises the scientific study of nature, but there only in the conventional praise of God in nature.

This on the whole suspicious attitude toward the sciences does not, however, deter him from assimilating a good bit of current scientific speculation into his own thinking. This is especially true in his reflections on cosmogony and eschatology, where he follows many of his contemporaries in seeking natural causes for events that traditionally belonged to Revelation. Already in the shorter poems there were references to the fiery origin of the world and to the cataclysms that took place prior to the completion of creation. In the longer poems this theme receives further treatment. In "Die Gräber" we are reminded of the upheavals of land and sea of earliest times such as the deluge in Noah's times. In "Lucrezische Gedanken", in his account of the creation, we found references and allusions to theories of Newton, Burnet, and Whiston, and speculations about the the malleability of the species in prehistoric times. As far as final things are concerned, in "Der Tod" and in "Lucrezische Gedanken", the final conflagration is pictured as caused by a gradual shortening of the earth's orbit about the sun, which again is an attempt to give a natural explanation for what hitherto had been an article of faith.

Related to this theme is the representation of nature as creator, sustainer, and destroyer of all things, almost as if it were an autonomous agent. On the one hand, nature's harmony makes it the model for the artist as in the forword to "An die Dichtkunst". Yet, on the other hand, "In einer stillen Nacht" shows us nature constantly destroying and building up with the ruins of destroyed worlds. In "Die Gräber" nature as sustainer of all things finds expression through the "Weltgeist", and nature's permanence amidst change is described as "ein penelopisches Gewebe", and again in "Versuch vom Menschen" we saw nature secluded in her workshop, tearing down and building up.

The ladder of nature and man's place on it also played an important role. With this image Creuz reminds his readers that man belongs to the same domain of living beings as plants and animals, that man is a part of nature.

Another theme which Creuz shares with his contemporaries is the worship of Newton. In "Die Zukunft" he speaks of "die erhabensten Neutonischen Gedanken", in "Die Gräber" it is Newtons "göttliche Gedanken" and in "Lucrezische Gedanken" we read "Newtons Ziffern" in the heavens. Even when the limitations of science are exposed, it is Newton who is taken as the best that science has to offer, as toward the end of "Lucrezische Gedanken" where Newton's lack of self-knowledge is decried.

Since this survey of Creuz' works has revealed such a variety of scientific themes, it is surprising that none of the critics who have examined his works mentioned this phase of the poet at all. They cover at length Creuz' position in regard to the philosophic, religious and psychological currents and controversies of the time, but seem to be oblivious to the fact that the sciences played such an important role in the thought of a man who was neither a professional nor even an amateur scientist.

19. Johann Jakob Dusch (1725–1787)

Johann Jakob Dusch was a pre-classical poet and critic who already in his lifetime was relegated into the background by the greater writers like Lessing and Herder. The histories of literature rarely mention him and those few publications that examine his works are not very revealing.[1] From the point of view of literary history several of his works are of value and deserve more careful attention. Our task, however, is to examine his treatment of scientific subject matter.

Dusch's best known didactic poem is "Die Wissenschaften".[2] It is a long poem in eight cantos each of which has a distinct theme. The first canto describes man in his primitive condition, in a state of nature. Man was ignorant and had no appreciation for the beauty and wisdom of nature. In this barbarous state there was no poetry or song, no love or friendship. In the second canto this misery is interrupted by the descent of the Muses. The lyrics of Orpheus, the tragedies of Sophocles and the epics of Homer awake in man new sentiments and virtues; art gives birth to humanity. In the process of discussing the humanizing effect of poetry, he gives a brief survey of lyric, dramatic and epic poetry from antiquity to the present. In the first two cantos, we thus have a secular history of man in his primitive and civilized circumstances.

In the next four cantos there is a presentation of "Weltweisheit", that is, the secular sciences. The presentation follows roughly the Wolffian system in that there is a theoretical part including logic, metaphysics and natural science in cantos three and four and a practical part including ethics and politics in cantos five and six. Canto seven has Revelation as its subject which as in the Wolffian system is the capstone of "Weltweisheit". Dusch briefly tells the history of man according to the Biblical story. In the last canto he praises the sciences and the enlightened society which permits them to flourish.

This is the general outline of the poem. An outstanding feature of the poem is the interweaving of history with the non-historical, formal philosophic system of Wolff. This is all the more striking since with all his interests Wolff entirely neglected the history of man, his arts and institutions.

Let us return to the fourth canto which deals entirely with the natural sciences, astronomy, natural history, physics. The canto opens with the appearance of astronomy:

---

1 Gustav Deicke's dissertation *Johann Jakob Dusch* (Strassburg i.E., 1910) is useful in its examination of Dusch's reception by his contemporaries. Yet he has avoided examining and explaining Dusch's most significant works. Vontobel, in his book on didactic poetry, charges that Dusch's work cannot be understood as "Selbstverwirklichung". That is true but beside the point.

2 *Vermischte Werke* (Jena, 1754), pp. 11–122.

Bewunderung im Gesichte, kam die Astronomie,
Ein Sehrohr in der Rechten, die Meskunst führte sie.
Ihr Geist misst ferne Welten, bezeichnet ihrer Reise
Der flüchtigen Bewegung unwandelbare Gleise.
Bis in den letzten Himmel hebt sie ihr Flug empor.
Sie zählet jedem Sterne des Umlaufs Schritte vor,
Giebt jedem die Gespielen, durchspannet ihre Weiten,
Weissaget Finsternissen, und theilt das Jahr in Zeiten. (49)

Astronomy surveys the heavens, measures the unchanging orbits of worlds far
away and predicts eclipses. Thereupon the author leaves the distant worlds and
turns his attention to earth, always fruitful, always rejuvenated. In describing the
qualities of the earth, he does not stress mathematical law and measurement as
before, but instead he sees in vegetation the plentitude and fruitfulness of
nature. He then begins a survey of the natural phenomena of the four elements.
In discussing the waters of the earth, he uses the analogy between the circulation
of the water of the earth with that of the blood in the body:

Doch wer hiess dein Gewässer unsichtbar Wege nehmen,
In Millionen Adern die Erde zu durchströmen?
Erstaunenswerthe Weisheit, die deinen Lauf regiert,
Und das, was du vergossen, in dich zurücke führt.
Ein stets sich gleicher Kreislauf im Kleinern, wie im Grössern,
Durchströmt mit Blut den Körper, die Erde mit Gewässern. (57)

In a footnote he raises the questions of the source of these waters, whether
they come through canals or because of rain, snow and dew. He leaves the
matter up to the reader and refers him to Pluche's *Schau-Platz der Natur*.

When discussing fire he turns to another popular interest of the time, namely,
that there are two sources of heat for man, the sun and the hot interior of the
earth:

O Flamme, reich an Wohlthun, doch mächtig zu zerstören,
Wie würde ohne Wärme der Erden Schoos gebähren?
Wer hätte seit der Stunde, wo sich die Welt gewälzt,
Die lange Nacht erleuchtet, ihr ewig Eis geschmelzt? (64)

As further proof of the interior source of heat, he discusses the devastating
fiery volcanoes. He also raises the controversy concerning light: "Nicht nur in
jenen Kreisen des Himmels eingeschlossen; / Das Licht ist allerorten rund um uns
ausgegossen" (63). Again in a footnote Dusch discusses the controversy over
whether light is a stream which perpetually flows out of the sun, the Newtonian
understanding, or whether there is a special light material which fills space and
which requires some motion for light to become visible to us. He cites Voltaire's

Eléments de la Philosophie de Newton as support of the first. He maintains, however, that as long as both are still hypotheses he is at liberty to choose between them and thus has adopted the second explanation.

He concludes this discussion of natural science with a typical expression of faith in the interrelatedness of all natural phenomena:

Erstaunlich die Verwandschaft des Grossen mit dem Kleinen!
Kom, zähle doch die Gaben, womit das Feld sich deckt;
Berechne die Geschöpfe vom Menschen zum Inseckt!
Durchschaue das Gefolge in Thieren, in den Pflanzen:
Kein Theil ist hier entbehrlich, und alle dient dem Ganzen.
In allem siehst du Nutzen, Kunst, und Zusammenhang. (67)

In other didactic poems an element of pessimism appears concerning human reason and the sciences. In the poem "Vernunft" (219—244) he maintains that reason is a much less reliable guide for man than the instincts are for the animals. To show the achievements of human reason he gives a brief history of philosophy from antiquity to modern times when Descartes and especially Bacon, Locke and Newton brought new insights:

Cartes zerreisst die Fesseln, die mancher schon genagt,
Er zweifelt, und sucht Gründe; er findet, und es tagt.
Der Weisheit Genius steigt aus des Moders Hügeln,
Und schüttelt mit Gewalt den Schulstaub von den Flügeln,
Ein Bakon, Lock, und Neuton ersetzt was noch gebricht;
Natur, Verstand, und Sitten und alles wurde Licht. (235)

At the same time, moderns like Descartes, Burnet and Whiston, in trying to explain everything, transcend the limitations of reason: "Was er [Descartes] mit Müh erschuf, das reisset Burnet nieder, / Zerstört die erste Welt, und baut die andre wieder. (238) He concludes that the practice of virtue is true rationality. In "Aberglauben, Glauben, Unglauben" (245—278) and "Der Weise" (311—322), he refers to the paradox of the scientist who knows so much about abstruse and distant things but so little about himself.

Dusch's *Schilderungen aus dem Reiche der Natur und der Sittenlehre*[3] is one of the most ambitious attempts to praise God in nature since Brockes' "physikalische und moralische Gedichte". The work has many precursors as Dusch himself admits in his preface. The division of the work according to the months of the year is clearly in imitation of Thomson's *Seasons*. James Hervey's *Meditations* was another one of his models. Yet he maintains that whereas Hervey seeks primarily to teach Christian morality from a contemplation of

---

[3] *Schilderungen aus dem Reiche der Natur und der Sittenlehre durch alle Monate des Jahres* (Hamburg and Leipzig, 1757—1760).

nature, he wishes to study nature for its own sake and lead his readers up the ladder of nature to God. He lists other poets and philosophers who have instructed as well as pleased their readers and thus have served as models for his work: Pluche, Réaumur, Fontenelle, Pope, Polignac, Kleist and Zachariä.

In the preface Dusch stresses the importance of the imagination in a description of nature. Because he wishes to appeal to the imagination he uses poetic prose in these essays about nature. Furthermore, since he is writing for the layman he has provided footnotes which clarify technical points. He warns that the scientist should not expect any new discoveries in this work and should read it only if he wishes to be entertained. The layman can expect both instruction and amusement.

Entirely in the Brockes tradition is the interest in astronomy which recurs throughout the text. Like so many of his contemporaries, Dusch delights in picturing our solar system with the planets revolving about the sun:

> Majestätisch dreht sich im Mittelpuncte jedes Sonnensystems, seine Seele, die Sonne; und um sie, von ihren Gespielen begleitet, die dunklen Planeten, alle vom Morgen zum Abend. Am nächsten um sie wandelt der einsame Merkur, und stufenweis folgen in weitern Kreisen, bis zum Saturn, die andern Planeten, die ihr Licht von der Sonne empfangen, mit ihren Gespielen. (Der April, 136)

He talks about these orbits not simply as dry technical facts but attempts to visualize the relative movements and distances of the heavenly bodies. For example, in comparing the orbit of the earth with that of Saturn, he says: "... und wenn sich die Erde bald zum neun und zwanzigstenmale durch ihren Cirkel gewälzet, fängt der Saturn erst zum zweytenmal an seinen jährlichen Lauf zu beschreiben." (Der April, 137). After the survey of this solar system, he directs his attention beyond it. To indicate the enormous distances involved, he compares the distances between the sun and its farthermost planet and between the sun and its nearest star. From there he turns to the millions of solar systems possibly inhabited by creatures of different degrees of perfections:

> Millionen von Sonnensystemen wälzen sich da, wohin noch kein bewaffnetes Auge geschauet hat, mit Geschöpfen bevölkert, die, vielleicht, von Stufe zu Stufe, sich der höchsten Vollkommenheit nähern." (Der April, 137)

Comets are also described according to modern astronomy as heavenly bodies with enormous yet calculable orbits and subject to the same gravitational force as the planets:

> Weit durch den hohen Äther, wo die Ferne und der Raum das Auge betrieget, und wo die Planeten ihren ordentlichen Lauf fortsetzen, nehmen sie ihren schnellen Lauf, doch nicht durch labyrinthische Wege, die keinem Gesetze

gehorchen, sondern in einer eccentrischen Bahn, nach einer untrüglichen Regel der anziehenden Kraft". (Der Jenner, 152)

The above statement about gravitational force is one of many references to the work of Isaac Newton. In one of his imaginative episodes, the author invokes Urania, the muse of astronomy. She had always taught men the mysteries of the heavens but only in recent times has she revealed through Newton truths unknown to the ancients: "Aber du hast späteren Zeiten die Geheimnisse vertraut, die jene nicht begreifen, und Newton, dein Liebling, wurde der Priester der Natur". (Der Jenner, 145).

He then enumerates the accomplishments of Newton, the priest of Nature:

Er öffnete den weiten Himmel, und wog dieses System in der Schaale. Er setzte die Gesetze der Bewegung der Sterne fest, und erklärte die Geheimnisse der Erscheinungen. . . . .

. . . .

Newton wies uns den Weg der feurigen Cometen, und nahm seinem flammenden Schweife die Schrecken, welche den abergläubischen Haufen der ältern Zeiten erschreckten. Er erklärte den feyerlichen Gang der Königin der Nacht, der silbernen Phöbe, der den Weisen der Alten dunkel blieb, und ihren Berechnungen sich nicht unterwerfen wollte. Von ihm lernte die Welt, mit was für Kräften der Mond in seiner Wanderschaft das weichende Meer drückt, dass seine Wogen bald ans Ufer schwellen, bald von den trocknen Küsten zurück treten. Er vertrieb die Wolken und erklärte, was der Gelehrte so lange vergebens gesucht hatte. (Der Jenner, 145–146)

By revealing these laws of the heavens, he continues, Newton is an even greater benefactor to man than those ancients who first instituted law and order in human society or those who invented writing and the arts. But not only the Newton of the *Principia* is celebrated, but also the Newton of the *Opticks:*

Aber siehe, der Geist des Newtons dringt in die heilige Nacht, die um ihre Werkstadt die geheime Natur gezogen, tiefer, als kein Sterblicher drang. Er fängt ein Gemische von Strahlen in sein künstliches Glas auf, spaltet das Chaos aus einander, und entdeckt die Farbe von jeglichem Strahle, der durch neue Gläser gebrochen, unveränderlich bleibt. Jeder hat seine eigene Farbe, und färbet den Körper verschieden, der ihn gebrochen in dein Auge zurück schickt. Also färbet die kommende Sonne den Schauplatz der Welt mit den Farben des Lichtes, das sie ihm sendet; und also empfindet der Mensch die Pracht der ganzen Natur. (Der April, 155)

Newton, the priest of nature, has discovered the secrets of nature in heaven and on earth. The extravagent statements about Newton's achievements are representative of the deification of the English scientist that had taken place in Europe by the middle of the century.

Another Englishman who receives Dusch's attention is Thomas Burnet, whose theory concerning the origin of mountains he rejects emphatically. In "Der May" he describes the beauties and uses of mountains and then turns with wrath to the theory of Burnet for whom mountains are primarily a reminder of Noah's flood: "Trauriger wandelt ein Burnet auf dem Rücken des Berges . . . und dünkt sich auf dem Raume der ersten Welt, zu wandeln, die der Zorn des Schöpfers in den Wellen des Weltmeers ersäufte". (Der May, 274). In a brief footnote Dusch gives a concise but thorough explanation of Burnet's theory:

> Er lehret mit vieler Beredtsamkeit, dass die Oberfläche der Erde vor der Sündfluth eben gewesen, und dass damals die Achse der Erden, die itzo mit der Ecliptik einen Winkel von 23 Gr. 28 Min. 30 Seconden machet, auf die Fläche der Erdbahn rechtwinkelicht gestanden; dass sich unter der äussersten allgemeinen Rinde eine grosse Wassersammlung befunden, und dass zur Zeit der allgemeinen Sündfluth die äusserste Rinde durch die natürliche Wirkung der Sonne, die wegen des gemeldeten Standes der Erdachse, durch keine Veränderung von Jahrszeiten, durch keinen Schlagregen oder Stürme geschwächt wurde, eingestürzt und gebrochen ist; dadurch ist die bis dahin eingeschlossene See zum Vorscheine gekommen, und die hervorragenden Stücken der eingestürzten Rinde haben die Gestalt von Bergen, Inseln und Halbinseln angenommen. (Der May, 275)

His main argument against theories like those of Burnet and Whiston is that they attempt to explain natural phenomena according to a preconceived mechanistic system: ". . . so wird man finden, dass sie sich erst einen Entwurf gemacht haben, wie sich die Erde wohl überschwemmen liesse, und nach diesem Entwurfe ihre Erde genau bildeten, damit sie sie gewiss zerstören könnten". (Der May, 279). Another argument against Burnet is that his theory violates the purposefulness which is apparent in all natural phenomena including mountains which are needed to circulate the water throughout the earth: "Der Kreislauf der Dinge hatte die erhabenen Schultern der Berge nöthig, ihnen die schiffende Last von Wassern zu vertrauen". (Der May, 281). A third argument is that certain animals exist only on mountains and if Burnet's theory were right, then "Diese Thiere müssten also erst nach der Sündfluth erschaffen seyn, oder sie müssten ihre erste Natur verändert haben". (Der May, 289). Since he believes in the fixity of species created in the beginning according to the Genesis account, these alternatives are unacceptable.

Another major concern of Dusch in this work is natural history. It is in this area rather than in astronomy that he develops conceptions of nature more representative of the interests of the second half of the century. In this connection he emphatically rejects mechanistic explanations of the world because natural history reveals to him a nature so mysterious and wise that mechanistic philosophies are exposed as mere human contrivances.

Dusch's conception of nature is most interesting when he discusses the mysteries and beauties of plant life. For example, the preformation theory of plant reproduction leads him to speculations of a general nature:

Alles hat er auf einmal erschaffen! Überlege den Satz, und erstaune, phlegmatischer Mensch! Jede erst erschaffene Pflanze trug in ihrem ge-bährenden Schoosse alle künftige Erndten ihrer Gattung! Unbegreifliche Zahlen von Dingen, die in einer unendlichen Reihe in Dingen stecken! Solch ein Gedanke ist der Allmacht und Weisheit eines Gottes würdig. (Der März, 96—97)

In a footnote in support of the text he continues his speculations about the seed and the implications of the scientists' discoveries about the seed:

Die Naturlehre überhaupt öffnet dem Menschen gleichsam erst recht die Augen, und ist voll von Wahrheiten, die die erhabensten und grössten Begriffe erregen müssen. Die Erhaltung und Fortpflanzung der Pflanzen ist gewiss eine davon. Da es sowol der Schrift, als der Vernunft nach angenommen werden muss, dass Gott alle Gattungen auf einmal erschaffen hat, und nichts neues mehr erschafft, so leitet uns dieses auf eine Folge, worüber wir erstaunen müssen. Die Schöpfung im Kleinen ist ein eben so erstaunliches Werk Gottes, als die Schöpfung im Grossen. Man überlege nur den Gedanken, dass in ein jedes erstes Saamenkorne, das erschaffen worden, sein ganzes folgendes Geschlecht gelegt ist, um auf einen Begriff des undenklich Kleinen zu kommen! (Der März, 96—97)

The encapsulation theory that all future plants are encapsuled in the first seed suggests to him that a seed is as much a world as any planetary world:

Welch ein künstlich Gebäude, welch ein unbegreifliches Magazin für künftige Jahre ist das kleine, kaum sichtbare Saamenkorn! Alle künftige Kinder stecken in ihm; eine unbeschreibliche Zahl, die die Zunge nicht aussprechen kann. Dieses Körnchen, das wie ein Stäubchen das Auge verliert, diess Behältniss einer künftigen Erndte im Kleinen muss gegen die zärtlichen Kinder in seinem Schoosse eine Welt seyn! (Der März, 98)

This thought about the world in a seed brings him again to the conception of a ladder of things from the smallest to the largest, each segment of which is unique yet subject ultimately to the same laws: "Wie tief an dem Nichts hebt die Staffel der Dinge, heben die Verhältnisse an, von Kleinem zum Grossen!" (Der März, 99).

Throughout his many discussions of plant life he makes it clear that God is the Creator who has endowed nature with all its order, harmony and variety. Yet very often God, the Author of nature, is left in the background and nature is described almost as if it were autonomous, almost as if it, itself, were endowed with divine qualities.

The autonomy and divinity of nature is suggested in an imaginative episode in which the author encounters a hermit who shuns human society to devote himself to a communion with and study of nature. In his long conversation about nature with this pious man, God is never mentioned; but nature, according to the qualities he attributes to it, seems truly omnipotent and omniscient. To begin with, the pious hermit acquired his piety not from religion but from a scientific study of nature. In his garden, which interferes with nature's way as little as possible, he admires and studies nature's art in its unlimited plant and animal species:

> Jetzo betrachte ich die Schöpfungskunst der Natur ... Was für Triebwerke und Kräfte sind nöthig, die schlechteste Blume aus den Saamen zu treiben, und zur Vollkommenheit zu bringen! Was für eine Baukunst entdeckt jede Pflanze von der Wurzel an, wodurch sie ihre Nahrung aus der Erde trinkt, bis auf die Frucht, die sie säuget! (Der October, 147)

The hermit is by no means merely an enthusiastic admirer of nature. His inquiring mind raises many questions which can be answered by the scientist:

> Was ist die Ursache, dass aus einem Saamen, den Regeln der Schwere zuwider, die Pflanze in die Höhe steigt? Was belebet das todte Saamenkorn? Durch welch einen Trieb wendet das ausgestreuete Korn sich um, wenn es etwas verkehrt in den Acker gefallen ist, und kehret die Wurzel immer Erdenwärts, und den Keim zum Himmel? Was treibt den Saft in die Wurzel, und in den Gipfel wolkenhoher Eichen, wider alle Gesetze der Schwere? Wie findet jede Pflanze ihren eigenen Saft, und wie bereiten ihn ihre Gefässe zu verschiedenen Blüthen, Blättern und Früchten? (Der October, 147–148)

Yet he does more than raise questions; he occupies his time in pursuing answers by the application of scientific method:

> Also beschäftige ich mich immer mit neuen Erfindungen, vergnügt, der Natur auf ihren Spuhren zu folgen. Jede Stunde ist reich an neuen Wundern, und mit den Wundern wächst die Neubegierde, und der Wissensdurst wird immer unersättlicher.
>
> .....
>
> Wie kann ich dir beschreiben, was für Versuche ich anstelle, und wie ich die Natur nöthige, vor meinen Augen einen Theile ihrer Schöpfung zu verrichten, und wie unter diesen lehrreichen Geschäfften die flügleschnellen Stunden dahin eilen! (Der October, 149–150)

Thus for the hermit nature is a synthesis of art, science and religion such as cannot be found in the contrivances of man, his works, his institutions.

Shortly after leaving the hermit, the author falls into a deep sleep and dreams of the temple of nature in which once again the synthesis of art, science and religion appears. A "Genius" appears to serve as a guide through the temple where there are allegorical representations of the various philosophies of nature from antiquity to the present. He explains the shortcomings of these philosophies, the chief of which was that they were too speculative and metaphysical; they transcended the limitations of reason and did not rely on experience enough. The moderns, however, receive his praise. He cites Bacon as the first one who threw off the fetters of prejudice and dared to think for himself: "Erfahrung und Vernunft waren die beyden sicherern Wegweiser des Verulam. Angestellte Versuche gaben ihm gewisse Gründe, woraus er die Wahrheit herleitete und erwies." (Der October, 187). This independence of the moderns to use their own judgment based on reason and experience, to bind themselves to no school or sect has been decidedly fruitful:

Was für Erfindungen wurden jetzo gemacht, die Werke und Begebenheiten der Natur besser zu betrachten, ihre Kräfte zu messen, und sie beynahe in ihren Geheimnissen zu behorchen! Einer bestimmte die Schweren der Elemente, und wog die Luft; jener spaltete den Strahl der Sonne, oder zog aus den Körpern den electrischen Funken. Dieser maass die Erde, und bestimmte ihre Figur, indem ein anderer in den Thälern und auf Gebirgen das Reich der Pflanzen untersuchte. Noch andere wandten ihre Aufmerksamkeit auf den Himmel, zähleten die Sonnen, und Monde, maassen ihren Abstand, und bestimmten die Zeiten ihres Laufes. (Der October, 189)

Discoveries in the telescopic world were supplemented by discoveries in the microscopic world:

Erstaunlich ist die Schöpfung im Grossen, und eben so erstaunlich im Kleinen. Alles ist der Betrachtung werth, und in dem Baue des kleinsten Insectes, das der Wanderer zertritt, liegen eben so grosse Wahrheiten für den Verstand verborgen, als in ganzen Weltkörpern. Die Erfindung der Gläser setzte die Neubegierde in den Stand, auch das Kleinste in der Natur zu entdecken. Alle diese gemeinschaftlichen Entdeckungen machten andere fähig, die Hauptwahrheiten zu sammlen, und aus allen Theilen der Naturlehre ein System zu erbauen. (Der October, 190)

Within the temple of nature the dreamer became aware of two mighty windows which revealed a wide view of a field of immeasurable distance. There he saw natural phenomena not depicted by man's art but in their original form. He beheld innumerable species of mineral, plant and animal life. The "Genius" instructs him concerning the natural order of these infinite phenomena:

Siehe nun, wie das Reich der Pflanzen in das Gebiethe der Thiere fliesst. Indem er dieses sagte, veränderte sich der Schauplatz, und ich sahe theils Pflanzen, theils lebendige Geschöpfe. Jene . . . nähern sich schon dem Leben durch Grade der Empfindung, und diese Geschöpfe sind halbe Pflanzen, und halbe Thiere. So steigt die Kette der Schöpfung von kleinern zu grössern Graden der Vollkommenheit. (Der October, 199—200)

The above reference to the chain of creation is one of many references to this image which recurs throughout the work in several variations.

Though this work is not outstanding for its originality, it is representative of the transition to a "romantic" conception of nature. Possibly that is why Lessing criticized the work so severely in his forty-first "Literaturbrief". From the point of view of this study the work is highly significant. It shows us a man of letters who is very well informed in the natural sciences and who has integrated science into his poetic conception of the world. Thus science plays an important role in his prose and poetry whether he writes as an "Aufklärer" in "Die Wissenschaften" or as a "romantic" in his *Schilderungen*.

Finally, we should like to refer to his critical work, *Briefe zur Bildung des Geschmacks*[4] which should find a place in histories of German literary criticism. In this six volume work, the first two volumes are devoted almost entirely to a critique of didactic poems from antiquity to the present. Especially interesting are his two letters on Lucretius' *Die Natur der Dinge*. Though he repudiates the Roman poet's atheism, he evaluates the poem from a purely aesthetic point of view. In his discussion he also inserts long passages of the poem in his prose translation. Any treatment of Lucretius in eighteenth century German literature should take these essays into consideration.

---

4 (Leipzig and Breslau, 1764—1773).

20. Johann Friedrich Löwen (1727–1771)

Johann Friedrich Löwen is known primarily for his work in the theatre. He studied "Theaterwissenschaft" and literature at the universities in Helmstedt and Göttingen and was elected to membership in the learned literary societies there. In 1766 he wrote a *Geschichte des deutschen Theaters* and the following year he was appointed director of the National Theater in Hamburg. His lengthy comic poem "Die Walpurgisnacht" of 1756 is mentioned occasionally in the histories of literature. Though he had no scientific training, his poetry reveals that he had assimilated some scientific material.

His earliest collection of poems, *Poetische Nebenstunden,*[1] contain a few themes worthy of consideration.

"Die Weisheit Gottes" is about the greatness of God in his creation and at the same time the transcendence of God in his creation. All the measurements designed by man are insufficient to encompass even a single aspect of His greatness (2). But if man seeks evidence of God's majesty and wisdom, he need only look at the orderly progression of innumerable heavenly bodies. Once again the vast number of suns and planets and the order they follow are used as visible signs of the invisible God. And once again the insufficiency of human science to grasp what is beyond nature is asserted.

In "Der Religionsspötter" the unbeliever is exhorted to lift up his eyes and behold the order that prevails among the thousands of heavenly bodies:

Dort hängt die Feste, die wir sehen,
Um die sich tausend Körper drehen,
Die Ordnung macht den Lauf geschwind. (12)

No idol, he concludes, no chance happening could have created such a structure, but only an eternal being.

In "Das Unbegreifliche" the author takes to task the pomposity and presumption of the learned, among them also scientists and philosophers:

Wenn Newton, Buffon, Wolf und Clark
Die Bahn gemeiner Geister fliehen,
Die Wahrheit als ihr Augenmerk
Aus Nacht und Nebel glücklich ziehen:
So denkt man: das ist ihre Pflicht.
Doch, dass sich ein Magister blähet,
Der kaum die Würde sich erzankt,
Sich stolz auf dem Catheder drehet,
Den Alten nichts, ihm alles dankt;
Nur das begreif ich nicht. (112)

1 Johann Friedrich Löwen, *Poetische Nebenstunden* (Leipzig, 1752).

He has no quarrel with those who have true learning, like Newton, Buffon, Wolff and Clarke, but only with the hordes of their semi-learned followers, who deem themselves wise simply by advocating the new and rejecting the old. Löwen doesn't reject modern learning but does view with suspicion the half-learned who follow modern trends instead of acquiring true learning.

In his *Schriften*[2] the didactic poem, "Der Billwerder", contains some interesting material. He undertakes an imaginative journey in which his "Genius" transports him from the corrupt life in the city and at the court into arcadian natural surroundings where he proceeds to compare the purity of the life there to the life he has left behind. Of interest to us are his reflections on the natural objects that surround him. From the summer house in an idyllic garden he extols the splendors of creation:

> Wie prächtig mahlt die Sonne diese Flur:
> Schön durch die Kunst, noch schöner von Natur.
> Wohin sich auch mein gierig Auge wendet,
> Seh ich die Pracht der Schöpfung fast verschwendet; (84)

The blending of art and nature in the garden, with nature making the superior contribution, had become a familiar theme by the middle of the century, as had the theme of nature's excessive bountifulness.

Garden contemplations frequently lead to observations that reflect the work of the natural historians, as we find it in the following passage:

> Der feiste Stier, der schwer den Klee durchwadet,
> Die Lerche, die im Sonnenstrahl sich badet,
> Der Fische Volk, die Milbe, die kaum lebt,
> Der kleinste Wurm, der seine Wohnung webt,
> Die, Schöpfer! sind dein Inbegriff, dein Spiegel,
> Sind deiner Macht und Weisheit stärkstes Siegel.
> Hier öffnest du, Natur, dein grosses Buch;
> Dann schwinden Wahn, und Zweifel und Betrug.
> Die Wissenschaft, wo wir nicht Gründe borgen,
> Lehrt mich das Land, und jeder Frühlingsmorgen. (85)

Not only God's wisdom and might are revealed in this survey of living species, but also the book of nature which in contrast to society is straightforward and certain. It is out of this book of nature that he learns science, uncomplicated by presupposition and argument, simple and immediate. Natural history is taken as the model for science rather than the mechanical and mathematical systems of the Cartesians and Newtonians.

---

2 Johann Friedrich Löwen, *Schriften,* Theil I (Hamburg, 1765).

He continues his contrast between nature and society by presenting caricatures of types prevalent in his society. One of those of interest to us is a philosopher who has an eye only for abstractions and distant spheres but neglects completely the revelations of nature close to him:

Marphurius vergnügt sich — aber wie?
Nur ganz Idee und ganz Philosophie,
Entzücken ihn nicht Gärten, Feld und Bäume;
Er sitzt im Busch und träumt Platonsche Träume.
Wie, öffnet ihm nicht die Natur ihr Buch? —
Ja, — doch umsonst im duftenden Geruch
Des Rosenstrauchs; nicht in den reifen Ähren,
Nein, in dem Raum unkenntbar ferner Sphären.
Er geht aufs Land, der tiefgelehrte Mann,
Damit er dort sein Sehrohr brauchen kann;
Ist zu gelehrt dem Landmann abzulernen
Kennt nicht die Welt; und wandelt unter Sternen. (91)

The other-worldliness of men of learning is here ridiculed. The deeply learned man who goes into the country simply to use his telescope to view far away things rather than what is before him is treated as an absurdity.

Another figure of interest to us is a collector of natural curiosities whose absurdity again lies in his lack of proportion:

Turpil, der Freund von Muscheln und von Schnecken,
Geht auf das Land ein Würmchen zu entdecken;
Versäumt die Pflicht, ein Mensch und froh zu seyn,
Und schliesset sich bey Schmetterlingen ein.
Wie sein Insect bekriecht er nur von weiten
Von der Natur die äusserlichen Seiten;
Ihr wahres Bild wird nie sein Auge sehn;
Nie wird für ihn die schönste Scene schön. (94)

The ridiculous collector knows many facts, but he has no real insight into nature; because of his pettiness he neglects his own humanity as well as the beauties of nature. He has lost his faculty for a true grasp of nature because of his exaggerated interest in precious and insignificant aspects of nature. However, Löwen qualifies his contempt of the collector of natural curiosities with the following interesting footnote: "Meine Leser sind gewiss so billig, von mir zu glauben, dass ich hier nicht den edlen Naturforscher, sondern einen Thomas Raupe, lächerlich zu machen suche .... Einen Pluche, Needham, Réaumur, Reimarus, Lesser, und andere mehr zu studiren, die Natur auch in ihren unendlichen Kleinigkeiten kennen zu lernen, die allemal die grössten Wunderwerke bleiben, ist das Geschäffte eines Weisen; allein mit der Sammlung der

Insecten und Schmetterlinge Zeit und Geld verschwenden, und darüber den wahren Genuss des Lebens vergessen, ist das Geschäffte eines Narren." (94)

The true scientists are defended, even when their study leads them into the endless details of nature. What he objects to is the popular craze for collection of curiosities unrelated to a serious and purposeful study of nature.

Thus, there are several familiar themes recurring in the works of Löwen. God is praised in His works in the heavens and on earth. The order in the vast heavens is seen as evidence that there is a God, creating and sustaining. The work of the natural historians, however, leads the poet not only to the recognition of the Creator in His works, but also serves to heighten his reverence for nature itself, its abundance, artistry and wisdom. Finally the poet aptly satirizes the pseudo-learned who approach nature with heart and senses closed.

21. Christoph Martin Wieland (1733—1813)

Young Wieland at the age of seventeen was inspired to write a long anti-Lucretian poem "Die Natur der Dinge"[1] which is distinguished from other anti-Lucretian poems primarily by its author's idealistic orientation. He was a devoted student of Plato and Leibniz and their idealism permeates the work. The sometimes puzzling mixture of Plato, Leibniz and Wieland's own uniqueness is very ably discussed by Gode-von Aesch[2] and Ermatinger.[3] However, these authors have failed to point out the many scientific themes in the poem which are not unique to Wieland but were quite common among the poets of the Enlightenment. Our discussion of the poem shall be confined to these themes.

In the first three books, Wieland opposes a variety of philosophies and cosmogonies of ancient and modern writers. The fallacies of the atomists, mechanists, pantheists, emanationists, materialists are exposed. In the fourth and fifth books, he presents his own philosophy and there we find many contemporary scientific themes.

In the second book of the poem there is one reference to modern scientific achievements when he maintains that love and desire for fame are the two strongest motivations; it is the latter that led to the important scientific discoveries of Galileo, Guericke and Newton:

Durch sie hat Pisens Preis der Sterne Glanz vermehrt,
Und dich, Uranie, durch Gläser sehn gelehrt.
Durch sie zwang Gerike die Luft vor ihm zu fliehen,
Und liess verborgne Glut aus Körpern Funken sprühen.
Dem Newton zeigte sie im weissen Sonnenstral
Durch ein dreyeckicht Glas der ersten Farben Zahl;
Von ihr gelehrt, hiess er in abgemessnen Sphären
Bestralte Welten sich zu ihrem Brennpunct kehren. (50)

Here Wieland joins a host of his contemporaries in praising Galileo's telescopic discoveries, Guericke's experiments with the air pump and Newton's two-fold achievement with his theories of color and gravitation — all crucial scientific events.

---

[1] According to Karl Walter in his *Chronologie der Werke Christoph Martin Wielands* (Greifswald, 1904), Wieland conceived the plan of the poem in August, 1750 and wrote it from January to April, 1751. It appeared in print in January, 1752 with a preface by G.F. Meier dated September 27, 1751. All quotations from "Die Natur der Dinge" are from *Gesammelte Schriften,* Erste Abteilung, Erster Band (Berlin, 1909).

[2] Alexander Gode-von Aesch, *Natural Science in German Romanticism* (Columbia University Press, 1941), pp. 39—52.

[3] Emil Ermatinger, *Die Weltanschauung des jungen Wieland* (Frauenfeld, 1907), pp. 9—54.

The fourth book contains the main body of Wieland's own world system. The underlying conception of his system, that there is a gradation of beings from the lowest to the highest, again is common to the period. Our solar system is characterized as encompassing the lowest spiritual beings:

Der ganze Kreis, der sich, voll von ätherischer Fluth,
Um unsre Sonne dreht, (die in dem Brennpunct ruht,
Und ihr heilsames Licht zu sechzehn Erden sendet,
Die ein geheimer Zug in eignen Bahnen wendet;)
Scheint vom Unendlichen der schlechtste Theil zu seyn,
Und schliesst die niedrigsten der Geistigkeit ein. (75)

The first four lines refer to the Cartesian aether, the Copernican system and the mysterious "Zug", attractive force, that keeps the planets in their orbits and is presumably Newton's gravity.

After an invocation of Clio, the Muse of history, he begins his discussion of living beings with those at the very bottom of the scale, unknown to man until Leeuwenhoek revealed them through his magnifying glasses:

Du, Leeuwenhök, zeigst uns mit scharf bewehrten Augen,
Was Menschblicke sonst nicht zu bestralen taugen.
Du zeigst den ganzen Stoff durch Gläser nur belebt,
Und wie der harte Fels selbst von Gewürmen webt.
Vor deines Scharfsinns Stral ist unsre Nacht verschwunden,
Der Erde kleinsten Punct hast du bewohnt gefunden. (76)

There are creatures so small, he adds, that no magnifying glass could bring them to view. For practical purposes, however, he begins with those worms of which Hooke and Swammerdam discovered millions in a drop of water:

Hingegen das Gewürm, wovon im Tropfen Nass
Ein Hook, ein Swammerdam, viel Millionen maass,
Lässt ein sichtbarer Leib in schärfre Augen dringen,
Ein Leib, der fähig ist, sich zeugend zu verjüngen;
Diess zeigt, dass unter ihm noch tiefre Classen gehn.
Doch endlich bleibt der Geist bey einer Gattung stehn . . . . (77)

Beyond the microscopic creatures he turns to the plant kingdom: "Um einen Grad erhöht beseelt das Pflanzenreich / Ein besseres Geschlecht, doch Thieren noch nicht gleich." (78) He does not describe specific species of plants, as many didactic poets do, but stresses the immense variety in the plant kingdom:

Auch dieses Hauptgeschlecht giesst sich, dem Meere gleich,
In tausend Arme aus, und ist an Arten reich.
Vom niedrigsten Gewächs, das Linnen selbst entgangen,

Bis zu der Cedern Haupt, die in den Wolken prangen,
Steigt eine ewge Zahl von neuen Arten auf . . . . (80)

The reference to Linnaeus, "Linnen selbst", is an example of the acceptance of his system of classification by the middle of the century.

The transition from plants to the animal kingdom is indicated by the molluscs which closely resemble plants: "Der Muscheln stachlicht Heer naht sich noch sehr dem Kraut" (80). He also describes worms, fish, quadrupeds and birds. Each animal, he maintains, is such a masterpiece that it points to God as Creator:

". . . Wie zeigt nur eine Mücke,
Ein ungeachtet Thier, im schönsten Meisterstücke
Des gliedervollen Leibs, dass sie ein Gott gebaut!
O hättest du, Lukrez, mit Hookens Aug geschaut,
Du hättest dich bemüht, mit deinen süssen Weisen,
Ein deiner werther Ziel, den Schöpfer selbst, zu preisen. (81)

It is doubtful that Lucretius would have praised God in nature even if he had looked through Hooke's microscope. It is again significant that Wieland subscribes to the very popular practice of praising God in nature.

In reflecting about the nature of animals in general, he stresses that man has much in common with the animals and that neither man's art nor science raises him as decisively above the animals as he thinks. In fact, animals have some valued qualities that man lacks: "Du bist von gleichem Stamm mit dem verworfnen Vieh, / Ja oft nimmts dir den Preis, und du bedenkst es nie" (82).

From these considerations of living beings on earth he turns to the earth itself:

Diess ist der Arten Zahl, aus der der Ball besteht,
Der langsam sich verzehrt, indem er uns erhöht.
Ihn heisst ein innrer Zwang in schneckengleichen Kreisen,
Um Titans feurgen Sitz, mit gleichem Wälzen, reisen. (86)

He shows how the earth's motions cause changes on the earth and discusses phenomena on earth related to the seasons. Then he turns to the heavenly bodies beyond the earth which are inhabited by spirits of a higher level. When man's spirit has left his place on earth and found his new home among the stars, he will have deeper insight:

Er wiegt der Wesen Kraft, er fasst den Stoff in Zahlen,
Dringt in der Dinge Mark und hängt sich nicht an Schalen.
Nie hemmt des Körpers Last des Geistes freyen Lauf;
Von neuen Sinnen fasst er neue Bilder auf;
Manch fühlend Gliedmass zeigt ihm neue Eigenschaften,
Die, unsichtbar für uns, an andern Körpern haften:

Vielleicht dass manche nur ein Sinn der Welt verbindt,
Und der nur durchs Gesicht, der nur durchs Ohr empfindt. (90)

Here are again several themes recurring since the 1720's: new insights into nature after death, discovery of new senses after death, the possibility that some creatures find one sense adequate.

Thus, Wieland's system of the world as it is found in the fourth book resembles that of many of his contemporaries. Most of the above themes are present in Brockes' poetry. In fact, in Wieland's early youth Brockes was his favorite poet as he states in a letter to Bodmer, dated March 6, 1752: "Brockes war mein Leibautor. Ich schrieb eine unendliche Menge von Versen, besonders kleine Opern, Cantaten, Ballette mit Schildereyen nach Art des Herrn Brockes".[4]

In the fifth book, in which he continues to develop his system of the world, there are further scientific themes of interest that are also common to the period. In the beginning of the book he reflects on the relativity of size suggested by microscopic observations. The worms observed by Needham in a drop of water are infinitely small; similarly we may appear as small to an interplanetary spirit:

Der Wurm, den in der Fluth ein Needham spielen sieht,
Der, zwar unendlich klein, doch Ströme von sich sprüht,
Ist in dem Tropfen Nass, der ihm ein Weltmeer dünket,
Was uns ein Wallfisch ist, der ganze Seeen trinket.
Selbst in der Glieder Bau zeigt sich die Ähnlichkeit,
Die Einfalt der Natur, der gleiche Unterschied;
Das klein're Seegeschöpf, unsichtbare Tritonen,
Und alle schreckt sein Grimm, die sein Gebieth bewohnen,
Und so, wie Needhams Blick, durch zauberisches Glas,
Ein solch kaum sichtbar Meer mit einem Sandkorn maass:
So hält ein Dämon, der durch Zwischenwelten steiget,
Wenn er sein leuchtend Haupt zu seinen Füssen neiget,
Und ihn ein ähnlich Glück die Erde finden lässt,
Der Menschen Sammelplatz für ein Ameisennest. (99)

A theme not common in the German poets prior to 1750, and strongly developed by Wieland is the mobility of the species, their capacity to move from the lower to the higher rungs of the ladder:[5]

---

[4] *Ausgewählte Briefe von Christof Martin Wieland,* edited by H. Gessner (Zürich, 1815), Vol. I, p. 46.
[5] Gode-von Aesch discusses these verses as an example of what Lovejoy calls the temporalizing of the Chain of Being, *Natural Science in German Romanticism,* pp. 47–49.

So wachet allgemach und nach der Ordnung Lauf
Das unterste Geschlecht vom alten Schlummer auf,
Und mehrt der Pflanzen Schaar; bewegt von Frühlingswinden
Beleben sie das Thal, und blühen in den Gründen.
Der Floren düftig Volk hebt sich durch gleiches Recht,
Wenn es verblühend stirbt, zum thierischen Geschlecht. (107)

The evolution here described is, however, a purely spiritual evolution. The
spirit of a member of any species after the death of its physical form undergoes a
development that prepares it to assume a new physical form on a higher level:

Wer zählt die Stufen ab, durch den ein Geist muss gehn,
Bis wir in gleichem Leib, ihn uns verbrüdert sehn?
Denn uns ersetzt der Tod, was wir durch ihn verlieren,
Aus Classen niedrer Art und anverwandten Thieren. (107)

Wieland had maintained already in the fourth book, as he does in the fifth
book also, that animals do not differ from man as much as man thinks. In the
above quotation, however, he asserts that the spirit or soul of an animal has
capacities to become human. Ermatinger cites as a source for this notion a work
by Georg Friedrich Meier, whom Wieland himself mentions in the poem:

O Meyer, den mit Lust das kluge Deutschland liest,
Von dessen weisem Mund platonscher Honig fliesst,
Wie deutlich hast du uns die Möglichkeit gelehret,
Dass sich auch in dem Vieh der Seele Werth vermehret. (109)

In his work on the animal soul, *Versuch eines neuen Lehrgebäudes von den
Seelen der Thiere* (Halle, 1750), Meier maintains that animals have all the
qualities human souls have, including immortality; they lack only the capacity
for abstract thought. He also maintains, as does Wieland above, that through
death the souls of animals ascend to humanity.[6]

Toward the end of the fifth book he turns to a related theme, namely, the
death and destruction of planets through a comet. He describes the fiery
destruction a comet causes in a planet by approaching too closely. He gives
another example of a planet passing only through the tail of a comet which
caused a flood similar to the one the earth experienced:

Dort sinkt sein blasser Schweif, ein ausgespanntes Meer,
Das halbe Wirbel füllt, von Glut und Dünsten schwer,
Auf eine Erde hin, zerborstne Wolken fallen
Aus der zu leichten Luft mit Blitz und holem Knallen.
So schwamm einst unser Ball in allgemeiner Fluth,

6 See Ermatinger, pp. 25–27 for a discussion of Meier's concept of the animal soul.

Die Erde floss, das Meer verdrang der Ufer Schutt,
Der Marmor selbst ward weich, und strömte von den Höhen,
Und donnernd wälzten sich die aufgebirgten Seeen. (113)

Here we recognize the Whistonian theory which Wieland undoubtedly learned from Bodmer who used it in his *Noah*. Another allusion to Whiston's theory is the reference to the comet as a dying planet: "Und dieses Übel wirkt ein sterbender Planet, / Der, ob er uns gleich irrt, doch nach Gesetzen geht, . . ." (113).

In another work of his youth, "Zwölf moralische Briefe in Versen" (1752),[7] there are a few further popular scientific themes. In the first letter he expresses a sentiment reminiscent of Haller, namely, that the scientist turn from his extended interests to a search for self-knowledge:

Steig Huygen, steig Cassin, von der ätherschen Bahn
In dein verkenntes Herz, und lass Cometen irren,
Der eignen Triebe Lauff sorgfältig zu entwirren,
Und führ, an jener statt, dein Herz, mit besserm Glük,
Von seines Brennpuncts Flucht zu seiner Sonn' zurük.

As the sun is the focal point of a comet's orbit so is God the focal point of man's life. It is a unique image with which to exhort man to leave his erring ways and turn to God.

In the seventh letter he describes the idyllic life of a wise man who, among other things, also studies the sciences:

Denn führt ein Bacon ihn durchs Feld der Wissenschaften,
Und stürzt die Götzen um, vor die die halbe Welt,
Zur Schande der Vernunft, abgöttisch niederfällt.
Denn folgt er erstaunt dem Solon der Planeten,
Er sieht (und zittert nicht) die schweiffende Cometen,
Und wie die Welten sich, wie durch Gewichte ziehn, . . . (267)

"Solon der Planeten" is Newton who calculated the paths of comets and discovered the laws of the mutual attraction of heavenly bodies. "Wie durch Gewichte" is an attempt to illustrate Newton's mysterious gravitational force.

In the twelfth letter there is the popular theme of a dream voyage to an idyllic society on a distant heavenly body: "Es war, so dünkte mich, schon lange dass ich flog / Als mich ein heller Mond von ferne zu sich zog." (303)

The subject of the inhabitation of other heavenly bodies by spiritual beings different from and usually better than man occurs several times in Wieland's "Briefe von Verstorbenen an hinterlassene Freunde" (1753).[8] In the third letter

---

7 *Gesammelte Schriften*, Erste Abteilung, Erster Band, pp. 223—307.
8 *Gesammelte Schriften*, Erste Abteilung, Zweiter Band, pp. 1—102.

Charicles describes to Laura the beneficent circumstances of his new home, the sun. In the fourth letter Theagenes pictures to Alcindor the panorama of a plurality of worlds in the universe and explains the gradations of beings and worlds. He also tells of the inhabitants of two planets in his solar system who, though they have only one sense, smell or hearing, are harmoniously attuned to the nature they perceive. In the ninth letter Theotima tells Melinde of a planet in one of the Milky Way's solar systems whose inhabitants, though tempted by Satan, have not fallen from innocence.

The scientific themes that have been found in young Wieland's verse are common property of the German poets in the period under consideration. His idealism, his development of the theme of spiritual mobility of the species up the ladder of creation, his emphasis on the human spirit point beyond our period to the age of Goethe.

22. Other German poets whose works contain some relevant
scientific material

In the case of the following poets, I shall indicate briefly with some excerpts what scientific themes appeared in their works. Many of the themes are the same as those already considered in the poets treated at length above. It is valuable to call attention to them, however, to note the extent to which these ideas were cultivated by the poets of this period. At the same time, there are some original formulations and unique treatments of recurrent themes. The presence of this material in over thirty more poets is a necessary supplement to the story of science in the poetry of the German Enlightenment. I shall again proceed chronologically.

Sonderbare Licht- und Wetter-Philosophie Gewisser Einwohner auf einer Neu-entdeckten Insul im Südländischen Meer (1741) is an anonymous parable in verse about an island near the south pole, so completely enveloped by a haze that none of the heavenly bodies are visible. Their scientists seek to understand the causes of light, heat, seasonal and weather changes, as do European scientists. They have an ancient tradition about distant heavenly bodies, of which one in particular, the sun, is supposed to be the source of many natural phenomena on their island. The enlightened moderns, however, reject this tradition and attempt to explain all these phenomena as originating out of the immediate, perceivable atmosphere. The parable is directed against the atheists, deists and naturalists who believe that nature is autonomous and that the faith mediated by tradition is unnecessary and contrary to reason and science.

Philipp Balthasar Sinold's (1657—1742) *Amadei Creutzbergs Seelen-er-quickende Himmels-Lust auf Erden* (Berlin, 1728)[1] is an example of the pre-Brockes version of the tradition of praise of God in nature. The work is divided into eight parts according to the four seasons and the four elements, so that we have the following sequence: "Frühling", "Luft", "Sommer", "Wasser", "Herbst", "Erde", "Winter" and "Feuer". Sinold's two hundred prose meditations are evenly distributed, twenty-five to each section. Preceding each section there are selections from Brockes' *Irdisches Vergnügen in Gott*. Since 214 pages of the 914 page book are devoted to excerpts from Brockes' poetry, it is clear that Sinold valued his poetry. Nevertheless, Sinold's own meditations exhibit little of Brockes' spirit. About one half of the meditations take as their point of departure some natural object or phenomena. With a few exceptions, however, the natural object is no more than an occasion for Sinold to turn to a religious theme which then takes up the remaining portion of the meditation. The personal encounter with the world of nature and the open, naive, delighted response to that world are lacking. There is almost no scientific material in his meditations.

1 A later edition (Berlin, 1742) was available for this study.

Hiob Gotthardt's von Tschammer und Osten (1674–1735) *Geistliche und Weltliche Gedichte* (Breslau, 1739) include one sonnet entitled "Natur" of relevance to our study:

Des Wesens rechter Grund, die güttige Natur
Ist keinmahl herrlicher als in geringen Dingen,
Wo man es nicht gedenkt, da sieht man ihre Spur,
Sie sucht den Überflus gar offt hervor zu bringen;
Jedoch sie zeiget nicht die wundervolle Cur,
Warum? sie lässt sich schwer zu solchen Sachen zwingen.
Sehr viele Zeit verlief, eh' es die Welt erfuhr
Wie Wachsthum, Stärke, Krafft in ihr zusammen hiengen.
Sie lässt nicht allemahl was man verlanget, sehen,
Sie spielt sie drücket ab und zeiget was sonst blüht,
Dahero kan es leicht so dort als hier geschehen,
Dass dieses oder das einander ähnlich sieht,
Sie leget allemahl den Grund zu vieler Kunst,
Denn diese macht für sich fast nichts als lauter Dunst. (55)

The central theme of the sonnet is nature from a purely secular perspective. Nature is benevolent, all-pervasive, superabundant, mysterious, spontaneous. In lines four to eight, he depicts nature as reluctantly revealing the secrets of its inner workings to the modern scientists.

In Michael Richey's (1678–1761) *Deutsche Gedichte* (Hamburg, 1764), there is a "Singgedicht" dated 1756 in which Sophronicus, a wise man, takes Furius, a freethinker, to task for his irresponsible life and ideas. In regard to the latter, Sophronius says:

Du hast das Rund der Welt in platter Form gedrücket,
Und iedem Wandelstern Bewohner zugeschicket;
Cometen müssen einst uns zu verbrennen dienen;
Die Seel ist cörperlich; die Menschen sind Maschinen;
Du klärest alles auf, Magneten, Farb und Licht:
Wir sehen, was du meynst, doch noch die Wahrheit nicht. (II, 228)

Sophronius equates scientific achievements like the discovery of the true shape of the earth and the nature of light and color with speculative hypotheses about the inhabitation of planets, the cometary cause of the final conflagration and the mechanical nature of man. He has placed Newton and Maupertuis in the same company with Whiston, Heyn and La Mettrie. His intention is to damn those who believe everything can be explained mechanically and who reject the Bible and Revelation.

In Johann Ulrich von König's (1688–1744) *Gedichte* (Dresden, 1745), a collection of occasional poems, there is one poem celebrating the marriage of his

friend Kirchbach, "Auf das Hochadeliche Kirchbach- und Vitzthumische
Beylager", which is pertinent to our study. The poet tells of a dream in which
the spirit of poetry leads him into a mine where he encounters an allegorical
representation of the Art of Mining, "Die Bergwerkskunst":

> Da sah ich aufgeklärt in Wunder-hellem Lichte
> Die unterirrdische geheime Bergwerkskunst.
> Ihr lag zur linken Hand Maass, Zirkel und Gewichte.
> Zur Rechten konnte man den Bergcompass ersehn,
> Womit der Bergmann pflegt den Abgrund durchzugehn,
> Und seine Fahrt vermag so sicher anzustellen,
> Als mit dem Seecompass ein Schiffer durch die Wellen.
> .....
> Dass grosse Wunderbuch, worinn ein jedes Blat
> Ein neu Geheimniss zeigt, und neue Lehren hat,
> Das Kunstbuch der Natur lag vor ihr aufgeschlagen,
> Weil sie gewohnt, darinn sich stündlich zu befragen. (246–7)

The poet stresses here that the art of mining involves a scientific study of
nature. Kirchbach appears in the dream as one who is devoted to the scientific
spirit:

> Doch bliebst du nicht vergnügt mit dem, was man nur sieht,
> Dein niemals-satter Geist war eiferigst bemüht,
> Durch die Erfahrung selbst in Stollen, Schacht und Gründen,
> Der Würkung Ursach' auch nachforschend auszufinden. (249)

The Art of Mining praises Kirchbach's diligence which revealed to him
nature's treasures beneath the ground; its metals, minerals and precious stones.
He even found traces of nature's creative processes:

> Hier, sprach die Bergwerckskunst: Hier findest du die Spur,
> Wie sonder Unterlass ihr edles Handwerk treibet
> Die aus dem Abgrund selbst stets würkende Natur,
> Die der Unfruchtbarkeit geschworne Feindin bleibet.
> Wie sie stets schwanger ist und stets Gebährerin,
> Und unverhinderlich aus Mütterlichem Sinn
> Erwärmt, befestiget, begränzt, erzeugt, verhüllet,
> Besaamet und erhält, befeuchtet und erfüllet. (252)
> ....
> Der Weltgeist hat als Mann hier die Natur zur Frauen,
> Sein Zeugungssaamen ist das Feuer und die Glut,
> So wie der ihrige die salzigt-fette Fluth, . . . (253)

The dream concludes with the encounter between Kirchbach and a mountain nymph who was his bride of the Vitzthum family.

Johann Michael von Loen's (1694–1775) *Moralische Gedichte* (Frankfurt, 1751) contains one cycle of poems entitled "Damons Land-Lust; nach Broks irrdischem Vergnügen". "Der Garten" and "Die Bienen" in this cycle are clearly imitations of poems by Brockes.

There are a few scientific themes in the poetry of Johann Christian Günther (1695–1723), and a few indications that he subscribed to the philosophy of the Enlightenment as represented by Leibniz and Wolff. However, there is no evidence to support the contention of Wilhelm Krämer, the editor of the critical edition of Günther's works that he is "... der dichterische Verkünder des Leibniz-Wolffschen Weltbildes".[2] Israel S. Stamm cites two passages in which Günther mentions Leibniz and Wolff by name, and on the basis of these and a few other passages concludes that Günther believed in "... the doctrine of nature as a lawful system". He thus agrees with Krämer.[3] A passage such as:

Die Bücher der Natur, die gross- und kleine Welt,
Verdienen überhaupt viel Sorgfalt im Betrachten;
Schau, wie ein jedes Ding Zeit, Ziel und Ordnung hält,
Und lerne so wie ich die Eitelkeit verachten. (II, 75)

shows that Günther was in favor of the modern approach to nature, as does the following passage in which he castigates physicians for their shoddy training and practice and exhorts them to a more scientific approach to medicine:

Mit dem Doctor kaum zwey Jahr flüchtig durch den Sennert laufen,
Hunde würgen, Feuer sehn, Pillen drechseln, Kräuter raufen,
Auf Gerathewohl verschreiben, andre neben sich verschmähn
Und sich bey dem Sterbebette in der Staatsperrüque blehn,
Ist so thöricht als gemein, thut auch selten grosse Wunder.
Bücher, Tiegel, Glas und Ring sind zusammen nichts als Plunder,
Wenn man die Gesundheitsregeln nicht vorher in Kopf gebracht
Noch auch durch vernünftig Schliessen die Erfahrung brauchbar macht.
Will man nun den Stümpern gleich nicht an jeder Klippe scheitern,
So bemüh man sich zuerst, Sinnen und Verstand zu läutern:
Man erforsche die Geseze, die der Bauherr schöner Welt
Ehmahls zwischen Geist und Cörper ewig gleich und fest gestellt.
Dies erfordert etwas mehr als in alten Schwarten wühlen
Und mit Knochen, Stein und Kraut oder heissem Erze spielen.
Wer die Wissenschaft der Grösse und der Kräfte nicht versteht,
Kan den Leib unmöglich kennen, der wie Wasseruhren geht. (201–2)

---

2 *Sämtliche Werke,* 6 Bände (Leipzig, 1930–1937), II, p. XX.
3 "Günther and Leibniz-Wolff," *Germanic Review,* XXIII (1948), 30–39.

There are a few more passages like these; however, this hardly permits the conclusion that he was "der dichterische Verkünder des Leibniz-Wolffschen Weltbildes".

In Johann Christian Müldener's *Geanders von der Ober-Elbe poetische Kleinigkeiten* (Dresden, Leipzig, 1753),[4] there is an essay "Ruhm derer Berge" (62–73), dated 1731, in which he describes the many uses of mountains. He mocks those "träumende Gelehrte" (68) who see in mountains only the ugly remains of the havoc caused by the Flood. Instead, he considers mountains magnificent decorations of our planet.

In Christoph Dietrich's von Böhlau (1707–1750) *Poetische Jugend-Früchte* (Leipzig, 1740) human foibles are satirized by being projected to a society in the moon. A letter, written in verse, from "Luna Katschaka, die Hauptstadt im Mond", describes some of the marital problems the inhabitants of the moon have in common with those on earth (315–320).

Johann Christian Cuno's (1708–1780) *Ode über seinen Garten: Nachmals besser* (Amsterdam, 1750) is in the Brockes tradition. Although there are references to the countless stars and suns, the world of natural history is the main subject of the poem. Flowers, birds, bees and horses are described with the awareness of a natural historian. Though there are moral and religious reflections, the revelation of nature's qualities, wisdom, plentitude and incorruptibility predominates throughout the poem. Included with Cuno's work in the second edition is the long physicotheological poem, "Beweis der Gottheit aus dem Grase" by Johann Daniel Denso (1708–1795) who edited several popular scientific periodicals.

Christoph Eusebius Suppius' (1709–?) *Der Inselberg* (Gotha, 1745) describes the beauties of this highest mountain in the Thuringian forest and praises the way of life of its inhabitants. Since he refers to the mountain as "Du, des dritten Schöpfungstages hochgebohrner Erdensohn" (2), it is clear that he does not subscribe to Burnet's mountain theory. When he reaches the mountain's peak, he is overwhelmed by his view of the heavenly bodies about him. He reflects about their orderly movements and praises Copernicus and Newton who revealed to men the mysteries of the heavens. He himself is eager to follow their example:

> Mein bewafnet Auge sieht manche dichte Kugel schwimmen,
> Doch der Geist beschäftigt sich Bahn und Lauf ihr zu bestimmen,
> Und indem ich sie verfolge, so empört sich mancher Schluss,
> Dass ich ihr, wie unsrer Erde, alles zugestehen muss,
> Wie entzückt mich dieses doch! dass ich meinen Stand vergesse,
> Wo ich gegenwärtig bin, und den Weg hinüber messe
> Bis zu unserm nechsten Nachbar, dem auch unsre Sonne scheint,

---

4 There was a first edition (Dresden, 1729).

Wo vielleicht ein Sternerforscher uns jetzt zu entdecken meynt,
Ob, und wie, und was wir sind . . . . . (20)

Johann Gottlob Krüger's (1715–1759) *Träume* (Halle, 1754)[5] is an imaginative work by a perceptive scientist and social observer. His 165 dreams cover a variety of subjects in the areas of society, philosophy and science. In dreams eighteen to twenty-two he becomes a space traveler like Kepler and Huygens before him and visits the planets of our solar system. His observations and conversations with the inhabitants include astronomic lore as well as social satire. One of his favorite themes is the relativity of knowledge and the importance of perspective. The above dreams exemplify that very well. In the seventeenth dream he finds himself transformed into a fish, and in the one hundred and eighth dream into a tiny insect, each time experiencing a new point of view. In the fiftieth dream he encounters five individuals each lacking one of the five senses. The dreamer then tries to elicit from each what his conception of the sensation he lacks would be. In dream one hundred and thirteen he marvels at the worlds revealed by the microscope and the telescope and concludes that there are no limits to nature and that the scientific knowledge gained so far is insignificant compared to what is yet to be learned. Along with the many other contemporary themes it contains, Krüger's *Träume* serves as a good mirror of the times.

Christian Fürchtegott Gellert's (1715–1769) *Moralische Vorlesungen*[6] is a collection of lectures he gave at the University of Leipzig during the last decade of his life. The lectures are intended as exercises to cultivate the heart and mind for right conduct. In the tenth and the seventeenth lectures, he shows how the study of nature can contribute to that goal. In the tenth lecture he offers a "moralische Bibliothek" containing books by Sulzer, Wolff, Derham, Pluche, Hervey, Nieuwentyt, Ray and Bonnet – all works that present science within a religious framework. In the seventeenth lecture, entitled "Von der Anwendung unsres Verstandes auf die Erkenntniss und Betrachtung der Natur", he reflects on natural history, biology and astronomy. The reflections include familiar themes: praise of God in nature, purposefulness in nature, the numerous species arranged by gradations from the lowest to the highest, the nature of the animal soul and the inhabitation of the planets. It is a beautifully written essay whose content is representative of the popular thought of the Enlightenment.

Ewald Christian von Kleist's (1715–1759) *Sämtliche Werke* (Berlin, 1761) contain several poems with scientific themes. In "Der Frühling" of 1745 he describes the beauties of nature and the variety of living beings with the eyes of a natural historian. In "Lob der Gottheit" he traverses the various realms of nature in heaven and on earth to praise God in His works. In "Die

---

5 The second edition (Halle, 1758) was available: a third edition appeared in 1764.
6 *Sämtliche Werke*, VI and VII (Leipzig, 1770).

Unzufriedenheit des Menschen" he justifies God in His creation which extends
far beyond man's senses:

> ..... Durchfleuch erst
> die blauen Gefilde
> Mit Sonnen und Erden durchsät, den milchfarbnen
> Gürtel des Himmels,
> Die Luftsphär' jeglichen Sterns; betrachte des
> Ganzen Verbindung.
> Samt allen Federn der Räder und andrer Planeten
> Naturen,
> Die Arten ihrer Bewohner, ihr Thun und Stufen-
> gefolge,
> Ergründ mit kühnem Gefieder des dunkeln Geister-
> reichs Tiefe,
> Sieh Wesen ohne Gestalten, merk ihre Abhäng
> und Kräfte,
> Steig auf der Leiter der Dinge selbst bis zum
> Throne der Gottheit:
> Dann strafe, woferne du kannst, die Vorsicht, und
> Ordnung der Erde. (146–147)

He also wrote an Anacreontic poem, "Gedanken eines betrunkenen Sternsehers", in which he pays tribute to the Copernican system:

> Mich wundert nicht, dass sich,
> Ihr Freunde, wie ihr seht,
> Die Erde dreht;
> Kopernik hat fürwahr kein falsch System ersonnen.
> Doch –– dort seh ich
> Am Himmel gar zwo Sonnen!
> Ey! Ey! das wundert mich. (49)

Johann Just Ebeling (1715–1783) with his three volumes of poetry,
Betrachtungen aus dem Buch der Natur und Schrift (Hildesheim, 1747) is an
imitator of Brockes. As a clergyman, the praise of God in nature is a recurrent
theme. Nevertheless, like his model he is fascinated by the worlds revealed
through the microscope and the telescope and is familiar, in a general way, with
the new scientific learning in astronomy and natural history. As in Brockes there
is a strong didactic element. Poems like "Die wunderbahre Bienenstatt" (III,
196–214) and "Die Grösse Gottes in Steinen gebildet" (III, 326–344) convey
much information about their respective subjects.

In Johann Matthias Dreyer's (1716–1769) *Gedichte* (Altona, 1771) there are
occasional themes praising God in nature. In "Morgengedanken" (10–13) the

Creator is recognized in the plurality of worlds, in comets, in living beings large and small. In one of his dramatic poems "Die Vernunft" and also in "Der Fleiss", he praises the triumph of reason and science over superstition (47—53). In "Das Gebirge" (257—259) the theme is nature's mysteries in mountains and the value of science to the miner:

Die Wissenschaft, die ewig ist,
Den ganzen Himmel kennt und misst,
Muss auch des Bergmanns Fleiss regieren;
Durch Zahl und Maass lernt er die Spur,
Der tief verborgenen Natur,
Und kann den Erztgang ihr entführen. (258)

Christoph Joseph Sucro's (1718—1751) *Versuch in Lehrgedichten und Fabeln* (Halle, 1747) is a collection of didactic poems inspired by Albrecht von Haller's poetry. Sucro's "Versuch vom Menschen", dedicated to Haller, contains anatomical descriptions of the human body and references to microscopic studies in natural history.

In Johann Wilhelm Ludwig Gleim's (1719—1803) *Sämtliche Werke*[7] there is one anacreontic poem, "Der Sternseher" (I, 40—44) in the section entitled "Versuch in scherzhaften Liedern, 1744—1753". In the poem the poet visits an ascetic astronomer who seeks new suns and worlds so assiduously that he has abandoned all earthly joys. That particular evening when the astronomer begins to study the moon he makes an unexpected observation:

"Da will ich" sprach er, "oben,
"Im Monde, Berg' und Thäler
"Und Meer' und Flüsse suchen;
"Ich will die Berge messen
"Und alle Fluren zählen!" —
Er zählte, schon bis zwanzig,
Da hört' er auf, und lauter
Als Wächter rufen, rief er:
"Im Monde wohnen Mädchen!"

The self-denying astronomer who had never before even smiled began to laugh and rejoice at the spectacle he beheld:

"Ha, welche kluge Mädchen!
"Sie tanzen unter Knaben
"Nach richtigen Figuren,
"Nach Winkeln und Quadraten,

---

[7] (Halberstadt, 1811—1813), 7 vols.

"Und spielen mit Quadranten,
"Und stehn auf hohen Gipfeln,
"Und sehn mit längern Augen,
"Als Euler und Kopernik!
"Ich habe nie mit Mädchen
"Getanzt, noch nie gespielet;
"O könnt' ich doch im Monde
"Mit jenen Mädchen spielen!"

The poet, however, had in the meantime caught sight of a beautiful lady here on earth and called out to the astronomer:

... "Sternbeschauer,
"Mein Auge soll nicht wachsen;
"Statt aller deiner Mädchen
"Im Monde, nehm' ich dieses!"

Abraham Gotthelf Kästner (1719–1800) has already been encountered as a poet and a popularizer of science. Though his scientific publications and translations of scientific works are well known, there is no bibliography of his many reviews of scientific books, prefaces to scientific works and contributions on scientific subjects in periodicals. In Carl Becker's *A.G. Kaestners Epigramme* (Halle, 1911), there is a bibliography of his literary works and contributions to periodicals on literary subjects. I have already discussed his popular didactic poem on cometary theory, "Philosophisches Gedicht von den Kometen". His most successful literary achievements were in essays and epigrams. Several of his epigrams have scientific themes.[8] "Auf Kepler" (3) praises Kepler's intellectual achievements and laments that his countrymen let him starve. "An Herrn Christlob Mylius" (6) is again about Kepler to whom he refers as "der Lehrer Newtons". The epigram accompanied a copy of Kepler's *Harmonice Mundi* which Kästner sent to Mylius. "Auf Christlob Mylius" (14) written after the latter's death, praises his work as a scientist and poet: "Als Physikus wusst' er zu observiren, / Und wie ein Dichter hielt er Haus". "Über den Eintritt der Venus in die Sonne den 3. Juni 1769" (46) celebrates the transit of Venus as follows: "Ich thäte selbst, wenn ich Cytheren hätte, / Was Phöbus thut: er geht mit ihr zu Bette". In "Auf Newtons Grabmal" (59) he pays tribute to Newton's synthesis but doesn't fail to mention his "Lehrer Kepler". The epigram "Dörfel" (64) refers to Samuel Dörfel's successful calculation of a cometary orbit in 1680 several years before Newton did so. "Der Venustrabant" (80) is one of his longer epigrams:

---

8   All page references to Kästner's epigrams are from the first part of his *Gesammelte Poetische und Prosaische Schönwissenschaftliche Werke,* 4 Theile (Berlin, 1841).

Dass ihr Adonis noch am Himmel um sie geht,
Von Wahlen ward zuerst Cythere so geschmäht
Sie haben freilich stets die Weiber im Verdacht;
Manch Sternrohr hat umsonst den Cicisbee bewacht.
Zu zeigen hat sich ihn einst Lambert unterstanden,
Und die Verläumdung ward zu Schanden.
So ist's am Himmel nur; man sieht Trabantenheere
Auf Erden leicht um jede Cythere.

He is referring to efforts to find a satellite of Venus. In the footnotes he explains that the two Italians, "Wahlen", Francesco Fontana and Domenico Cassini, were the first to raise this question. The German astronomer Johann Heinrich Lambert also had expected to find the satellite.

Magnus Gottfried Lichtwer's (1719—1783) *Das Recht der Vernunft* (Leipzig, 1758) is a didactic poem whose central theme is Christian Wolff's practical philosophy which is concerned with politics and ethics. There are occasional references to the enlightenment that the sciences have brought (30, 32, 37, 38, 65, 83, 87).

In Johann Nathanael Reichel's *Schriften vor den Wiz und das Herz* (Leipzig, 1756) there are physicotheological reflections in verse about plant life in "Lehrende Betrachtungen über Grass und Blumen" (51—60), written in imitation of Brockes whom he mentions by name. In the poem "Gedanken über den Donner und Bliz" (61—67) he takes issue with those who maintain that an explanation of the natural causes of thunder and lightning precludes a divine purpose. He asserts that any natural phenomena could still carry out God's design though the immediate natural causes are known. The poem "Die Berge" (152—160) expresses the author's sense of awe and joy inspired by mountains. He also describes the uses of mountains and the treasures in metals and stones that can be found there. In a long footnote he disagrees with Thomas Burnet's theory about mountains. At the same time, he shows that there is a paradox in Burnet's thinking. He gives examples, with excerpts from Zimmermann's translation, of Burnet's praise of the majesty of mountains on the one hand and on the other, descriptions of mountains as chaotic, disorderly phenomena that are a blight on creation.

In Johann Arnold Ebert's (1723—1795) *Episteln und vermischte Gedichte* (Hamburg, 1789) there is a poem dated 1749 and dedicated to "Philander" which possibly is the pseudonym of Ernst Christoph von Manteufel (1676—1749), an enlightened aristocrat dedicated to philosophy and science. In the poem the count's spirit which had always striven for knowledge is depicted being led by the angels from sphere to sphere and receiving enlightenment from them:

Dort zeigten sie ihm oft in Werken der Natur,
Am meisten in ihm selbst, des grossen Schöpfers Spur;
.....
Dort, wo ein Newton sieht, wie sehr er hier geirrt,
Ein Leibnitz sich verliert, und Lock' ein Schüler wird, ... (295)

In Friedrich Gottlieb Klopstock's (1724–1803) *Der Messias*[9] there are several examples of the new astronomy and related themes such as vast cosmic space, countless inhabited worlds and the perspectives of rational creatures in different planets. In the first canto the archangel Gabriel hurries through space and we get a glimpse of the enormity of creation:

Unterdess eilte der Seraph zur äussersten Gränze des Himmels
Wie ein Morgen empor. Hier füllen nur Sonnen den Umkreis.
Und gleich einem von Lichte gewebten ätherischen Vorhang,
Zieht sich ihr Glanz um den Himmel herum. Kein dämmernder Erdkreis
Naht sich des Himmels verderbenden Blick. Entfliehend und ferne
Geht die bewölkte Natur vorüber. Da eilen die Erden
Klein, unmerkbar dahin, wie unter dem Fusse des Wandrers
Niedriger Staub, von Gewürmen bewohnt, aufwallet und hinsinkt.
Um den Himmel herum sind tausend eröfnete Wege,
Lange, nicht auszusehende Wege, von Sonnen umgeben. (10–11)

In the same canto Gabriel descends to the center of the earth where there is an interior sun providing another source of heat for the earth (27). Hell, we learn in the second canto, is not in the interior of the earth but at the remotest corners of creation, immeasurable distances away from the outermost stars (43). In the sixth canto while God passes through the milky way we learn of a planet in one of the solar systems whose first man had not fallen as Adam did. We hear him tell his children of the fall from innocence of the earth's inhabitants, of the consequences that followed and of the promise of salvation.

Historischmoralische Schilderungen zur Bildung eines edlen Herzens in der Jugend (Helmstädt, 1753) by Johann Peter Miller (1725–1789) is a series of dialogues between an instructor and his pupil. Conversation four is entitled "Die Gartenlust" or "Von der Weisheit Gottes" and conversation five, "Der gestirnte Himmel" or "Die Allmacht des Schöpfers". These are popular treatments of natural history and astronomy such as we can find in Derham, Fontenelle and Brockes. Scientific material is conveyed in an entertaining manner and written within a pious framework.

Johanne Charlotte Unzer (1725–1782), wife of the famous physician Johann August Unzer, wrote poetry as well as the popular scientific works referred to in

---

[9] (Halle, 1760), second edition.

part I. In her *Versuch in sittlichen und zärtlichen Gedichten* there are a few themes of interest.[10] "Vom Daseyn Gottes" (3–10) and "Lob Gottes" (11–19) give praise to God in nature, in the millions of worlds in space as well as millions of living creatures in a drop of water. In "Das Schicksal" (22–29) she cites examples that show that the lawfulness of nature is God's design and purpose. "Über die Verwesung" (30–42) reveals the knowledge of anatomy in describing the decay of the human body in death. In "Aufmunterung zum Vertrauen auf Gott" (80–84) she gives an account of the creation, following both Genesis and current cosmogonies which maintain that the Biblical story applies only to the creation of this planet and that the earth existed in a chaotic lifeless state before God's act of creation. She also refers to a theory that while the earth was in this pre-creation state of chaos the planet Mars was its satellite: "Mars, der in jener Zeit, eh ihm ein Zufall wehrt, / Trabant der Erde war, des treuern Monds Gefährt, . . ." (82).

Christian Felix Weisse's (1726–1804) *Die unerwartete Zusammenkunft oder der Naturaliensammler*[11] (1764) is a comedy revolving about a country gentleman's passion for collecting natural curiosities about which he understands very little. His daughter's suitor uses both the gentleman's passion and ignorance to his advantage by ingratiating himself with gifts of phony fossils. The gentlemean recognizes his folly in the end, but until then acts out an amusing caricature of a role well known in the eighteenth century.

Just Friedrich Wilhelm Zachariä's (1726–1777) *Tageszeiten* (1755) and *Die Schöpfung der Hölle* (1760) modelled after Thomson's *Seasons* and Milton's *Paradise Lost* respectively contain familiar themes from astronomy: millions of suns, boundless space, countless systems of planets, myriads of inhabitants, the orbit of the earth.[12] In "Die Nacht", the last section of *Die Tageszeiten,* he celebrates modern astronomy's triumph over its crude beginnings of fables and superstitions. In the following passage the discoveries of Copernicus, Hevel, Galileo, Huygens, Cassini and Newton are cited as the foundation of the new astronomy:

Kühn befreyte Copernick zuerst die belästigte Sonne
Von dem beschwerlichen Weg um unsern geringeren Erdball;
Liess sie nun wieder im Mittelpunkt ruhn, und besser die Erde,
Zu den Planeten gesellt, sich um die Sonne bewegen.
Auch eroberte Hevel den Mond; sah Alpen und Seen,
Auf der fleckigten Kugel, und nante die Länder mit Namen.
Galiläi erblickte zuerst die Jupitersmonden,

10 (Halle, 1754). The second edition (Halle, 1766) was used.
11 *Sammlung der besten deutschen prosaischen Schriftsteller und Dichter,* Band 76: *Weissens Lustspiele,* pp. 121–208.
12 *Poetische Schriften.* 9 Bände in 3 (Amsterdam, 1767).

Und Saturns Trabanten und Ring Huygens und Cassini.
Newton verfolgte sogar den Lauf des schnellen Kometen
Über die fernesten Grenzen des Weltgebäudes hinüber; . . . (161)

Conrad Stephan Meintel (1728—1764) has much nature poetry in his
Vermischte Gedichte (Nürnberg, 1764). Although he says in his preface that he
seeks traces of the Creator in nature, when he describes natural phenomena, God
is left out of the picture. In a poem such as "Der Frühling", in which he
describes a variety of plants and flowers, there is an involvement in detail and
enjoyment of sense perception.

A few poems which Gotthold Ephraim Lessing (1729—1781) wrote in his
youth contain scientific themes. Most of these appeared in Christlob Mylius' *Der
Naturforscher* (1747—1748) and are written in the spirit of the Anacreontic
poets who stressed the virtues of wine and love. The Anacreontic poems with
scientific themes are the following: "Die Planetenbewohner" (75), "Die drey
Reiche der Natur" (95), "Die Wetterpropheceyung" (127) and "Der neue
Welt-Bau". (127)[13] In the last poem — the only one which did not appear in *Der
Naturforscher* — he maintains that Copernicus was under the influence of wine
when he realized that the sun stood still and the earth moved:

Der Wein, der Wein macht nicht nur froh,
er macht auch zum Astronomo.
Ihr kennt doch wohl den grossen Geist,
nach dem der wahre Welt-Bau heisst?
Von diesem hab' ich einst gelesen,
dass er beym Weine gleich gewesen,
    als er der Sonne Stillestand,
    die alte neue Wahrheit fand. (127)

In "Die drey Reiche der Natur" he substitutes for the Linnaean system of
classification his own: The difference between the three realms of nature is that
men and animals drink and love, plants only drink and stones do neither; thus,
any creature that neither loves nor drinks belongs to the stones.

"Die lehrende Astronomie" (124—126) is a serious poem. Contemplation of
the stars, he maintains, teaches the wisdom of humility. Since virtue is lacking in
this world, he hopes that it exists in those better worlds among the distant stars.
He sends his thoughts ahead to those better spheres with the expectation of
following soon.

His most significant poem from the point of view of our subject is the
fragment "Aus einem Gedichte an den Herrn M *** (243—247) which appeared
in *Der Naturforscher* in 1748. The subject is the quarrel between the ancients

13 All page references are to volume I of Karl Lachmann's edition of Lessing's
Sämtliche Schriften, 23 Bände (Stuttgart, 1886—1924).

and the moderns. Lessing maintains that nature dispenses its gifts evenly and that at all times there are creative spirits. However, in antiquity the best minds turned to poetry, whereas now they turn to science:

> Das Alter wird uns stets mit dem Homer beschämen,
> Und unsrer Zeiten Ruhm muss Newton auf sich nehmen.
> Zwey Geister gleich an Gröss, und ungleich nur im Werk,
> Die Wunder ihrer Zeit, des Neides Augenmerk.
> Wer zweifelt, dass Homer ein Newton worden wäre,
> Und Newton, wie Homer, der ewgen Dichtkunst Ehre,
> Wenn dieser das geliebt, und dieses der gewählt,
> Worinne beyden doch nichts mehr zum Engel fehlt? (243)

Newton and Homer are spirits of equal stature but chose one area rather than the other. His position in the quarrel, then, is that the ancients are superior in poetry and the moderns in science. The modern poet who claims to imitate nature never gets beyond appearances, "Ins innre der Natur dringt nie dein kurzer Blick" (244). The modern scientists on the other hand, are the real creative spirits of today:

> Er, der zuerst die Luft aus ihrer Stelle jagte,
> Und mehr bewies, als man je zu errathen wagte;
> Er, der im Sonnenstrahl den Grund der Farben fand,
> Und ihre Änderung in feste Regeln band;
> Er, der vom Erdenball die platten Pole wusste,
> Eh ein Maupertuis sie glücklich messen musste;
> Hat die kein Schöpfergeist bey ihrer Müh beseelt: . . .? (247)

Guericke's experiments with the air pump, Newton's color theory, his calculation that the earth was flattened at the poles, later verified by Maupertuis' expedition to Lapland — these are the creative deeds with which the moderns have surpassed the ancients as ancient poets still surpass the moderns:

> Stagirens Ehr ist jezt den Physikern ein Kind,
> Wies unsre Dichter noch bey alten Dichtern sind . . . (247)

In Salomon Gessner's (1730–1788) *Schriften*[14] there is an idyll "Die Gegend im Gras" (III, 142) in which the poet describes natural phenomena with the precision of the natural historian. In a pastoral play, "Evander und Alcimna", there is a caricature of a scientist who knows only useless things. He does not know medicine, agriculture, politics, or poetry; what he does know is the following: "Ich rechne den Sternen ihren Lauf aus; ich kenne Sprachen, die

---

14 Zürich, 1762).

entfernte Nationen reden; ich habe berechnet, wie viele Sandkörner auf einer Meile Landes liegen, und hab' erst vor kurzem noch einen Flek im Mond entdekt, den Endymion selbst nicht gekannt hat" (IV, 52).

Johann Friedrich von Cronegk (1731—1758), a friend of Lessing, was at his untimely death considered one of the promising poets of the day. In "Einsamkeiten in zween Gesängen" (II, 41—76) and in "Lob der Gottheit" (II, 151—154) we find a cosmic view of immeasurable space, enormous heavenly bodies orbiting harmoniously and inhabited by souls who have attained varying degrees of enlightenment. In his didactic poem "An Herrn K **" he uses Newton's color theory as an image to describe the relativity of human happiness:

> Der hohe Neuton drang in ew'ger Weisheit Rath,
> Und fand, dass an sich selbst kein Wesen Farben hat:
> Bloss von der Sonnen Licht, nachdem es auf ihn strahlet,
> Wird jeder Gegenstand verändert und bemahlet.
> So ist der Menschheit Glück: auf unsern eignen Wahn
> Kömmt Hoheit, Niedrigkeit, Glück oder Unglück an. (139)

Again in "Das Glück der Thoren", in speaking of the relativity of wisdom and folly, he says "Selbst Neuton ist vielleicht ein Thor in bessern Welten". (111).

Part III:
A SUMMARY OF SCIENTIFIC THEMES

In the second part I examined the profiles of poets in regard to the scientific themes in their poetry. In part III I have selected the most significant themes and trace them through the poetry considered in part II. This summary and survey will demonstrate, from a different point of view, the variety and recurrence of scientific themes in the poetry of the German Enlightenment. I have selected the following nine topics or categories: (1) attitudes toward science, (2) Newton, (3) cosmogony, (4) astronomy, (5) phenomena pertaining to the earth sciences, (6) plant life, (7) animal life, (8) attitude toward nature and (9) comic episodes. These categories, although not all-inclusive of the themes examined in part II, do encompass the most important scientific material.

(1) Attitudes toward science

The attitudes toward science encountered in the poetry are both positive and negative. Generally, the attitude is favorable toward the new sciences, though repeatedly doubts and criticisms are expressed.

Brockes praises modern scientists for having learned so much about plants that they can be classified better. Drollinger praises scientific achievements in astronomy as an indication of the grandeur of the human spirit. Nevertheless, he warns that the scientist who is so proud of his exact measurements and calculations may have neglected self-knowledge. He refers to the uselessness and impracticality of scientific knowledge. In Spreng's dedicatory poem, Drollinger is depicted as having attained both scientific knowledge and self-knowledge.

Triller was very critical of science in his later years. He depicts the scientists who claim to know so much as touching only the surface of natural phenomena. Triller taunts scientists for their evasive answers to fundamental questions. The true task of science and philosphy should be the teaching of self-knowledge.

Scheibel completely subscribes to the scientific enterprise in his long didactic poem on weather phenomena. However, at one point he casts the modern scientist in the role of Prometheus impiously trying to transcend the limitations of human nature.

Gottsched praises the new sciences for ushering in the new age of enlightenment. He enumerates some of the greatest achievements of the new sciences.

Hagedorn enumerates scientific achievements and praises scientific studies for raising man above the controversies of daily life. He expresses his faith in the new learning which has enlightened man about the cosmos. However, he also expresses serious doubts as to whether science can give man real happiness. He depicts the sciences as extraneous to man's life and extolls the practical arts like agriculture.

Haller enumerates some of the extraordinary scientific achievements, but warns that this success may distract man from self-knowledge. He grants that scientific knowledge can inculcate piety by leading men to a recognition of God, the Creator.

Zernitz praises and describes man's scientific achievements but also insists that self-knowledge has priority over all other kinds of knowledge. He asserts that a contemplation of purpose in nature can lead man to a proper understanding of self. Knowledge of final causes, he maintains, together with efficient causes constitutes man's comprehension of nature.

Uz asserts that the art of attaining happiness presupposes the acquisition of wisdom which includes a study of the sciences. Giseke warns that scientific learning can make one too pretentious to experience ordinary human feelings.

Creuz believes that science can lead man to God. He warns that the victory of science over superstition has not given man certain knowledge. The scientists who measure and count know only the outer garment of nature. The main justification of science is its practical and utilitarian aspect.

Dusch praises modern science for having abandoned the speculations of the ancients in favor of reason and experience. König praises the seeker for truth who turns to the empirical study of nature. Lessing maintains that the best minds today turn to science rather than poetry.

Thus, as positive attitudes can be cited the praise of science for abandoning false speculations, for bringing enlightenment, for lifting man above the controversies of daily life and for leading him to piety by a recognition of purpose in nature. The critical attitudes are the assertions that science does not lead to self-knowledge, that it is useless and impractical in contrast to the practical arts like agriculture, that science leads only to a superficial understanding of nature and that it inculcates an exaggerated pride in human achievements.

(2) Newton

The scientist most frequently alluded to by the poets of our period was, without question, Isaac Newton. He was the scientist who represented the method and the success of modern science. I shall consider the references to his color theory, those to his theory of gravity and numerous other statements glorifying him and his achievements.

His color theory concerning the composite nature of white light is cited by several poets as one of the greatest scientific achievements: Triller, Gottsched, Haller, Wieland and Richey. Bodmer, in his 1752 edition of *Der Noah,* makes a parenthetical comment about Newton being the first to discover the true nature of light and color. Sendel has in his verse compendium of science two detailed descriptions of color phenomena according to the Newtonian theory. Zernitz refers to Newton's attempts to imitate the Creator by reproducing the colors of the rainbow in a darkened room. Dusch describes Newton's experiments on color. Lessing mentions Newton's color theory as an example of the creativity of modern science. Cronegk uses the color theory as an image to describe the relativity of human happiness.

There are numerous references to Newton's theory of gravity, though in the first half of the century some express doubt about the nature of the force involved. Drollinger speaks of the balance which Newton established in the heavens. Triller praises Newton's achievement but maintains he took refuge in occult qualities with his concept of gravity. Gottsched alludes to the theory of gravity with his reference to planetary orbits that maintain a balance of centripetal and centrifugal forces. He also refers to a magnetic force that prevails throughout the universe. Haller describes as Newton's supreme achievement, his discovery of a force inherent in matter which moves planets in their orbits and causes tides on our planet. Lange says Newton revealed nature according to number, weight and mass, and discovered the parabolic nature of cometary orbits. Mylius cites Newton's discovery of the mutual attraction between all bodies which he compares to magnetic attraction. Creuz attributes gravitational attraction to the primeval particles at the beginning of creation. Dusch stresses Newton's calculations of the orbits of planets and comets and his discovery of the force that causes tides. Wieland mentions Newton's calculations of planetary and cometary orbits about the sun and refers to his discovery of the laws of the mutual attraction of heavenly bodies. Kästner praises Newton for his discovery of that single force by which planets and comets remain in their orbits and by which bodies tend to the center of the earth.

In connection with Newton's theory of gravity the references to the Lapland expedition of Maupertuis can also be mentioned. Newton and Huygens had maintained on the basis of the theory of gravity that the earth was flattened at the poles. In 1735 the Académie des Sciences sent expeditions to Peru and Lapland to measure meridian arcs in different latitudes. The measurements made at Torneå in Lapland in 1736 under the direction of Maupertuis verified that the earth was flattened at the poles. These results were hailed as a verification of Newton's theory of gravity.

Scheibel refers to the results of the expedition, which he accepts as valid, but questions whether the cause of the flattening at the poles is known. As a Cartesian he could not accept the gravitational force as an explanation. Zernitz describes the expedition, its dangers, its sponsorship by the king, the primitive Lapps and the expedition's success in verifying Newton's and Huygens' calculations. Mylius mentions the expedition to Kittis near the North Pole where Maupertuis proved what Newton knew long ago. Mylius expresses the wish that his own speculations about comets will one day be verified just as was the case with Newton. Leinker cites the contention of Picard and Cassini that the earth was egg shaped and the Maupertuis expedition which disproved it. Richey makes a brief comment about the expedition and Lessing refers to Newton's knowledge of the figure of the earth before Maupertuis' measurements.

There are numerous other references to Newton, glorifying him and his achievements. Triller cites Newton as that mortal who came closest to the mysteries of nature; he dreamt true dreams. Gottsched refers to the telescope as "Neutons Röhren". Hagedorn in his speculations about inhabited worlds conjectures that they too may have their Newtons. According to Haller, Newton gave man the tablets of eternal laws which God implanted in nature. Yet, science has its limitations and Newton, the model scientist, knew it. Uz speaks of "Neutons Pfad", that is, the system by which the order in the heavens is plotted. Mylius envisions encountering after death the spirit of Newton, the greatest of all astronomers. He refers to "Newtons Kunst" by which comets were proven to have measurable orbits like planets. Creuz speaks of "die erhabensten Neuto-nischen Gedanken", "Newtons göttliche Gedanken" and "Neutons Ziffern". Dusch refers to Newton as "der Priester der Natur" and Wieland calls him "Solon der Planeten". Kästner pays tribute to Newton's synthesis in his epigram "Auf Newtons Grabmal". Lessing describes Homer and Newton as spirits of equal stature. Overbeck compares Newton's reformation in the sciences to Luther's in religion.

(3) Cosmogony

Not unrelated to Newton and his system of the world is the interest in cosmogony and related themes. There were numerous theories that attempted to account for the creation of the universe and cataclysmic events such as Noah's flood and the final conflagration, according to natural laws. We shall again turn to our poets and summarize their reflections on cosmogony and related themes, that is, those dealing with the creation and destruction of the world or worlds and transformations on the face of the earth.

Bodmer follows Whiston's cometary theory closely in explaining Noah's flood as being caused by a comet. The rains start when the earth passes through the comet's tail, and the comet's gravitational pull forces the waters in the interior of the earth to flood the land. Bodmer, also in accordance with Whiston's theory, brings the comet back a second time in its ascent from the perihelion to cause ninety more days of rain.

Gottsched considers the possibility that stars perish and thus as suns would each time signify the destruction of a solar system. He also describes comets as planets that are in the process of perishing – an allusion to Whiston's cometary theory.

Anna Dorothea Lange, in describing Noah's flood, refers to the speculations presumably of Burnet and Whiston, that the interior of the earth had to supply the huge quantities of water necessary to cover the entire globe. As evidence that the flood was universal, she cites the transformations that have taken place on the earth's surface as indicated by the presence of fossils. She also alludes to Burnet's theory that mountains appeared during the cataclysms caused by the deluge. Lange, in his poem "Der Komet", refers to the speculation of Whiston and Heyn that a comet is a planet in a state of chaos.

Zernitz sees a constant change in nature, and God is perpetually creating new worlds out of old substances. Thus, nothing ever perishes; there are simply continuous transformations. In his considerations on death he cites the probability that stars perish, and with them the inhabited planets dependent on them for heat and light. He maintains that the destruction of worlds is a part of God's design as well as in accord with natural laws. He also raises the question of the age of the earth in connection with the widespread presence of marine fossils, which suggest to him a gradual transformation of the surface of the earth.

Mylius explains the cometary theory of Whiston and Heyn in his three didactic poems on the subject: "Lehrgedicht von den Bewohnern der Planeten", "Auf dem Tod weyland Herrn Johann Heyns" and "Vom Vorspiel des jüngsten Gerichts". Especially the latter is about the creation of the planet, the deluge and the final destruction – all involving a comet.

In Leinker's poetry several aspects of Whiston's theory appear: comets are planets in a state of chaos, a comet imparted a diurnal motion to the earth after Adam's fall, and a comet caused the deluge. He also refers to Burnet's theory concerning the flood, namely, that the waters in the interior of the earth broke through the crust. He cites fossils as evidence that the surface of the earth has undergone radical changes.

Creuz' poetry abounds with cosmogonic themes. There is a reference to the final conflagration, whose immediate natural cause is the slowing down of the earth's orbit, thereby forcing it to plunge into the sun. He considers evidence that suggests the fiery origin of the earth and the vast changes that have taken place on our planet since the creation. He depicts nature as constantly creating new worlds and destroying old ones. He speaks of colossal changes that have taken place on the surface of the earth, such as the universal deluge during which the waters from the interior of the earth broke through the crust, suggesting

Burnet's theory. Elsewhere he alludes to the sudden creation and destruction of mountains, the replacement of sea by land, and the creation and destruction of stars. In the primeval beginnings of creation, the ultimate particles were being attracted to one another according to a Newtonian attraction. Life was created in the sea and there underwent many transformations. He cites the polyps as vestiges of this early period of creation out of chaos. He alludes to one aspect of Burnet's cosmogony by suggesting that the surface of the earth before the deluge was a thin crust composed of oil and dust particles. He refers to Whiston's theory that the earth was originally a comet and that the flood was caused by a comet. Finally, he suggests that the final conflagration of the earth will be caused by its gradual approach to the sun.

Müldener mocks those scholars — presumably Burnet among them — who see in mountains only the ugly remains of the havoc caused by the deluge. Reichel, in a long footnote, disagrees with Burnet's theory about the origin of mountains.

(4) Astronomy

The scientific themes most popular with the poets of our period are those related to astronomy. The first German to write extensively about matters pertaining to astronomy was Barthold Heinrich Brockes. In my brief treatment of scientific themes in his *Irdisches Vergnügen in Gott,* I cited only a fraction of the passages dealing with astronomy. During the four decades after the publication of the first volume of Brockes' work in 1721, many German poets followed his example, as we can see in the poetry that has been considered where astronomic themes abound. I shall briefly summarize the themes that recur repeatedly.

The Copernican theory is mentioned and alluded to frequently. Astronomers who worked in support and development of the theory are cited by name and their contribution briefly described. Among the poets after 1720, there is no dissent from the heliocentric system.

Contemplation of the heavens and enumeration of the facts of the new astronomy often lead the poet to religious sentiments. Praise of God in nature and a recognition of His wisdom, power and goodness are frequently the conclusion of a poet's excursion into the field of astronomy.

There is a great fascination with measurements and telescopic observations. Poets delight in describing the sizes of planets and stars, the distances between the planets and stars and the vast number of stars. These facts and figures often bring the poet to an awareness of the vastness of space which some consider unlimited and infinite.

The belief in a plurality of worlds appears in much of the poetry. Every one of an unlimited number of stars is a sun and center of a planetary system. The poets delight in surveys of heavenly bodies. They usually start with our solar system, consider the sun, then each of the planets and their satellites, comets and beyond to the fixed stars and infinite space.

The sun, the earth and the moon receive special attention. There are references to solar and lunar eclipses, sun spots, speculations about the surface of the sun and descriptions of the surface of the moon as seen through the telescope. The motions of the earth are very popular themes. Especially Brockes, but many others as well, picture the earth's daily rotation about its axis and its annual revolution about the sun.

There are several themes involving astronomy which I shall summarize in greater detail and with reference to the authors in whose works they appear. These themes are: the inhabitation of planets, imaginary space voyages, the enlightenment a human spirit enjoys after death, and the awareness of difference in perspective, that is, the relativity or subjectivity of man's view of the universe. All four themes are related and represent the attempt to go from the known to the unknown, from the seen to the unseen, to extend nature or to conceive of nature beyond our three dimensional world.

The belief in the inhabitation of the planets of this solar system, of their satellites and of the planets and satellites of the countless other solar systems — even comets and suns themselves are sometimes included — is a widespread belief found in the prose and poetry of our period. Here we shall refer primarily to poetic statements of this theme.

Brockes extends the ladder of creation beyond man, which leads him to speculate about the nature of inhabitants on other planets. He reasons that since nature on our planet is observed to be inexhaustible and versatile, we can expect nature to be just as inventive there and provide those many planets with a variety of creatures. This theme appears many more times in his *Irdisches Vergnügen in Gott,* as for example: I, 436; IV, 236, 334; V, 14—23; VI, 321; VIII, 146.

In Bodmer's *Der Noah,* we learn that the souls of the damned find their new home on a lonely uninhabited satellite of an uninhabitable planet of a star at the very edge of the aether. The inhabitants of our sun are depicted as being a much happier community.

Gottsched's arguments for the inhabitation of the planets is teleological: Since the other planets share with the earth those motions that create conditions for life, then there must be life there, for God would not have created them so without a purpose.

Hagedorn asserts his belief in the existence of a plurality of inhabited worlds, and in a footnote refers to the ancient and modern writers with whom he shares this belief.

316 A Summary of Scientific Themes

Sendel emphatically affirms his belief that all the planets are inhabited by rational creatures. He even rejects Huygens' doubts about the inhabitability of the moon. The main argument that underlies his conviction is the analogy between the planets and the earth.

Uz raises himself up to a cosmic perspective and sees a host of inhabited heavenly bodies, of which the earth is one of the most insignificant.

Mylius in his essay, "Von der Unendlichkeit der Welt", speculates about the millions of inhabited worlds that exist in an infinite universe. In his "Lehrgedicht von den Bewohnern der Kometen", he argues with conviction for the possibility and probability that comets are inhabited.

Leinker accepts the inhabitation of planets, for could they have been created without a purpose, he asks. Creuz refers to countless inhabited heavenly bodies.

Wieland conjectures about the beneficent circumstances that inhabitants of different heavenly bodies might enjoy. He also pictures the panorama of a plurality of worlds and explains the gradations of beings and worlds.

Richey characterizes the belief in the inhabitation of planets as one of the achievements which have deluded men into thinking that they have attained truth.

Gellert reflects about the inhabitants of other planets in his *Moralische Vorlesungen,* and Ewald von Kleist alludes to the theme in his poem "Die Unzufriedenheit des Menschen".

In Klopstock's *Der Messias,* the perspective of a plurality of inhabited worlds is an essential part of the cosmic panorama in which the action of his epic unfolds. The same can be said of Zachariä's Biblical epic, *Die Schöpfung der Hölle,* as well as his *Tageszeiten.*

Cronegk expresses a cosmic view in which a plurality of inhabited worlds is accepted.

Closely related to the theme of the inhabitation of planets, are the imaginary space voyages. Brockes in his poem, "Traum-Gesicht", dreams of journeys to other planets, whose inhabitants have only one of the five senses. He communicates telepathically with an inhabitant of Jupiter who informs him that earth creatures are on a level between animals and the higher beings on Jupiter.

In Bodmer's *Der Noah,* the archangel Raphael and Lamech, Noah's father, move freely through space stopping at various inhabited heavenly bodies.

Sendel's Sternlieb, an amateur astronomer, discourses about astronomy with an inhabitant of the moon whom he meets on a dream journey to the satellite. Before he leaves, the moon inhabitant hands him a work on astronomy which the dreamer understands, because it is written in the universal language of astronomy.

Uz describes the flight of the Muse Urania through space. She moves to far away solar systems never viewed by earth astronomers and attains a cosmic perspective.

Mylius expresses the wish to soar through the heavens to inspect the many orbiting bodies. He expresses his faith in man's capacity to provide the means some day for space flight.

In the last of Wieland's "Zwölf moralische Briefe in Versen", he goes on a dream voyage to an idyllic society on a distant heavenly body.

In dreams eighteen to twenty-two of his *Träume,* Krüger becomes a space traveler and visits the planets of our solar system. His observations and conversations with the inhabitants are about astronomy and society.

Another theme involving astronomy is the attempt of the poets to imagine the enlightenment a spirit experiences after death. Brockes considers the possibility of spirits after death acquiring new senses and thus perceiving more than here on earth. We find also the theme of the spirit after death ascending and surveying the numerous heavenly bodies and seeing clearly what he could only surmise here (I, 140; II, 391; III, 649–653).

Triller pictures the spirit of the deceased Hermann Boerhaave in full knowledge of planetary orbits, the nature of light, the origin of comets and realizing with amazement that Newton's dreams were almost true.

In Gottsched's poem in praise of Count Manteufel, we see the latter's spirit attain a more enlightened condition in which he swiftly sees the truth which he so diligently sought on earth. Similarly, in another poem the spirit of a princess who had in her life applied herself industriously to the sciences is delighted with a fulfillment of her quest.

In Mylius' "Gedanken von dem Zustande der abgeschiedenen Seelen", Damon is enthusiastic about the prospect of joining the souls of the greatest astronomers of the past, especially Newton, in a perfect contemplation of the universe.

In "Der Tod", Creuz contrasts the uncertainty of our knowledge here on earth with our state after death when our spirits will move swiftly to inevitable conclusions, unencumbered by preconceptions.

Wieland imagines that once man's spirit has left his place on earth and found his new home among the stars, he will have deeper insight; he will then penetrate to the essences and not be confined to the periphery. New senses may then unfold to reveal reality to him.

Ebert shows us the spirit of an enlightened aristocrat, who had always striven for knowledge, being led by the angels from sphere to sphere, receiving enlightenment from them.

Finally, there is the theme of the awareness of the relativity or subjectivity of man's view of the universe. The cosmic perspective of the new astronomy suggested the possibility of other and more expanded points of view.

Brockes delights in lifting up his mind to a cosmic perspective. In "Das Grosse und das Kleine", he surveys the heavenly bodies by stages, from the earth, to the moon, to the planets and beyond our solar system to the stars. In "Traum-Gesicht" he considers the possibility of rational creatures on other planets who may have less than or more than our five senses and, consequently, see reality from a perspective different from ours. He considers this a possibility in view of the variety found in the kingdom of nature. In "Die Zeit" he claims that time is not something absolute and real. It is a subjective factor caused by the daily and annual motions of our planet which gives us an awareness of change. Thus our sense of time is no more than our perspective, our point of view.

Sendel has his character Sternlieb on the moon view the cosmos through a moon telescope. Among other things, he sees the earth revolve about its axis and thereby gains a new perspective. Later Urania explains that Saturn can also be inhabited, for though it is far removed from the sun, its substance is such that the sun's rays suffice to impart life. Thereby, Urania indicated that we cannot judge all parts of the cosmos solely from our perspective here on earth.

Uz in his "Theodicee" elevates himself to a cosmic view from which our planet appears diminished in size and significance.

Mylius in "Von der Unendlichkeit der Welt" expands his cosmic perspective to stars of the sixth magnitude and conjectures about the many stars, unknown to us, but perceived by the inhabitants of solar systems in the Milky Way.

Creuz, in "Die Gottheit", considers the vastness of the universe which we cannot grasp due to the limitations of our senses and our narrow perspectives. When we conceive of the immensity about us, we realize the insignificance of our globe. Again in "Die Zukunft", he asserts that our knowledge is confined by our condition here on earth. We see only a small part of vast space and measure everything according to our limited perspective.

Wieland suggests that after death, new senses are discovered which expand the perspective. He also reflects on the relativity of size which is suggested to him by microscopic observations. The living organisms in a drop of water are infinitely small; similarly, we may appear as small to an interplanetary spirit.

(5) Phenomena pertaining to the earth sciences

Now let us turn to natural phenomena studied by the earth sciences and the life sciences. The former, which shall be considered first, are divided in the compendiums of science either according to the four elements, or as to whether they exist or occur on the surface of the earth, about it, or beneath it.

Brockes treats earth phenomena in the manner of the compendiums of science in his long didactic poems. In "Die Erde", "Die Luft", "Das Wasser", "Das Feuer", the nature of the elements is examined, then specific phenomena and their use to man. In "Das Wasser" he studies the tides, floods, different bodies of water like oceans and rivers, lists several specific rivers, and describes sea animals and sea vegetation. "Das Feuer" considers various theories about fire, circumstances under which fire arises, volcanic eruptions, subterranean fires and the effect and power of fire. In "Die Erde" he examines the size of the earth, the nature of gravity, the interior of the earth, metals, minerals, stones and subterranean fires and waterways. In "Die Luft" he stresses the importance of that element to all life, he describes the expansion and contraction of the air under different circumstances thereby causing phenomena like clouds, snow, hail, dew, fog and wind. In another long didactic poem, "Die drei Reiche der Natur", he considers the mineral kingdom, which he divides into five classifications: metals, half metals, earth, salts and stones. He enumerates many kinds in each classification and gives the salient characteristics of each.

Triller's "Die Luft" is a didactic poem in which he describes the properties of air and many of its functions. "Der Ursprung des Blitzes und Donners" is another didactic poem in which the natural causes of thunder and lightning are explained.

Scheibel's *Die Witterungen* is a long didactic poem in which weather phenomena, agriculture and a variety of related themes are discussed.

In Zell's "Gottes Grösse in den Wassern", we have a description and explanation of ocean tides from a Cartesian point of view, according to which the moon presses on the air which in turn presses on the earth's waters.

Gottsched states the new belief in the lawfulness of nature and describes some of the natural phenomena on earth whose laws are now understood: motion, thunder and lightning, tides, storms and earthquakes.

In a poem appearing in the first edition of his poems in 1729, Hagedorn praises the wise man who searches for the causes of natural phenomena such as tides, wind, weather, thunder, lightning, motion, heat, light, sound and pressure.

In Haller's "Die Alpen", there are discussions of the treasures in the interior of the earth, mineral springs, weather phenomena, tides.

In Sendel's compendium of science in verse, we find descriptions of atmospheric and weather phenomena, mountains, metals, minerals, stones, the properties of water and various manifestations of water.

In a poem by Anna Dorothea Lange, the subject of fossils and the origin of mountains is taken up.

Zernitz includes the natural phenomena associated with the elements, air, fire, earth and water in his description of the success scientists have had in seeking knowledge about nature.

In "Die Kunst stets fröhlich zu seyn", Uz returns to earth from a journey in the vastness of space, to consider the orderliness of natural phenomena on earth, in which he includes atmospheric phenomena such as snow, wind, thunder, lightning.

Leinker examines theories concerning the origin of the earth and then turns to an exploration of natural phenomena on earth which he divides according to the four elements in the manner of compendiums of science. He considers metals, minerals, stones, volcanoes, earthquakes; he describes floods, the sudden appearance and disappearance of islands, lists some of the marine life and enumerates the many forms in which water appears and the benefit man derives from them; among air phenomena he mentions atmospheric phenomena like rain, hail, snow, northern lights, halos, rainbows and speaks of the many useful phenomena associated with air; finally, he discusses the qualities of fire and its uses to man.

Creuz refers to water phenomena as examples of the interdependence of natural phenomena: rivers are fed by vapors arising from the oceans and oceans are replenished by the rivers; the earth is nourished by dew which the sun draws upwards again.

In the fourth canto of Dusch's "Die Wissenschaften", the poet discusses, among other things, natural phenomena on our planet, dividing them according to the four elements in the manner of the compendiums of science. He compares the circulation of the planet's waters to the circulation of the blood in the human body; he also raises the question of the sources of the waters on earth. In connection with fire phenomena he subscribes to the belief in a source of heat in the interior of the earth which is as necessary to life as the heat of the sun. He cites volcanoes as evidence of such an interior source of heat.

Wieland in his "Die Natur der Dinge" shows how the earth's motions cause changes on the earth and discusses phenomena on earth related to the seasons.

In one of König's poems, in a dream experience, the art of mining is characterized as requiring a scientific study of nature. To one so trained, nature's treasures beneath the ground, its metals, minerals and precious stones, will be revealed.

Both Müldener and Suppius praise the beauties of mountains and reject Burnet's thesis that they are merely ugly remains of the flood. Müldener considers mountains magnificent decorations and, moreover, very useful to man. Also Dreyer in his poem "Das Gebirge" refers to nature's mysteries in mountains and praises the miner who uses science to reveal those mysteries.

The subject of mountains occurs also in Reichel's "Die Berge" in which he expresses the sense of awe and joy which they inspire in him. He also describes the uses of mountains and the treasures in metals and stones that can be found there. He rejects Burnet's theory about mountains, and also maintains that Burnet had an ambivalent attitude toward his subject.

(6) Plant life

Following the ladder of creation and the order of the compendiums of science, I shall turn from the earth sciences to the life sciences, namely, the kingdom of plants and the kingdom of animals. Plant life did not inspire as many controversial issues as astronomy; nor did it provide as much substance to the imagination. Nevertheless, natural history was eagerly cultivated by many amateurs. The study of plants brought the amateur as well as the scientist into a direct encounter with nature and evoked a response to nature that led to an organismic rather than a mechanistic view of nature.

Next to astronomy, plant life is the most popular subject in Brockes' *Irdisches Vergnügen in Gott*. His detailed knowledge of this kingdom of nature, his descriptions of individual plants, sometimes purely didactic, sometimes with great aesthetic merit, characterize his sense of immediacy for nature.

In his elaborate didactic poem "Die drei Reiche der Natur", he discusses the anatomy of plants, describing the parts and functions that plants have in common. He also enumerates twenty-two species of plants with many more sub-species. He takes up many individual plants, especially flowers and fruits. Plant life is often mentioned in connection with his numerous reflections about the world of minute phenomena, the world of the microscope. A typical example is the poem "Das Grosse und Kleine" in which he swings from the world of astronomy and the telescope to the world of natural history and the microscope. The image of the ladder of creation is then used to show the continuity in nature.

Plant life is one of the favorite themes in the poetry of Drollinger, an amateur botanist. In his letter, "Über die Aurikeln", he describes his own observations of the auriculas, and then tells a charming Ovidian tale about the metamorphosis of this plant from a simple healing herb to its present beauty. He discusses at length the theory of preformation and encapsulation, namely, that the whole plant is contained in the seed and, moreover, that all future plants exist already in the seed. Drollinger raises questions about the validity of the theory, although most of his contemporaries accepted it. In his poem "Auf eine Hyacinte", he offers fine poetic description of the drama of a plant's growth.

Zell's interest in the plant kingdom is exemplified in his poem, "Der Saamen der Pflantzen", in which he describes the wonders in a seed as revealed by the microscope. In the poem he also alludes to the preformation theory.

In Bodmer's *Der Noah,* the Noachides are depicted as natural historians who know as much about the history of plants as Malpighi or Ray. Sipha especially distinguishes himself in these studies with his lenses that have both microscopic and telescopic capacities.

In Haller's "Die Alpen", he describes the work of an unlearned villager who as an amateur natural historian appreciates the beauties of nature, classifies plants and knows their medicinal virtues.

In Sendel's compendium of science in verse, the plant kingdom is treated at length. He gives a detailed description of the parts of plants and the structures and functions of those parts. He explains the processes by which plants receive nourishment and grow. In connection with the question of the birth of plants, he explains and accepts the theory of preformation and encapsulation. In Behr's *Die Gottheit,* another compendium of science, the plant kingdom is also treated, but not nearly as thoroughly as in Sendel's work.

Uz stresses the lawfulness of nature which the scientist studies; he includes the natural historian who studies the lawfulness underlying the growth of plants.

Mylius, one of the many amateur natural historians of the time, demonstrates his interest in the subject, in his poem "Auf die Gegend bey Gera". He compares Leipzig's artistically designed gardens with Gera's unadorned beauty, and concludes that nature is the greater artist.

Leinker in his compendium of science in verse surveys the kingdom of plants in the manner of the natural historian by enumerating individual species.

Creuz sees in the plant kingdom primarily evidence of the greatness of God, as, for example, in the poem "Frühlingsgedanken" in which Damon invites Thyrsis to contemplate nature where even a blade of grass is a mirror of the Divine.

In the fourth canto of Dusch' "Die Wissenschaften", vegetation is described as an example of nature's plentitude and fruitfulness. In his *Schilderungen aus dem Reiche der Natur,* he repeatedly uses plant life to characterize his view of nature as wise, mysterious and almost endowed with divine qualities. He also adheres to the preformation and encapsulation theories, which suggest to him that a seed is as much a world as any planetary world.

Wieland discusses vegetation in his ascent up the ladder of creation. He does not describe specific species of plants, as many didactic poets do, but stresses the immense variety in the plant kingdom. He also refers to the Linnaean system of classification.

Cuno's *Ode über seinen Garten* celebrates the world of natural history with descriptions of numerous plants and flowers. The theme of nature's plentitude and incorruptibility pervades the work. By contrast, Denso's "Beweis der Gottheit aus dem Gras" is primarily a physicotheological poem.

In his *Moralische Vorlesungen,* Gellert sees in the plant kingdom an occasion to praise God in nature and evidence of purposefulness in nature. Similarly, Ebert praises God in the plant kingdom and the world revealed by the microscope.

Reichel imitates Brockes with his physicotheological reflections in verse about plant life, his "Lehrende Betrachtungen über Grass und Blumen". Similar is Miller's didactic "Die Gartenlust", a conversation between pupil and teacher about topics in natural history.

Finally, there is Salomon Gessner's "Die Gegend im Gras" in which the poet describes natural phenomena with the precision of the natural historian.

(7) Animal Life

Scientific interest in animals was widespread in our period, and, as in the case of plant life, offered a more immediate contact with living nature than did the study of heavenly bodies. The mathematical, mechanistic approach to nature, so successful in astronomy, had little effect in the study of the animal kingdom. Examinations of microscopic life, anatomy, the study of structures and functions of the parts of animals, descriptions of individual species, classification of animals, their arrangement on the ladder of nature and the nature of the animal soul are the principal themes appearing in the poetry.

Brockes treats the animal kingdom in his verse compendium of science, "Die drei Reiche der Natur". He discusses functions such as the circulation of the blood, nourishment, digestion, reproduction and the parts of the body that are involved. He gives a classification of animals and enumerates and describes dozens of individual animals. Another theme pertaining to the world of animals is microscopic observations of minute life. These observations often lead to reflections about the continuity of the kingdoms of nature, frequently characterized by the image of the ladder of creation.

Among Triller's didactic poems, there is one describing the behavior and habit of bees and another which gives a detailed account of the mating habits of frogs. Other didactic poems demonstrate his medical knowledge with accounts of the anatomy of the human body and some of its functions (230—1).

In Zell's oratorio "Die Erschaffung der Welt", Adam is depicted as a pious eighteenth century natural historian who notes the animals on land, in the sea and the air, and is led thereby to recognize God, the Creator.

In Bodmer's Der Noah, the animals enter the ark according to the classification of the Linnaean system. The animals appear by classes — mammals, birds, amphibians, worms, insects — with several species described according to their distinguishing characteristics in each class. In his comments on insects, he refers to the work of the entomologist Réaumur, who revealed the complexity in these tiny creatures. Japhet is pleased at the prospect of living in the ark, for to him it is a cabinet of living natural curiosities where he can study the ladder of creation.

Gottsched in his description of scientific achievements cites the studies of human anatomy that have set forth the parts of the body and the functions of the organs.

In Hagedorn's fabels there are frequent references to insects and animals, supplemented by explanatory footnotes in which he quotes from natural historians like Réaumur and Pluche. In his poem "Die Thiere", he takes up the problem whether animals have the capacity to think and judge or are mere machines as Descartes had maintained. Like most of his contemporaries, he rejected Descartes' position and concluded that animals share with humans some capacity to reason.

In Sendel's treatment of the animal kingdom, there is no enumeration of classes and species of animals but only an account of what they have in common. He discusses in detail the structures and functions of the parts of animals. There are two further sections on the human body in which the physician Sendel gives us a medical text for the layman in verse. He concludes by surveying the entire animal kingdom, indicating the similarities and differences between man and the species beneath him.

Behr's procedure with the animal kingdom is to enumerate individual animals and to describe what is unique about their physical structures, habits and environment. The descriptions, though not precisely scientific, suffice for this natural history in verse. The footnotes refer the reader to more scientific accounts of each subject.

Zernitz raises the question of the nature of the animal soul in his philosophical poem, "Gedanken von den Endzwecken der Welt". Like most of his contemporaries, he rejects Descartes' point of view and tries to show that the difference between man and the animals is only one of degree. He offers numerous examples from the animal kingdom, descriptions of the behavior of various animals, their responses to various situations to force recognition of the presence of feelings and thoughts in animals. Animals, he maintains, have their own uniqueness and excellence which are different from those of man, but to which they have as much right as man to his.

Leinker in his verse compendiums treats the animal kingdom in the manner of the natural historian by enumerating individual species. In the second part, he describes, with considerable detail, the parts and life processes of the human body.

Creuz also denied a fundamental difference between man and other living forms. He maintains on the basis of many similarities that physiologically man belongs to the animal kingdom. He returns to this theme later with the daring thought that man was once what animals are now. Though he implies a transformation of the species in the course of time, Creuz may have meant only a spiritual evolution. He also implies that at one time the ladder of creation was in a formative state in which new species were created; now, however, he continues, the species are fixed and will remain so until the final conflagration. He cites the polyps as vestiges of this early period of creation.

Dusch also refers to the animal kingdom in connection with the temple of nature episode where the continuity of nature from the lowest forms to the highest is depicted.

Wieland treats the animal kingdom within the context of the ladder of creation. He begins with those tiny worms studied by Leeuwenhoek, Hooke and Swammerdam, and after considering the plant kingdom, deals with the transition to the animal species. He also takes up the mobility of the species, that is, their capacity to move from the lower to the higher rungs of the ladder, though only in a spiritual sense. In the poem he refers to Georg Friedrich Meier's work on the animal soul, in which the latter maintains that animals have all the qualities human souls have, including immortality; they lack only the capacity for abstract thought. He also claims that through death the souls of animals ascend toward humanity.

(8) Attitudes toward nature

In connection with the scientific themes discussed up to now, various attitudes toward nature are expressed. I shall now trace through the poetry several of these attitudes such as: the lawfulness of nature, purpose in nature, nature's versatility and incessant activity, nature's superiority over art, religious sentiments in regard to nature, nature as a model for human conduct, nature as wise and mysterious.

The lawfulness of nature is especially stressed in the numerous descriptions of the regular orbits of heavenly bodies. Gottsched, in one of his occasional poems, asserts the lawfulness of nature in the earth's planetary orbit, as well as in some of the earth phenomena whose natural laws are now understood such as motion, thunder and lightning, tides, storms and earthquakes. Haller refers to the lawfulness in nature that Newton had discovered in the heavens and on earth. Zernitz explains the orderliness and interrelatedness of natural phenomena by picturing the chaos that would result if the earth's orbit were to be shifted only slightly. Uz refers to nature's order found by the astronomer in the planetary orbits, by the physicist who studies weather phenomena, and by the natural historian who studies the growth of plants. Giseke rejoices that nature is not subject to man's whim and fancy, but is governed by laws which are not of man's design. He refutes freethinkers with the argument of the all-pervading lawfulness of nature which he finds in the tiniest, as well as in the grandest natural phenomena. Unzer cites examples to show that the lawfulness of nature is God's design and purpose.

A recurring theme is the demonstration of purpose, design and inter-relatedness in nature. Zernitz believes the realization that nature is permeated with purpose imparted to it by God can give man a natural religion which could bring order to his moral life. However, he makes it clear that his conception of teleology is not an anthropocentric one. His goal is not to show that man is the main recipient of God's design in nature, but to demonstrate God's wisdom as revealed in the design. Dusch concludes his discussion of the natural sciences in his poem, "Die Wissenschaften", with an expression of faith in the interrelated-ness of all natural phenomena. He surveys the kingdoms of nature in which every part is necessary because it serves the whole. For Gellert the presence of purpose in nature is an article of faith to which he often returns. Reichel argues that an empirical explanation of a natural phenomena does not preclude the teleological, for any natural phenomena could still carry out God's design, even though the immediate natural causes are known.

Many poets depict nature as versatile, ever active and full of variety. Brockes expects planets to be inhabited, because nature on our planet is versatile and inexhaustible. For Zernitz there is constant change in nature. However, there is no real destruction either; substances simply undergo a transformation of form. In his principle of conservation both change and permanence characterize nature. He also stresses variety in nature which is limited only by the fact that each species reproduces according to its kind. Mylius maintains that relativity is a rule in nature and that even within the limited perspective on our planet we can perceive nature's inexhaustible capacity for variety. Creuz refers to nature's variety, abundance and incessant activity in describing the continuous process of destruction and building that goes on in nature. König describes nature's processes as constantly active and fruitful.

Nature as a model and guideline for art is also a theme that occurs in the context of general reflections about nature. Drollinger's advice to the artists is to follow nature: it never errs, it is a clear unchanging light, it imparts life and beauty to all, it is at the same time the source and purpose of art. Creuz reflects on the abundance which is prevalent everywhere and concludes that the arts flourish when man becomes aware of the artistic design in nature. He urges that we learn art in the school of nature rather than in schools of man. Dusch's pious hermit studies nature's art in the unlimited plant and animal species of his garden which interferes with nature's way as little as possible. Löwen also uses the garden theme to demonstrate a blending of art and nature, with nature making a superior contribution. Leinker maintains that scientific truths impart to poetry a quality of depth; thus nature and our scientific knowledge of it is a most fitting subject for poetry. In his description of the mechanism of the human body, he asserts that nature's wisdom and art as seen in the human body should be a model for man's art and technology.

Reflections about nature occasionally give rise to religious sentiments. Behr praises God in nature as do so many of his contemporaries, but goes further in claiming that God stands behind every natural phenomena. In Zernitz' poetry we find an example of nature viewed as holy, as a creation of God. Nature is called the temple of God and thus, is a reliable and consistent source of God's revelation. Giseke is convinced that a proper study of nature's wonders must always lead to a recognition of God. Dusch considers God as the Creator of nature, but often leaves Him in the background, so that nature is described almost as if it were autonomous and endowed with divine qualities. The pious hermit, in this connection, acquired his piety not from religion but from a scientific study of nature. In the hermit's dream of the temple of nature, we find a synthesis of art, science and religion.

There are a few other characterizations of nature to be considered. Zell describes nature as a mysterious, invisible power, the source of life and growth. Zernitz recommends that man should imitate nature in his own moral life. The wisdom and rationality that pervade nature can serve as a guideline for man in the organization of his own life. Dusch rejects mechanistic explanations of the world because the study of natural history reveals to him a nature that is mysterious and wise. In Gotthardt von Tschammer und Osten's sonnet "Natur", nature is described as benevolent, all-pervasive, superabundant, mysterious, spontaneous.

Finally, I shall cite several poetic statements of the image of the ladder of creation which appears so often in the poetry and prose of our period. It is one further expression of the belief in continuity and order in nature. By means of this image, a vast accumulation of data about the kingdoms of nature, about the worlds of the telescope and microscope, about nature extended beyond the senses is integrated into a coherent pattern that also seems to be wise, just and good.

Brockes is led by his reflections about the vast world of solar systems in the heavens and the world of minute phenomena on earth to use the image of the ladder of creation to combine the two worlds. He extends the ladder beyond the visible to the possible by trying to conceive of the nature of intelligent beings above man that might inhabit other planets.

In Bodmer's *Der Noah*, Sipha is also brought by his speculations about the worlds of the telescope and the microscope to the vision of a continuity in nature that extends beyond man to the angels. Sipha describes nature as having made numerous attempts before it finally fashioned man; nor did it stop there but continued until every gradation was occupied. When Japhet sees the ark filled with animals he is enthusiastic over the prospect of studying this chain of beings, this ladder of creation.

Uz turns from a cosmic perspective to the earth with a realization of our planet's insignificance. He makes a plea for tolerance of all creatures on our earth, no matter how small, because all creatures have their proper place on the golden ladder of creation.

Creuz, in his use of the image of the ladder, states that the animals and man stand on the same ladder and that what the animals now are we once were, suggesting that the element of time plays a role in nature's continuity.

Dusch's thoughts about the world that exists in a tiny seed also brings him to the conception of a ladder of things from smallest to the largest, each segment of which is unique yet subject to the same laws. In the temple of nature, Dusch beholds the innumerable species of mineral, plant and animal life which he sees arranged in a continuity from the lowest to the highest. The chain of creation, as he describes this continuity, extends beyond the lower forms to higher degrees of perfection.

In young Wieland's system of the world, the underlying conception is again a gradation of beings from the lowest to the highest, with mankind constituting merely some of the lesser forms. In another statement of the ladder of creation, he maintains that there is not only continuity but also mobility of the species, that is, they have the capacity to move from the lower to the higher rungs of the ladder in the course of a spiritual evolution.

(9) Comic episodes

Finally, I shall summarize several comic episodes involving scientific themes which were encountered in the poets. In Gottsched's *Das Neueste aus der anmuthigen Gelehrsamkeit,* there appeared a fable in verse to explain why the transit of Venus on June 6, 1761 was not visible in Leipzig. We learn that Apollo, undaunted by a previous experience of Mars, was about to embrace Venus when he noticed an intruder, namely, the English astronomer, Jeremiah Horrox, the first to observe a transit of Venus in 1639. Since then mortals have been spying on Venus and have prophesied that the lovers will meet again. Apollo, however, eludes once more with the help of a cloud.

Lange's *Der Komet* is a comic tale in rhymed verse about a comet who is exorcised and forced to reveal the story of his origin. He turns out to have been a poet who ruined his fame by writing too much, especially after his limited talent was exhausted. He then ceased to be a star generating its own light and became a mere comet with a diluted light trailing behind it. Before Lange gives his poetic vision of the exorcised comet's own account, he refers to the theories of Whiston and Newton about comets.

Mylius in his essay, "Sendschreiben von dem Aufnehmen der Naturlehre", offers several tongue-in-cheek proposals to enlist the foibles and vices of men in the service of science simply by having them do what comes most naturally to them. His "Anfangsgründe der Physikopetitmaitrick" is a parody of the practice of his time to construct systems with the pretense of scientific and mathematical accuracy. His new science, complete with axioms, postulates, theorems, observations and experiments demonstrates that the amorous adventures of young gentlemen are actually scientific experiments.

Löwen in "Der Billwerder" ridicules the other-worldliness of men of learning. He presents a caricature of an astronomer who goes into the country simply to use his telescope to view far away things rather than what is before him. Similarly, he shows us a ridiculous collector of natural curiosities who knows many facts, but neglects his own humanity as well as the beauties of nature, because of his exaggerated interest in precious and insignificant aspects of nature. Gessner's pastoral play, "Evander und Alcimna", presents a caricature of a scientist who knows only useless things and is ignorant about practical matters.

Weisse's Der Naturaliensammler is a comedy revolving about a country gentleman's passion for collecting natural curiosities about which he understands very little. He acts out an amusing caricature of a type well known in the eighteenth century.

Gleim's "Der Sternseher" depicts an ascetic astronomer who seeks new worlds so assiduously that he has abandoned all earthly joys. However, one particular evening, his phantasy more than his telescope reveals to this self-denying astronomer dancing girls on the moon.

Ewald von Kleist in his Anacreontic poem, "Gedanken eines betrunkenen Sternsehers", pays tribute to the Copernican system by personally experiencing that the earth moves, though he cannot quite explain the two suns.

Lessing in his youth also wrote some Anacreontic poems with scientific themes. In "Der neue Welt-Bau" he maintains that Copernicus was under the influence of wine when he realized that the earth moved. In "Die drey Reiche der Natur", he substitutes for the Linnaean system of classification his own, according to which the capacity to drink and to love become distinguishing characteristics.

CONCLUSION

In presenting the material in parts one, two and three, I have been as comprehensive as is reasonably possible and desirable. I have avoided confining myself to any single theme or set of themes like astronomy or natural history, for in the research it soon became clear that the scientific themes were interrelated. Thus, I have limited the topic only as regards the period, namely, 1720—1760. In the early 1720's, Christian Wolff began to publish his German works and Brockes his *Irdisches Vergnügen in Gott* — two very significant formative influences for the next few decades. By the 1750's their influence had waned and by the 1760's a new age, the age of Goethe, was beginning to take shape. The period, 1720—1760, has a distinct continuity of subject matter, though it is clear that its roots extend far into the past and its influence on into the future.

The sources for this study have been more than a hundred popular writings and the works of more than fifty poets. Most of this material has received little or no attention in professional publications by historians of any discipline. There are several reasons why these works had fallen into oblivion. First, the literary and social history of the German Enlightenment has been neglected in favor of the age that followed it. Next, there has been relatively little interest in popular literature; it does not really belong to the domain of any historical discipline. Then, the history of the natural sciences has been closed to historians of literature until recently. Finally, many of the books which were used are relatively inaccessible.

These labors have been directed toward a twofold goal. I have told the story of the diffusion of the sciences in Germany through popular literature from 1720 to 1760. Secondly, I have demonstrated the wide spectrum of scientific interests of men of letters as reflected in the variety of scientific themes in their poetry. It is furthermore of utmost significance that the scientific themes found in the popular literature in part one appear so consistently in the poetry examined in parts two and three. The demonstration of a continuity of scientific themes in the popular literature and the poetry of the German Enlightenment summarizes best this work's contribution to scholarship. I shall cite several outstanding examples of this continuity.

Among the German translations of popular scientific works by foreign authors, there were several which exerted much influence on the poets, directly and indirectly. Burnet, Whiston, Derham, Fontenelle and Huygens were, without question, the most influential. They are frequently mentioned by name in German prose and poetry. Their interests, mostly related to cosmogony and astronomy, are among the most popular with the poets.

The popular compendiums of science by Scheuchzer, Wolff, Gottsched and Krüger found their poetic counterparts in verse compendiums of science by

Brockes, Sendel, Behr and Leinker. They are similar in their structure and didactic intent. Since the prose compendiums were written before 1740 and the verse compendiums after 1740, it is likely that the former inspired the didactic poetry of the latter.

Strongly represented in both popular literature and poetry is the physico-theological tradition. Though this tradition is frequently mentioned by historians of the eighteenth century, it has usually been derided for its naive theology and thus not taken seriously. I have found it necessary to do so, because these works contributed so much to the dissemination of science.

Corresponding to these physicotheological treatises, there is the physico-theological poetry which praised God in His works and thereby taught much scientific material. It combined the teaching of science with the teaching of piety. Brockes was the most effective of these poets and throughout his life, his influence on German poetry was enormous. Of the poets that have been treated the following can be mentioned as belonging to the physicotheological school with clear indications of the Brockes influence: Drollinger, Triller, Scheibel, Zell, Bodmer, Sendel, Behr, Leinker, Sinold, Richey, von Loen, Cuno, Denso, Ebeling and Meintel.

Brockes stands out as the poet who is most honored by all the physico-theological authors. They frequently pay tribute to him for the inspiration of his poetry which they quote liberally throughout their works. J.A. Fabricius lauds Brockes and his poetry. It was Brockes, he informs his readers, who constantly inspired and encouraged him in his translation of the Derham works. The amateur natural historian, Rösel von Rosenhof, cites Brockes' poetry as the influence that turned him to his nature studies. Brockes was indeed the shining light of the physicotheological tradition which enjoyed its heyday during the years of publication of the *Irdisches Vergnügen in Gott,* 1721–1748. It was a movement that spread to many levels of the population. Participants in it were clergymen, educators, physicians, scientists and men of letters.

The fusion of science and letters is very ably represented in the works of Gottsched, Kästner and Mylius. Though they did not reject the physicotheological orientation, their intent was more secular; they were truly "Aufklärer". With their translations, periodicals, compendiums of science, essays and poetry, they constitute a distinct formative influence in the German Enlightenment. They are the best examples of men of letters as popularizers of science.

Of the numerous scientific themes that appear consistently in the popular literature and the poetry, I should like to single out the praise and worship of Newton. The period under consideration has been called the age of Newton. The reception of Newton in England and France is mentioned in most histories of Western civilization. I have found ample material that tells the story of Newton in Germany. In part one, I frequently noted the attitudes of the popular writers toward Newton's *Optics* and *Principia*. In part three, I demonstrate the extent to which these attitudes are reflected in the poetry. Moreover, it became clear that by the middle of the century, Newton had become more than just a mathematician and a scientist; he was *the* scientist, the symbol of the new sciences and their success in revealing the mysteries of nature.

When we consider the entire spectrum of scientific themes in the poetry, as summarized in the third part, it is remarkable to note the unanimity of scientific material in both the poetry and popular literature. The poets' breadth of interest — cosmogony, astronomy, earth and life sciences — suggests the "Faustian" urge of the age, to know all things in heaven and on earth. At the same time, there are numerous warnings about science. Its validity is questioned and doubts are raised whether science is an adequate means to understand nature. Furthermore, the virtues of piety and self-knowledge are advocated in contrast to the dubious value of the scientist's superficial knowledge.

Finally, as regards the continuity of subject matter in popular literature and poetry, there are several traditional themes that received a new emphasis in this period. First, there is the ancient tradition of didactic poetry with scientific content. In the eighteenth century this tradition is continued, but with material derived from the new sciences. The praise of God in nature is another old tradition, as the Fabricius bibliography in his translation of Derham's *Astro-Theology* shows. In the eighteenth century, this tradition is vigorously perpetuated with the aid of the new sciences. The plurality of inhabited worlds is also a tradition that can be traced back to antiquity. In this period and supported by the new scientific outlook, the existence of a plurality of inhabited worlds becomes one of the most popular speculations and, to many, an article of faith. Finally, there is the image of the chain of beings, whose history Professor Lovejoy has written so comprehensively. It frequently appears in the German poetry of our period, but usually in the form of a similar image, the ladder of nature, which likewise characterizes the order and continuity of nature. Thus, we find in this period several traditional themes perpetuated in prose and poetry with material from the new sciences.

The diffusion of the sciences and science in German literature did not, of course, stop with the year 1760. In fact, there is good reason to believe that science and letters attained a heightened fusion and interrelatedness in the age of Goethe. This study has attempted to provide the necessary background for a systematic examination of the relations of science and literature in the age of Goethe.

BIBLIOGRAPHY

A. Primary Sources

Anon. *Sonderbare Licht- und Wetter-Philosophie Gewisser Einwohner auf einer Neu-ent-deckten Insel im Südländischen Meer* (1741)

Arndt, Johann. *Vom Wahren Christentum.* Schwabach, 1737. The first edition appeared 1605—1609.

Der Arzt. Eine medicinische Wochenschrift. Hrsg. von Johann August Unzer. Hamburg, 1759—1764.

Barth, Johann Matthaeus. *Physica Generalior, oder kurze Sätze von denen natürlichen Körpern überhaupt.* Regensburg, 1724.

Behr, Georg Heinrich. *Die Gottheit oder Lob und Erkänntniss des Schöpfers aus seinen Geschöpfen.* Frankfurt und Leipzig, 1752.

— *Die schwache Wissenschaft der heutigen Ärzte.* Strassburg, 1753.

Belustigungen des Verstandes und des Witzes. Hrsg. von Johann Joachim Schwabe. Leipzig, 1741—1745.

Beyer, Johann. *Beschreibung einer Himmels- und Erd-Kugel.* Hamburg 1718.

Bibliothek der schönen Wissenschaften und der freyen Künste. Hrsg. von Friedrich Nicolai und Moses Mendelssohn. Leipzig, 1757—1767.

Der Biedermann. Hrsg. von Johann Christoph Gottsched. Leipzig, 1727—1728.

Bodmer, Johann Jakob. *Der Noah.* Zürich, 1752.

— *Der Noah.* Zürich, 1765.

Böhlau, Christoph Dietrich von. *Poetische Jugend-Früchte.* Leipzig, 1740.

Der Brachmann. Hrsg. von Johann Georg Altmann. Zürich, 1740.

Briefe, die neueste Literatur betreffend. Hrsg. von Lessing, Mendelssohn, Nicolai. Berlin, 1759—1765.

Brockes, Barthold Heinrich. *Irdisches Vergnügen in Gott, bestehend in Physikalisch- und Moralischen Gedichten.* 9 Bände. Hamburg, 1721—1748. The volumes used were dated as follows: I, 1737; II, 1734; III, 1736; IV, 1736; V, 1735; VI, 1740; VII, 1746; VIII, 1746; IX, 1748.

Buffon, Georges Louis Leclerc, Comte de. *Allgemeine Naturgeschichte.* Eine freye mit einigen Zusätzen vermehrte Übersetzung, nach der neuesten französischen Ausgabe von 1769, von Friedrich Heinrich Wilhelm Martini. 7 Bände. Berlin, 1771—1775.

— *Naturgeschichte der vierfüssigen Thiere.* Übersetzt von Friedrich Heinrich Wilhelm Martini und Bernhard Christian Otto. 23 Bände. Berlin, 1771—1801.

— *Naturgeschichte der Vögel.* Übersetzt von Friedrich Heinrich Wilhelm Martini und Bernhard Christian Otto. 37 Bände. Berlin, 1772—1829.

Burnet, Thomas. *The Sacred Theory of the Earth: Containing an Account of the Original of the Earth, and of all the general Changes which it hath already undergone, till the Consummation of all Things.* 2nd ed. London, 1690—1691.

Creuz, Friedrich Carl Casimir Freiherr von. *Oden und andere Gedichte.* Neue und vermehrte Auflage. Frankfurt und Mainz, 1753.

— *Oden und andere Gedichte.* 2 Bände. Frankfurt, 1769.

Cronegk, Johann Friedrich von. *Schriften.* Hrsg. von Johann Peter Uz. 2 Bände. Leipzig, 1760—1761.

Cuno, Johann Christian. *Ode über seinen Garten: Nachmals besser.* 2. Auflage. Amsterdam, 1750.

Derham, William. *Astrotheologie, oder Himmlisches Vergnügen in Gott, bey aufmercksamen Anschauen des Himmels, und genauer Betrachtung der Himmlischen Cörper.* Übersetzt von Johann Albert Fabricius. Hamburg, 1732.

— *Physicotheologie, oder Natur-Leitung zu Gott.* Übersetzt von Johann Albert Fabricius. Hamburg, 1732.

Deutsche Acta Eruditorum oder Geschichte der Gelehrten, welche den gegenwärtigen Zustand der Litteratur in Europa begreifen. Hrsg. von Justus Gotthard Rabener, Christian Schöttgen, Johann Georg Walch. 20 Bände. Leipzig, 1712—1739.

Discourse der Mahlern. Hrsg. von Johann Jakob Bodmer und Johann Jakob Breitinger. Zürich, 1721—1723. A later edition appeared under the title: *Der Mahler der Sitten.* Zürich, 1746.

Doppelmayr, Johann Gabriel. *Ausführliche Erklärung über 2 neue Homännische Charten, als über das System Solare et Planetarium Copernico—Hugenianum.* Nürnberg, 1707.

Dreyer, Johann Matthias. *Vorzüglichste deutsche Gedichte.* Altona, 1771.

Drollinger, Carl Friedrich. *Gedichte.* Hrsg. Johann Jakob Spreng. Frankfurt, 1745.

Dusch, Johann Jakob. *Briefe zur Bildung des Geschmacks.* Leipzig und Breslau, 1764—1773.

— *Schilderungen aus dem Reiche der Natur und der Sittenlehre durch alle Monate des Jahres.* Hamburg und Leipzig, 1757—1760.

— *Vermischte Werke.* Jena, 1754.

Ebeling, Johann Just. *Betrachtungen aus dem Buch der Natur und Schrift.* 3 Bände. Hildesheim, 1747.

Ebert, Johann Arnold. *Episteln und vermischte Gedichte.* Hamburg, 1789.

Eberhard, Johann Peter. *Erste Gründe der Naturlehre.* 4. Auflage. Halle, 1774.

Fabricius, Johann Albert. *Hydrotheologie, oder Versuch durch aufmerksame Betrachtung der Eigenschaften, reichen Austheilung und Bewegung der Wasser die Menschen zur Liebe und Bewunderung ihres . . . Schöpfers zu ermuntern . . .* Hamburg, 1734.

— *Pyrotheologie oder Versuch durch nähere Betrachtung des Feuers, die Menschen zur Liebe und Bewunderung ihres . . . Schöpfers anzuflammen.* Hamburg, 1732.

Fénelon, François de Salignac de La Mothe. *Traité de l'existence et des attributs de Dieu.* In *Oeuvres de Fénelon,* I. Paris, 1865.

Fontenelle, Bernard Le Bovier de. *Dialogen über die Mehrheit der Welten.* Übersetzt von Johann Elert Bode. Berlin, 1780.

— *Gespräche von mehr als einer Welt.* Thomas Fritsch: Leipzig, 1698.

— *Gespräche von mehr als einer Welt.* Übersetzt von Johann Christoph Gottsched. 2. Auflage, 1730; 4. Auflage, Leipzig, 1751; 5. Auflage, Leipzig, 1760.

Freymüthige Nachrichten von neuen Büchern und andern zur Gelehrtheit gehörigen Sachen. Hrsg. von Johann Jakob Bodmer, Zürich, 1744—1763.

Frisch, Johann Leonhard. *Beschreibung von allerley Insecten in Teutsch-Land,* Leipzig und Berlin, 1720—1738.

Gellert, Christian Fürchtegott. *Moralische Vorlesungen.* In *Sämtliche Werke,* VI, VII. Leipzig, 1770.

Genest, Abbé Charles Claude. *Grund-Sätze der Welt-Weisheit des Herrn Abts Genest.* Übersetzt von Barthold Heinrich Brockes. 3. Auflage. Hamburg, 1736.

Der Gesellige, Eine Moralische Wochenschrift. Hrsg. von Georg Friedrich Meier und Samuel Gotthold Lange. 6 Teile. Halle, 1748—1750.

Gesellschaftliche Erzählungen für die Liebhaber der Naturlehre, der Haushaltungs-Wissenschaft, der Arzney-Kunst und der Sitten. Hrsg. von Johann August Unzer. Hamburg, 1753.

Gessner, Salomon. *Schriften.* Zürich, 1762.

Giseke, Nikolas Dietrich. *Poetische Werke.* Hrsg. von Carl Christian Gärtner. Braunschweig, 1767.

Gleim, Johann Wilhelm Ludwig. *Sämtliche Werke.* Erste Original Ausgabe aus des Dichters Handschriften durch W. Körte. 7 Bände. Halberstadt, 1811—1813.

Der Glückselige, eine Moralische Wochenschrift. Hrsg. von Georg Friedrich Meier und Samuel Gotthold Lange. Halle, 1763—1768.

Göttingische Zeitung von gelehrten Sachen. Hrsg. von W.B.A. von Steinwehr. Göttingen, 1739—1752.

Gottsched, Johann Christoph. *Erste Gründe der gesammten Weltweisheit.* 2 Bände. 2. Auflage. Leipzig, 1735; 5. Auflage, 1748; 6. Auflage, 1756.

— *Gedichte.* 2 Bände. 2. Auflage. Leipzig, 1751.

Gundling, Nikolas Hieron. *Historie der Gelahrtheit.* 5 Bände. Frankfurt, 1734—1746.

Günther, Johann Christian. *Sämtliche Werke.* Hrsg. von Wilhelm Krämer. 6 Bände. Leipzig, 1930—1937. (Bibliothek des literarischen Vereins in Stuttgart. Publikation Nr. 275, 277, 279, 283, 284, 286).

Hagedorn, Friedrich von. *Poetische Werke*. 3 Theile. Hamburg, 1769.
— *Versuch einiger Gedichte*. Hamburg, 1729. *Deutsche Literaturdenkmale des 18. Jahrhunderts*, Nr. 10. Hrsg. von Bernhard Seuffert, Heilbronn, 1883. This is a reprint of the original 1729 ed.
Hagelganss, Johann Georg. *Kurtze doch Gründliche aus der Übereinstimmung des Lichts der Natur und Offenbahrung geleitete Vorstellung des Welt-Gebäudes*. Frankfurt, 1736.
— *Machina Mundi Sphaerica cum Planisphaerio, oder Vollständige Beschreibung einer . . . zweyfachen Welt-Kugel*. Frankfurt, 1738.
Haller, Albrecht von. *Tagebuch seiner Beobachtungen über Schriftsteller und über sich selbst*. Hrsg. von Johann Georg Heinzmann. Bern, 1787.
— *Versuch Schweizerischer Gedichte*. 11. Auflage. Bern, 1777.
Hamburgisches Magazin, oder gesammlete Schriften zum Unterricht und Vergnügen aus der Naturforschung und den angenehmen Wissenschaften überhaupt. Hrsg. Abraham Gotthelf Kästner. 26 Bände. Hamburg und Leipzig, 1747—1767.
Heyn, Johann. *Gesamlete Briefe von den Cometen, der Sündflut und dem Vorspiel des jüngsten Gerichts*. Berlin und Leipzig, 1745.
— *Versuch einer Betrachtung über die Cometen, die Sündflut und das Vorspiel des jüngsten Gerichts, nach astronomischen Gründen und der heiligen Schrift angestellet*. Berlin und Leipzig, 1742.
Hoffmann, Johann George. *Kurtze Fragen von den natürlichen Dingen, oder Geschöpfen und Wercken Gottes*. 6. Auflage. Halle, 1770.
Huygens, Christian. *Celestial Worlds Discovered*. London, 1698.
Jablonski, Johan Theodor. *Allgemeines Lexicon der Künste und Wissenschaften*. Leipzig, 1721.
Kant, Immanuel. *Allgemeine Naturgeschichte und Theorie des Himmels*. In *Sämtliche Werke*, I. Leipzig, 1867.
Kästner, Abraham Gotthelf. *A.G. Kästners Epigramme*. Hrsg. von Carl Becker. Halle, 1911.
— *Gesammelte Poetische und Prosaische Schönwissenschaftliche Werke*. 4 Theile. Berlin, 1841.
Kindermann, Eberhard Christian. *Die Geschwinde Reise auf dem Lufft-Schiff nach der obern Welt*. 1744.
— *Reise in Gedancken durch die eröffneten allgemeinen Himmels-Kugeln*. Rudolstadt, 1739.
— *Vollständige Astronomie oder Sonderbare Betrachtung derer vornehmsten an dem Firmament befindlichen Planeten und Sternen*. Rudolstadt, 1744.
Kleist, Ewald Christian von. *Sämtliche Werke*. Berlin, 1761.
Knorr, Georg Wolfgang. *Auserlesenes Naturaliencabinet, welches aus den drey Reichen der Natur zeiget, was von curiösen Liebhabern aufbehalten und gesammlet zu werden verdienet*. 2. Auflage. Nürnberg, 1766—1767.
König, Johann Ulrich von. *Gedichte*. Dresden, 1745.
Krüger, Johann Gottlob. *Geschichte der Erde in den allerältesten Zeiten*. Halle, 1746.
— *Naturlehre*. Halle, 1740.
— *Träume*. 2. Auflage. Halle, 1758.
Lambert, Johann Heinrich. *Cosmologische Briefe über die Einrichtung des Weltbaues*. Augsburg, 1761.
Lange, Samuel Gotthold. *Horatzische Oden*. Halle, 1747.
— *Der Komet, mein letztes Gedicht*. In *Almanach der deutschen Musen auf das Jahr 1770*. Leipzig, 1770.
Ledermüller, Martin Frobenius. *Mikroskopische Gemüths- und Augenergötzungen*. Nürnberg, 1760—1765.
— *Physikalische Beobachtungen derer Saamenthiergen*. Nürnberg, 1756.
— *Versuch zu einer gründlichen Vertheidigung derer Sammenthiergen*. Nürnberg, 1758.
Leinker, Johann Siegmund. *Die Körperwelt und ihre Einwohner der Mensch*. Frankfurt und Leipzig, 1759.
Lesser, Christian Friedrich. *Insecto-Theologia, oder Vernunfft- und Schrifftmässiger Versuch, wie ein Mensch durch aufmercksame Betrachtung derer . . . Insecten zu . . .*

Erkänntniss und Bewunderung der Allmacht, Weissheit, der Güte und Gerechtigkeit des grossen Gottes gelangen könne. 2. Auflage. Frankfurt und Leipzig, 1740.

— *Kurzer Entwurf einer Lithotheologie, oder eines Versuches, durch natürliche und geistliche Betrachtung der Steine, die Allmacht, Güte, Weissheit und Gerechtigkeit des Schöpfers zu erkennen, und die Menschen zur Bewunderung, Lobe und Dienste desselben aufzumuntern.* Nordhausen, 1732.

— *Lithotheologie, oder naturhistorische und geistliche Betrachtung der Steine.* Hamburg, 1751.

— *Testaceo-Theologia, oder Gründlicher Beweis des Daseyns und der vollkommensten Eigenschaften eines göttlichen Wesens, aus natürlicher und geistlicher Betrachtung der Schnecken und Muscheln.* Leipzig, 1744.

Lessing, Gotthold Ephraim. *Sämtliche Schriften.* Herausg. von Karl Lachmann. 23 Bände (Stuttgart, 1886—1924).

Lichtwer, Magnus Gottfried. *Das Recht der Vernunft.* Leipzig, 1758.

Loen, Johann Michael von. *Moralische Gedichte.* Frankfurt, 1751.

Löscher, Valentin Ernst. *Die merckwürdigen Wercke Gottes in denen Reichen der Natur.* Dresden, 1724.

Löwen, Johann Friedrich. *Poetische Nebenstunden.* Leipzig, 1752.

— *Schriften.* Hamburg, 1765.

Ludovici, Carl Günther. *Ausführlicher Entwurf einer vollständigen Historie der Wolffischen Philosophie.* 3. Auflage. Leipzig 1738.

Meier, Georg Friedrich. *Versuch eines neuen Lehrgebäudes von den Seelen der Thiere.* Halle, 1750.

Meintel, Conrad Stephan. *Vermischte Gedichte.* Nürnberg, 1764.

Der Mensch, Eine Moralische Wochenschrift. Hrsg. von Georg Friedrich Meier und Samuel Gotthold Lange. 12 Teile. Halle, 1751—1758.

Miller, Johann Peter. *Historischmoralische Schilderungen zur Bildung eines edlen Herzens in der Jugend.* Helmstädt, 1753.

Müldener, Johann Christian. *Astronomischer und geographischer Begriff, von dem natürlichen Zustande unserer Welt und Erdkugel, in 17 Schreiben, einer auf dem Lande wohnenden Frau von Stande eröffnet.* Dresden, 1729.

— *Geanders von der Ober-Elbe poetische Kleinigkeiten.* Dresden und Leipzig, 1753.

Musschenbroek, Pieter van. *Grundlehren der Naturwissenschaft.* Nach der 2. Lat. Ausgabe. Übersetzt von Johann Christoph Gottsched. Leipzig, 1747.

Mylius, Christlob. "Tagebuch seiner Reise von Berlin nach England, 1753." In Johann Bernoulli's *Archiv zur neuern Geschichte, Geographie, Natur und Menschenkentniss,* V—VII. Leipzig, 1786—1787.

— *Vermischte Schriften.* Hrsg. Gotthold Ephraim Lessing. Berlin, 1754.

Nachrichten von merkwürdigen Büchern. Hrsg. von Siegmund Jakob Baumgarten. 12 Bände. Halle, 1752—1758.

Der Naturforscher, eine physikalische Wochenschrift. Hrsg. von Christlob Mylius. Leipzig, 1747—1748.

Neue Zeitungen von gelehrten Sachen. Hrsg. von J.G. Krause; ab 1735; Joh. Burck. Mencke; sp. Otto Mencke (u.a.). 70 Bände. Leipzig 1715—1784.

Neuer Büchersaal der schönen Wissenschaften und der freyen Künste. Hrsg. von Johann Christoph Gottsched. 10 Bände. Leipzig, 1745—1750.

Das Neueste aus der anmuthigen Gelehrsamkeit. Hrsg. von Johann Christoph Gottsched. 12 Bände. Leipzig, 1751—1762.

Nieuwentyt, Bernhard. *Die Erkänntnüss der Weissheit, Macht und Güte des Göttlichen Wesens, aus dem rechten Gebrauch derer Betrachtungen aller irrdischen Dinge dieser Welt.* Übersetzt von Wilhelm Conrad Baumann. Frankfurt und Leipzig, 1732.

Der Nordische Aufseher. Hrsg. von Johann Andreas Cramer. 3 Bände. Kopenhagen und Leipzig, 1758—1761.

Der Patriot. Hrsg. von Michael Richey, Barthold Heinrich Brockes, (u.a.) 3 Bände. Hamburg, 1724—1726.

Philosophische Untersuchungen und Nachrichten von einigen Liebhabern der Weisheit. Hrsg.

von Christlob Mylius und Johann Andreas Cramer. 6 Teile. Leipzig, 1744—1746.
Physikalische Belustigungen. Hrsg. von Christlob Mylius und Abraham Gotthelf Kästner. 3 Bände. Berlin, 1751—1757.
Der Physikalische und oekonomische Patriot. Hrsg. von Johann August Unzer. Hamburg, 1756.
Pluche, Abbé Antoine. *Historie des Himmels nach den Vorstellungen der Poeten, der Philosophen und des Moyses betrachtet.* Aus dem Franz. übersetzt. Dresden und Leipzig, 1740.
— *Schau-Platz der Natur, oder Gespräche von der Beschaffenheit und den Absichten der natürlichen Dinge.* Aus dem Franz. übersetzt. 8 Bände. I, II, Frankfurt und Leipzig, 1760; III—VIII, Wien und Nürnberg, 1751—1755.
Preu, Johann Samuel. *Versuch einer Sismotheologie, oder physikalisch-theologische Betrachtung über die Erdbeben.* Nördlingen, 1772.
Rathelf, Ernst Ludwig. *Akridotheologie, oder historische und theologische Betrachtungen über die Heuschrecken.* 2 Bände. Hannover, 1748, 1750.
Ray, John. *Drey Physico-Theologische Betrachtungen von der Welt Anfang, Veränderung und Untergang.* Aus dem Englischen übersetzt von Theodor Arnold. Leipzig, 1732.
— *The Wisdom of God Manifested in the Works of the Creation.* 12th edition. London 1759.
Das Reich der Natur und der Sitten, eine Moralische Wochenschrift. Hrsg. von Georg Friedrich Meier. 12 Teile. Halle, 1757—1762.
Reichel, Johann Nathanael. *Schriften vor den Wiz und das Herz.* Leipzig, 1756.
Reimarus, Hermann Samuel. *Allgemeine Betrachtungen über die Triebe der Thiere, hauptsächlich über die Kunsttriebe derselben.* 2. Ausgabe. Hamburg, 1762.
— *Die vornehmsten Wahrheiten der natürlichen Religion.* 4. Auflage. Hamburg, 1772.
Reimmann, Jacob Friedrich. *Versuch einer Einleitung in die Historiam Literariam derer Teutschen.* 6 Bände. Halle, 1708—1713.
Richey, Michael. *Deutsche Gedichte.* 3 Bände. Hamburg, 1764.
Richter, Johann Gottfried Ohnefalsch. *Ichthyotheologie oder Vernunft- und schriftmässiger Versuch aus Betrachtung der Fische zur Bewunderung, Ehrfurcht, und Liebe ihres grossen, liebreichen und allein weisen Schöpfers zu führen.* Leipzig, 1754.
Rohr, Julius Bernhard von. *Physikalische Bibliothek, worinnen die vornehmsten Schriften die zur Naturlehre gehören, angezeiget werden.* Hrsg. von Abraham Gotthelf Kästner. 2. Auflage. Leipzig, 1754.
— *Phyto-Theologia, oder Vernunfft- und Schrifftmässiger Versuch, wie aus dem Reiche der Gewächse die Allmacht, Weisheit, Güte und Gerechtigkeit des grossen Schöpfers und Erhalters aller Dinge von den Menschen erkannt und Sein allerheiligster Nahme hievor gepriesen werden möge.* Frankfurt und Leipzig, 1740.
Rösel von Rosenhof, August Johann. *Insecten-Belustigungen.* 4 Bände. Nürnberg, 1746—1761.
Rost, Johann Leonhard. *Astronomisches Handbuch.* 2. Auflage. Nürnberg, 1726.
— *Der Aufrichtige Astronomus.* Nürnberg, 1727.
— *Compendiöse Vorstellung des gantzen Welt-Gebäudes.* Nürnberg, 1743.
Sammlung Einiger Ausgesuchten Stücke der Gesellschaft der freyen Künste zu Leipzig. Hrsg. von Johann Christoph Gottsched. 3 Teile. Leipzig, 1754—1756.
Sammlung von Natur- und Medicin-, wie auch hierzu gehörigen Kunst- und Literatur-Geschichten . . . Hrsg. von J. Kanold, et al. 19 Bände. Breslau, 1718—1736.
Scheibel, Gottfried Ephraim. *Die Witterungen. Ein Historisch- und Physicalisches Gedicht.* Breslau, 1752.
Scheuchzer, Johann Jacob. *Jobi Physica sacra, oder Hiobs Natur-Wissenschafft verglichen mit der Heutigen.* Zürich, 1721.
— *Kupfer-Bibel, in welcher die Physica Sacra, oder geheiligte Natur-Wissenschaft derer in Heiliger Schrifft vorkommenden natürlichen Sachen deutlich erklärt und bewährt.* Augsburg und Ulm, 1731—1735.
— *Physica oder Natur-Wissenschaft.* 3. Auflage. Zürich, 1729.
Schirach, Adam Gottlob. *Melitto-Theologia, die Verherrlichung des glorwürdigen Schöpfers*

aus der wundervollen Biene, nach Anleitung der Naturlehre und Heiligen Gottesgelahrheit. Dresden, 1767.

Schmidt, Johann Jakob. *Biblischer Physicus oder Einleitung zur Biblischen Natur-Wissenschaft.* Leipzig, 1731.

— *Biblischer Mathematicus oder Erläuterung der H. Schrift aus den Mathematischen Wissenschaften.* 2. Ausgabe. Züllichau, 1749.

Der Schriftsteller Nach der Mode, I. Hrsg. von Christian Nicolaus Naumann. Jena, 1748–1749.

Scriver, Christian. *Gottholds Zufälliger Andachten.* 13. Auflage. Helmstädt, 1706.

Semler, Christian Gottlieb. *Astrognosia Nova oder Ausführliche Beschreibung des gantzen Fixstern und Planeten Himmels.* Halle, 1742.

Sendel, Christian. *Der Fromme Naturkundige, eine Wochenschrift in Versen.* Danzig, 1740.

Sinold, Philipp Balthasar. *Amadei Creutzbergs Seelen-erquickende Himmels-Lust auf Erden.* 2. Auflage. Berlin, 1742.

Stolle, Gottlieb. *Anleitung zur Historie der Gelahrheit.* 3. Auflage. Jena, 1727.

Sucro, Christoph Joseph. *Versuch in Lehrgedichten und Fabeln.* Halle, 1747.

Sulzer, Johann Georg. *Unterredungen über die Schönheit der Natur.* Berlin, 1750.

— *Versuch einiger moralischen Betrachtungen über die Werke der Natur.* Berlin, 1740–1745.

Suppius, Christoph Eusebius. *Der Inselberg.* Gotha, 1745.

Swammerdam, Jan. *Bibel der Natur, worinnen die Insekten in gewisse Classen vertheilt, sorgfältig beschrieben, zergliedert, in saubern Kupferstichen vorgestellet, mit vielen Anmerkungen über die Seltenheiten der Natur erleutert, und zum Beweis der Allmacht und Weisheit des Schöpfers angewendet werden.* Aus dem Holländischen übersetzt. Leipzig, 1752.

Triller, Daniel Wilhelm. *Poetische Betrachtungen über verschiedene aus der Natur- und Sittenlehre hergenommene Materien.* 6 Bände. Hamburg, 1725–1755. The editions used were dated as follows: 1750, 1746, 1750, 1766, 1751, 1755.

Tschammer und Osten, Hiob Gotthardt von. *Geistliche und Weltliche Gedichte.* Breslau, 1739.

Uffenbach, Zacharias Conrad von. *Merkwürdige Reisen durch Niedersachsen, Holland und Engelland.* 3 Bände. Ulm, 1753–1754.

Unschuldige Nachrichten oder Sammlung von Alten und Neuen theologischen Sachen, Büchern, Urkunden. Hrsg. von Valentin Ernst Löscher, ab 1751: von Joh. Elias. Kapp und Joh. Rud. Kiessling. Leipzig, 1702–1761.

Unzer (geb. Ziegler), Johanne Charlotte. *Grundriss einer Weltweisheit für das Frauenzimmer.* Halle, 1751.

— *Versuch in sittlichen und zärtlichen Gedichten.* 2. Auflage. Halle, 1766.

Uz, Johann Peter. *Sämtliche Poetische Werke.* Hrsg. August Sauer. In *Deutsche Literaturdenkmale des 18. und 19. Jahrhunderts,* XXXIII–XXXVIII. Stuttgart, 1890.

Walch, Johann Georg. *Bibliotheca Theologica.* 4 Bände. Jena, 1757–1765.

— *Philosophisches Lexicon.* 2. Auflage. Leipzig, 1733.

Walpurger, Johann Gottlieb. *Cosmotheologische Betrachtungen derer wichtigsten Wunder und Wahrheiten im Reiche der Natur und Gnaden.* 4 Teile. Chemnitz, 1748–1759.

Weisse, Christian Felix. *Der Naturaliensammler.* In *Sammlung der besten deutschen prosaischen Schriftsteller und Dichter,* LXXVI: *Weissens Lustspiele.* Carlsruhe, 1778.

Whiston, William. *Neue Betrachtung der Erde.* Übersetzt von Michael Swen. Frankfurt, 1713.

Wiederburg, Johann Bernhard. *Astronomisches Bedenken . . .* Neue und vermehrte Auflage. Jena, 1744.

— *Einleitung zu denen Mathematischen Wissenschaften . . .* Jena, 1726.

Wieland, Christoph Martin. *Abhandlung von den Schönheiten des epischen Gedichts 'Der Noah'.* Zürich, 1753.

— *Gesammelte Schriften.* Hrsg. von der Deutschen Kommission der Königlich Preussischen Akademie der Wissenschaften. Berlin, 1909–.

Wilkins, John. *Vertheidigter Copernicus.* Aus dem Englischen übersetzt von Johann Gabriel Doppelmayr. Leipzig, 1713.

Wolff, Christian. *Allerhand nützliche Versuche, dadurch zu genauer Erkänntniss der Natur und Kunst der Weg gebähnet wird.* 3 Bände. 3. Ausgabe. Halle, 1745—1747.

— *Die Anfangs-Gründe aller mathematischen Wissenschaften.* 4 Theile. Halle, 1710.

— *Ausführliche Nachricht von seinen eigenen Schrifften.* 2. Ausgabe. Frankfurt, 1733.

— *Mathematisches Lexikon.* Leipzig, 1716.

— *Vernünfftige Gedancken von den Würkungen der Natur.* 3. Auflage. Halle, 1734.

— *Vernünfftige Gedancken von den Absichten der natürlichen Dinge.* Halle, 1724.

— *Vernünfftige Gedancken von dem Gebrauche der Theile in Menschen, Thieren und Pflanzen.* 3. Auflage. Frankfurt und Leipzig, 1737.

— *Vernünfftige Gedancken von der Menschen Tun und Lassen.* 4. Auflage. Frankfurt und Leipzig, 1733.

— *Vernünfftige Gedancken von Gott, der Welt und der Seele des Menschen.* 3. Auflage. Frankfurt und Leipzig, 1725.

Woodward, John. *An Attempt towards a Natural History of the Fossils of England.* 2 volumes. London, 1728—1729.

— *Essay toward a Natural History of the Earth.* London, 1695.

Zachariä, Justus Friedrich Wilhelm. *Poetische Schriften.* 9 Bände in 3. Amsterdam, 1767.

Zedler, Johann Heinrich. *Grosses vollständiges Universal Lexicon aller Wissenschaften und Künste.* 64 Bände. Leipzig, 1732—1754.

Zell, Albrecht Jacob. *Erweckte Nachfolge zum Irdischen Vergnügen in Gott, bestehend in Physikalisch- und Moralischen Gedichten.* Hamburg, 1735.

Zernitz, Christian Friedrich. *Versuch in Moralischen und Schäfergedichten.* Hamburg und Leipzig, 1748.

Zimmermann, Johann Georg. *Das Leben des Herrn von Haller.* Zürich, 1755.

Zimmermann, Johann Jacob. *Astronomischer Beweissthum des Copernicanischen Welt-Gebäudes aus Heiliger Schrifft.* Frankfurt und Leipzig, 1691.

Zorn, Johann Heinrich. *Petino-Theologie, oder Versuch die Menschen durch nähere Betrachtung der Vögel zur Bewunderung, Liebe und Verehrung ihres Schöpfers zu ermuntern.* 2 Bände. I, Pappenheim, 1742; II, Schwabach, 1743.

Zuverlässige Nachrichten von dem gegenwärtigen Zustande, Veränderung und Wachstum der Wissenschaften. 18 Bände. Leipzig, 1740—1757.

B. Secondary Sources

Adams, Frank Dawson. *The Birth and Development of the Geological Sciences.* Dover Publications, New York, 1954. Reprint of the first edition, Baltimore, 1938.

Albertsen, L.L. *Das Lehrgedicht.* Aarhus, 1967.

Allen, Don Cameron. *The Legend of Noah. Renaissance Rationalism in Art, Science and Letters.* University of Illinois Press, 1963. Originally published as Vol. 33, Nos. 3—4 in the *Illinois Studies in Language and Literature.*

Allgemeine Deutsche Biographie. Hrsg. durch die Historische Commission bei der Königl. Akademie der Wissenschaften (Bayern). 56 Bände. Leipzig, 1875—1912.

Arnold, Robert F. *Allgemeine Bücherkunde zur neueren deutschen Literaturgeschichte.* 3. Auflage. Berlin und Leipzig, 1931.

Baldinger, Ernst Gottfried. *Biographien Jetztlebender Ärzte und Naturforscher in und ausser Deutschland.* Jena, 1772.

Batt, Max. *The Treatment of Nature in German Literature from Günther to Goethe's "Werther".* Diss. Univeristy of Chicago, 1901.

Bieder, Gertrud. *Natur und Landschaft in der deutschen Barocklyrik.* Zürich, 1927.

Boas, George. *The Happy Beast in French Thought of the Seventeenth Century.* The Johns Hopkins Press, 1933.

Bodenheimer, F.S. *Geschichte der Entomologie bis Linné.* 2 Bände. Berlin, 1928—1929.

Bruford, W.H. *Germany in the Eighteenth Century: The Social Background of the Literary Revival.* Cambridge, 1939.

Burdach, Karl Friedrich. *Die Literatur der Heilwissenschaft,* I. Gotha, 1810.

Bush, Douglas. *Science and English Poetry: A Historical Sketch.* Oxford University Press, 1967. (A reprint of the 1950 edition).

Cassirer, Ernst. *Die Philosophie der Aufklärung.* Tübingen, 1932.

Collier, Katherine Brownell. *Cosmogonies of our Fathers.* New York, 1934.

Dannemann, Friedrich. *Grundriss einer Geschichte der Naturwissenschaften.* 2 Bände. Leipzig, 1896—1898.

Danzel, Theodore. *Gottsched und seine Zeit.* Leipzig, 1855.

Darmstaedter, Ludwig. *Handbuch zur Geschichte der Naturwissenschaften und der Technik.* Berlin, 1908.

Deicke, Gustav. *Johann Jakob Dusch.* Strassburg i.E., 1910.

Dillenberger, John. *Protestant Thought and Natural Science: A Historical Study.* New York, 1960.

Dudley, Fred A. *The Relations of Literature and Science: A Selected Bibliography 1930—1967.* University Microfilms, Ann Arbor, 1968.

Ermatinger, Emil. *Die Weltanschauung des jungen Wieland.* Frauenfeld, 1907.

Faber du Faur, Curt von. *German Baroque Literature.* New Haven, 1958.

Feess, Kurt. *Charles Claude Genest.* Köln, 1912.

Fränzel, Walter. *Geschichte des Übersetzens im 18. Jahrhundert.* Leipzig, 1913.

Fraunberger, Fritz. *Elektrizität im Barock.* Köln, 1964.

Fromm, Hans. *Bibliographie deutscher Übersetzungen aus dem Französischen 1700—1948.* 6 Bände. Baden-Baden, 1950—1953.

Fulton, John F. *The Great Medical Bibliographers. A study in humanism.* Philadelphia, 1951.

Fusil, Casimir Alexandre. *L'Anti-Lucrèce du Cardinal de Polignac.* Paris, 1918.

— *La poésie scientifique de 1750 à nos jours.* Paris, 1918.

Gode-von Aesch, Alexander. *Natural Science in German Romanticism.* Columbia University Germanic Studies, N.S., No. 11. Columbia University Press, 1941.

Goedeke, Karl. *Grundriss zur Geschichte der deutschen Dichtung,* IV. 3. Auflage. Dresden, 1916.

Gove, Philip Babcock. *The Imaginary Voyage in Prose Fiction.* New York, 1941.

Guerlac, Henry. "Newton's Changing Reputation in the Eighteenth Century". In *Carl Becker's Heavenly City Revisited.* Ed. Raymond Oxley Rockwood. Cornell University Press, 1958. 3—26.

— *Science in Western Civilization: A Syllabus.* New York, 1952.

Haber, Francis C. *The Age of the World: Moses to Darwin.* The Johns Hopkins Press, 1959.

Haller, Elisabeth. *Die Barocken Stilmerkmale in der englischen, lateinischen und deutschen Fassung von Dr. Thomas Burnets "Theory of the Earth".* Bern, 1940.

Hartmann, Carl. *Friedrich Carl Casimir Freiherr von Creuz und seine Dichtungen.* Heidelberg, 1890.

Hastings, Hester. *Man and Beast in French Thought of the Eighteenth Century.* The Johns Hopkins Press, 1936.

Hazard, Paul. *European Thought in the Eighteenth Century.* Cleveland and New York, 1963. Translated from the French *La Pensée Européenne au XVIIIème Siècle.* Paris, 1946.

Heinsius, Wilhelm. *Allgemeines Bücher-Lexikon.* 4 Bände. Leipzig, 1812.

Hettner, Hermann. *Geschichte der deutschen Literatur im Achtzehnten Jahrhundert.* 7. Auflage. Hrsg. von Ewald A. Boucke. 3 Bände in 4. Braunschweig, 1925—1926.

Hirsch, August. *Biographisches Lexikon der hervorragenden Ärzte aller Zeiten und Völker.* 6 Bände. Wien und Leipzig, 1884—1888.

Hochdoerfer, Margarete. *The Conflict Between the Religious and Scientific Views of Albrecht von Haller.* Nebraska University Studies in Language and Literature. No. 12. Lincoln, Nebraska, 1932.

Irsay, Stephen d'. *Albrecht von Haller, eine Studie zur Geistesgeschichte der Aufklärung.* Leipzig, 1930.

Jöcher, Christian Gottlieb. *Allgemeines Gelehrten-Lexikon.* 4 Bände + 7 suppl., Leipzig, 1750—1819.

Johnson, Francis Rarick. *Astronomical Thought in Renaissance England.* Baltimore, 1937.

Jones, Richard Foster. *Ancients and Moderns.* 2nd edition. St. Louis, 1961.

Jones, William Powell. *The Rhetoric of Science.* University of California Press, 1966.

Jördens, Karl Heinrich. *Lexikon deutscher Dichter und Prosaisten.* 6 Bände. Leipzig, 1806—1811.

Junker, Christof. *Das Weltraumbild in der deutschen Lyrik von Opitz bis Klopstock.* Berlin, 1932.

Kayser, Christian Gottlob. *Vollständiges Bücher-Lexikon,* enthaltend alle von 1750 bis zu Ende des Jahres 1832 in Deutschland und in den angrenzenden Ländern gedruckten Büchern. 2 Bände. Leipzig, 1832.

Kiernan, Colm. *Science and the Enlightenment in eighteenth-century France.* Studies on Voltaire and the Eighteenth Century, LIX. Genève, 1968.

King, Donald Lawrence. *L'influence des sciences physiologiques sur la littérature française de 1670 à 1870.* Paris, 1929.

Kirchner, Joachim. *Die Grundlagen des deutschen Zeitschriftenwesens.* 2 Bände. Leipzig, 1928—1931.

Klemm, Friedrich. "Martin Frobenius Ledermüller: Aus der Zeit der Salon-Mikroskopie des Rokoko," *Optische Rundschau,* Sonderdruck aus Nr. 45 bis 48, Jahrg. 1927. Schweidnitz, 1928.

— "Die Physik im Zeitalter der Aufklärung," *Die BASF (Zeitschrift der Badischen Anilin- und Soda-Fabrik),* Jg. 8 (1958), Heft 3, 99—108.

Koyré, Alexandre, *From the Closed World to the Infinite Universe.* New York, 1958. Reprinted from the first edition, The Johns Hopkins Press, 1957.

Kronick, David A. *A History of Scientific and Technical Periodicals.* New York, 1962.

Lempp, Otto. *Das Problem der Theodicee in der Philosophie und Literatur des 18. Jahrhunderts.* Leipzig, 1910.

Lovejoy, Arthur O. *The Great Chain of Being.* Harvard University Press, 1936.

Manikowsky, Fritz von. *Die Welt- und Lebensanschauung in dem "Irdischen Vergnügen in Gott"* von Barthold Heinrich Brockes. Diss. Greifswald, 1914.

Marsak, Leonard M. *Bernard de Fontenelle: The Idea of Science in the French Enlightenment.* Transactions of the American Philosophical Society, N.S. Vol. 49, Part 7. Philadelphia, 1959.

Martens, Wolfgang. *Die Botschaft der Tugend. Die Aufklärung im Spiegel der deutschen Moralischen Wochenschriften.* Stuttgart, 1968.

McColley, Grant. "The Seventeenth Century Doctrine of a Plurality of Worlds," *Annals of Science,* I (1936), 385—430.

Meadows, Arthur Jack. *The High Firmament. A Survey of Astronomy in English Literature.* Leicester University Press, 1969.

Meusel, Johann Georg. *Das gelehrte Teutschland oder Lexikon der jetzt lebenden Teutschen Schriftsteller.* Lemgo, 1776.

— *Lexicon der vom Jahr 1750 bis 1800 verstorbenen teutschen Schriftsteller.* Leipzig, 1802.

Meyer, Heinrich. *The Age of the World, A Chapter in the History of Enlightenment.* (Multigraphed at Mühlenberg College, Allentown, Pa., 1951).

Miller, Minnie M. "Science and Philosophy as Precursors of the English Influence in France", *Publications of the Modern Language Association of America,* XLV (1930), 856—896.

Mornet, Daniel. *Les sciences de la nature en France au dix-huitième siècle.* Paris, 1911.

Naïs, Hélène. *Les animaux dans la poésie de la Renaissance: science, symbolique, poésie.* Paris, 1961.

Nicolson, Marjorie Hope. *The Breaking of the Circle.* The Northwestern University Press, 1950.

— *Mountain Gloom and Mountain Glory.* Cornell University Press, 1959.
— *Newton Demands the Muse.* Princeton University Press, 1946.
— *Science and Imagination.* Cornell University Press, 1956.
— *Voyages to the Moon.* New York, 1948.
Ornstein, Martha. *The Role of Scientific Societies in the Seventeenth Century.* London, 1963 (Reprinted from the third edition of 1938).
Philipp, Wolfgang. "Physicotheology in the age of Enlightenment: appearance and history", *Studies on Voltaire and the Eighteenth Century,* LVII (1967), 1233—1267.
— *Das Werden der Aufklärung in theologiegeschichtlicher Sicht.* Göttingen, 1957.
Poggendorff, Johann Christian. *Biographisch-Literarisches Handwörterbuch zur Geschichte der exacten Wissenschaften.* 2 Bände. Leipzig, 1863.
Price, Mary Bell and Laurence M. Price. *The Publication of English Humaniora in Germany in the eighteenth Century.* Berkeley and Los Angeles, 1955.

Reichel, Eugen. *Gottsched.* 2 Bände. Berlin, 1908, 1912.
Reicke, Emil. *Neues aus der Zopfzeit. Gottscheds Briefwechsel mit dem Nürnberger Naturforscher Martin Frobenius Ledermüller.* Leipzig, 1923.
Richter, Karl. "Die kopernikanische Wende in der Lyrik von Brockes bis Klopstock", *Schiller-Jahrbuch,* 1968, 133—169.
Ritterbush, Philip C. *Overtures to Biology: The Speculations of Eighteenth-Century Naturalists.* Yale University Press, 1964.
Rosenfield, Leonora C. *From Beast-Machine to Man-Machine.* New York, 1941.
Sarton, George. *A Guide to the History of Science.* New York, 1952.
Schimank, Hans. "Stand und Entwicklung der Naturwissenschaften im Zeitalter der Aufklärung", *Lessing und die Zeit der Aufklärung.* Göttingen, 1968. 30—76.
Schmid, Christian Heinrich. *Anthologie der Deutschen.* Frankfurt und Leipzig, 1770.
Schmidt, Albert-Marie. *La poésie scientifique en France au seizième siècle.* Paris, 1939.
Schneider, Ferdinand J. "Kometenwunder und Seelenschlaf", *Deutsche Vierteljahrschrift für Literaturwissenschaft und Geistesgeschichte,* XVIII (1940), 201—231.
Shorr, Philip. *Science and Superstition in the Eighteenth Century.* New York, 1932.
Sprengel, Kurt Polycarp Joachim. *Geschichte der Botanik.* Altenburg und Leipzig, 1817—1818.
Stimson, Dorothy. *The Gradual Acceptance of the Copernican Theory of the Universe.* New York, 1917.
Strodtmann, Johann Christof. *Beyträge zur Historie der Gelahrtheit.* Hamburg, 1748—1750.
Thyssen, Erwin. *Christlob Mylius.* Diss. Marburg, 1912.
Vartanian, Aram. *La Mettrie's "L'Homme Machine". A Study in the Origins of an Idea.* (Princeton University Press, 1960).
— "Trembley's Polyp, La Mettrie, and Eighteenth-Century French Materialism", *Journal of the History of Ideas,* XI (June, 1950), 259—286.
Vontobel, Willy. *Von Brockes bis Herder.* Bern, 1942.
Wagman, Frederick Herbert. *Magic and Natural Science in German Baroque Literature.* Columbia University Press, 1942.
Walter, Karl. *Chronologie der Werke Christoph Martin Wielands.* Greifswald, 1904.
Waniek, Gustav. *Gottsched und die deutsche Literatur seiner Zeit.* Wien, 1897.
Westen, Lois Armour. *"Melitto-Logia" The Mythology of the Bee in Eighteenth-Century German Literature.* Diss. University of Illinois, 1952.
White, Andrew Dickson. *A History of the Warfare of Science with Theology in Christendom.* New York, 1896. Reprinted by the Dover Press, New York, 1960.
Willey, Basil. *The Eighteenth Century Background.* London, 1940.
Winter, Ernst. *Tschirnhausen und die Frühaufklärung in Mittel- und Osteuropa.* Akademie-Verlag, Berlin, 1960.
Wolf, A. *A History of Science, Technology and Philosophy in the XVIth and XVIIth Centuries.* New York, 1959. Reprinted from the second edition, 1950.
— *A History of Science, Technology and Philosophy in the XVIIIth Century.* New York, 1961. Reprinted from the second edition, 1952.

Wolff, Hans M. *Die Weltanschauung der deutschen Aufklärung in Geschichtlicher Entwicklung*. 2. Auflage. Bern und München, 1963.

Woolf, Harry. *The Transits of Venus. A Study of Eighteenth-Century Science*. Princeton University Press, 1959.

Zinner, Ernst. *Entstehung und Ausbreitung der Copernicanischen Lehre*. Erlangen, 1943.

Zöckler, Otto. *Geschichte der Beziehungen zwischen Theologie und Naturwissenschaft*. 2 Bände. Gütersloh, 1877—1879.

INDEX OF NAMES